The Holy Spirit

The Holy Spirit
Classic and Contemporary Readings

Edited by
Eugene F. Rogers, Jr.

WILEY-BLACKWELL
A John Wiley & Sons, Ltd., Publication

This edition first published 2009
© 2009 Eugene F. Rogers, Jr.

Blackwell Publishing was acquired by John Wiley & Sons in February 2007. Blackwell's
publishing program has been merged with Wiley's global Scientific, Technical,
and Medical business to form Wiley-Blackwell.

Registered Office
John Wiley & Sons Ltd, The Atrium, Southern Gate, Chichester, West Sussex,
PO19 8SQ, United Kingdom

Editorial Offices
350 Main Street, Malden, MA 02148-5020, USA
9600 Garsington Road, Oxford, OX4 2DQ, UK
The Atrium, Southern Gate, Chichester, West Sussex, PO19 8SQ, UK

For details of our global editorial offices, for customer services, and for information about
how to apply for permission to reuse the copyright material in this book please see
our website at www.wiley.com/wiley-blackwell.

The right of Eugene F. Rogers, Jr. to be identified as the author of this work has been asserted in
accordance with the Copyright, Designs and Patents Act 1988.

Library of Congress Cataloging-in-Publication Data
The Holy Spirit : classic and contemporary readings / edited by Eugene F. Rogers, Jr.
p. cm.
Includes bibliographical references (p.   ) and index.
ISBN 978–1–4051–3623–5 (hardcover : alk. paper) — ISBN 978–1–4051–3624–2 (pbk. : alk. paper)
1. Holy Spirit. I. Rogers, Eugene F.
BT121.3H66 2009
231'.3—dc22
2009001935

A catalogue record for this book is available from the British Library.

Set in 10/13pt Sabon by Graphicraft Limited, Hong Kong
Printed in Singapore by Ho Printing Singapore Pte Ltd

01   2009

For my father,
Eugene F. Rogers,
who taught me how to use rhetoric,
or the spirit of the words

Contents

List of Illustrations   x
About the Authors   xi
Acknowledgments and Sources   xiii
Introduction   1

I Late Twentieth-Century Questions

1 You Wonder Where the Spirit Went, *Robert W. Jenson*   9
2 Trinity, *Richard Norris*   19
3 Living into the Mystery of the Holy Trinity: Trinity, Prayer, and
   Sexuality, *Sarah Coakley*   44
4 Word and Spirit, *Rowan Williams*   53
5 Charismatic Experience, *Church of England Doctrine Commission*
   (*Sarah Coakley*)   68
6 Vatican Clarification on the Filioque, *Pontifical Council for
   Promoting Christian Unity*   81
7 Matter and Spirit, or What is Pauline Participation in Christ?
   Stanley Stowers   91

II Syriac Resources

8 *from* Hymn on Virginity, 7, *Ephrem the Syrian*   109
9 [Eating Love], *Isaac of Nineveh*   111
10 *from* The Holy Spirit in the Syrian Baptismal Tradition,
   Sebastian Brock   113

III   Early Greek Resources

11 *from* Catechetical Orations, *Cyril of Jerusalem*   131
12 *from* Orations against the Arians, *Athanasius of Alexandria*   136
13 *from* On the Holy Spirit, *Basil of Caesarea*   141
14 *from* On Holy Baptism *and* On Pentecost, *Gregory of Nazianzus*   149

IV   Latin Resources

15 Homily on the First Epistle of John, *Augustine of Hippo*   165
16 *Veni Spiritus* Hymns   174
17 [The Holy Spirit Hovers over Baptism], *Rupert of Deutz*   177
18 Fourth Sermon for Palm Sunday, *Guerric of Igny*   180
19 *from* Summa Theologica, *Thomas Aquinas*   185

V   German Resources

20 *from* The Last Words of David, *Martin Luther*   195
21 *from* Mysterium Paschale, *Hans Urs von Balthasar*   205
22 *from* The Trinity and the Kingdom, *Jürgen Moltmann*   209

VI   Russian and Romanian Resources

23 *from* The Comforter in *The Pillar and Grand of the Truth*,
    Pavel Florensky   217
24 Redemption and Deification, *Vladimir Lossky*   237
25 *from* Trinitarian Relations and the Life of the Church,
    Dumitru Staniloae   247

VII   Mystical Resources

26 *from* The Discourses, *Symeon the New Theologian*   261
27 *from* The Spiritual Espousals, *John Ruusbroec*   272
28 *from* The Inhalation of the Air in *The Spiritual Canticle*,
    St John of the Cross   278
29 [The Spirit as Bride] in *A Manual of Catholic Theology*,
    Matthias Scheeben   281
30 *from* Prayer in the Trinity, *Adrienne von Speyr*   285

VIII   Late Twentieth-Century Applications

31   *from* How the Spirit Reads and How to Read the Spirit,
     Stephen E. Fowl   301
32   *from* The Epistemic Role of the Spirit, *Bruce D. Marshall*   316

Further Reading   322
Scripture Index   326
General Index   330

Illustrations

(between pages 176 and 177)

1. Icon with the Hospitality of Abraham.
   Benaki Museum, Athens, Greece.
   (Photo Credit: Scala / Art Resource, New York)

2. Master of the Berthold Sacramentary, thirteenth century: *The Trinity*, from a missal, Germany (Abbey of Weingarten), *ca.* 1200–32. M.710, f.132v.
   The Pierpont Morgan Library, New York.
   (Photo Credit: The Pierpont Morgan Library / Art Resource, New York)

3. Gian Lorenzo Bernini (1598–1680): *Beata Ludovica Albertoni*.
   San Francesco a Ripa, Rome.
   (Photo Credit: Biblioteca Herziana)

4. Hanging silver dove, probably a pyx (container for consecrated bread), sixth to seventh century, early Byzantine, North Syrian, made in Attarouthi.
   Metropolitan Museum of Art, New York.
   (Photo Credit: Image copyright © The Metropolitan Museum of Art / Art Resource, New York)

About the Authors

Eugene F. Rogers, Jr. is Professor of Religious Studies at the University of North Carolina at Greensboro.

Robert W. Jenson is Senior Scholar for Research, Emeritus, Center of Theological Inquiry, Princeton, NJ.

Richard Norris (1930–2005) was Professor of Church History at Union Theological Seminary in New York.

Sarah Coakley is Norris-Hulse Professor of Divinity at Cambridge University.

Rowan Williams is Archbishop of Canterbury, formerly Lady Margaret Professor in Divinity at Oxford University.

Stanley Stowers is Professor and Chair of Religious Studies, Brown University.

Ephrem the Syrian (ca. 306–73), Syrian theologian and hymnographer in Nisibus and Edessa (now Nusaybin and Urfa, Turkey).

Isaac of Nineveh (flourished ca. 680), Syrian mystical theologian, briefly bishop of Nineveh (now Mosul, Iraq).

Sebastian Brock was formerly Reader in Syriac Studies, the Oriental Institute, Oxford.

Cyril of Jerusalem (ca. 313–ca. 386/7), theologian and bishop of Jerusalem.

Athanasius of Alexandria (295–373), theologian and archbishop of Alexandria.

Basil of Caesarea (ca. 329–79), theologian and bishop of Caesarea (in present-day Turkey).

Gregory of Nazianzus (329–89), theologian and bishop of Constantinople (now Istanbul).

Augustine of Hippo (354–430), theologian and bishop of Hippo (in present-day Algeria).

Rupert of Deutz (1075–1129), abbot of a Benedictine abbey near Cologne.

Guerric of Igny (1070/80–1157), Cistercian homilist and abbot of Igny (France).

Thomas Aquinas (1225–74), Dominican theologian and doctor of the Catholic Church, who taught at the University of Paris.

Martin Luther (1483–1546), first Protestant reformer, who taught at the University of Wittenberg.

Hans Urs von Balthasar (1905–88), Swiss Catholic theologian and publisher.

Jürgen Moltmann (b. 1926) is a German Protestant theologian at Tübingen and Emory University, Atlanta.

Pavel Florensky (1882–1937), Russian philosopher, poet, electrical engineer, aesthetician, and theologian.

Vladimir Lossky (1903–58), Russian Orthodox theologian who wrote in Paris.

Dumitru Staniloae (1903–93), Romanian Orthodox theologian.

Symeon the New Theologian (949–1022), Eastern Orthodox mystic, theologian, and abbot of St Mamas monastery in Constantinople.

John Ruusbroec (1293–1381), Dutch theologian and mystic.

St John of the Cross (1542–91), Spanish Carmelite reformer, theologian, poet, and mystic.

Matthias Scheeben (1835–88), German Catholic dogmatician and mystic.

Adrienne von Speyr (1902–67), Swiss theologian and mystic under the spiritual direction of Swiss theologian Hans von Balthasar.

Stephen Fowl is Professor of New Testament and Chair of Theology at Loyola University, Baltimore.

Bruce D. Marshall is Professor of Historical Theology at Perkins Divinity School of Southern Methodist University.

Acknowledgments and Sources

I wish to thank students of my Holy Spirit seminars at the University of Virginia and the University of North Carolina at Greensboro and the librarians who made hard-to-find texts available to them. I am grateful to UNC Greensboro for a Regular Faculty Grant in 2005–6 to study images of the Holy Spirit in their liturgical contexts and for a Research Assignment in 2007–8 that allowed me to get the manuscript off my desk. I am grateful to Pat Bowden, Amanda Hughes, Tamara Bryant, and especially Jeff Mortimore, Elizabeth Currin, Mary Dortch, and Caroline Sain for painstaking planning, scanning, converting, correcting, editing, and other help in the preparation of the manuscript. I am grateful despite myself to a pesky reader for the press who made excellent concrete suggestions for additions after I thought the book was done. I am grateful to Dean Timothy Johnston for providing an institutional home to teach and write without commuting. Finally, I am grateful to Derek Krueger for patience, support, and love.

The material in this anthology has appeared earlier as follows:

1   "You Wonder Where the Spirit Went," by Robert W. Jenson, *Pro Ecclesia: A Journal of Catholic and Evangelical Theology* 2 (1993): 296–304. © 1993 by the Center for Catholic and Evangelical Theology. Reprinted with permission from Rowman & Littlefield Publishing Group.

2   "Trinity," by Richard Norris. First published in this volume.

3   "Living into the Mystery of the Holy Trinity: Trinity, Prayer and Sexuality," by Sarah Coakley, *Anglican Theological Review* 80 (1998): 223–32. © 1998 by *Anglican Theological Review*. Reprinted with permission from the author and *Anglican Theological Review*.

4   "Word and Spirit," by Rowan Williams, in *On Christian Theology* (Oxford: Blackwell, 2000), pp. 107–11, 115–27. © 2000 by Rowan Williams. Reprinted with permission from Blackwell Publishing.

5   "Charismatic Experience: Praying 'In the Spirit'," by the Church of England Doctrine Commission / Sarah Coakley, in *We Believe in the Holy Spirit* (London: Church House Publications, 1991), pp. 17–36. © The Central Board

of Finance of the Church of England, 1991; The Archbishop's Council, 1999 and reproduced by permission.

6   "The Greek and Latin Traditions Regarding the Procession of the Holy Spirit," by the Pontifical Council for Promoting Christian Unity, *L'Osservatore Romano*, Weekly English Edition, 20 September 1995, no. 38, pp. 3 and 6. © *L'Osservatore Romano*.

7   "What is Pauline Participation in Christ?" by Stanley Stowers, in *Redefining First-Century Jewish and Christian Identities: Essays in Honor of Ed Parish Sanders*, ed. Fabian E. Udoh, *et al.* (Notre Dame, IN: University of Notre Dame Press, 2008). © 2008 by University of Notre Dame Press. Reprinted with permission from Notre Dame Press.

8   Excerpt from *Hymns on Virginity*, no. 7, by Ephrem the Syrian, in Sebastian P. Brock, *Studies Supplementary to Sobornost*, 2nd edn. (London: The Fellowship of St Alban and St Sergius, 1983), pp. 48–9, 51. © 1983 by Sebastian P. Brock. Reprinted with permission from the author.

9   [Eating Love] by Isaac of Nineveh, in *Mystical Treatises*, trans. A. J. Wensinck (Amsterdam: Koninklijke Akademie von Wetenschappen, 1923), pp. 211–12. Public domain.

10 *The Holy Spirit in the Syrian Baptismal Tradition*, by Sebastian P. Brock., 2nd rev. and enlarged edn., The Syrian Churches Series, vol. 9, ed. Jacob Vellian (Poona, India: Anita Printers, 1998), pp. 1, 4–11, 27–36. © 1998 by Sebastian P. Brock. Reprinted with permission from the author. (Rev. 3rd edn., Piscataway, NJ: Gorgias Press, 2008).

11 Excerpt from the *Catechetical Orations*, by Cyril of Jerusalem, in *A Select Library of the Nicene and Post-Nicene Fathers of the Christian Church*, Second Series, ed. Philip Schaff et al., in several editions, vol. 7. Public domain.

12 Excerpt from *Orations against the Arians*, by Athanasius of Alexandria, in *A Select Library of the Nicene and Post-Nicene Fathers of the Christian Church*, Second Series, ed. Philip Schaff et al., in several editions, vol. 5. Public domain.

13 Excerpt from *On the Holy Spirit*, by Basil of Caesarea, in *A Select Library of the Nicene and Post-Nicene Fathers of the Christian Church*, Second Series, ed. Philip Schaff et al., in several editions, vol. 8. Public domain.

14 Excerpts from *On Holy Baptism* and *On Pentecost*, by Gregory of Nazianzus, in *A Select Library of the Nicene and Post-Nicene Fathers of the Christian Church*, Second Series, ed. Philip Schaff et al., in several editions, vol. 7. Public domain.

15 *Homilies on the First Epistle of John*, no. 7, by Augustine of Hippo, in *A Select Library of the Nicene and Post-Nicene Fathers of the Christian Church*, First Series, ed. Philip Schaff et al., in several editions, vol. 7. Public domain.

16 *Veni, Creator Spiritus* and *Veni, Sancte Spiritus*, traditional Latin texts in multiple translations and editions: *Veni, Creator Spiritus* in the translation by John Dryden, and *Veni, Sancte Spiritus* in the translation by J. M. Neale. Public domain.

17 Excerpt from *De divinis officiis*, book 7, by Rupert of Deutz, in *Corpus christianorum continuatio mediaevalis*, vol. 7, ed. Hrabanus Haacke (Turnhout: Brepols, 1967), pp. 225–8. My translation, first published here.

18 Sermon 32, Fourth Sermon for Palm Sunday, in *Liturgical Sermons*, by Guerric of Igny, translated by the monks at Mount Saint Bernard Abbey (Kalamazoo, MI: Cistercian Publications, 2006), vol. 2, pp. 73–9. © 2006 by Cistercian Publications. Reprinted with permission from Liturgical Press.

19 Excerpt from the *Summa Theologica*, by Thomas Aquinas, from the translation of the Fathers of the English Dominican Province (New York: Benziger Brothers, 1947–8). Public domain.

20 "The Last Words of David," by Martin Luther in *Luther's Works*, vol. 15, ed. and trans. Jaroslav Pelikan and Hilton C. Oswald (St Louis, MO: Concordia Publishing, 1972), pp. 276, 280, 289–90, 301–9, 310–12, 315–16. From *Luther's Works*, vol. 15. © 1972 by Concordia Publishing House. Used with permission.

21 *Mysterium Paschale*, by Hans Urs von Balthasar, trans. with an Introduction by Aidan Nichols (Grand Rapids, MI: Eerdmans, 1990), pp. 203, 210–12. © 1990 by T. & T. Clark Ltd. Reprinted by permission of Continuum International Publishing Group and Ignatius Press.

22 *The Trinity and the Kingdom*, by Jürgen Moltmann, trans. Margaret Kohl (Minneapolis: Fortress Press, 1993), pp. 64, 81–3, 88–90, 94, 104–5. © 1981 in the English translation by SCM Press. Reprinted by permission of SCM-Canterbury Press and Augsburg Fortress Publishers.

23 "The Comforter," chapter 6 in *The Pillar and Ground of the Truth*, by Pavel Florensky, trans. Boris Jakim (Princeton, NJ: Princeton University Press, 1997), pp. 80–3, 85–99, 101–5. © 1977 by Princeton University Press. Reprinted by permission of Princeton University Press.

24 "Redemption and Deification," by Vladimir Lossky, in *In the Image and Likeness of God*, ed. John H. Erickson and Thomas E. Bird (Crestwood, NY: St Vladimir's Seminary Press, 1974), pp. 97–110. Originally translated by Edward Every in *Sobornost*, series 3, vol. 2 (1947), pp. 47–56. © 1974. Reprinted with permission from St Vladimir's Seminary Press.

25 "Trinitarian Relations and the Life of the Church," by Dumitru Staniloae, in *Theology and the Church*, trans. Robert Barringer (Crestwood, NY: St Vladimir's Seminary Press, 1974), pp. 11–15, 20–9, 40, 43. Originally published in Romanian in *Ortodoxia* 19 (1967): 503–25. © 1974. Reprinted with permission from St Vladimir's Seminary Press.

26 Excerpts from *The Discourses*, by Symeon the New Theologian, trans. C. J. deCatanzaro (Mahwah, NJ: Paulist Press, 1980), pp. 195–6, 198–203, 339–46. Copyright © 1980 by the Missionary Society of St Paul the Apostle in the State of New York. Paulist Press, Inc., New York/Mahwah, NJ. Reprinted by permission of Paulist Press, Inc. www.paulistpress.com

27 Excerpts from *The Spiritual Espousals*, by John Ruusbroec, in *The Spiritual Espousals and Other Works*, translated and with an Introduction by James A. Wiseman, OSB (New York: Paulist Press, 1985), pp. 41–2, 75, 77, 78–81, 113–16. Copyright © 1985 by James A. Wiseman, OSB. Paulist Press, Inc., New York/Mahwah, NJ. Reprinted by permission of Paulist Press, Inc. www.paulistpress.com.

28 "The Inhalation of the Air," in *The Spiritual Canticle*, by St John of the Cross, commentary on Stanza 39. My translation, first published here.

29 [The Spirit as Bride], by Matthias Scheeben, in *A Manual of Catholic Theology Based on Scheeben's "Dogmatik,"* 3rd, rev. edn. by Joseph Wilhelm and Thomas B. Scannell (London: Kegan Paul; New York: Benziger Brothers, 1906), pp. 333–6. Public domain.

30 "Prayer in the Trinity," by Adrienne von Speyr, in *The World of Prayer* (San Francisco: Ignatius Press, 1985), pp. 28–37, 40–2, 57–67, 69–72. © 1985 by Ignatius Press. Reprinted with permission from Ignatius Press.

31 "How the Spirit Reads and How to Read the Spirit," by Stephen E. Fowl, from *Engaging Scripture* (Oxford: Blackwell, 1998), pp. 97–9, 113–27. © 1998 by Stephen E. Fowl. Reprinted with permission from Blackwell Publishing.

32 "The Epistemic Role of the Spirit," by Bruce D. Marshall, in *Trinity and Truth* (Cambridge: Cambridge University Press, 2000), pp. 180–2, 204–7, 211–12. © 2000 by Cambridge University Press. Reprinted with permission from the author and Cambridge University Press.

Introduction

In the period before the *doctrine* of the Trinity became a rule about how Christians ought to talk, the three *names* of the Trinity formed a pattern of speech and liturgy. Christian thought and practice insist on a Trinity of Father, Son, and Holy Spirit. Christianity also enjoys a second-order practice *about* its practices to regulate and reflect on them, called theology. Theology is a practice of thought that reflects on other things Christians do, like prayer, liturgy, invocation, sacraments, feast days, catechesis, argument, iconography, interpretation, commentary. But theology has had trouble – for how long? – explaining what the Holy Spirit adds, no matter that pattern and invocation always included it. In modern Christian theology, anything the Spirit could do, Christ could do better, even if traditional Christians would be surprised to hear it put that way. Despite itself, recent academic theology has sounded like the duet from *Annie Get Your Gun*:

> Anything Spirit can do, Son can do better
> Son can do anything better than She.[1]

Is the Spirit superfluous? Academic theology has all but answered yes.

The trouble arises in part because academic theology tends to regard the Trinity in linear fashion, as crossing a distance. In that model, Jesus comes down from heaven and crosses an infinite distance between God the Father and the world. The Holy Spirit then crosses a distance of a different sort between the exterior history of the Son and the interior of the human heart. But believers tend to minimize the second distance and the Spirit with it. It's just a few inches.

Why not let Jesus do that too? "Let Jesus into your heart." Even committed trinitarians see little reason not to identify Christ as the crosser also of the second distance. If Christ can descend from the Father, he can enter the heart. If he enters the heart – and why not? – then the Spirit looks superfluous. If the way of the Son reaches into the far country of creation, then it can also cross the heart's frontier. Anything the Spirit could do, Christ could do better.

That conclusion presses especially hard on one prevailing version of the distance-crossing model. In that version, the crossing amounts to the transmission of information. On that view, what Christ brings down from heaven and deposits in the heart is just revelation, the knowledge that saves. You might use information to transform. You might even identify what Christ brings down as itself transformative and self-involving, like compassion. But academics prefer the distance-crossing model because it reduces – not necessarily, but all too easily – to the provision of information. We academics deal well with information. And as long as we're dealing with information transfer, we do well to eliminate middlemen. If we could get down to one mediator, wouldn't that count as an improvement? Not that anyone would admit trying to eliminate the Spirit. But the distance-crossing model can obscure why the Spirit might be a good thing, especially when it's revelation that makes the trip. In that case Christ can bring it better, even into the heart.

If Son and Spirit cross a distance and transmit information, then theologians can also ignore interpretations of scripture in interactive narrative and visual art. But those interpretations also show what most theologians are missing. If the Son and the Spirit appear on stage together in visual art or dramatic narrative, then neither reduces to the other. They do more than pass on information, they interact. If they interact, they reveal, not just information, but something of their relationship. They unveil, not a text to interpret or even an object to behold, but a community to join. If they commune, neither is dispensable; if they interrelate, neither is superfluous. Like the rivals in *Annie Get Your Gun*, when they interact on stage, they involve the audience. Iconic New Testament scenes interpreted in art and story show how the Son cannot replace or dispense with the Spirit, when the two interact. Sermons, poetry, hymns, treatises, rules, icons, mosaics, sculptures, narratives, paintings, vestments, winged fonts, and dove-shaped pyxes – not all illustrated here – imply or insist upon their interaction, especially in the Annunciation, the Baptism of Jesus, the Transfiguration, and in Ascension-and-Pentecost taken as a pair. Commentary in art and narrative help texts give up their secrets.

Christian images and narratives of the Son and the Spirit suggest two distinct practices of entry into the divine life, if not more. In the more linear pattern I described above, the Spirit leads a human being to the Son, who presents that one to the Father. In a more incorporative pattern, the Spirit introduces the human being into the interior of a relationship among Father, Son, and Spirit. This book suggests that the second, incorporative pattern solves problems raised by the first, distance-crossing one. Images and narratives of the Son and the Spirit interacting together provide both evidence for that assessment and contemplative practices for seeing the difference.

This book, an anthology, follows *After the Spirit*, a monograph. In their different ways, both books show how varying strains of Christian thought perceive the Holy Spirit as distinct from the Son, but this book argues by display what that one argued by exposition. That book, like this, proposes that Christian practices like prayer, reading, and icon-veneration take the goal of contemplation in at least two ways, and that the way of incorporation makes better sense of those practices than the way of traversal.

The way of traversal suggests that the Son crosses a distance. He makes his way into the far country of the human heart. He enters it largely as information. If the Spirit also indwells the heart, she looks superfluous – and thus dispensable – since Jesus is already there.[2] The way of incorporation, on the other hand, suggests that the Spirit joins human beings to a community or to its shared life. She shows them Jesus himself stretched out for them as a way into God.[3] She introduces them into God as participants. In this version, *they* are superfluous – as grace is – since the Spirit is already there. Dispensability becomes gratuity; waste becomes abundance; and superfluity turns out to be a good thing. The cup of the Spirit runs over.

At its best, the distance-crossing pattern specifies a case of the incorporative one. Then saving knowledge does not reduce to gnosis in a Gnostic sense. The Son provides information by which the Spirit engages the heart. The patterns need not conflict, since the traversal can take place within the trinitarian embrace.

Interpretive pieces in this book come both from classic traditions of Greek, Latin, and German Christianities and from understudied Syriac and Russian texts. This book makes crucial texts more available; it sounds more voices than one; it prompts other uses than mine. Both books present research, and both defend a thesis, but this one allows teachers and others to form their own judgments and serve their own purposes.

Both books argue, from classic texts and images, several further theses. (1) The Spirit makes sense only when paired with bodies: the bodies of individuals, communities, sacraments. (2) Christian thought succeeds in distinguishing the Spirit from the Son *just when* both appear together, as I said above: when they interact. When the Spirit interacts with the Son, the Spirit differs from the Son. When both appear on stage, then Christian art and texts treat the Spirit as neither dispensable nor superfluous. (3) Theses 1 and 2 go together. In Christian texts and art, the Spirit characteristically rests not just on any body, but on "the body of Christ."

In a pattern familiar to students of religion, that body bears many meanings. Thus Christians refer to the body of the historical Jesus as the body of Christ, to the Church as the body of Christ, and to the bread and wine of the sacraments as the body of Christ. The Spirit rests on the body of Christ in the narrative figure of Jesus at his conception, baptism, transfiguration, and resurrection; the Spirit rests on the body of Christ in the community of the Church; and the Spirit rests on the body of Christ in the sacraments. This anthology does not, therefore, collect merely texts. It looks deeply into both texts and images to defend a thesis about how scholars of religion ought to understand Christian talk about the Holy Spirit. It pursues that thesis just when theologians themselves seem unsure whether Christianity gives the Holy Spirit anything distinctive to do.

In many cases, the Holy Spirit does not float free of bodies, but befriends and accompanies them, paraphysically as it were,[4] coming to rest on holy places, holy people, holy things. In baptism, the Spirit alights on the body of a person. In the Eucharist, it inhabits the body of Christ as fire in the bread and wine. In unction, it covers a body by means of oil. The Spirit hovers over the waters of creation, of Mary's womb, of the Jordan, of the font, resting on the body of Christ in the world, in the womb, in the river, and in the church. The Spirit befriends the body as light, fire, incense, wine, and song. The Spirit transcends things, so that it can also inhabit them.

Meanwhile, nineteenth- and twentieth-century North Atlantic academic theologians called time and again to revive trinitarian thinking. But they (always?) went on to focus on Jesus at the Spirit's expense. New Testament scholars sought the Jesus of history, while mainstream believers sought the Christ of faith, leaving the Spirit to marginal groups. Even the defenders of the Trinity had little to say for the Spirit. Trinitarian revivals only exposed their difficulty.

The order of pieces began as the order in which I taught them in class, and changed a bit as I imagined how others might use or read them differently. In the end, readers and teachers will create their own orders by design or by accident. The categories, notional at best, raise as may questions as they solve: why class Symeon the New Theologian with the mystics, and not with the Greeks? Why separate von Balthasar from von Speyr? I have tried to resist confessional identities by grouping readings by language or area instead of by creed. Many of the pieces should, like *Don Quixote*, never be read for the first time: on second readings, various themes will suggest themselves, including the role of the Spirit in the Trinity, in deification, in prayer, in disputed questions. The introductions substitute for a first reading. If you read the introductions, then you will begin to get a sense of whether and in what order you might want to read the articles and excerpts that they introduce. The introductions are very directive; they identify themes and arguments; they do not address historical development except incidentally. If you are more interested in the problems, start with Jenson or Coakley; if you are more interested in exposition, start with Norris.

As there is no one correct ordering, there is no hope of exhaustiveness. I chose the readings to be interesting and to do conceptual work. Many important and interesting works – from Athanasius' *Letters to Serapion on the Holy Spirit* to the works of Karl Barth often mentioned here – abridge badly and demand to be read at length on their own. In those cases, I have attempted substitutions. So we have a short extract from Athanasius' *Orations against the Arians* instead of a long one from his *Letters to Serapion*; Robert Jenson about Barth instead of Barth himself; Symeon the New Theologian instead of Gregory Palamas; Lossky and Staniloae instead of Bulgakov: pieces both interesting in their own right, as well as for their relation to others. The cuts to those included have been cruel: Basil cuts like butter, and Weinandy (*The Father's Spirit of Sonship*) cut like diamond – which is to say that I couldn't figure out how to cut it at all, and had to leave it out, to be read whole as a separate book. In general I have cut evidence in favor of argument, and footnotes with or without notice. No course of reading would be complete in one volume; no course of reading would be complete without some of those longer treatments suggested in For Further Reading.

Different audiences can read this book (and its fellow) in different ways. Within Religious Studies, the books reflect on indigenous Christian accounts of experience, community, identity formation, ritual practice, economic activity, and material culture. All those matters prompt native Christian accounts to invoke the Holy Spirit.

Within Christian theology, the same accounts prompt further reflection on how the Spirit functions in the Trinity and interacts with Jesus. The anthology enlarges the audience and refashions the argument in a more subtle and multi-voiced way. Scholars all over the university – from politics to medicine – have much to learn about how Christian practices pursue the Spirit to engage and befriend human bodies.

Notes

1   For more about this problem, and an attempt to solve it, see my *After the Spirit: A Constructive Pneumatology from Outside the Modern West* (Grand Rapids, MI: Eerdmans, 2005; London: SCM Press, 2006).
2   As already Jerome noted (*In Isa.* [*On Isaiah*] XI, on Isa. 40: 9–11), three traditions of Christian thought used different pronouns for the Spirit, because the word had masculine, feminine, and neuter genders in Latin, Syriac, and Greek. All Christian traditions agreed that God transcends gender. For more, see Sebastian Brock in this volume, as well as Sebastian Brock, "The Holy Spirit as Feminine in Early Syriac Literature," in *After Eve*, ed. Janet Martin Soskice (London: Marshall-Pickering, 1990); Susan Ashbrook Harvey, "Feminine Imagery for the Divine: the Holy Spirit, the Odes of Solomon, and Early Syriac Tradition," *St Vladimir's Seminary Quarterly* 37 (1993): 111–39; and Gabriele Winkler, "Further Observations in Connection with the Early Form of the Epiklesis," in *Studies in Early Christian Liturgy and its Context*, Variorum Collected Studies Series, no. 593 (Aldershot, UK: Ashgate, 1997), pp. iv, 66–80, esp. pp. 69–73, 79–80, on invocations of "the Mother, the Spirit of holiness," p. 69.
3   Thomas Aquinas, *Summa Theologica*, Part I, proemium to Question 2.
4   The attempt to recover the language of *para phusin*, which Paul uses for the work of the Spirit in Romans 11, appears in Eugene F. Rogers, Jr., "The Spirit Rests on the Son Paraphysically," in *The Lord and Giver of Life*, ed. David H. Jensen (Philadelphia: Westminster John Knox Press, 2008), pp. 87–95.

I
Late Twentieth-Century Questions

1

Robert W. Jenson, "You Wonder Where the Spirit Went"

Robert W. Jenson is one of the most rigorous and creative theologians writing in English. His article "You Wonder Where the Spirit Went" crystallizes an unease about successive nineteenth- and twentieth-century trinitarian revivals: whether they have much interesting to say about the Holy Spirit; whether, indeed, they tend (despite themselves) to reduce the Spirit to a function or "power" of the Son. He poses that question by focusing on the greatest and most ambitious of those revivals, that of Karl Barth.

Barth is a theologian's theologian. Some students have read thousands of pages by him. Some have yet to read any. But both can learn from Jenson's analysis things they can learn almost nowhere else. Why study an article devoted largely to someone you haven't read? Because sometimes the omissions and tendencies of the greatest inspire the best thinking among their critics. They require those who find fault to think through why.

In thinking through why, Jenson identifies the impediments he suspects of obstructing robust Spirit-talk. Barth's Spirit-talk shows a tendency to announce the Spirit but discuss the Son. He exhibits a kind of theological speech impediment: almost involuntary pauses in speaking of the Spirit, filled in by repetitions in speaking of the Son. The obstacles must be powerful indeed, if they hinder Barth. Why read Jenson on Barth on the Spirit? Because Jenson can diagnose what stumps Barth.

The case of Barth suggests, according to Jenson, that views like these will impede a theologian's Spirit-talk. These, according to Jenson, are the problems:

1   The Spirit is a something rather than a someone.
2   The Spirit is no agent in itself, but God's capacity to "echo" in some *other* agent (Jesus, the human being, the Church). The echo is unreliable or too hard to discern – "subjective" – in any agent but Jesus.

Robert W. Jenson, "You Wonder Where the Spirit Went," *Pro Ecclesia: A Journal of Catholic and Evangelical Theology* 2 (1993): 296–304.

3   Therefore the Spirit echoes rather than acts in human experience. Thus it reduces all too easily to human experience, rather than becoming objective in the Church.
4   The Spirit echoes rather than acts in human history. Thus the Church reduces all too easily to church history, rather than mediating salvation.
5   The Spirit echoes rather than acts at Pentecost. Thus Pentecost marks the denouement of the stories about Jesus, rather than a new initiative of the Spirit.

Jenson's diagnosis raises two questions of its own. (1) To what extent does Barth avoid the Spirit only as a corrective to Schleiermacher? Would Barth have allowed the Spirit more scope, if he had fought an opponent on a different front? (2) Can Jenson talk about the objectivity of the Spirit in the Church, and still allow God to correct the Church?[1]

Karl Barth (1886–1968) was the greatest Protestant theologian of the twentieth century, and arguably the greatest *Christian* theologian of that century. He revived trinitarian thinking to propose new and powerful answers to questions that had not been thoroughly thought through in trinitarian fashion before. Doctrines as diverse as revelation, election, creation, and redemption were to be judged by how trinitarian they were, where the opposite of "trinitarian" was "abstract."

Yet the trinitarianism usually served to distinguish the Son from the Father. So not only was the Father the revealing God, but the Father was revealing himself in the Son. Not only was the Father the electing God, but the Son was the electing God and the elect human being in One. Not only did the Father create, but it was characteristic of the Father to desire a created other to himself because he had an uncreated other to himself in the Son. Not only did the Son redeem, but in him the human being participated in the judgment of the Father.

You might expect pneumatological analogates of those moves. Sometimes you get them telegraphed; sometimes you don't get them at all. Barth makes the Holy Spirit responsible for the human being's "readiness" for revelation, or for God's involving or engaging the human being in revelation. But you do not hear that the Holy Spirit is the electing God; it falls to Jenson, in another piece, to develop that insight.[2] You scarcely hear that the role of the Holy Spirit in creation is to create witnesses. You hear about the role of the Holy Spirit in redemption, but that turns out to reduce, Jenson notes, to "the power of Jesus Christ."

Barth avoided the Holy Spirit, he makes clear, because he thought that Schleiermacher had made it too easy for the Spirit to cover anthropocentrism. You might read Jenson's career as devoted to the theology of the Holy Spirit. On the way, he proves in the doing that you get off the seesaw between Schleiermacher's anthropocentrism and Barth's avoidance of it. You could have a doctrine of the Spirit – or any of several interesting doctrines of the Spirit – without reducing the Spirit either to the Son or to the human being. Like Luther, Jenson generates new ideas with delight and phrases them with compression, often leaving it to others to fit them together. More than any other theologian after Barth, he exercises the theologian's license to argue *thesenhaft*, in elegant and provocative theses. Among his more interesting proposals about the Spirit are these: The Spirit is the electing God. If God is the one who was, and is, and ever shall be, the Spirit corresponds to the future, to what God shall be. If the Father is the source of divinity, the *fons deitatis*, the Spirit is the goal of divinity, the *finis deitatis*. The Spirit liberates the Father.[3]

You Wonder Where the Spirit Went

Robert W. Jenson

Karl Barth is the initiator and model (the *image*, in his own sense!) of this century's renewal of trinitarian theology. He is moreover a giant of the Reformed theological tradition, famous always for its witness to the Spirit. The near-unanimity is therefore remarkable, with which a recent meeting of the Karl Barth Society of North America agreed that long stretches of Barth's thinking seem rather binitarian than trinitarian. What can be the explanation? This paper is the result of the Society's assignment, that I should seek one.

There are at least three modes of trinitarian reflection in the *Kirchliche Dogmatik* [*Church Dogmatics*]. First, Barth so locates the doctrine of Trinity systematically as to make it *identify* the God whose ways the *Kirchliche Dogmatik* will seek to trace. The biblical narratives claim to identify a particular God, and therefore claim to be true of him in a way that specifies his hypostatic being. Barth sets his analysis of this phenomenon in the very prolegomena of his dogmatics, to make it plain that it is *this* God of whom also his subsequent dogmatic propositions are to be true. Barth's observation – so easy to make once he had made it – that the doctrine of Trinity is Christianity's *identification* of its God, and the amazing resolution with which he exercises that insight throughout his dogmatics, would be epochal theological contributions had Barth made no other.

Second, in I/1, §§8–12, Barth develops a full technical doctrine of Trinity. This *locus* is, I think, problematic in part. §8, "God in his Revelation" has been itself a revelation for many: the way in which the trinitarian mandates are laid one upon another, by each time asking what must be true if God is truly to *be* exactly as he is in revealing himself, has burned itself into the thinking of serious late 20th-century theology. But the §§ in which Barth then develops what he calls the "churchly doctrine" itself, are perhaps less rewarding as a whole. Though they are of course filled with remarkable individual insights, it cannot be said that they are either as creative or as knowledgeable as we expect from Barth.

Barth says that the three in God are foundationally to be understood "from their . . . variously specific genetic relations to each other,"[4] but in the actual development of the doctrine he makes little or no use of this principle, in practice substituting "analogy" for "relation" – that analogy is itself a relation does not change the point. Again, Barth takes the traditional founding of the three in their mutual relations as a reason for preferring "modes of being" to "persons" for the three. Surely, however, precisely "persons" are constituted in mutual relation – exactly according to Karl Barth! – in a way harder to grasp for "modes of being." My suspicion is that these questions are not unrelated to the question which directly occasions this essay.

Third, throughout the *Kirchliche Dogmatik* Barth indeed *uses* the church's and his insight into God's triunity. This paper is devoted to a problem encountered just here. But that is only to say that the paper is devoted to nit-picking. For Barth is the theologian and the *Kirchliche Dogmatik* the book by which Western theology rediscovered that the doctrine of Trinity, while indeed a mystery, is not a puzzle, that instead it is the frame within which theology's mysteries can be shown and its puzzles solved. If some of his own solutions are incomplete or even misleading, that remains a secondary matter. To be sure, if the nit I will pick turns out to be the one biting it is a sizeable varmint, and lively on the ecumenical scene.

II

The *Kirchliche Dogmatik* presents a smorgasbord of cases in which the doctrine of Trinity, as *used*, seems to be rather a doctrine of binity. Let me mention three, at this point merely to instance the problem. Of these, the latter two are especially alarming. The Karl Barth Society's attention was drawn to the problem by the case of Barth's trinitarian grounding of female-male community. As the Father and the Son are to one another, so therefore are Christ and humanity to one another, and so therefore within humanity are male and female to one another.[5] Since there are only two sexes – at least in the strange world of the Bible or of Barth – it is plain that the Spirit's appearance as a party in these analogies would be disruptive. But a theology's power at any point is perhaps best shown by its ability to profit from disruptions.

A second instance of apparent binitarianism occurs in IV/3, §69, 1, 2, 4. In these daring and in many ways even beautiful pages, Barth conducts a probing and systematically way-breaking discussion of the "objectivity" of the proclamation. Surely he is right: to be faithful to the logic of the gospel, we must think of the gospel's occurrence also *pro nobis* as itself a salvation-historical event antecedent to its sounding in any set of our ears, as itself an "external" reality. Perhaps we will be especially sensitive to this logic, if we have been attending to Orthodox ecumenical initiatives. Both common teaching and Orthodox urging will then make us expect Barth to designate the Pentecostal coming of the Spirit as the event just posited. Instead, Barth conducts some of the most tortuous dialectic in the *Kirchliche Dogmatik*, in order to locate the proclamation's objectivity in the Resurrection of the Son. Does Barth suppose that an act of the Spirit cannot transcend subjectivity?

Barth's more specific location of the proclamation's objectivity in the "universal prophetism" of the risen Lord would then, to be sure, more than recoup the pneumatological loss, if in Barth's description of this prophetism itself, the Spirit had the role which surely he should have in description of a "prophetism." But despite the title of §69, 4, *Die Verheissung des Geistes* [The Promise of the Spirit], the Spirit hardly appears in the story.

Our third instance occurs in the same volume,[6] under the title "The Holy Spirit and the Mission of the Christian Congregation." Barth here undertakes nothing less than an exegesis of the novelty which the church presents in universal history. The piece is a marvel. But he manages to write it entirely without mention of the Spirit – which must be an equal marvel, given who and what the Spirit is in Scripture.

III

I must turn to diagnosis. The present section is preliminary. It is regularly observed that Barth's developed doctrine of Trinity is, despite the new insights on which it is based and despite some new insights scattered also in it, thoroughly Western-traditional in its general contour. The triune God as such is personal in a modern sense, while the three are otherwise characterized. The *filioque* is used systematically. Of the classic heresies, modalism is the temptation.

Notoriously, traditional Western teaching has its drawbacks, in my judgment one principally. Any theologian for whom the doctrine of Trinity is more than a relic, that is, any theologian who *uses* the doctrine of Trinity outside its own *locus,* is repeatedly led – indeed, compelled – to treat the three as *parties* of divine action, and that also "immanently." Not only those with a "social" doctrine of Trinity do this sort of thing – for my own part, I was initiated into the possibility by my orthodox Lutheran and otherwise adamantly Augustinian *Doktorvater,* Peter Brunner. The problem with the Western form of teaching is that it offers little or no justification for this necessary practice; indeed, it seems actually to have quenched the practice in Western theology.

Notoriously also, difficulties of this sort are especially severe in the case of the Spirit – whether or not Eastern attribution of all Western problems to the *filioque* is correct. Augustine himself felt and remarked a special difficulty with the Spirit, and so have many successors.

The general problem is plainly present in Barth. The three in God are not to be regarded as "persons" in a modern sense, but rather as the "modes" in which the one God "is three times differently God" (*dreimal anders Gott*);[7] in this systematically decisive definition Barth moreover intends the "is" as an active verb with the one God as its subject, so that the being of three is adverbial. Such a doctrine of Trinity can offer no better support for the actual use which Barth elsewhere makes of God's triunity than Western teaching in general does for such use. For also Barth's use invariably depends on taking the Father and the Son as *parties* of an action in God.

The drawbacks of Western-style trinitarianism are not necessarily fatal to theology that labors under them. That not every conceptual practice that a theologian finds necessary is fully supported by his/her general system is probably, indeed, a distinguishing virtue of theology. Moreover, Eastern forms of trinitarian teaching present equal if different drawbacks. So probably would any such future revised or ecumenical form as Pannenberg or I have been working on.

But within Barth's system, Western hindrances may obstruct more mischievously than elsewhere, just on account of his achievements. Barth envisions the entire history of salvation as eternally actual in God, in whom it is divine history posited in God's triunity. Therefore the way in which the immanent Trinity is interpreted must more directly determine the way in which God's triune work is grasped, than is usual in Western theology. This is profoundly to the good. But therefore again – and this is my preliminary diagnosis – in Barth's theology, Western trinitarianism's common difficulty in conceiving the Spirit's specific immanent initiative in God must become a difficulty in conceiving the Spirit's entire salvation-historical initiative.

It is not, of course, that Barth *wants* to conceive such a salvation-historical personal initiative of the Spirit and is hindered from doing so. He denies that there is any such thing to conceive: "The New Testament knows . . . of only one coming of the One who has come. . . . It is not thereby excluded that this . . . occurs in differing forms, at times he . . . chooses and in circumstances he orders. . . . It occurs . . . in the time of the church . . . also in the form of the sharing of the Spirit. . . . And it will again occur in other form . . . as his coming to inaugurate the general resurrection. But in all these forms it is one single event (*ein einziges Ereignis*)."[8] What Barth is hindered in, is supposing that he *ought* to conceive a specific salvation-historical initiative of the Spirit.

IV

I will now concentrate my analysis on a decisive mark of Western trinitarianism and principal bone of contention with the East. In normal Western trinitarianism, characterization of the Spirit as the *vinculum amoris* between the Father and Son is systematically central. Barth is no innovator or exception at this point. Indeed, his great attachment to this theologoumenon is his stated reason for supporting the *filioque*.

Barth writes, "The *filioque* expresses our knowledge of the fellowship between the Father and the Son: the Holy Spirit is the love that is the essence of the relation between these two modes of God's being."[9] Confirming Orthodoxy's worst suspicions, he continues with the explicit proposition that this "perfect consubstantial fellowship between the Father and the Son" is "the being of the Spirit . . ." and that precisely these propositions make the point "on which everything seems to us to depend . . ."[10]

The "inner-divine" fellowship of Father and Son in the Spirit is explicitly described as "two-sided," since the Spirit is the fellowship itself. Precisely this merely two-sided fellowship is then the eternal ground for there being fellowship between God and humanity,[11] first between God and the Son Jesus and then between God in Jesus and Jesus' sisters and brothers. But that is to say that this merely two-sided fellowship is the eternal ground of all salvation-history. Moreover, the way this grounding works is that each two-sided fellowship is the *archetype* of the thereby next grounded such pairing,[12] so that the two-sidedness reproduces itself at every ontological level.

One passage must be quoted *in extenso*: "The Holy Spirit is the power and his action is the work of *coordination* between the being of Jesus Christ and that of . . . his congregation. Just as he as a divine 'person,' i.e. mode of being, as Spirit of the Father and of the Son (*qui ex Patre Filioque procedit*) is the bond of peace between the two, so in the historical work of atonement he is the constituent and guarantee of the *unity* of the *totus Christus* . . ."[13]

According to Barth, the triune reality of God is actual as the event of election, of the decision made "before all time" in God. And that is to say, the triune reality of God is actual as an eternal meeting between the Father and the Son, a meeting in which, as in all personal meetings, something is decided. What is decided is that the eternal relation of the Father and the Son is in fact the relation between the Father and the man Jesus and so also a covenant between God and Jesus' sisters and brothers.[14] I think this complex theologoumenon precisely and simply true. But again, it may be that just the precision and depth of his understanding make Barth's participation in the common difficulties of Western theology more than usually consequence-laden.

Some of the pressure on Barth's ability to identify the Spirit's actuality may come from a residue of the traditional Calvinist teaching of predestination. That doctrine, for all that can otherwise be said in its praise, described the event of election much in the protological past tense and little in the eschatological future tense. Within Barth's correct identification of the event of election with the actuality of triunity, Calvinist presuppositions about election must exercise a reverse pressure on the interpretation of triunity. And if the Trinity's actuality thereby comes to be thought definitively in the past tense, the Spirit is left without that mode of God's time in which the Bible locates him.

But my guess is that the *vinculum*-doctrine is the chief Jonah. Precisely in that the inner-trinitarian relations do gloriously become concrete and alive in Barth, so that the Father and the Son *confront* one another, the actuality of a *vinculum* between the two parties Father and Son must be their I–thou relation itself. Thus the very reality of the Spirit excludes his appearance as a *party* in the triune actuality.

In formal doctrine, Barth calls all three hypostases *modi essendi* [modes of being]. In his *use* of trinitarian insight, he nevertheless speaks freely of the personal immanent intercourse of the Father and the Son. But the Spirit is condemned by the vinculum-doctrine to remain a *modus* only. The concretion of triunity is a history in God in which the Spirit does not appear as an historical party. Appropriately, the causative relation of this history to a reality *ad extra* [toward the outside] is an impersonal principle, of image-analogy.

It is again tempting to speculate that the pressure may work backwards, here from a merely two-sided understanding of human community and so of historical reality, inherited from the "I–Thou" tradition of 19th-century German philosophical anthropology, to a merely two-sided understanding of trinitarian community and history. Were this the case, it would be the symptom of a deep flaw indeed. It would mean that Barth's use of the image-analogy principle had opened a channel in his thinking for projection of perceived human value onto God, for theological analogy in which a human phenomenon is the primary analogate also in the order of being. I will not pursue this horrid possibility.

V

It is surely with the doctrine of the church that a discussion of this matter must terminate. The discussion of the church in IV and particularly in IV/3 finds its warrants at every step in descriptions of a meeting in God between the Father and the Son. An alternative possibility of course would to find such warrants in description of a meeting between the Spirit on the one hand and the Son with the Father on the other.

The ecclesiology which would result from this alternative move has the recommendation of ecumenical urgency. For it is precisely that currently being pressed on the Western church by Orthodoxy and increasingly found salvific also in Catholic/Protestant dialogues – though not often by Protestant churches reacting to the dialogues. What according to Orthodoxy must be apprehended is that the Pentecostal coming of the Spirit is "a new intervention of the Holy Trinity in time . . ." and that on this occasion the intervention "issues from the third Person of the Trinity. . . ."[15] When this specific role of the Spirit is not grasped, the Western pendulum between Catholic institutionalism and Protestant spiritualist individualism must, according to Orthodox polemic, necessarily ensue. When it is grasped, an ecclesiology of *communion* ensues.

This leads to a final speculation – which I offer with quite intense suspicion that it is true. Perhaps the final reason for the whole web of Spirit-avoidance in the *Kirchliche Dogmatik* is avoidance of the *church*. For if the Pentecostal creation of a structured continuing community were identified as the "objectivity" of the gospel's truth *pro nobis*, then this community itself, in its structured temporal and spatial extension, would be seen as the *Bedingung der Möglichkeit* [condition of the very possibility] of faith. Or again, if the Community between the Father and the Son were himself an *agent*[16] of their love, immanently and economically, then the church, as the community inspirited by this Agent, would be the active *mediatrix* of faith, in precisely the way demanded by Catholics and resisted by Protestants in every chief dialogue.

Catholic commentators have notoriously found many approaches in the *Kirchliche Dogmatik* to Catholic patterns of thought. The point at which approach would become arrival has been defined by no less than Joseph Cardinal Ratzinger: "For the Catholic, the church is itself comprised in the deep source of the act of faith: it is only in that I believe with the church that I share in that certitude in which I may rest my life."[17] Union with the church constitutes a "new and wider self" of the believer; and it is this self that is the subject of faith, "the self of the *anima ecclesiastica*, that is, the self of that person through whom the whole community of the church expresses itself. . . ."[18] May Karl Barth's impulsion to practiced binitarianism be in fact the last resistance of his Protestantism?

I must finish by considering the chief passage in which Barth states the ecclesial reality of the Spirit theoretically, IV/3, 867–872. The mystery of the church is the "identity of her being with that of Jesus Christ."[19] But this identity obtains only as it *happens*; i.e., insofar as it is "work of the Spirit."[20] So far, one might think, so plain. But then two phenomena appear.

The personal agent of this work in fact turns out at every step of Barth's argument to be *not* the Spirit, as advertised, but Christ; the Spirit is denoted invariably by impersonal terms. The Spirit is "the power of Jesus Christ's being";[21] "the Holy Spirit is the godly power (*Gottesmacht*) unique to the being of Jesus Christ, in the exercise . . . of which he lets his congregation become what it is";[22] the Spirit is what happens when "Jesus Christ makes use of his power. . . ."[23] This work in itself is the *coordination* of "heavenly and earthly activity . . . ," in which their difference is – in good Western fashion – strictly maintained. And then we discover that the earthly activity in question is the "*subjective*" side of the knowledge of God.[24]

It seems unavoidable: in Barth's system, the Spirit is precisely the *Geschichtlichkeit* of "the relation of the being of Jesus Christ to that of his congregation . . . ."[25] The Spirit is the capacity of God as archetype, at whatever ontological level, to evoke an echo in some subjectivity. When does the Spirit disappear from Barth's pages? Whenever he would appear as someone rather than as something. We miss the Spirit at precisely those points where Bible or catechism have taught us to expect him to appear as someone *with capacities*, rather than as sheer capacity – in the archetype/image scheme, as himself an archetype.

It is of course a generally unsolved problem, felt from the earliest days of Christian theology: How is the Spirit at once his own person and what "all three" hypostases actively are together? How is the Spirit at once one who has power and that power itself? It is no general refutation of Barth, that he too has left a few problems unsolved. But interaction between this unsolved problem and Barth's particular achievements produces an especially painful set of symptoms.

Notes

1   For an example of a Jenson protégé arguing that the Church is the hypostasis of the Spirit, see Reinhard Huetter, *Suffering Divine Things: Theology as Church Practice*, trans. Douglas W. Stott (Grand Rapids, MI: Eerdmans, 1999).

2   Robert W. Jenson, "The Holy Spirit," in Robert W. Jenson and Carl Braaten, *Christian Dogmatics*, 2 vols. (Philadelphia: Fortress Press, 1984), vol. 2, pp. 101–82.

3   Robert W. Jenson, *The Triune Identity* (Philadelphia: Fortress Press, 1982), last chapter; *Unbaptized God: The Basic Flaw in Ecumenical Theology* (Minneapolis: Fortress Press, 1992), Part III.

4   Karl Barth, *Die Kirchliche Dogmatik*, 4 vols. in 13 (Zurich: Evangelischer Verlag/Zollikon, 1932–70). English edn.: *The Church Dogmatcks*, 4 vols. in 13, trans. G. W. Bromiley et al. (Edinburgh: T. & T. Clark, 1936–75), I/1, 382.

5   III/2, §45.

6   IV/3, §72.

7   I/1, 380.

8   IV/3, 338.

9   I/1, 504.

10 I/1, 505.

11 I/1, 504.

12 I/1, 505.

13   IV/3, 870.

14   For all this, I may perhaps be permitted to refer to my first book about Barth, *Alpha and Omega* (New York: Nelson, 1963), especially chapters 3 and 5.

15   Nikos Nissiotis, *Die Theologie der Ostkirche im ökumenischen Dialog* (Stuttgart: Evangelisches Verlagswerk, 1968), pp. 74f.

16   I do not yet know how to work out this proposition conceptually.

17   Joseph Cardinal Ratzinger, "Luther und die Einheit der Christen," *Communio* 12 (83): 575–6.

18   Joseph Cardinal Ratzinger, *Église, Oecuménisme et Politique*, trans. P. Jordan, P.-E. Gudenus and B. Müller (Paris: Fayard, 1987), p. 173.

19   *KD*, IV/3, 867.

20   Ibid., 868.

21   Ibid.

22   Ibid., 869.

23   Ibid., 870.

24   Ibid., 871.

25   Ibid., 868.

2

Richard Norris, "Trinity"

It is commonplace among certain twentieth-century writers on the Trinity – including Robert Jenson, Sarah Coakley, Rowan Williams, David Yeago, J. A. DiNoia, Adrienne von Speyr, Thomas Weinandy, and myself – that the Trinity is less an object to observe than a community that joins human beings to itself. This article, by Richard Norris, makes one of the clearest arguments for that sort of view. "Christians do not 'worship' the Trinity in the sense that they stand, as it were, off from it and gawk reverently from a safe distance," Norris writes. "On the contrary, their worship is a kind of participation in the relations among the members of the Trinity." Arguing for rather than assuming that view, Norris presents more evidence than one sometimes finds. For the claim that Christian worship participates in the Trinity rather than gazing at it, Norris offers three other claims in support, each with its characteristic evidence. (1) "[T]he words of one reasonably representative eucharistic prayer" imply that the Eucharist is somehow taken up into the praise and celebration that occupy the members of the Trinity and takes place within their activity, because in it "believers ascribe 'all honor and glory' to God the Father 'through Christ and with Christ and in Christ' and 'in the unity of the Holy Spirit.'" (2) The characteristic appearing of Father, Son, and Spirit at Christ's baptism involves other human beings in the relationship of beloved sonship there displayed. And (3) Irenaeus and the Cappadocians interpret God as neither identical nor contrary to the world but as a sort of place, activity, or love *embracing* and *engaging* the world, in which the world lives, moves, and has its being. Each of those supporting claims unpacks a way in which Christian worship participates in the Trinity rather than gazing at it from a safe distance. The argument centers on the second claim, that the baptism of Christ sets the pattern for Christian worship in the Trinity.

First published in this volume.

The baptism of Christ, according to Norris, does not just display the Trinity in a tableau, but "catches" the Trinity "in the very act of 'doing its thing,'" enacting the relationship among Father, Son, and Spirit. The voice of the Father, the receptivity of the Son, and the descent of the Spirit in the form of a dove manifest the Trinity as one who blesses, one who receives blessing, and one who rests or spreads or celebrates as blessing. Or, in the more concrete terms of Irenaeus of Lyon and Basil of Caesarea, the Three are the Anointer, the Anointed, and the Unction with which he is anointed. That interaction does not take place at a distance, but in such a way as to involve others in it. Christ receives as human what he enjoys as God – just so that other human beings can receive it after his pattern. What the Father does for Christ he does after that pattern also for other human beings. As the Spirit befriends or accompanies the body of Christ she befriends or accompanies or spreads over – after that pattern – additional members of the body of Christ. The baptism of Christ is also, by the spreading of the Spirit, a great inclusion of other human beings into the trinitarian embrace. It is that baptismal pattern that continues to unfold when other Christian practices, from the celebration of the Eucharist to the exposition of divinity, come to make sense as ways of incorporating the participant in the Trinity's life.

Trinity

Richard Norris

"What is the Trinity?" asks the Catechism in the current American *Book of Common Prayer*. It then answers its own question, as catechisms do: "The Trinity is one God, Father, Son, and Holy Spirit."[1] This brisk statement is perhaps not very helpful to inquirers, any more than is the fuller affirmation in *The Thirty-Nine Articles of Religion*: "There is but one living and true God . . . , and in the unity of this Godhead there be three Persons, of one substance, power, and eternity; the Father, the Son, and the Holy Ghost."[2] But if these statements are not very helpful, because they assert something puzzling without explaining it, they are very clear on one basic point. The word "trinity" as they understand it refers to – is simply another word for – God. In other words, the Trinity[3] is not a doctrine. It is what Christians worship, as the ancient hymn *Te Deum* asserts:

> Throughout the world the holy Church acclaims you;
> Father, of majesty unbounded,
> your true and only Son, worthy of all worship,
> and the Holy Spirit, advocate and guide.[4]

More than this, Christians do not "worship" the Trinity in the sense that they stand, as it were, off from it and gawk reverently from a safe distance. On the contrary, their worship is a kind of participation in the relations among the members of the Trinity. Otherwise, what is to be made of the words of one reasonably representative eucharistic prayer, which has believers ascribe "all honor and glory" to God the Father "through Christ and with Christ and in Christ" and "in the unity of the Holy Spirit"?[5]

It is no surprise, then, that there is a *dogma* regarding the Trinity: that is to say, a teaching that is both traditional and official. For how should an historical community like the Church not be clear about *what* and *how* it worships? One of the plainer formulations of this dogma, if not the most familiar, is contained in a decree (380 CE) of the Emperors Gratian, Valentinian, and Theodosius:

> We command that all churches be forthwith delivered up to the bishops who confess the Father, the Son, and the Holy Spirit to be of one majesty and power, of the same glory and of one splendor; making no distinction by any profane division, but rather harmony by the assertion of the trinity of the persons and the unity of the Godhead . . .[6]

That, if read carefully, states the dogma of the Trinity without wasting words; and if it is not enough, one can go on to consult the "Athanasian" Creed,[7] or even the Niceno-Constantinopolitan Creed, which speaks of God, of God's unique Son who is "true God from true God," and finally of the Holy Spirit who "proceeds from the Father" and is "worshiped and glorified together with the Father and the Son."

Now it would be silly to announce, at this juncture, that there is nothing more to be said about the Trinity. Dogma – what Christian tradition has *defined* as essentially belonging to the faith – is always something rather terse, stark, and straightforward. A dogma tends to say as little as possible, but to assert it very definitely. *Hence a dogma is not an explanation.* It is a determination of a particular issue, like certain judicial verdicts. It may raise all sorts of questions. It may, and probably will, require interpretation. Once the move is made from formula to interpretation, however, one leaves the realm of dogma and enters that of catechetical *doctrine* and ultimately of *theology*, whose typical product is not a terse assertion but a two-volume treatise. One thus crosses into a realm in which people differ because they expound the dogma from different points of view, and on the basis of different insights. There is no necessary harm in this: as Richard Hooker once said, we should "take comfort in this variety"; for as long as the explications in question are honest efforts to be true to the dogma, what emerges is the *richness and depth* of the reality that the dogma engages.

What will be undertaken here, therefore, is not a full-blown and authoritative elaboration of the doctrine of the Trinity, but an arguable, perhaps illuminating, but in any case relatively brief, *interpretation* of its classical formulation. To be specific, we shall ask where the idea of the God as Trinity is rooted, and answer this question by allusion to a passage in Irenaeus of Lyon (d. *ca.*195) which itself looks back to the New Testament. Then, as we explore this formulation, we will comment on it in the light of the settlement that emerged out of the fourth-century Arian controversy – i.e., the doctrine as set forth by the Cappadocian fathers;[8] and at the same time, weigh some of the problems and interpretations that are being discussed in contemporary talk about the Trinity.

1. Roots of the doctrine of the Trinity

It would be wrong to begin this enterprise without a straightforward acknowledgment that nowadays the doctrine of the Trinity strikes most people as a difficult, speculative, and superfluous afterthought. The very terms it employs – "substance," e.g., or "hypostasis" – present themselves as abstractions from abstractions; and to many folk, the whole affair seems to be no more than a bit of bad arithmetic or a ghostly metaphysical speculation whose connection with, or relevance to, human life and experience is difficult to specify. Moreover, to the Enlightenment tradition, which still shapes Western culture where questions of religion are concerned, the doctrine of the Trinity represents the acme of religious particularism and obscurantism; and this perception of it is by now a part of the cultural air that Christians breathe. To see one effect of this tradition, one has only to consider Friedrich Schleiermacher's influential work titled *The Christian Faith* (1821). That work treated the dogma of the Trinity as material for a mildly disparaging appendix, thus marking it as a near irrelevance if not an embarrassment in any serious account of Christian life and belief.

It was around a century later that, at least in Protestant circles, a revival of interest in the doctrine of the Trinity got under way. To correct the prevalent depreciation of that doctrine, the Swiss theologian Karl Barth, abruptly and without warning, repositioned it. He plucked it out of Schleiermacher's appendix and set it right at the opening of the work he called *Church Dogmatics*. Barth expounded the doctrine of the Trinity in the introductory volume (1932) of this monumental *opus*; and he expounded it not as an "item" in a list of Christian doctrines, but as an immediate implication of the foundational reality of Christian faith: the self-revelation in and through which God is made known to human persons as one whom they may deeply trust, gladly obey, and joyfully thank. This self-revelation in which "God reveals Himself as the Lord" shows itself, Barth said, to be the revelation of a threefold Deity; for God is manifested as *the One who reveals*, as *the One who is revealed*, and as *the One who is the givenness of this revelation for us*: in Barth's words, as Revealer, Revelation, and Revealedness – Father, Son, and Spirit. These are the same God repeated three times; for on any other hypothesis it would be impossible to say that a revelation of *God* has in truth occurred. Thus a form of the doctrine of the Trinity, it seems, is presupposed in the very relationship that God, in the act of self-revelation – the act of speaking *God's* Word and making it heard – establishes with human persons.

In developing this line of thought, Barth made allusion to some words of Irenaeus of Lyon – a Greek Christian writer of the late second century CE – in the latter's work *Against Heresies*.[9] On closer examination, these words indicate, better perhaps than Barth saw, the *historical* roots of the sort of argument he himself develops; for Irenaeus is arguably the earliest Christian author to evolve a reflective, though certainly not a perfectly self-consistent or fully developed, account of the Trinity.

In the passage Barth cited, Irenaeus argues that whenever Paul employs the title "Christ" ("anointed one," "messiah"), his reference is to "Emmanuel," i.e., to "God-with-us" (Matt. 1: 23; cf. Isa. 7: 14) or, as Irenaeus then rephrases his thought, to "the Son of God made son of man." Further, he argues that this is what the title "Christ" properly signifies. For, says Irenaeus, "in the name 'Christ,' there is understood by implication the Anointer, the Anointed, and the Ointment itself with which he is anointed: but the Anointer is the Father, while the Son is anointed with the Spirit who is the Ointment, as the Word says through Isaiah: *The Spirit of the Lord is upon me, for he has anointed me*" (Isa. 61: 1; cf. Ps. 45: 7). Two centuries later, the point was reiterated by Basil of Caesarea in Irenaeus' own terms. Basil explained that to describe baptism as "into Christ" is to say everything: "For the naming of Christ is the confession of the whole [Trinity], manifesting as it does the God who gave, the Son who received, and the Spirit who is, the Ointment."[10]

Barth's interest in this passage lay in its intimation that the focal center of the doctrine of the Trinity is "the question of the divinity of Christ." For present purposes, however, it is more relevant to note that what lay in the back of Irenaeus' mind was the Gospel scene in which John the Baptist washes Jesus in the waters of the Jordan river. This story is told in all four Gospels, and in all of them it is understood to mark the first occasion on which Jesus was manifested as "Christ," a manifestation that in effect intimates the character of his coming ministry. Thus it sets before readers the very sort of thing Barth was talking about, namely, an *event of revelation*, the revelation of the Anointed One.

If this is the case, however, it is worthwhile to weigh the manner in which this revelation is said to have come about. If we ignore John himself and the onlookers whose presence the story seems to presuppose, there are three participants in this scene. There is God, whose word from on high presents him as Father of this Son. Then there is the Son himself, Jesus, who has God as his Father. And finally there is that descending dove, the symbol of the invisible Breath or Spirit of God who comes down upon Jesus as the divine "ointment" that marks him as the Christ.[11] It requires little or no ingenuity, then, to see that this scene, the scene of Jesus' revelation as God's Christ, is at the same time a manifestation of the Trinity, and indeed of the Trinity caught in the very act of "doing its thing."[12] What is more, if any ingenuity *is* required, Irenaeus has already supplied it. The "Son" in this scene, he insisted, is one individual, yet at the same time one in whom two realities are somehow wedded, so that a person who contemplates this "Son" experiences a form of double vision. For as Irenaeus tells us, there is on the one hand, the eternal Son or Word of God and, on the other, the human, finite Son of Man, Jesus, in whom other human beings can easily recognize one of themselves; and yet these two somehow stand in together, as the shared title "son" indicates.

Here, then, is an intimation of the *nature* of the relationship that is established through God's self-revelation and self-giving to human persons in baptism. A full account of it would require an explication of the whole "work" of Christ, and therefore, in the end, of the whole creedal and scriptural narrative whose meaning is recapitulated in the action of baptism. What Irenaeus says about the baptism of Jesus, however, indicates what is to be the *fruit* of Christ's work. It is the lifting-up of human beings into the life of God, their "sharing through grace" – not merely or even primarily as individuals but as a common *body* – in the identity and the destiny of Christ. Needless to say, the basis of such a possibility – the *reality* that grounds it – is, as Irenaeus saw, twofold. First, there is the union of God and humanity in Christ, or, to employ the language of the fourth Gospel, the becoming flesh of the Word of God. If the Word and Son of God truly takes on and shares the conditions of a particular human existence, that action implies, conversely, that human beings can in their own way, but for all that a new way, live their life, individual and common, in the power of God's life and in union with the eternal Word of God. This very statement, however, points to a second "moment" in this relationship with God: the gift of the Spirit, by which humanity is empowered to live out the Christ-life as its own.

Furthermore, it is essential to insist that Jesus' baptism in "water and the Spirit" (cf. John 3: 5; Acts 2: 38) does not stand alone in early Christianity. Others – disciples of the first and later generations – marked their solidarity with him by accepting just such a baptism as their own, though only (as far as one can tell) after his resurrection. And what is one to make of that? Paul answers the question: "For as many of you as were baptized into Christ have put on Christ. There is neither Jew nor Greek, there is neither slave nor free, there is neither male nor female; for you are all one in Christ Jesus" (Gal. 3: 27–8; cf. 1 Cor. 12: 12–13). In other words, the baptism that disciples receive dresses them up, collectively and individually, as Christ. It so identifies them with him that other identities, ethnic identities, for example, or gender identities, tend to have their importance discounted. Baptism even occasions believers to share Christ's death to sin, so that they may further share his resurrection (cf. Rom. 6: 3–4). And all this Paul sums up in the words: "God has sent the Spirit of his Son into your hearts, crying, 'Abba! Father!'" (Gal. 4: 6).[13] "The Spirit of his Son" – that is, the same Spirit that anointed Jesus at *his* baptism[14] – here manifests the disciples of Jesus as God's *adoptive* children, as siblings by grace of the Son of God, and even, according to Irenaeus, as "gods."[15] The baptism of Christians, then, is a reiteration of, and a sharing in, the baptism of Christ; and indeed Irenaeus asserts that the Spirit descended on the Christ precisely in order that he in turn might share it with believers.[16] Active in this baptism are the same God and Father, the same Son and Word, the same Spirit of holiness – taking human beings into their company on the ground of the identification of the eternal Word of God with Jesus, who somehow is, and represents, "us," and whose identity "we" can share.[17]

It was thus Irenaeus' belief that from the first moment of creation, and then throughout the long and checkered history of humanity with God, the Son and the Spirit are, in one way or another, under one set of circumstances or another, the constant companions of the human race: in other words, that the picture of God's relationship to humanity conveyed by the story of Jesus' baptism supplies, as we have said, the paradigm for the structure of that relationship not only in baptism and in creation, but in every time and circumstance.[18]

Let us, then, be a little more specific than Barth. Let us agree that the occurrence of revelation presupposes, generally and in principle, a threefoldness in the manner of God's self-giving to faith, and therefore, if that self-giving is to be real, in the God who is thus conveyed; but let us add that this general truth is concretely instantiated in New Testament accounts of the baptism of Jesus as well as in the baptisms of those who have set out to follow him. Then it becomes clear, as Barth wanted to insist, that the doctrine of the Trinity is anything but an airy and derivative speculation. It is in the first instance *a statement of the structure of humanity's relation to God in Christ*: that is, a statement that articulates and specifies both the other *term* of this relation (God the Trinity) and the pattern and logic of the relationship itself. The ultimate "root" of Christian trinitarianism, then, is baptismal; for it is in baptism that this relationship is established and sealed.

2. On the meaning of "God" in this account

The first and most central question that must be raised in connection with this account of the Trinity has nothing directly to do with "threes" and "ones," but rather with the very *connotation* of the word "God." In this context it of course *refers*, together and severally, to the Father, the Word whom the Father speaks, and the Spirit whom the Father breathes. But both Irenaeus in his conflict with Christian Gnostics and the Cappadocians in their later conflict with Arianism dealt with opponents whom they took to work with a dangerously false understanding of God – or, as the Cappadocians would put it in what was to become a technical term in the vocabulary of the doctrine of the Trinity, a false understanding of God's *ousia* [being].[19]

First, then, Irenaeus' Christian Gnostics had raised a question about the *identity* of God. They had little respect for the one they called the "artisan"-God – the Deity whose doings are recounted in the creation story of Genesis 1–2. Indeed the very term "artisan" (*dêmiourgos*) was, on their lips, a put-down. They contended that this creator-figure could not be the same as the good Father known and proclaimed by Jesus, but was a being of a much lower grade. For this reason, Irenaeus had to insist – at length and with much repetition – (a) that the Creator God of Genesis 1 is indeed the one and only God; and (b) that this God is, therefore, the very "Father" alluded to in the stories of Jesus' baptism – the one who sent his own Son and Word as his self-revelation, and who at the same time sent the Holy Spirit to "adapt" humanity-in-Christ to its new life with God as thus revealed.

Irenaeus' criticism of his opponents' view amounted to an attack on their separation of the Creator from the ultimate, good, transcendent Deity. If, he argued, this ultimate God bears no responsibility for the visible cosmos that the artisan-Creator has formed, if the creation of that material cosmos really was just an unfortunate, even malignant, error, then not only does the Creator figure fail to qualify as God, but so does the (allegedly) ultimate and hidden Deity who is the source of the spiritual cosmos. They are like two artists who share the same studio, each of whom spends all his or her time defacing the work of the other. He thinks, in other words, that the two gnostic God-figures limit each other, with the consequence that neither one can satisfy the conditions for being called "God" in the proper sense.

Thus when Irenaeus speaks of God, he wants to speak of one unenclosed, illimitable, incomprehensible God, who is the sole author of everything there is, spirit and matter alike: that is the connotation of "God," as he understands the word. His opponents, to be sure, had employed the same sort of apophatic language about their ultimate Father; but there were things – anything material, for example – that they sought in the end to exclude from the scope of the ultimate Deity's responsibility. Irenaeus therefore argues in effect that they did not understand the implications of the language they were using. Their two divine figures, since they were pictured as strictly contrary to each other, might perhaps, supposing they were real, be conceived as important cosmic "powers"; but *cosmic powers are not God*. The true Deity, says Irenaeus, is strictly unlimited, infinite and immeasurable, because God "contains all things without being contained by any."[20] This formula, derived from Hellenistic Jewish sources, implies for him (a) that "in his greatness, God is unknown to all his creatures" but is known by them through his love;[21] and (b) that God is not "in" the world (or for that matter "outside" it).[22] On the contrary, the world is "in" God, who is the "place" in which the finite order is set, and is therefore non-mediately present to it: and that, oddly enough, explains why "no one has seen God at any time" (John 1: 18). As the world's medium and context, its ground, God does not belong in the same file-folder with created things – or, for that matter, in any file-folder at all. God is everything's holder and upholder.

This account of the reference and meaning of the word "God" was not, in any of its components, new with Irenaeus; and much later it was reiterated by the Cappadocian fathers as an essential premise of any Christian account of the Trinity. Indeed it was as important to them as to Irenaeus, though for slightly different reasons. The notorious fourth-century Arian or "trinitarian" controversy was originally focused on the location or status of the Logos or Word of God in the relation between God and the created order. In other words, the turf over which the controversy initially moved was, roughly speaking, the field defined by the picture of creation conveyed, e.g., in 1 Corinthians 8: 6 or John 1: 3 or Proverbs 8: 22. These texts were normally taken, at the beginning of the fourth century, to assert that the divine Word or Wisdom or Son, the one *through* whom God creates, is a *derivative* and *mediatorial* figure, one that played the role of a buffer-state between the ultimate Deity and the created order. Arius, starting in about 318, had in effect protested this established picture by insisting that the title "God" had no business being applied to a secondary figure of this sort – as though there could be such a thing as a descending hierarchy of degrees or "grades" of divinity. He preferred, Arius said, to acknowledge what must be the true case – that the Logos was not God in any sense, but was instead the highest and noblest of created beings.

This teaching, as we know, was repudiated in no uncertain terms by the Council of Nicaea (325). Many years, however – years that were to be filled with misunderstanding, argument, and political conflict – had to pass before the old-fashioned "conservative" view that there are descending "grades" of Deity, just as there are grades, say, of beef or of motor-oil, could be rejected and displaced as the only, and the only correct, alternative to Arianism. It was the task of Athanasius of Alexandria and, later, of the Cappadocian fathers, to defend a third position: (a) that the Logos is neither a creature nor a secondary, slightly watered-down Deity, but *God* in the same sense as the ultimate God; and (b) that the same is true of the Holy Spirit (who had scarcely been mentioned at all in the first stages of the controversy, no doubt because the scriptural "creation" texts that shaped its agenda did not mention the Spirit).[23]

The opponents that Basil and the two Gregories faced, however, were a different breed, whose position historians have come to label as "Neo-Arianism." This movement did not simply reproduce Arius's views or even those of the old-fashioned conservatives (who were often, though perhaps unjustly, called "Semi-Arians"). On the contrary, the deacon Aëtius of Antioch and his disciple Eunomius, who circulated in Asia Minor during the lifetimes of the Cappadocians, argued not only that the Logos and the Spirit are creatures, but that they have to be understood and defined as strictly *unlike* God, not in the old-fashioned sense that they represent different *degrees* of Deity, but in the radical sense that they are *different sorts of things entirely*. Father, Son, and Spirit on this view would be like an apple, an alligator, and an acid: three quite different *kinds of beings* (*ousiai*). So much for Nicaea's famous formula, "of one being": *homoousios*. And indeed, so much for Arius's view that God is so grand – so transcendent – as to be beyond the comprehension even of the Logos. For the interesting thing about Neo-Arianism was that its argument turned on the assumption that "God" – the "nature" or "being" of God – can be *defined*. Eunomius in fact insisted that the mind which has clearly grasped the concept of the "ingenerate" or "unbegotten" has grasped the essence of *what it is to be God*; and that since Son and Spirit are *not* described as ingenerate, they are not and cannot be, even in some vague sense, "the same sort of thing" as God. Hence Neo-Arian use of the epithet "unlike."

Oddly enough, though no one noticed it, this position had something in common with that of Irenaeus' Gnostics. The Neo-Arian argument assumed that the negative terms traditionally employed of God in theological discourse – terms like "immutable," "incorporeal," or "timeless," but above all, in their particular case, "unbegotten" – imply that a strict *contrariety* obtains between God and any finite being. In a word, they pictured their definable Deity as the *opposite* of everything creaturely and therefore as *inconsistent*, and by nature incompatible, with it[24] – just as the earlier Gnostics had postulated a divorce of sorts between the spiritual (divine and light-filled) world and the material (dark and empty) world and the different God-figures that ruled them. What the Neo-Arians apparently did not notice was that this understanding of God's transcendence is not only open to Irenaeus' criticism of his Gnostics' teaching, in that it would render God limited or finite, but also that it renders God supremely lonely and isolated – untouching and untouchable.

The Cappadocians sensed the futility of this Neo-Arian position. Because (a) it pretended to define the nature of God, and (b) did so on the assumption that the differences between Creator and creature make them out to be contraries, it *really* succeeded only in "finitizing" God by suggesting that God can be limited just as created "natures" are mutually limiting.

Moreover, the alternatives the Neo-Arian vision presupposed – i.e., inconsistency or consistency, to put the matter as crisply as possible – had consequences that are echoed in much modern thought, and consequences that illustrate, if nothing else, the annoying persistence of this issue. On the one hand, if one sets about trying to express the transcendence of God in negatives understood as the Neo-Arians had understood them, what one ends up with is not so much a transcendent God as a merely isolated God. On the other hand, if, frustrated by this outcome, one demands that the negatives, implicit or explicit, be dropped, so that God can be "closer" to human beings and their affairs, a God so conceived will no doubt cease to be isolated (at least to some degree), but will nonetheless continue to be *one thing among others*, differing only by being bigger, more powerful, better intentioned, and so on. In other words, both of these models of God, if actualized, would result in a finite Deity; and that, whatever else it might be, would not be God. Yet this paradoxical situation seems to be the one in which much current theology finds itself, as it forever trades in a false transcendence or a reductionist immanence, or *vice versa*.

The Cappadocian solution to this issue – a solution whose implications are not frequently enough pondered – was to assert, with Irenaeus (and others), the incomprehensibility and infinity of God and hence of the divine "nature." God's perfection as "the good" consists, argued Gregory of Nyssa, in the strict *infinity* of God's goodness: one cannot get to the end of it, and it is thus in the strictest sense unfathomable.[25] Hence the first principle of the Cappadocian account of the Trinity was the proposition that *the "nature" or "being" of God cannot be grasped conceptually by the human mind* because – as Gregory of Nyssa added – it has no borders, internal or external. Just as Irenaeus had said bluntly that "in his greatness, God is unknown to all his creatures," so Gregory of Nazianzus stated: "What God is in nature and essence, no one has ever yet discovered or can discover."[26] But then just as Irenaeus had added that God is known through his "love," so too Nazianzen asserts that God is discerned in "the glory which is manifested among the creatures," a glory that is "the back parts of God . . . , tokens of himself."[27]

To understand this, it is important to recall that by the fourth century the idea – which Irenaeus may have taken over from Hermas' *Shepherd*[28] – of God as the one who *contains all things without being contained* had become something of a commonplace. This way of speaking was employed originally to provide an answer to the question how God could be said to be "in" the world as in a "place," or in some particular place in the world, as the Scriptures seemed often to suggest. The answer given, as we have said, was that God is not "in" the world as one of the items it contained; rather it had to be said that God is the "place" in which the world exists – a way of speaking that was meant precisely to *deny* that God is an item within, or a dimension or region of, the created order while at the same time asserting the unbreakable intimacy between the Creator and the creation. God is *always* present and "walking in the Garden in the cool of the day" (Gen. 3: 8), yet not in the sense that God is *in* the Garden, but in the sense that God is the Garden's proper "place," its "where."[29] If this is correct, however, then the notion that God is the world's – and therefore humanity's – contrary needs to be entirely rethought; and this remains true even though the Cappadocians and their posterity could on occasion, unaware of the implications of their own teaching, revert, tacitly or explicitly, to the rhetoric of incompatibility.

In other words, this picture – for that is what it is – of God as the world's "place," containing and embracing the world as its Creator and Sustainer, suggests a possible solution to the problem about contraries. It does not seek to rule out the so-called "negative" – apophatic"[30] – theology: quite the contrary. It does however demand that such language be understood in a different way. To envisage God and world as contraries is to make a very fundamental mistake: it is to speak of the Creator's relation to the creation as if it could be reliably and literally character-ized in the very same terms that are employed to characterize the relations of cre-atures to one another. It is, in a word, to set them on a level. But if we mentally construct the relation between God and creature as if it were simply another instance of a type of relation that can, and often does, obtain between finite beings, then we talk as though God were indeed another individual item on a list of "the things there are." In other words, we end up, inevitably, engaging in what was once called "idolatry." We erect some finite reality as our God, not unlike the Israelites in the wilderness, whose anxiety and impatience once led them to construct an ill-fated golden calf.

But the original aim of the "negative" theology as used in Jewish and Christian circles was to say that God is *not* limited by the world or any of its "contents," in the way that things in the world limit one another, and so has no business being *opposed* to them in the manner of a logical contrary. In other words, the negative theology spoke of God dialectically, by way of denial (*apophasis*) that depends upon and presupposes an original affirmation. It was intended, in short, to school believers away from idolatry. It meant to say that God's being is *not* another species of the same genus as the created order, but that it is strictly *on another level* from created being in the sense that it does not belong to *any* "kind"; and this in turn implies that God's "otherness" in relation to creatures must never be construed as inconsistency, but rather as something that goes beyond what we perceive as consistency and inconsistency. The finite cannot contain the infinite; but of the infinite one says both (a) that it *is not* finite, and (b) that *for just that reason* it makes room for the finite and is that with which the finite is most deeply *at home*, even as the doctrine of creation affirms. "No one has seen God at any time," says the Fourth Gospel, but the divine Word, the only-begotten Son made flesh, "has made him known" (John 1: 18). This sounds like mere paradox – especially if one under-stands that the presence of the Son *is* the presence of the Father; but the point of the paradox is to stress that God's self-identification in and with "flesh" marks a work far beyond what might be possible for *either* a merely transcendent deity, who cannot come "downstairs" without losing face, *or* a merely immanent deity who has no business getting above himself by venturing "upstairs." The God that is Trinity is immanent precisely in its transcendence and transcendent precisely in its immanence. Basil of Caesarea captures this strange thought neatly. He writes that what most truly attests God's "excellency" is the fact that

> God, being incomprehensible, should be able, impassibly, through flesh, to have come into close conflict with death, to the end that by his own suffering he might give us the boon of freedom from suffering.[31]

The incomprehensible God is beyond suffering, and yet – or perhaps therefore – can take on human suffering. Indeed that is in part what is meant by talk of divine incomprehensibility: not that one cannot ever speak of God in a way that gets God right, but that what one has to say in order to do so is something that does not always "fit" the ordinary rules of our (finite) thinking and speaking. The divine work of creation and redemption can only be the work of one who does not inhabit our time but makes his own time ours, who is himself our "place," and who is closer to us than we are to each other in virtue of being at *every* moment (a) the "Other" that calls us into being, (b) the "Other" that represents for us the being that is to be ours, and (c) the "Other" that is communicating this being to us.

The proposition, then, that God contains all things without being contained by any intimates first of all that God's "difference" from finite beings is a very different kind of difference from the kind to which they are accustomed. But second, it goes hand in hand with insistence upon a "negative" or "apophatic" theology whose point is not to pen God up in heaven, but to supply a corrective to the mental fashioning of a limited God: to point faith beyond every finite reality to the "Other" in whom alone it is at every point grounded, formed, and affirmed, and in whose being its finite existence is a kind of participation. Thus the Cappadocians followed Irenaeus' lead:[32] they envisaged a God that (1) stands in non-mediated relationship with every created being, but (2) is no part of the finite order nor subject to its conditions. Their "negative theology," indeed, seems implicitly to presuppose that (2) above is some sort of condition for the truth of (1).

3. The "threefoldness" of God

This unique and unfathomable Deity, then, is nonetheless the One who eternally speaks a self-objectifying Word in an act of self-conferral, and at the same time breathes a life-giving Spirit that carries and so affirms the Word thus spoken and, in doing so, conforms human beings to it. And so we come to the question of the threefoldness of God asserted in the doctrine of the Trinity: or, to use more familiar language, the threesome of "persons," by each of whom the one illimitable divine being is completely shared.

Irenaeus did not use any settled, technical term to denote the members of the Trinity – certainly not "person" (for he did not write in Latin), nor even the Greek term whose equivalent it was later taken to be, i.e., *hupostasis*. Instead he used the range of definite descriptions that had become traditional in Christian talk: e.g., "God" or "Father"; "Word" or "Son" or "Only-begotten"; "Spirit" – i.e., "Breath" – or "Wisdom."[33] With or without technical terms, however, Irenaeus' account of Word and Spirit is clearly a doctrine of divine threefoldness (and not of three Gods). This is made plain enough by his image of the "two hands" of God. Thus he asserts that the "one God made and ordered everything by his Word and Wisdom";[34] but for him this means the same as "by God's two hands," which are the Son and the Spirit, "through whom and in whom he made all things freely and of himself." Son and Spirit, then, are not helpers hired, as it were, at some cosmic labor-exchange. They are simply the one Deity itself in other modes; that is the primary point of the "hands" metaphor. They are God's own, indeed they are God, and therefore what they do amounts simply to specific forms of God's doing. In the Father, says Irenaeus, is the *being* of all things; in the Son, their *model*; and in the Spirit their *form*:[35] a transposition, this, of the picture of God that emerges in the story of Jesus' baptism into the key of a discourse about creation. The members of the Trinity are here identified by their complementary and reciprocal ways of participating in the single business of creation; and this activity of creation Irenaeus understood to be continued in a new form by the same threefold God, no doubt in the same threefold manner, for the purpose of bringing a now fallen humanity to the end originally intended for it – the new creation begun in baptism. For "God . . . is one and the same. It is he who *rolls the heaven up as if it were a book* [Isa. 34: 4] and *renews the face of the earth* [Ps. 104: 30]. It is he who made the things of time for the sake of humanity, so that, coming to maturity amongst them, it might bring forth the fruit of immortality."[36]

Hence for Irenaeus, the Son is always the one through whom God brings the created order into being: Irenaeus has read John 1: 3 and 1 Corinthians 8: 6 and internalized them thoroughly. The Son is the *objectification* of God – God's self reproduced, the measureless measured, God's mind and purpose rendered articulate – God, one might say, self-expressed with creation in view. It is for this reason that Irenaeus can call the Son or Word – God's image and self-communication – *exemplum*, "model." Not only is the Son the model for humanity, that image of God after which Adam was fashioned, but the Son is for all practical purposes the "Wisdom" – "the first-born of all creation" (cf. Col. 1: 15–16) – that models God's purpose for the entire created order. Thus the realization of God's will in creation is the actualization in finite form of the Wisdom and Word of God ("God said, and it was so"). Or put it another way: the self-objectification of God in the Son is not only God's eternal self-expression, but also – and for just that reason – the act that eternally grounds the creation of a finite cosmos and, indeed, represents the – logical not chronological – first step of it. It is not possible, save by deliberate abstraction, to talk of God without talking also about what God does with, and holds in, those two "hands."

Furthermore, in Irenaeus' scheme – whose baptismal root is evident in the way he supplements John 1: 3 and 1 Corinthians 8: 6 – the Spirit appears not as next after the Word in a descending series of divine "persons," but as the Word's divine correlate: like one hand to the other (to use Irenaeus' metaphor), or (to alter the metaphor slightly) like a forefinger to the Son's thumb. If God is objectified (for himself and for creatures) in the Word, God is also "subjectified" in the Spirit as the divine gift and power by which (a) the Word himself is affirmed as God's self-expression, and (b) believers are conformed to their identity in the Word or Son. Indeed the Spirit is the power by which all the works of God, posited by the Father and given form in God's Word, are affirmed and conformed to their inward identity. Thus Irenaeus writes in his *Proof of the Apostolic Preaching*:

Paul well says: *one God, the Father, who is above all and with all and in us all* (cf. Eph. 4: 6); for "above all" is the Father, but "with all" is the Word, since it is

> through him that everything was made by the Father, and "in us all" is the Spirit, *who cries, Abba, Father*, and has formed man to the likeness of God. So the Spirit manifests the Word, and therefore the prophets announced the Son of God; but the Word articulates the Spirit, and therefore it is himself who gives their message to the prophets, and takes up man and brings him to the Father.[37]

Hence the Spirit is the one that brings about "increase" in believers, "preparing humanity for the Son of God" and for the vision of God.[38] If the Word is truly the image of God, and the destiny of humanity is to be conformed to that image, then it is the Spirit who enables human persons to actualize that destiny.

But how was this idea of the equality of the three "members" of the one God understood and expressed by the Cappadocian fathers? The heart of the Cappadocians' trinitarianism lay in the way they distinguished between the two Greek terms *ousia* and *hupostasis*: terms which Irenaeus' account of the Trinity did not employ, but which had become central in the fourth-century debate. In ordinary speech the meanings of these two words often overlapped. They could and did, for certain purposes, function as synonyms. Indeed they had been employed as synonyms in one of the propositions condemned by the creed of the Council of Nicaea.[39] This terminological vagueness was one of the sources of misunderstanding among the various parties to the trinitarian debate; and it was only made worse by the fact that Latin translated both of these Greek words by the one term *substantia*. The Cappadocians, therefore, inherited the task of clarifying the language of the debate, which they did by asserting or assuming that *ousia* was an abstract word that denoted the form of an answer to the question "*What* is this?" The *ousia* of something is its "what," its *nature*, as we say. To speak of the *ousia* of God, then, is to refer to *what God is*.

But what of the term *hupostasis*? This was the term that had come to denote the "three" that were called "Father," "Word," and "Spirit." What is more, it had for some time been employed consciously and deliberately with view to insisting that these words name *realities*: distinct, objectively existent "things" with particular identities, and not simply appearances or aspects of God. The Cappadocians, thinking this over, came initially to believe that for the purposes of trinitarian discourse *hupostasis* should be understood to refer to a concrete *instance* or *exemplification* of some nature. Thus, it was argued, Peter, Paul, and John are three instances of what it is to be human; and in the same way, the hypostases of the Trinity are three instances of what it is to be God.

But there are two difficulties here: and one of them is glaringly obvious. On this view, or at least on the most obvious understanding of it, the three hypostases of the Trinity would be three Gods and not one, just as Peter, Paul, and John are three human beings and not one. Furthermore (and this difficulty is not so obvious), that which distinguishes the three instances or hypostases from one another would have to be some individuating attribute – a quality of some sort, like red hair, say, or an acerbic wit – that makes the "what" of Peter, say, different from that of John or Paul. But by hypothesis, *the "what" of God does not differ from one hyposta-*

sis to another; in other words, Deity is not an abstract "kind." It is one given "thing," one reality: God's self. More than that, the Cappadocians were clear, as we have seen, that the "what" of God cannot be grasped by any human conceptual apparatus. God is non-finite, non-comprehensible, and non-definable; so that when one speaks of the *ousia* of God one is referring (a) to something one cannot grasp in human terms save by indirection, i.e., by analogy, negation, or metaphor; and (b) to something that cannot be supplemented or diminished.

Hence to the question what differentiates the three hypostases or "persons" from one another (i.e., the characteristic that "individuates" each of them: *idiotês*), they returned in the end the answer that whatever it is, it could have nothing to do with the category of *ousia*. "The difference" between Father and Son, says Gregory of Nazianzus, "is external to the nature [*ousia*]."[40] The hypostases are in the end *not* to be differentiated – and to that extent constituted – as different *species* or different particular *instances* of the genus "God." Rather they gradually came to be called, though not explicitly by the Cappadocians, *tropoi huparxeôs*, "modes of [God's] existence."[41] Hence what constitutes and differentiates them is not of the order of a "what," but, as Gregory of Nyssa says, making the same point in his own terminology, of the order of a "how" (*pôs einai*).[42] It is their *relations* – i.e., *how* they exist *in relation to one another* – that constitute one as Source, one as Offspring, and one as Gift; but each of them is the same thing, the same identical "what," i.e., God. "Father is not the name of a nature [*ousia*] or of an activity [*energeia*] . . . But it is the name of the relation in which the Father stands to the Son, and the Son to the Father."[43]

Further the Cappadocians argued, as we know, that human knowledge of God is not knowledge of the infinite and unutterable *ousia* of God: "what" God is. Rather, they thought, it is focused on the *energeia* of God: what God *does*. Human beings speak of God on the basis of God's activity or working – in creation, in the sustaining of the natural order, and in redemption; and the rule of such speech is ultimately the language of the Scriptures.[44] But the Cappadocians asserted that this "energy" or "activity" of God is nevertheless the direct expression and revelation of God's "nature" or "self": what God does follows upon who and what God is.[45] Therefore, just as the three hypostases are not three different "whats," so the divine activity is not three different activities, one for each "person" of the Trinity. God's *doing* is a single activity that happens triadically just as God's *being* happens triadically: a reiteration, this, of a point already made in effect by Irenaeus. This of course does not mean that there is no difference to be observed between the working of the Father, of the Son, and of the Spirit. It means that these differences too are of the order of "how" and not of the order of "what." *What* the three hypostases are correctly said to do – e.g., create, redeem, or sanctify, to allude to a formula now current – is one thing; but the *how* of their doing it involves three coordinate *ways* of working to accomplish that one thing.[46]

Thus Basil of Caesarea can in principle simply repeat Irenaeus on the score of the "working" of God in self-revelation: for, reflecting, among other texts, on 1 Corinthians 12: 3 ("No one can say, 'Jesus is Lord,' except by the Holy Spirit"), he writes:

the way of the knowledge of God lies from the one Spirit, through the one Son, to the one Father; and conversely, the natural goodness and inherent holiness and the royal dignity extend from the Father through the Onlybegotten to the Spirit. Thus there is both acknowledgment of the hypostases, and the true dogma of the [one God] is not lost.[47]

4. Questions and perplexities

This teaching about the hypostases, then, performs a twofold function. When it defines the *particularity* of each member of the Trinity through its *relation* to the others, it is doing two jobs at the same time. It asserts at once the many-ness of God on the one hand, and the one-ness of God on the other. It discerns the unity of God *in* the threefoldness of the hypostases (because their very differences, being relational, assure their union); and it roots the threefoldness of God *in* the unity of the divine nature (because the hypostases are, in their mutual relations, reiterations of one divine reality). The problems commonly faced by trinitarian theology are therefore problems about maintaining this balance between unity and threefoldness.

The most obvious of these problems, and one that has figured prominently in discussions since the late twentieth century of trinitarian doctrine, is a distinction between the "economic" and the "immanent" (or sometimes "ontological") Trinity. The phrase "immanent Trinity" refers to threefoldness as proper to Deity considered simply in and of itself – proper, that is, to God *absolute*, God *abstracted from* any relationship to anything other than God. Conversely, "economic Trinity" refers to threefoldness as discerned or manifested in God's engagement with humanity and its world in the "economies" of creation and redemption, that is, to God-*in-relation*. The distinction tacitly presupposes, then, that God's relations to the created order are more or less what, in cinema advertisements, used to be called an "extra added attraction." Whence there arises the question whether the divine threefoldness is real *apart from* those relations – whether, in a word, it may not be a merely secondary quality or phase of Deity and not "original" to God at all. On that view, God is *really* a unitary being, and the threefoldness is a cosmetic, and by so much a deceptive, addendum.

There is of course at least one further alternative. This distinction may be one that exists only in the mind of the person who makes it: useful, perhaps, for some purposes, but not corresponding to any real division or separation. After all, the two terms of this distinction cannot coincide either (a) with the difference between essential "nature" and contingent "accident,"[48] or, for that matter, (b) with the difference between "being" and "doing" (*energeia*). The divine unity, after all, is said to be threefold in the sense that God "happens" in three ways. For that reason – i.e., because they are the modes or the "hows" of God's being – the hypostases cannot be secondary or merely "accidental," even though they do not *define* God's "what" but only embody it in different manners. By the same token, the threefold "personhood" of God represents not God's "doing" (*energeia*) as distinct from God's "being," but the "hows" of God's doing. That, no doubt, is why the tradition has taught that the ways in which God exists are *at the same time* the ways in which God acts.

Such being the case, it is easy to see that this distinction between *God absolute* and *God related* is a version of the ancient "Semi-Arian" creed, which set the Son or Word in a mediating position between the ultimate God and the created world, on the hypothesis that the Word is a sufficiently watered-down form of Deity to engage, and even to enter, the visible, created order. Both positions, ancient and modern alike, set real Deity – Deity-in-and-of-itself – off against a lesser type of Deity that is susceptible of relatedness to beings other than itself. The only difference between these two views is that the earlier one seems to trade on the distinction between the uttered "Word" and the divine "Speaker," while the more recent version trades on that between God's intrinsic and essential "being" and God's threefoldness in "person" or "hypostasis."

The antidote to this intellectual dissection of God is no doubt to assert, in the formula of Karl Rahner – by now a truism in theological circles – that "The economic Trinity is the immanent Trinity and the immanent Trinity is the economic Trinity." This formula, however, correct though it be, does not of itself show the way to overcoming what seems to be a settled disposition on the part of theologians of almost every ilk to suspect that *being God* and *being related* are difficult to reconcile.

Ancient and mediaeval thinkers laid great stress on what one might call the *reliability* of God. They insisted that God does not change, but simply *is*, at every moment and in the same way, whatever can properly be meant by "being God." These qualities of immutability and timelessness signify that God can be counted on: that, for example, the God whose name is "love" does not mutate into its opposite: does not have periodic fits of anger, or succumb permanently to vengefulness, not even when needled by the perverse behavior of finite agents. It also entails that God does not "just happen" – whether by chance or by reaction to the action of an "other" – to have this or that or *any* characteristic. God's identity is unchanging, and nothing that you or I do will change that identity (this, I take it, is what is meant by "impassibility"). It is concerns and ideas like these that underlie, for example, Thomas Aquinas' assertion that while creatures have a *real* relation to God, God does not have a real relation to the world, but only a relation *in thought*. The intent of this assertion was of course to affirm that God is not *passively reactive* to actions or events in the finite world, that God's being is not *relative to* creaturely actions or attitudes as that of creatures is to God. Certainly Aquinas did not have it in mind to deny God's connectedness to the world or God's active concern for it. Nevertheless his language has a touch of the absurd about it: how can one *not* affirm that Deity is related to its own creation?

No doubt for this reason as well as for cultural reasons, modern theologians have stressed the Trinity's relatedness to the creation – to nature as well as to human beings in their history, and above all in their conscious history with God; and some have insisted that God *becomes* whatever it is to be God in and through these relations in time to finite beings, thus dispensing with divine immutability. For it is now an axiom that things – and especially "persons" – are constituted, at least in part, by their relations with others,[49] with the result that where Aquinas subordinated relatedness to "being" (*substantia*, "what-ness"), his posterity now subordinates "being" to relations. In this theological analogue of the debate between nature and nurture, then, stress tends now to be laid not only on the deep involvement of God with creation, but on what one might call the *responsiveness* of God to finite events and agencies – a quality which must surely qualify as a criterion of moral goodness. The off-chance that the change that this risky involvement brings about in God may be a change for the worse is discounted, perhaps because there lurks somewhere in a corner of theologians' minds a shadow of the classical belief that, at least basically, God does not change *very much*.

The fact seems to be that these two starkly opposed attitudes terminate in each other, rather like life and death; for each of them, when pressed to its logical conclusion, dissolves into nagging doubt, and it is always the other that must come to the rescue. The absolute God cannot be God in any serious sense save as *related* to the created "other"; and the related – should one say "relative"? – God cannot be God in any serious sense save as having a stable *identity* in relation to the created "other." Moreover, in an odd symbolic way this is conveyed by the very story to which this essay has appealed as revealing the root of trinitarian faith. In the Gospel accounts of Jesus' baptism, the Voice from the opened heavens which says plainly, "This is my beloved Son . . . ," and does this even as "the Spirit of God" descends "like a dove" upon the incarnate Word, belongs nevertheless to a Speaker that is not seen. The God who speaks is hidden even in this self-revelation, and remains in some fashion remote and mysterious, "beyond" human affairs despite intense involvement with them. This God embraces humanity – Adam – as represented in the person of Jesus, and through that humanity, as some would add, the natural order that is its matrix. That embrace, moreover, elevates humanity into the divine life. It is in this act, and not apart from it, then, that God's "relatedness" is discerned, but discerned precisely as the relatedness of the One who is timelessly "other": the "absolute." God sees and calls humanity in the Son and blesses and affirms it in that identity by conferring the life-giving Breath which is the Spirit. This is "relation" indeed; but it is the relation of the Mystery that creates *on its own* to the creation that owes it everything: the Mystery that is still shaping its creation as the Word that is God's self-objectification, and at the same time bringing it to perfection in the life-giving Spirit that God breathes.

The key to the unity of the "economic" and the "immanent" Trinity, then, must lie precisely in the "apophatic" or "negative" theology that is, as we have suggested, an essential element in the Irenaean and Cappadocian teaching about God. God is *not* related to the created order as entities within that order are related to each other. Yet as Creator, God *is* related to them in a manner that not only makes their mutual relatedness possible but marks it out as an image of, and a participation in, the way that God exists in the relations of "persons." By the same token, God is not subject to the successiveness of past, present, and future as are the creatures for whose fulfillment God created time; yet for all that, since their time is a dimension of the finite reality that God creates, the Trinity's way of being is not inconsistent with temporality. God is able to embrace time, to act within it, and so to be made known to creatures, but always as the ever self-consistent Deity that is time's Alpha and its Omega. As always, then, the presupposition of this pattern of affirmation-and-denial, which is the proper form of what is called "apophatic" theology, is the idea that the Trinity is the One who contains all things without being contained – or, in the more elegant language of some Greek poet whom Luke perhaps admired, the One in whom "we live and move and have our being" (Acts 17: 28), and therefore One to whom nothing finite is alien, even though nothing finite can fully or properly figure God.

How then is this triadic way of being world-related to be pictured? For if the nature of God on the one hand and the three "hows" of that nature on the other are in fact not to be classified as two different "forms" of God, the absolute and the related, but it is the absolute God who is eternally self-related to the finite order as its Origin, as its Model, and as the Empowerment of that Model, something has to be said about the divine "persons" in their relation to each other; and in this connection, the first question that arises is that of what "person" here denotes.

Present-day Christians have to make an effort to recall that "person" in the language of the fourth and fifth centuries bore none of the engaging, not to say endearing, connotations it has gradually acquired since Boethius defined it, in the sixth century, as meaning "individual substance of a rational nature." The Greek word spelled "hypostasis" in English in its classical usage had many senses, and it could certainly be employed to refer to individuals that *we* – nowadays – would call "persons." Nevertheless none of its connotations conveyed, in and of itself, the notion of being "personal." In the Latin-speaking west, as we have seen, *persona*, a rough equivalent of the Greek *prosopon* ("face," "outwardly manifested iden-tity," "role," "mask"), was employed instead of "hypostasis"; but the meaning of this term, first used in a trinitarian context by Tertullian in the third century, had not yet evolved to the point where it connoted a self-conscious center of thought and action. It meant an identity, or a party (as in "the party of the first part") – in any case, something one could refer to by a pronoun.

The question, then, whether the word "hypostasis" – and so in the West the word "person" – can legitimately be employed to denote the members of the Trinity as persons *in the modern sense of that term*, needs some weighing. They referred, as we have seen, to "somethings" that were differentiated only by their relations to each other. Hence terms referring to the three members of the Trinity stated, as we have indicated, *how* God *exists and acts* (i.e., in three distinct ways); and such a statement is of a different order from any assertion of *what* God *is*, i.e., *what* it is that exists in these three ways. To say, then, "The Father, the Son, and the Spirit are persons" would, in the terms of this classical trinitarian logic, imply that "person" is a label for a *way* of being God, but not a characterization of *what* God *is*.

There is, however, an obvious problem here. If "person" is applied to each of the hypostases in the same sense – as, for example, "God" or "creator" or "redeemer" are – the word would stand not for what distinguishes the hypostases from each other but for something they have in common. In that case, however, it would seem, "being personal" would belong to the divine nature rather than to the hypostases (this, incidentally, seems to have been Barth's conclusion); for it is the divine *ousia* that the latter have in common. Maybe then it would be better to say that the hypostases mark *three different ways in which God is personal*, just as they mark three different ways in which God exists and acts. In taking this view, however, one would have to remember that the words "ways" or "modes" (i.e., of existing or of being), when employed in connection with the Trinity, do *not* connote mere appearances or aspects of God, but characterize concrete and distinct *realities* ("somethings" = hypostases) that are differentiated from each other not by "what" they are but by "how" they are. If to be God is to be personal, then Father, Son, and Spirit are indeed *personal*, but in three different *ways*.

Given that qualification there is no reason to think that to speak of the members of the Trinity as "persons" in the later, modern sense is inconsistent with the traditional language of the doctrine. *Persona* and *hupostasis* could certainly be used, and were used, to refer to what moderns would call persons, even if that was not the going "dictionary" meaning of the words in the fourth century; and in any case, Jesus and God and the Spirit were addressed and answered and questioned – spoken *to*, and not just spoken *of* – in the Church's liturgical and biblical idiom. It is useful to note, moreover, that someone like Gregory of Nyssa ascribes will and self-motion to both the Word and the Spirit as well as to the Father.[50]

How then, to return to our original question, do the relations that mark the persons of the Trinity illuminate the relationship of God to the creation? If one looks closely at the line taken by the Cappadocians, one's initial impression is that the persons constitute a series in the order Father → Son → Spirit. They are even called, inevitably, "first," "second," and "third," though of course Basil of Caesarea insisted that such counting be done *reverently*, i.e., both done and denied, in the best apophatic fashion. Quite apart from Basil, however, this "serial" account of the Trinity ignores a further crucial element in the Cappadocians' picture of the relations among the persons. The Father generates the Son, to be sure; but it is also the Father who breathes the Spirit. The order, then, is not strictly serial, since the Spirit does not in the first instance proceed from the Son. Rather the two appear, as in Irenaeus, to be in a sense parallel and even coordinate; and this impression is reinforced when we discover that Gregory of Nyssa makes two distinctions with regard to the business of origination.[51] There is an initial distinction to be made between "the cause" and "that which is out of the cause," i.e., between the Father on the one hand, and Son and Spirit on the other. Then, he adds, there is a further distinction to be made *within* "that which is out of the cause," namely, between "what is immediately out of the original cause" (the Son) and "what is *through* that which is immediately out of the original [cause]" (the Spirit). In this form, the doctrine of double procession[52] emphasizes the close connection between the work of the Word and that of the Spirit – their coordination. Thus Gregory will say that the Spirit is "from the Father and of Christ," as the Scriptures teach. The "thirdness" of the Spirit has to do with his being the one that brings all the works of God to completion.

Moreover the three persons, on this account, are never apart from each other, but always together. One reason for this is that "The Father is never held in mind apart from the Son, nor is the Son grasped separately from the Spirit. For just as it is impossible to mount to the Father unless one has been lifted up by the Son's agency, so it is impossible to call Jesus 'Lord' save in the Holy Spirit." Hence Gregory continues:

> For the Father and the Son and the Spirit are acknowledged to be always with one another, in their sequence [*akolouthôs*] and in close union, in the full and perfect Trinity. Moreover, from before any creation and before all ages the Father is the Father, and in the Father is the Son, and with the Son is the Holy Spirit. It was not because he stood in need of assistance that the God who rules everything made all things through the Son, nor does the Only-begotten God accomplish everything in the Spirit because his power is inadequate to his project. No: but the wellspring of power is the Father, the power of the Father is the Son, and the spirit of power is the Holy Spirit; and the entire created order, perceptible and incorporeal alike, is the accomplished design of that power.[53]

In these words, one can see the basic principle that, in time, led to many other developments, or refinements, in trinitarian doctrine. The principle might be stated simply enough by repeating what was said at the beginning of this section: that the Trinity is a unity not only in being one "thing" but also in and through the relations of the persons. The Word is nothing and does nothing apart from the Father, and the Spirit is nothing and does nothing apart from the Word and the Father; and it follows that the Father is nothing and does nothing apart from Word and Spirit: *the three cannot even be thought without being thought together*. This point is reinforced by language which speaks of the Son's being eternally in the Father and the Spirit's being ever with the Son: the picture is essentially the Irenaean one, and was stated by Athanasius of Alexandria:

> For the holy and blessed Triad is indivisible and one in itself. When mention is made of the Father, there is included also his Word, and the Spirit who is in the Son. If the Son is named, the Father is in the Son and the Spirit is not outside the Word.[54]

The persons of the Trinity take each other in.

Thus that in respect of which God is one is threefold; and that in respect of which God is threefold is one. It is the former point that seems to have been the theme of the controversy that occupied the middle years of the fourth century. Each of the persons *is* the one God, though set apart from the others by the relation to them that defines it. The second of these points became central through reflection on the first, and was eventually articulated in the later doctrine of *perichoresis*.[55] This process of reflection began with the Cappadocians but came to its most stable expression in the work of John of Damascus, who appropriated the ideas – and indeed the words – of the unknown author of a treatise on the Trinity falsely (but usefully) attributed to Cyril of Alexandria (d. 444). It was this last-mentioned author who brought to expression the *reciprocal indwelling* of the three persons by adapting the idea of *perichoresis* to express it. "Where the Trinity is concerned, the three hypostases are and are called one God because of their identity of nature and their *perichoresis* within each other" – a *perichoresis* by which, it was said, they "hold on" to each other. The persons of the Trinity are so closely involved with each other that they really do constitute one thing without losing their individuality. Conversely, the difference of the persons is sustained by the communication from one to the other of the one nature.

Here then is a picture – sketched partly in a spatial metaphor, partly by way of an analogy with personal relations – of a God whose way of being is sharing and in whom, therefore, one-ness and many-ness, like the lion and the lamb, consent together. The original setting, however, in which this being-that-is-sharing is known and manifested is that of the water- and Spirit-baptism which Jesus shares with his disciples, a setting in which just such a way of being is opened to the participation of creatures – creatures that the God whose nature is inexpressible and whose name is unutterable created for just this purpose. Therefore it has to be said that the Trinity, though needing nothing and no one and being in that sense "absolute," quite naturally does what it is. For mere love's sake[56] it shares being and motion and life with a created order that participates in a multitude of different ways in God's own life, and, in the case of "personal" creatures, can image the very manner of God's being by being caught up in the identity of the Word of God through the Father's gift of the Spirit.

Notes

1   *Book of Common Prayer* (New York: The Church Hymnal Corporation and The Seabury Press, 1979), p. 852.
2   Article I, in *Book of Common Prayer*, p. 867.
3   The word "trinity" is from the Latin *trinitas*, itself a rendering of the Greek term *trias*. The words mean "threefoldness" and "threesome," respectively.
4   *Book of Common Prayer*, p. 95.
5   *Book of Common Prayer*, p. 375.
6   *Codex Theodosianus* 16.1.3 (addressed to Auxonius, Proconsul of Asia).
7   *Book of Common Prayer* I, pp. 864f.
8   This expression ordinarily refers to Basil of Caesarea, called "the Great" (d. 379); his friend and ally Gregory of Nazianzus (d. 389) called "the Theologian" because of his eloquent defense of the Nicene faith in a series of addresses given in Constantinople in 380; and Basil's younger brother, Gregory of Nyssa (d. *ca*.395).
9   For the quotations that follow, see Irenaeus, *Against Heresies* (hereafter *AH*) 3.18.3; cf. 3.6.1; 3.17.1.
10 *On the Holy Spirit* 28, in Nicene and Post-Nicene Fathers, second series (hereafter NPNF$_2$), 8: 18.
11 Cf. *AH* 3.9.3; 3.12.7; 3.17.1.
12 See Origen, *Homilies on Genesis* 2.5 (*Sources chrétiennes* 7 bis [Paris, 1976], p. 102): Origen speaks of the Marcan account of the Baptism of Jesus, "ubi et primum coepit sacramentum patescere Trinitatis" ("where the mystery of the Trinity first began to become manifest").
13 Note that allusions to baptism in Paul – and not Paul alone – regularly characterize its effect by reference to the members of the Christian Triad: e.g., "It is God who establishes us with you in Christ . . . he has put his seal upon us and given us his Spirit in our hearts as a guarantee" (2 Cor. 1: 21f.); "You were washed, you were justified, you

were sanctified in the name of our Lord Jesus Christ and in the Spirit of our God" (1 Cor. 6: 11); "To the exiles of the dispersion . . . chosen and destined by God the Father and sanctified by the Spirit for obedience to Jesus Christ and for sprinkling with his blood" (1 Pet. 1: 1f.). These are references, moreover, to the effects of baptism, to what happens in baptism, and not merely to the words of a baptismal "formula" or confession. Matthew 28: 19 is no doubt merely another, and somewhat less interesting, example of this sort of text.

14 See, e.g., Tertullian, *On Baptism*, 8.

15 *AH* 3.6.1; cf. Ps. 82: 6.

16 *AH* 3.17.1–2; and cf. *AH* 3.9.3 *ad fin.*

17 On this fundamental point it is useful to notice the words of Basil (*On the Holy Spirit* 61, in NPNF₂ 8, p. 38): it is the work of the Spirit that a person "who no longer 'lives after the flesh' but, being 'led by the Spirit' is called a son of God, and is 'conformed to the image of the Son of God.'"

18 On this point, see Colin Gunton, *The One, the Three, and the Many* (Cambridge: Cambridge University Press, 1998), pp. 158–60, with its discussion of Irenaeus and the idea of "economy."

19 This word has been variously translated as "substance," "stuff," "being," "subject," "essence," and "nature." Any of these is acceptable; which is correct must be determined contextually. The word is commonly thought of as a technical philosophical term, but it was in common use in a wide range of senses, and was in fact technical in about the same sense and to about the same degree as the English words like "real" or "reality."

20 E.g., *AH* 4.20.2; but see also, in particular, the opening chapters of *AH* 2.

21 *AH* 4.20.4.

22 It also implied for Irenaeus that God does not stand in want of anything: the world is not God's need-fulfiller, as some Gnostics had argued with regard to the artisan-Creator, maintaining that he as it were "uses" or milks the material creation for his own purposes. On the contrary, says Irenaeus, God created humanity "in order to have someone upon whom to confer benefits" (*AH* 4.14.1), and therefore creation is a purely positive act of love. Further, God does not "need" any helpers to carry through the business of creation, being quite capable of doing the whole job alone.

23 In the churches of the third century, Logos-language and Spirit-language seem as often as not to have got dissociated from each other to one degree or another, no doubt because they tended to be employed in different connections. The natural "field" of Logos-language was discourse about creation and incarnation. The natural "field" of Spirit-language was accounts of prophetic and apostolic inspiration on the one hand, and, on the other, discourse about baptism and about the shape of the new life of the people of God created by baptism.

24 See Gregory of Nyssa's discussion in *Against Eunomius*, 1.518 (and indeed the whole surrounding passage): NPNF₂ 5, p. 83 = GNO (Gregorii Nysseni Opera) 1: 176.

25 See, e.g., *Against Eunomius*, 1.291, in GNO 1: 112 = NPNF₂ 5, p. 62. "The primary Good is by nature unlimited; and for that reason the participation of the person who joys in that Good will also, of necessity, be unlimited. He will always be receiving more, and forever discovering something than more that which he has already taken in, and he will never be able to measure up to what he has received, since that in which he participates is unlimited, and on account of such participation, it can never stop growing."

26 Gregory of Nazianzus, *Oration*, 28.17.

27 Ibid., 28.3; cf. Exod. 33: 20ff. With this it worth comparing the language of Calvin (*Institutio*, I.5.1): "His essence is incomprehensible . . . But upon his individual works he has engraved unmistakable signs of his glory."

28 *The 'Shepherd' of Hermas*, Mandate 1, in K. Lake (ed.) *The Apostolic Fathers*, 2 vols. Loeb Classical Library (Cambridge, MA: Harvard University Press, 1959), vol. 2, p. 70.

29 See Philo's remarks on Genesis 3: 8 in *Allegories of the Laws*, III. 4–6.

30 The Greek word *apophasis* means "denial"; hence an "apophatic" theology is one that characterizes God by saying what Deity is not.

31 *On the Holy Spirit*, 18 (in NPNF$_2$ 8, p. 12).

32 See, e.g., Gregory of Nyssa, *Against Eunomius*, I.26.367, in NPNF$_2$ 5, p. 69 = GNO 1: 135.

33 Note that contrary to what was already customary in the NT Irenaeus identifies the figure of Wisdom (cf. Prov. 8: 22ff.; Wisdom 7: 22ff.) with the Holy Spirit rather than with the Christ. This is very likely attributable to the influence of Theophilus of Antioch. More oddly still, Irenaeus' account of the Word or Son of God nevertheless continues to endow the latter with the attributes of Wisdom, even though the title is assigned elsewhere.

34 *AH* 4.20.4; cf. 3.24.2.

35 *AH* 4.20.1. I follow here the text as reconstructed by A. Rousseau (*Sources chrétiennes*, 100, p. 626).

36 *AH* 4.5.1.

37 *Proof of the Apostolic Preaching*, 5, as translated by J. P. Smith in Ancient Christian Writers, no. 16 (Westminster, MD: Newman Press, 1952).

38 *AH* 4.20.5, 6.

39 The Council condemned the proposition that the Son "is from another *hupostasis* or *ousia*," i.e., other than the Father's.

40 Gregory of Nazianzus, *Oration*, 29.12.

41 On this phrase, see G. L. Prestige, *God in Patristic Thought* (London: SPCK, 1952), pp. 245–6, where the author points out the connection of the phrase with modes of origination. Karl Rahner (at least in English translation) rendered it as "modes of subsisting."

42 See Gregory of Nyssa, *To Ablabius, That There Are Not Three Gods*, in Edward Hardy, ed., *Christology of the Later Fathers*, Library of Christian Classics (hereafter LCC), vol. 3 (Philadelphia: Westminster, 1954), p. 266 = GNO 3.1: 56.

43 Gregory of Nazianzus, *Oration*, 29.16.

44 On this score, see Basil's account of the *energeiai* of the Holy Spirit: *On the Holy Spirit*, 49, in NPNF$_2$ 8, pp. 30f.

45 This of course is merely a paraphrase of Thomas Aquinas's nice Latin aphorism: "operatio sequitur esse."

46 This is a way of stating the principle famously formulated by Augustine in the words, "Opera trinitatis ad extra sunt indivisa" ("The activities of the Trinity are not differentiated in relation to what is outside of God"). He derived this principle from the Cappadocians; see, e.g., Gregory of Nyssa, *To Ablabius: That There Are Not Three Gods*, in LCC 3, pp. 261f. = GNO 3.1: 48.

47 *On the Holy Spirit*, 47, in NPNF$_2$ 8, pp. 29f. Cf. Gregory of Nyssa, *Against Eunomius*, 1.531, in NPNF$_2$ 5, p. 84 = GNO 1: 179f.

48 It needs to be observed, of course, that this distinction has ordinarily been declared alien to God, in whose "being" nothing is contingent or accidental.

49 See the influential and now surely classic study by G. H. Meade, *Mind, Self, and Society from the Standpoint of a Social Behaviorist* (Chicago: University of Chicago Press, 1934). For Aquinas, of course, "relation" was the name of a contingent or accidental modification of, or addition to, a creature's given "being" (*ousia*).

50 See his *Address on Religious Instruction* 1–2, in LCC 3, pp. 271, 273 = J. H. Srawley, ed., *The Catechetical Oration of Gregory of Nyssa* (Cambridge, 1956), pp. 9f., 15.

51 *To Ablabius*, in LCC 3, pp. 266 and GNO 3.1: 56.

52 See also Athanasius, *To Serapion*, 1.2: "the Spirit, who proceeds from the Father, and belonging to the Son, is from him given to the disciples and all who believe in him" (C. R. B. Shapland, ed., *The Letters of St Athanasius Concerning the Holy Spirit* [London: Epworth, 1951], pp. 64f.). The doctrine of the "double procession" of the Spirit is now best known in its embroidered Augustinian form, which is stated in a phrase that was inserted into the Niceno-Constantinopolitan creed in the West during the late fifth and following centuries. According to this phrase, the Holy Spirit "proceeds from the Father and the Son" – thus presumably having two simultaneous sources of his being. Gregory's formula – "from the Father" and "through the Son" – preserves the role of the First Person of the Trinity as the single source and original of the divine nature reproduced in Son and Spirit; but I am not sure whether the difference between the two formulations amounts to an inconsistency.

53 For these citations, see Gregory of Nyssa, *On the Holy Spirit*, in PNF₂ 5, pp. 319, 320 = GNO 3.1: 98–100. Cf. Athanasius, *To Serapion*, 1.9 (Shapland, *Letters*, p. 82): the Spirit, "in whom the Father, through the Word, perfects and renews all things."

54 Athanasius, *To Serapion*, 1.14 (Shapland, *Letters*, pp. 93f.).

55 *Perichoresis* is a rare word in Greek. It can mean "reciprocal alternation" (moving from one thing to another in circular fashion and coming back to the starting point of the motion); for the Greek verb *choreo* means to go forward or advance and the proposition *peri-* can mean "around." The verb, though, can also mean "contain" or "make room for;" and *perichoresis* can then connote something like "interpenetration" or "permeation."

56 Creation, then, can indeed be described as an act of God's will; but it is not the fruit of a process of argumentative deliberation – a distinction which, as the age-old critique mounted by Plotinus shows, is an important one.

3

Sarah Coakley, "Living into the Mystery of the Holy Trinity: Trinity, Prayer, and Sexuality"

Along with other contemporary authors – Richard Norris, Robert Jenson, David Yeago, Rowan Williams, and myself – Sarah Coakley follows Romans 8 to see the Trinity as a community of inclusion, where the Spirit incorporates the human being into the relationship between the Father and the Son. Coakley focuses on the experiential aspect of this inclusion: it happens in prayer, in the Spirit's praying for, with, and in human beings. It is not just that in the Spirit, God prays. It is almost as if, in the Spirit, "only" God prays, but the Spirit includes human beings in the praying of God to God. If human contemplative prayer joins the human being to God, that is only because the Spirit includes human beings in the intradivine prayer by which God joins to God, or one Person of the Trinity joins with another in an exchange of gift and gratitude. (Contemplative prayer is a prayer of intimate communion, relatively but not completely opposed to intercessory prayer that asks for things.)

Coakley finds a lonely predecessor in this approach in the early Christian thinker Origen. She finds, intriguingly, that Origen is anxious about interpreting the joining of the human being with God – which involves the Spirit's "groaning in travail" and giving birth to sons of God – in a sexual way. He instructs a married couple not to pray where they have sex, for example. But that means, according to Coakley, that Origen thinks of contemplative prayer and sexual expression as rivals for the same kind of energy. And that means that he thinks of them as having the same root. Both sexuality and contemplative prayer, she infers, join a human being with a personal object of desire, human or divine. Both sexuality and contemplative prayer partake, in short, of an erotic energy. Origen needs to distinguish them, precisely because he sees their deep connection. A different age, having lost that connection, may need to discover it anew.

Sarah Coakley, 'Living into the Mystery of the Holy Trinity: Trinity, Prayer and Sexuality', *Anglican Theological Review* 80 (1998): 223–32.

Living into the Mystery of the Holy Trinity: Trinity, Prayer and Sexuality

Sarah Coakley

In this presentation, I want to lay before you three theses about the Trinity which have been much exercising me in my recent theological research,[1] and which are, I believe, intertwined in a complex and fascinating way. They relate to what I see as the interlocked themes of the Trinity, prayer, and sexuality. Let me start with a succinct enunciation of my three theses, and then proceed to a slightly more ramified explication of each in the time available.

The first thesis is this: *that the revival of a vibrant trinitarian conceptuality, an 'earthed' sense of the meaningfulness and truth of the Christian doctrine of the Trinity, most naturally arises out of a simultaneous renewal of commitment to prayer, and especially prayer of a relatively wordless kind.* I shall try to explain why I think this is so with special reference to Paul's discussion of the nature of Christian prayer in Romans 8 as 'sighs too deep for words' (Rom. 8: 26), instituted by the Holy Spirit; and how I think this Spirit-leading approach to the Trinity through prayer is the only experientially rooted one likely to provide some answer to the sceptical charge: why three 'persons' at all? Why believe in a trinitarian God in the first place?

So that will be my first thesis: the inextricability of renewed trinitarian conceptuality and the renewal of prayer-practice, and I shall be arguing that Christian prayer-practice is inherently trinitarian.

The second thesis goes on from this, and is perhaps a little more surprising; it is that *the close analysis of such prayer, and its implicitly trinitarian structure, makes the confrontation of a particular range of fundamental issues about sexuality unavoidable.* (Note that I use 'sexuality' in a wider sense than is often employed in North America – not restricting it to actual genital sexual activity.) The unavoidability of this confrontation seems to me to arise from the profound entanglement of our human sexual desires and our desire for God; and in any prayer of the sort in which we radically cede control to the Spirit there is an instant reminder of the close analogue between this ceding (to the trinitarian God), and the *ekstasis* of human sexual passion. Thus it is not a coincidence that intimate relationship is at the heart of both these matters. That the early Fathers were aware of this nexus of associations (between trinitarian conceptuality, prayer of a deep sort, and the – to them – dangerous connections with issues of sex and gender), I shall illustrate with a particular example from the third-century Alexandrian theologian, Origen. What will emerge from this second thesis, I hope, is that no renewed trinitarian spirituality can *sidestep* these profound issues of the nature of sexual desire, issues which now so divisively exercise us in the Church's life, and are, in turn, of course, fundamentally connected with gender themes about women's roles, women's capacity for empowerment, and for professional equality.

In short, it is not a coincidence that 'Affirming Catholicism' works simultaneously for renewed spiritual practice, for enlivened trinitarian doctrine, and for an honest confrontation of tough questions in the contemporary Church about issues of sexuality and gender. For these three issues all belong together, and can be shown with a bit of delicate archaeological digging beneath the polite edifice constructed by the standard history-of-doctrine textbooks, to have accompanied one another all along. Or so I shall argue.

My third thesis, then finally, is not so much a finished proposition, but a task in progress for us all. It is the task of *rethreading the strands of inherited tradition on these three matters in such a way that enacted sexual desire and desire for God are no longer seen in mutual enmity, as disjunctive alternatives, with the non-celibate woman or homosexual cast as the distracter from the divine goal.* Rather, we are seeking a renewed vision of divine desire (a trinitarian vision, I suggest) which may provide the guiding framework for a renewed theology of human sexuality – of godly sexual relations – rooted in, and analogously related to, trinitarian divine relations. Again, I want to suggest, there are resources in the tradition for this task, even if one has to dig a bit.

Now this is rather a lot to tackle in one short lecture! But let me say at least a bit more about these three theses in turn, and where my research has led me.

The Trinity in prayer-practice

When we move to face the puzzling question of why perfect relationship in God was understood as triadic in the first place, I want to argue that an analysis of Christian prayer (especially relatively wordless contemplative or charismatic prayer) provides an acutely revealing matrix for explaining the origins of trinitarian reflection. Vital here is Paul's analysis of prayer in Romans 8, where he describes how, strictly speaking, we do not autonomously do the praying, for we do not even really know what to ask for; rather it is the 'Spirit' who prays in us to the ultimate source in God ('the Father',[2] or 'Abba', and does so with 'sighs too deep for words' transcending normal human rationality. Into that ceaseless divine dialogue between Spirit and 'Father' the Christian pray-er is thus caught up, and so transformed, becoming a co-heir with Christ and being fashioned into an extension of redeemed, incarnate life. Recall how Paul puts it:

> For all who are led by the Spirit of God are sons of God. For you did not receive a spirit of slavery to fall back into fear, but you have received a spirit of adoption. When we cry, 'Abba, Father!' it is that very Spirit bearing witness with our spirit that we are children of God, and if children, then heirs of God and joint heirs with Christ (Rom. 8: 14–17) . . . Likewise the Spirit helps us in our weakness; for we do not know how to pray as we ought, but that very Spirit intercedes with sighs too deep for words. And God, who searches the heart, knows what is the mind of the Spirit, because the Spirit intercedes for the saints according to the will of God. (Rom 8: 26–7)

Now it is important to underscore that what is going on here is not three distinguishable types of 'experience' (in the sense of emotional tonality), each experience relating to a different point of identity – 'Father', 'Son' and 'Holy Spirit'. This in any case would prove to be a 'hunting of the snark' from the perspective of later-developed orthodox trinitarianism, since the *homoousion* principle disallows that the different 'persons' should be experientially separate, or do different things. Rather, what is being described in Paul is *one* experience of an activity of prayer that is nonetheless ineluctably, though obscurely, triadic. It is *one* experience of God, but God as simultaneously (i) doing the praying in me, (ii) receiving that prayer, and (iii) in that exchange, consented to in me, inviting me into the Christic life of redeemed sonship. Or to put it another way: the 'Father' (so-called here) is both source and ultimate object of divine longing in us; the 'Spirit' is that irreducibly – though obscurely – distinct enabler and incorporator of that longing in creation – that which *makes* the creation divine; and the 'Son' *is* that divine and perfected creation, into whose life I, as pray-er, am caught up. In this sense, despite all the unclarity and doctrinal fuzziness of Romans 8, the prayer described here seems to be at least proto-trinitarian in its implications.

Now no one would suggest that most of our prayer, sweated out as it so often is in states of dryness and distraction, may clearly feel like this. But just occasionally, I submit (at least if we allow enough space in which we are not insistently setting the agenda – if we allow, that is, this precious *hiatus* for the Spirit), then we breathe the Spirit's breath in this way; we see briefly that this is, theologically speaking, the triadic structure of God's graced ways with us – what is always going on though we mostly cannot *see* it. As John of the Cross puts it in a lovely passage in *The Spiritual Canticle* (39.3.4), not coincidentally quoting Romans 8: 'the Holy Spirit raises the soul most sublimely with that His divine breath . . . that she may breathe in God the same breath of love that the Father breathes in the Son and the Son in the Father'.

The Spirit, on this view, note, is no redundant third, no hypostatized afterthought, no cooing 'feminine' adjunct to an established male household. Rather, experientially speaking, the Spirit is *primary*, just as Pentecost is primary for the church; and leaving noncluttered space for the Spirit is the absolute precondition for the unimpeded flowing of this divine exchange in us, the 'breathing of the divine breath', as John of the Cross puts it.

Now what we want to know next is this (and it brings us to our second thesis): What happened to exegesis of Romans 8 in the critical early-patristic period? Why was it not the wellspring of the turbulent conciliar discussion of the Trinity? And why, as it seems from the standard textbooks, did the Spirit get properly attended to only third and last (in the later fourth century) in the development of trinitarian doctrine in the crucial early-patristic period, when the equality of the rational Logos with the 'Father' was discussed and established so much earlier? Or was this really so? Was there perhaps a 'soft underbelly' history of the development of the doctrine of the Trinity which the textbooks have obscured, and in which the Spirit played a much more significant role from the outset?

The Trinity and sexuality

My answer to this last question, although it is a speculative answer, is 'Yes'. There *is* a 'soft underbelly' history of the early development of the doctrine of the Trinity which the Fathers had reason to push to one side. What I suggest is that there is an alternative account of the genealogy of the doctrine which only becomes clear once we see the covert entanglement of this genealogy with questions of sex and gender.

What is striking, first, is how little Romans 8 gets used as a basis for trinitarian argument and reflection in the early period (with some important exceptions in Irenaeus, Origen, and then the later Athanasius).[3] My hypothesis is that this is because this Romans 8 approach, fertile as it was theologically, proved a little too hot to handle. Why?

What I suggest here is that, from the second century on, there were both politico-ecclesiastical *and* gender reasons for keeping this approach to the Trinity away from the centre stage in the public conciliar discussions of the matter. For Paul's analysis of prayer in Romans 8 notably involves: (i) a certain loss of noetic control to the leading experiential force of the Spirit in the face of our weakness (8; 26); (ii) an entry into a realm beyond words, beyond normal rationality or *logos* (ibid.); and (iii) the striking use of a (female) 'birth pangs' metaphor to describe the yearning of creation for its 'glorious liberty' (8: 22). After Montanism (the prophetic and rigorist sectarian movement of the second century, ultimately condemned by Rome), it is not hard to see why any or all of these features could look less than attractive to developing mainstream 'orthodoxy', at least as a first basis for trinitarian reflection. The danger of ecstatic prophecy, when loosed from the primary control of an extrinsic Logos, was one matter. This had all the drawbacks of an essentially sectarian manifestation of the faith. The releasing of 'wretched women', as Hippolytus reports of early Montanism,[4] into positions of authority and prominence, was a second one. But there was a third danger, with which I think the third-century theologian Origen is primarily concerned (much more than he is with Montanism); and that is the danger, in any form of prayer that deliberately gives away rational mastery to the Spirit, of possible confusion between loss of control to that Spirit and loss of *sexual* control.

Let me just describe to you briefly what Origen says about prayer, trinitarianism and sexuality – all together in one nexus of association – in his fascinating treatise on prayer, the *De Oratione*.[5]

I shall just draw attention to the following four features of this work, especially of its opening sections, from which you will see how closely related they are to the themes I have just outlined:

(i) The work starts (I) with an insistence on the priority and primacy of the Holy Spirit in understanding the nature and purpose of prayer; and it stresses the capacity of the grace of God to take us beyond the 'worthless reasoning of mortals' to a sphere of unutterable mysteries (see 2 Cor. 12), where 'spiritual prayer' occurs in the 'heart'. Already, then, there is the explicit willingness to allow that the Spirit – although from the start a 'fellow worker' with the Father and Son – escorts us to a realm beyond the normal constraints of human rationality, even though in Origen's case there is no suggestion that the Spirit finally undermines the significance of the rational sphere. (ii) Exegesis of Romans 8 is central to the argument from the start, and citations are reiterated more than once; it is through prayer, and being 'mingled with the Spirit', that we become 'partakers of the Word of God' (X.2). (iii) This form of prayer is repeatedly, and strikingly, compared to sexual intercourse and procreation. Thus, for instance, Origen writes: 'just as it is not possible to beget children without a woman and without receiving the power that serves to beget children, so no one may obtain . . . requests . . . unless he/she has prayed with such and such a disposition' (VIII.1). The Old Testament figure of Hannah, on this view, becomes the supreme type of the pray-er who overcomes sterility through the Spirit (II.5, etc.). But finally (iv) (and this is where we see Origen putting the brakes on), an *absolute disjunction,* according to Origen, must be made between the sexual and procreative theme in its metaphorical force (as *we* would now call it), and in its normal human functioning. Thus Tatiana, the woman to whom (along with a man, Ambrose) this work is addressed, can be trusted with this approach only because she is 'most manly', and has gone beyond 'womanish things' – in the 'manner of Sarah' (Genesis 18: 11). And knowing how 'to pray as we ought' (Romans 8: 26, see II.2) is paralleled with an appropriately 'passionless', 'deliberate', and 'holy' performance of the 'mysteries of marriage', lest 'Satan rejoice over you through lack of self control'. Unsurprisingly too, then, Origen's daring treatment of Romans 8 also occasions an immediate reminder (with reference to 1 Timothy 2 and 1 Corinthians 11), that women should always wear modest apparel and cover their heads at prayer, lest their distracting presence lead to the same sort of loss of (male) sexual control. Later in the text, too, Origen advises against praying at all in a room in which sexual intercourse has taken place (XXXI.4). The intrinsic connections between (deep) trinitarian prayer and sex, it seems, are too close, but also too dangerous.

For Origen, the answer to this closeness between trinitarianism, contemplative ascent and sexuality, and the concomitant danger of a sinful confusion of the areas, must lie in allowing only advanced contemplatives ('enoptics') – those who have also shed actual physical sexual relations – into the circle of those who may safely use the erotic language of the Song of Songs to describe Christ's intimate mystical embrace of us.[6] Hence erotic language becomes the (finally) indispensable mode of speaking of our intimacy with God, but only at the cost of renouncing the physical or fleshly expressions of sexuality.

But it is precisely here that our third question presses, one to which I have no complete answer, but only some speculative suggestions.

Divine and human desires

My third thesis, you remember, is the call to rethread the strands of tradition on divine and human desires such that they are no longer set in fundamental enmity with one another, no longer failing in their alignment. For the fatal accompaniment of such a failure of alignment, as is all too clear in Origen (amongst others), is the denigration of nonvirginal woman, or indeed any humanly desirable person, as a distractor from the divine.

What has the Trinity got to do with *this?* Let me just suggest two programmatic points in closing:

The first is the hypothesis that unless we have some sense of the implications of the trinitarian God's proto-erotic desire for us, then we can hardly begin to get rightly ordered our own erotic desires at the human level. Put another way, *we need to turn Freud on his head.* Instead of thinking of 'God' language as really being about sex (Freud's reductive ploy), we need to understand sex as really about God, and about the deep desire that we feel for God – the clue that is woven into our existence about the final and ultimate union that we seek. And it matters in this regard – or so I submit – that the God we desire is, in Godself, a desiring trinitarian God: the Spirit who longs for our response, who searches the hearts, and takes us to the divine source (the 'Father'), transforming us Christically as we are so taken.

In this connection there is a wonderfully suggestive passage in the fifth-century pseudo-Dionysius (*Divine Names*, IV) where Dionysius speaks of this divine *ekstasis* and yearning of God for creation catching up our human yearning into itself: 'This divine yearning', he writes, 'brings ecstasy so that the lover belongs not to self but to the beloved . . . This is why the great Paul, swept along by his yearning for God and seized of its ecstatic power, has these inspired words to say: "It is no longer I who live but Christ who lives in me". Paul was clearly a lover, and, as he says, he was beside himself for God'.[7]

Now it needs to be admitted that this passage of Dionysius's is not worked out explicitly in trinitarian terms; indeed it is open to the charge of being more influenced by neo-Platonic notions of emanation and effusion than by a strictly Christian conceptuality. But I want to suggest here that it is at least capable of trinitarian glossing, according to the model provided in undeveloped form in Romans 8, and discussed above. And on this basis I suggest that we need to have a vision of trinitarian divine *ekstasis* if we are even to begin to construct a decent theology of human sexual desire that is in analogous relationship to divine desire.

Thus secondly, and lastly: if human loves are indeed made with the imprint of the divine upon them – vestigia of God's ways – then they too, at their best, will bear the trinitarian mark. Here we have to take off where Augustine left us, at that crucial moment in the *De Trinitate*, at the end of book VIII, when he rejects finally the analogy of 'the lover, the loved one, and the love that binds', as inadequate to the Trinity because it is bound to bodies. 'Let us tread the flesh underfoot and mount up to the soul', as he puts it (*De Trinitate*, VIII.14). But sexual loves *are* bodily, and if they are also to be godly, then they too should mirror forth the trinitarian image. And what would that involve? Surely, at the very least, a fundamental respect each for the other, an equality of exchange, and the mutual *ekstasis* of attending on the other's desire as distinct, *as other*. This is the opposite of abuse, the opposite of distanced sexual control; it is, as the French feminist Luce Irigaray has written, with uncanny insight, itself intrinsically trinitarian; sexual love at its best is not 'egological', not even a 'duality in closeness', but a shared transcendence of two selves toward the other, within a 'shared space, a shared breath'. 'In this relation', she writes, 'we are at least three . . . you, me, and our creation of that ecstasy of ourself in us (*de nous en nous*) prior to any child'.[8] As each goes out to the other in mutual abandonment and attentiveness, so it becomes clear that a third is at play – the irreducibility of a 'shared transcendence'.

To speak thus of the trinitarian nature of sexual love at its best is a far remove from the grimy world of pornography and abuse from which Christian feminism has emerged to make its rightful protest. Unfortunately, no language of *eros* is safe from possible nefarious application; and hence the feminist hermeneutic of suspicion can never come to an end. Even these reflections on divine trinitarian *eros* could, I am well aware, be put to potentially dangerous and distorted applications.[9] In this regard, Origen's caution about putting the Song of Songs into the wrong hands looks less completely wrong-headed than we might have suggested earlier. We do indeed play with fire when we acknowledge the deep entanglement of sexual desire and desire for God.

But what, finally, I have been trying to lay before you tonight, in these reflections on the Trinity, prayer, and sexuality, is that this potent nexus of themes is one that no serious renewed Catholicism can afford to ignore or repress; and that only the faithfulness of prayer that reveals the nexus in the first place can hope to deliver the insights we need in developing an adequately rich trinitarian theology of sexuality to confront the ecclesiastical ructions on matters of sex and gender that now so profoundly exercise us.

Notes

1 See Sarah Coakley, 'Can God be Experienced as Trinity?,' *The Modern Churchman* 28 (1986): 11–23; and 'Why Three? Some Further Reflections on the Doctrine of the Trinity', in Sarah Coakley and David A. Pailin (eds.) *The Making and Remaking of Christian Doctrine: Essays in Honour of Maurice Wiles* (Oxford: Oxford University Press, 1993); and Sarah Coakley, *God, Sexuality and the Self: An Essay 'On the Trinity'* (Cambridge: Cambridge University Press, forthcoming).

2 I do not here address the vexed issue of whether a feminist theologian should, under any circumstances, call God 'Father'. In *God, Sexuality and the Self* (see n. 1) I argue that in inner-trinitarian contexts there are theological reasons why it is difficult to insist on consistent substitutions for 'Father language; 'creator', 'redeemer', and 'sanctifier' , for instance, does not do the same theological work as 'Father', 'Son', and 'Holy Spirit'. In addition, the attempt to repress *all* 'Father' language out of liturgical usage may merely force paternal imagery underground, leaving it to continue its (often baleful) effects out of conscious sight. My solution is a multi-pronged one, including the use of deliberate illogical conjunction (maternal and paternal imagery combined) as a means of avoiding crass literalism in the attribution of parental characteristics; but I do not advocate the complete obliteration of 'Father' language, especially in the trinitarian context.

3 See, e.g., Irenaeus, *Adversus haereses* [*Against Heresies*], 5.20.2; Origen, *De oratione*, I. 3–6 (see discussion below); Athanasius, *Ad Serapion* [*To Serapion*], 1.6, 1.7, 1.19, 1.24, 1.25, 4.4. These passages are set in context in my article 'Why Three?' (see n. 1, above).

4 See Hippolytus, *Refutatio omnium haeresiorum* [*Against All Heresies*], 8.19; also discussed in 'Why Three?' (see n. 1, above).

5 I use here the English translation of the *De oratione* (and the section divisions) in Rowan A. Greer (ed.) *Origen* (New York: Paulist Press, 1979), pp. 81–170.

6   Origen makes this point emphatically at the opening of his *Commentary on the Song of Songs* (Prologue, I); see R. P. Lawson (trans.) *Origen: The Song of Songs Commentary and Homilies* (London: Longmans, Green and Co., 1957), pp. 22–3.

7   Pseudo-Dionysius, *The Divine Names*, 4.13; see Colm Luibheid (trans.) *PseudoDionysius: The Complete Works* (London: SPCK, 1987), p. 82.

8   Luce Irigaray, 'Questions to Emmanuel Lévinas', in Margaret Whitford (ed.) *The Irigaray Reader* (Oxford: Blackwell, 1991), p. 180.

9   The point about the *dangers* of some feminists' use of the 'erotic' as a positive and transformative category is well made in Kathleen M. Sands, 'Uses of the Thea(o)logian: Sex and Theodicy in Religious Feminism', *Journal of Feminist Studies in Religion* 8 (1992): 7–33.

4

Rowan Williams, "Word and Spirit"

Williams opposes a linear model of the Trinity because it depends on picturing God as distant from the human being. Precisely if God crosses a distance to come to human beings, the distance defines and constrains their relationship. How, Williams wonders, can we think of the Trinity as promoting intimacy between God and creatures? And not an intimacy that glories in the apparent *power* claimed by closeness to God. So Williams does not propose an alternative *model* to the linear one. Rather, he wants to *resist* models, in the name of an intimate or liberating spirituality. He wants to preserve a space for the Spirit to transform, free, love the human being into choosing the power*less*ness exemplified in the life of Christ. He describes that powerlessness as not passive but an engaged and constructive refusal to dominate. He wants to invite the reader into a form of life, to *suggest* what only the Spirit in a concrete human life could spell out. A theology of the Spirit, according to Williams, must not bypass the cross, but invite the human being into sharing Christ's vulnerability. Williams wants to steer a course between a model of the Trinity that defines the divine and the human in terms of either simple contrast (the distance model) or simple identity (a model of union), in favor of lives that are not theories at all, but venues in which the Spirit shapes Christlikeness under the conditions of engaged limit. In short: neither distance nor power defines the shape of the Trinity, but love incarnate and crucified. The distinctive advantages of Williams's approach are two: like Coakley, he ties together Spirit and spirituality; like von Balthasar, he ties together Trinity and cross. Many spiritualities of the Trinity are spiritualities of glory; this one is (also) a spirituality of the cross.

Rowan Williams, "Word and Spirit," in *On Christian Theology* (Oxford: Blackwell, 2000), pp. 107–11, 115–27.

Word and Spirit

Rowan Williams

Many writers have remarked a certain poverty in theological reflection on the Holy Spirit in Western Christianity over the last decades. Despite the enormous proliferation of literature concerned with the charismatic movement in recent years,[1] and despite the appearance of a number of more substantial essays in English on the Spirit,[2] it is hard not to feel that a certain unease persists. It is an unease reflected very clearly in the fact that more than one recent writer in the Anglican tradition seems to settle for a virtual binitarianism, a trinity of two persons (agents) and a force, or quality, or 'mode of presence'.[3] Looking further afield, it is notable that several of the greatest contemporary theologians on the Continent of Europe share something of this malaise. Barth's doctrine of the Spirit is, notoriously, one of the least developed areas of his system;[4] and this weakness is, if anything, accentuated in the work of perhaps his most distinguished pupil, Eberhard Jüngel.[5] In Roman Catholic theology, neither Rahner nor Küng has provided an independent treatise on pneumatology, and their respective essays in theological synthesis[6] contain only the most cursory treatment of the subject. Schillebeeckx's fine essay in Christology[7] touches the theology of the Spirit only tangentially.

One could go on quoting such instances (and it needs also to be said that there are some very notable exceptions, in the Protestant and Catholic worlds: the two intriguing and challenging figures of Jürgen Moltmann[8] and Hans Urs von Balthasar[9] stand out here), but it would not be particularly useful. What we need to be asking is why there should be such an awkwardness in this area. One fairly obvious answer might be that, in the present theological climate as seldom before, all the pressures are towards the concrete, the worldly – towards Christology, in fact. For those like Moltmann and Schillebeeckx who are profoundly engaged in dialogue with the Frankfurt School, Christology becomes, above all, the vehicle for coping with the most tormenting questions of our age about the *humanum* – what is it to be a human being after the Holocaust (or after Vietnam or Kampuchea)? The rejection and death of Jesus is in a sense the only *possible* theological datum now: to avoid Christology is to avoid the human question of how to talk of God in the shadow of hell. From this perspective (though Moltmann himself does not draw any such simple conclusion), pneumatology can very easily look both evasive and triumphalist: harsh remarks have sometimes been made (not entirely justly) about the emergence of vigorous charismatic groups in situations of acute social conflict (Latin America, Southern Africa) as a re-directing of frustrated energies unable to manage the realities of secular confrontation. Christology has a priority simply because there the question of God and the human is most directly raised. Pneumatology can be seen as raising only the question of God and certain limited kinds of human experience. A very acute observer of Roman Catholic pentecostalism in America wrote (several decades ago, surprisingly):

We have seen too often how 'religion' can become no more than an intellectual failure of nerve. How 'God' can become an emotional uplift for the 'gaps' in our lives. How 'Spirit' can become an unexamined blanket-word to cover a whole range of rich but too-fleeting experiences which may or may not be real (that is, true). For the perhaps unpleasant fact remains that no alert contemporary Westerner can really turn his back on science, on criticism, on *theoria* (in a word, on differentiated consciousness) even in his articulation of his 'moral', and 'Christian' life. More accurately, he can do so only at the price (too often and too willingly paid, I fear) of having that life, at first ecstatic, dissolve into the adventitiousness of a 'religious' atmosphere or a 'leisure' moment or harden into the brittleness of an ideology.[10]

Large questions here, needing very careful discussion. The implication is that what this writer calls 'Spirit-theologies' are in danger of trivializing the whole of theological anthropology: they have little or nothing to say to the *humanum* as such. And this is a very good reason for approaching the theology of the Spirit with reserve and caution. But it should also make us reflect how very odd it is that it should be possible so to separate Christology and pneumatology that the former is thought to be in itself an adequate response to the anthropological question while the latter has little bearing. It is an oddity pointed out very persistently by theologians of the Eastern Orthodox tradition,[11] for whom Western trinitarian theology is rendered hopelessly asymmetrical and 'Christomonist' by the *filioque*. And it suggests that our problem really lies at a deeper level.

What I should like to explore in this paper is the thesis that theologies of Spirit have generally suffered as a result of the predominance of one kind of trinitarian model in the formative ages of Christian reflection, a model which is constantly being questioned by a rather elusive alternative. This alternative is, in fact, the presupposition of a great deal of Christian language and practice, but is less easily manageable at the theoretical level. I should want to argue further that the first model pressed to its logical conclusion is potentially destructive of any kind of trinitarian theology;[12] and this is not an issue which all would find desirable. How far it is possible to give *systematic* shape to the 'alternative' remains to be seen.

I

The model of which I am speaking is roughly this: God communicates or 'interprets' himself to the world by the mediation of Word and Spirit. The problem to which trinitarian theology is the answer is the problem of revelation: how is God heard or seen to be present to the human world? This seems to me to be a perfectly proper question to ask, and it is clearly important that it was being asked with some seriousness in pre-Christian Judaism, as well as in the Hellenic world.[13] But the difficulties which arise in the early Church show very clearly the problem of fitting together the threefold formulae of the NT and liturgical practice with a basically *twofold* cosmological-revelatory theological picture. The tension has very frequently been noted and discussed,[14] but there a few points which I should like to underline anew. First of all, the model takes it for granted that the two primary terms are 'God' and 'the world': the revealing or mediating reality, the 'bridge-concept,'[15] must occupy a space *between* these terms. Secondly, the mediator is posited to answer the question of how *God* comes to *the world*; that is, the line runs from God 'downwards'. So that, thirdly, the relation between mediator and God is obscure and difficult to state: we do not know what sort of line runs from world *to* God through the mediator. In short, one of the difficulties in all this is that the understanding of God as such is not affected by the 'bridge-concept': the latter is instrumental to solving a problem which has two *clear* starting-points.

Furthermore, it is evident that this scheme strictly requires one mediator only. If we are to speak of a third divine hypostasis at all, Spirit as well as Logos, there is an immediate awkwardness. Second-century Christian writers in this tradition produce a wide and ingenious assortment of solutions, occasionally foreshadowing with remarkable accuracy some of the suggestions of more recent theologians. Thus Hermas cuts the Gordian knot by a straightforward assimilation of Logos and Spirit: the eternal and preexistent Spirit chooses to dwell in flesh; and as a result of the co-operation of the 'flesh' with the Spirit, it is taken up to God as Son, becoming a 'fellow-councillor' of God.[16] Exactly what status 'the Son' has in this passage and whether he is in any sense pre-existent is not at all clear; what is plain is that the Spirit is the cosmological mediator *par excellence*. Later, we find the *Son* as 'fellow-councillor' in the act of creation itself.[17] Obscure as this is, it does appear that we here have to do with a basically binitarian structure, in which the eternal Son is strictly the same as the Holy Spirit, but the assumption of Jesus into the heavenly realm adds some kind of 'third term' to the divine council. Whatever the correct interpretation,[18] this popular and widely diffused work illustrates quite clearly the degree to which a not very sophisticated theological mind of the second century could take it for granted that the structure of the divine economy was God 'plus' a mediator: how exactly Spirit and Son are to be accounted for separately does not trouble the author.

. . .

It is a logical outcome of the general tendency of the tradition we have been considering: the Trinity is a *sequence* of divine persons, successively revealed in a kind of hierarchically ordered illumination. The Spirit is 'nearest' to us; the Father, in whom resides the divine 'monarchy', the 'fount of godhead', is furthest from us. Growth in the knowledge of God is a penetration from forecourt to inner chamber.

II

I do not intend to argue that all this is an invalid or useless way of talking about God. The purpose of this long discussion of primitive trinitarian discourse has been to demonstrate the results in trinitarian theology of the dominance of an uncomplicated and readily available religious conceptual structure. 'God and his mediating agencies' is a model fairly conventional in the Jewish and Hellenistic worlds alike, as has already been remarked. It can appear most neatly and economically as 'God and his Logos', or in a more diffused form in some sort of doctrine of graded emanations or of divine 'powers' being distributed within creation.[19] The only structure which is satisfactorily triadic appears on the scene rather late in the day, in Plotinus's threefold cosmic process, and this – for various reasons – is taken up only very cautiously by Christian theologians. Otherwise, there is a real and evident difficulty in providing a rationale for *three* hypostases, no more and no less. Professor R. P. C. Hanson, in a sharp critique of Orthodox and Greek patristic pneumatology, asks; 'Why do we need two images, two revealers? Why should there not be an infinite series of images or revealers if there are to be more than one?'[20] But there seem to me to be weaknesses of a more than merely logical kind here: if we conceive the Spirit and the Word as illuminators, transmitters of saving knowledge, we are in danger of driving a wedge between the idea of 'Spirit' and the 'spirituality' of Christian people. If the Spirit simply instructs and guides, leads toward the Logos, it is less easy to talk about 'Spirit' as the constitutive reality or quality of Christian existence – Spirit as received in baptism, as invoked in liturgy, received and invoked not simply to instruct or inform but to *transform*. If the phrase 'in the Spirit' is reduced to designating simply the prophet who is receiving extraordinary communications of divine truth, the Pauline emphasis on the Spirit of sonship is seriously obscured. If the Spirit's role is to conduct us to the 'advanced class' where the Logos presides, Christian maturity 'in the Spirit' becomes a rather aridly intellectualist notion. In short, if the role of Spirit is *communication*, in a narrowly 'linear' sense, whether by ecstatic vision or noetic purity, an impoverished and abstract concept of the actual texture of Christian life and experience is likely to result.

I emphasize this point because at least some of our present difficulties about the doctrine of the Holy Spirit seem to rest upon one or other of these models of communication. Some varieties of 'charismatic' theology clearly operate with a doctrine of the Spirit whose focus is communication through prophecy and ecstatic utterance.[21] And – at the opposite extreme – the theology of Professor Geoffrey Lampe, one of the most distinguished exponents of a 'Spirit-centred' dogmatics,[22] rests upon the conviction that 'Spirit' is the term which may and should be used to cover all the ways in which God communicates himself to creatures; so that the 'pre-existent' and eternal Christ is in no sense an independent hypostasis, but only a strongly hypostatized metaphor for Spirit. Logos, in fact, is swallowed up in Pneuma, in a fashion a little reminiscent of Hermas. Once again, the general question here is one concerning the bridge between the world and the transcendent God; and for Professor Lampe, the superfluous term is the Word, conceived as eternally distinct from Spirit. God interprets himself through Spirit: Jesus as supremely the recipient and transmitter of grace, the paradigm of 'graced' relationship with God as Father (and Professor Lampe is very far from being arid or intellectualist here), is himself a source of grace because of his consistent 'transparency' to Spirit.

But of course it is not only a reduction of Word to Spirit that we have seen in contemporary dogmatics. It is at least possible to read Barth's early reflections on the Spirit, especially in I.1 and 2 of the *Church Dogmatics*, as a partial reduction of Spirit to Word. The Spirit is 'the subjective side in the event of revelation',[23] God in us receiving the Word which we cannot receive in our own right, 'the reality in which [God] makes Himself sure of us'.[24] It is indeed the Spirit of adoption, constituting us children of God,[25] and Barth's exegesis of the relevant Pauline and Johannine passages is superb. And the Spirit is 'the act of communion' between Father and Son, the gift given between them.[26] However, the whole discussion is conducted with reference to the problem of *revelation*: how do human beings come to hear the Word? The lengthy treatment in 1.2, 16 of the Spirit as 'subjective reality' and 'subjective possibility' of revelation is couched mostly in terms of the impossibility of there being any immanent or worldly or human ground for the hearing of the Word: 'subjective revelation', the hearing of the Word by this or that person, occurs only on the basis of 'objective revelation', the truth that there is an eternal Word, and an eternal witness to that Word.[27] The Spirit teaches us that 'we are not only approached' by the Word, but taken into Him, that He 'abides with us, and so becomes ours and we His'.[28] 'He is simply the Teacher of the Word';[29] strictly speaking, the 'subjective possibility of revelation' is not the Spirit as such, but the Spirit as making the Word present.[30] By the work of the Spirit, human beings come to recognize the Word as unavoidably 'master',[31] to recognize authority, command, the claim to obedience, to give our responsibility into the hands of the Word and be formed by Him, through the activity of the Spirit.

It seems, then, that for Barth Spirit is what closes the hermeneutical circle. The Word's interpretation of God the Father is interpreted in and to us by the Spirit, since we have no immanent possibility of interpreting any more than of hearing the Word. And what the Spirit realizes in us is our status as God's children, those who belong to God because their sin has been borne by Christ: in the Spirit, we are 'placed with' the Son in his cross and resurrection. We become free for God, *capaces Dei*, in and only in this 'form' of Christ's death.[32] We can interpret ourselves as God's, as belonging in God's realm or sharing in the fruits of God's work, only because of the Spirit. Here indeed we are 'made sure' of God because he makes sure of us.

I have attempted elsewhere[33] to discuss what seem to me to be some of the weaknesses of a scheme based so exclusively upon 'interpretation'. There is the familiar risk of turning sin into ignorance (though Barth generally avoids anything so crude); and, more significantly perhaps, there is the identification of the 'saved' condition as 'taking cognizance' of an existing state of affairs. The element of call is muted, the place of Christian *praxis* (as opposed to witness alone) is not clear. Barth, earlier in I. 1, describes the three modes of God's trinitarian being as 'form', 'freedom', and 'historicity':[34] it is the Spirit who constituted revelation as historical, capable of being responded to by individuals in specific contexts.[35] But the sense here given to 'historical' is very obscure, since it appears to have little to do with the actual continuing 'construction' of a human reality. In fact, we return again to our earlier point about the more obvious attractions of Christology for those at all seriously engaged with the *humanum*. Pneumatology looks uncomfortably like an exercise designed simply to explain how we know what Christ does (granted that we do not know it simply by historical inspection or by subjective intuition): the

Spirit is the seal of epistemological security, and Barth is perhaps nearer here to the theology of the Apologists than he might have cared to admit.

And yet the notion of Spirit as 'historicity' is tantalizing and deeply suggestive. What I hope to do in the remainder of this essay is to suggest how such a conception might be developed, with reference to the more subtle and elusive models of the divine Spirit in the New Testament. Part of our current *impasse* has to do with the fact that much pneumatology is cast in what might loosely be called a Lukan mould: the Spirit as continuator of Christ's work, filling a space left by Christ's exaltation, manifest in the conviction of extraordinary experiences.[36] It is an idea still well within the horizons of classical and intertestamental Judaism: in the last days, the visible workings of God return to the world, in miracle and prophecy, and this is the outpouring of Spirit. It has been pointed out[37] that the Spirit in the Acts of the Apostles occasionally seems to have the role of the *bath qōl* in later Judaism. And Luke is seldom so far from Paul as in his conception of Spirit. If we turn to the Pauline literature, it rapidly becomes clear that the eschatological character of the Spirit's presence, still firmly asserted, has nothing *intrinsically* to do with extraordinary charismata. The central eschatological reality is identification by grace with the obedience of God's Son, through which human beings are set 'on the far side' of judgement and condemnation; so that the Spirit's eschatological character is inseparable from the condition of life lived 'in Christ'. Thus the presence of the Spirit can be associated with 'freedom' (as in 2 Cor. 3: 17–18), the freedom from imperfect and alienating mediation between God and human beings, and of course, with adoptive sonship (Rom. 8: 14–17, Gal. 4: 6–7), the condition of maturity; the end of servitude, sharing in the quality of Christ's own life, in the tension between suffering and glorification. Emphasis upon the gifts of the Spirit, which are both 'charismatic' and more prosaic (see, notably, 1 Cor. 12: 28–30, where gifts of administration and glossolalia are juxtaposed), is balanced by emphasis upon *life* in the Spirit, with its moral and relational 'fruits' (Gal. 5: 22–3). The Spirit is no longer specified by, and thus potentially limited to, the extraordinary and episodic.

At first glance, the Johannine concept of the Paraclete can appear rather as a reflection of Luke's view of Spirit – the substitute mediator and continuator of Christ's work. However, the differences are clear on closer examination; and not the least important of these is the firm and consistent application (in John 14–16) of straightforwardly personal language to the Paraclete conceived as, in some sense, 'over against' Jesus and the Father. If Luke invariably sees Spirit as acting 'in a straight line', so to speak, from God and Jesus towards the human world, John sees the Paraclete as active in and with the disciples, moving them towards Father and Son, as well as acting simply *upon* them. The agency of the Paraclete is understood in terms of distance and response rather than simple identification with the agency of Father and Word; it cannot readily be seen in any kind of 'animistic' perspective, or even as a species of *bath qōl* intervention. It is nowhere associated with the extraordinary: the event within the Church's life with which 'holy spirit' is linked is simply the forgiveness of sins (20: 23). The test for the Spirit's presence (compare 1 Cor. 12: 3) is the confession of Christ's coining in flesh (1 John 4: 2; cf. 5: 6–9). 'The Spirit is the witness, because the Spirit is the truth' (1 John 5: 7):

the Paraclete is the spirit of truth, re-presenting the judging and convicting truth of Christ's own presence (John 16: 7–15), 'glorifying' Christ by his witness.

The parallels between Pauline and Johannine conceptions are fairly clear. For both, the Spirit is associated with the character of Christian existence as such, creating in the human subject response to, and *conformation* to, the Son. The Spirit's witness is not a pointing to the Son outside the human world, it is precisely the formation of 'Son-like' life in the human world; it is the continuing state of sharing in the mutuality of Father and Son; it is forgiven or justified life. It is also the assurance of the fact that mediation between God and the human is done away: the veil is lifted, truth stands in the midst of us. The distance between God and the world is transcended, so that the relation of slave to master is no longer the appropriate mode for the human apprehension of God. And if all this is, in whatever sense, the work of Spirit, it is clear that the association of Spirit exclusively or chiefly with the more dramatic charismata is a misunderstanding.

It is easy to see why the 'Lukan' model is at first more influential, why the idea of Spirit as substitute or secondary mediator is more readily grasped and developed in the early Church. The association of Spirit with 'adoption' in a very general way is indeed more elusive than its association with clearly defined phenomena, or with the transmission of knowledge of the Logos. The Pauline and Johannine alternative is not easily accommodated in the language of 'interpretation', or even of 'witness' in a simple sense: if the Spirit interprets anything, it is neither Father nor Word, but (as Hippolytus implies) the relation of Father and Son; and he interprets it by re-creating, *translating* it, in the medium of human existence. This is not simply to assimilate the Pauline–Johannine pneumatology to the later model of Spirit as *nexus amoris* in the Trinity; it is to recognize (what many patristic writers were slow to recognize) that the meaning of 'holy spirit' for the Christian cannot be divorced from the vision of Jesus' relation to his Father and all that flows from it. Nor can it be divorced, as Paul so frequently makes plain, from the vision of Christ risen, the Christian conviction that 'Jesus' relation to his Father' is not a contingent fact belonging to the human past alone. For John, the Spirit is not given before the passion and resurrection, because Jesus is not yet decisively 'with' his Father once more, not yet 'glorified' (John 7: 39). The Jesus who, as risen and exalted, is at the Father's right hand becomes the one who sends the Spirit into the hearts of believers: the Spirit in turn enacts in us the union of Jesus with the Father.

However, if the notions of 'adoption' and 'union' are not to be reduced again simply to the dimensions of limited 'religious experience', they need careful examination. And here Barth's all-too-brief discussion[38] of the crucial New Testament passages provides an indispensable starting-point. As he indicates, it is significant that the word *Abba* occurs on the lips of Jesus only in Gethsemane (Mark 14: 36): thus, to cry '*Abba*' with Jesus in the Spirit is not only to put on Christ's sonship but also to recognize that 'This child, sinful man, can meet this Father, the holy God, as a child meets its father, only where the only-begotten Son of God has borne and borne away his sin'.[39] It is the cry from the midst of temptation and despair (Barth quotes Luther's magnificent comments on Gal. 4: 6 to illustrate this), the human confession of dependence upon the saving grace of Christ. We can cry '*Abba*' because Jesus so cried in his suffering for us.

Barth, however, does not exhaust the significance of this occurrence of the term; for the cry of '*Abba*' in Gethsemane is surely part of a wider sense of the way in which Jesus' own sonship is inseparable from conflict, decision and suffering, from the cross. The paradox is that it is precisely Jesus' intimacy with the will of his Father that presses him towards the dereliction, the 'Godlessness', of the cross. To be 'Son of God' in the world of violence *is* to be the crucified victim; the sonship of Jesus is in no sense a 'cushion' between him and the felt absence of God in the world. To do the Father's will in the world is to refuse the authority of 'the kings of the Gentiles', and this leads inexorably to the impotence of suffering; and the Father cannot 'rescue' Jesus from outside because that would be the victory of coercion. We do not need (I believe) to talk, as Moltmann seems to wish to do,[40] of the Father's desertion or even annihilation of the Son: Dorothee Sölle's protest about 'theological sadism'[41] is valid and right here. We need rather to see the Father's weakness and powerlessness as the inevitable and necessary corollary of the Son's powerlessness in a world of corrupt and enslaving power. Father and Son are not to be set against each other at Calvary: the God who 'abandons' is the God of Caiaphas, the God whose relation to the world is that of master to slave. But Jesus is not slave but child, and *eldest* child, and adult 'child', and his Father is not the castrating despot of infantile nightmare. 'God' vanishes on the cross: Father and Son remain, in the shared, consubstantial weakness of their compassion. And the Father will raise the Son in the power of Spirit.

To speak of adoptive relation, then, is, in the light of the cross of Jesus, to accept the death of the distant and alien father-God,[42] to accept what might be called the poverty of the Father. The relation of adoption is a fact, a dimension of reality, not a solution or a promise of easy deliverance. Hence it is possible to see the logic of Paul's conclusion in Rom. 8, that to share Christ's relation to the Father is to share his sufferings, and to understand how 2 Cor. can juxtapose the condition of freedom and 'unveiled' vision with the experiences of humiliation, pain, frustration, and so forth (2 Cor. 6). The God who, as 'omnipotent Father' in the Freudian sense, can intervene to save and console from without, is illusory, a mask of God: his is a nature incompatible with the conviction that in Christ the veil is taken away. Another paradox (and one not, I think, alien to Luther's thought): that it is the God whose working is evident or simple to us that is the God whose face is veiled; the God who is Father and Son in the passion and resurrection is the God whose glory has been uncovered for us, whose face we see directly. 'Union' with him involves just this acknowledgement of an experienced absence of manifest power.

This may illuminate the tension in Christian spirituality between action and contemplation. The absence of God's manifest power is bound up (as in Gethsemane) with a decision *for* powerlessness, *against* the domination of the world by manipulation or fantasy. It is a decision for reality, for the acceptance of constraint and limit in the human world. But it is still a *decision*: that is to say, it is meant to determine, to create, a course of action, to engage with the constraint of reality, to shape within its boundaries one form of life rather than another. It is not a decision for passivity or disengagement, but a decision to live with and within the potentially hurtful and destructive bounds of the world, a decision not to escape. But because this is an option for *response* and not manipulation, it incorporates the dimension of contemplative receptivity. If the sonship of Jesus means the poverty and vulnerability of Jesus in the world, it is indeed both active and contemplative, both the taking of responsibility for one's place in the world and the refusal to interpret and enact this as coercive power. The modern apostles of non-violence are right to deny that non-violence implies indifference or passivity.[43] And we may look also to Péguy's celebrated affirmation of the continuity between *mystique* and *politique*.[44]

How are we to relate all this to the theology of the Spirit? It does at least suggest a way in which pneumatology might be reconnected with central Christological issues so as to bear more directly on the *humanum*; and it also points to the possibility of restating the classical argument that rests the claim for the Spirit's divinity upon his share in the work of salvation or divinization.[45] In this perspective, to see the Spirit in second-century style as a secondary mediator makes no sense: the work of Spirit, like the Son's work, is bound up precisely with the *loss* of mediatorial concepts designed to explain how the transcendent God (who is *elsewhere*) can be communicated *here*. The pivotal image of Jesus as Son radically changes the simple schema of God-and-the-world. Second-century theology is a witness to the extreme difficulty of assimilating such a shift, and it is not until the post-Nicene period that some of the necessary major reconstructions of language about God begin, slowly and awkwardly, to occur. We are, of course, ourselves part of that post-Nicene period. The notion of Spirit as simply 'communicator' accordingly recedes; and with it the idea that the work of Spirit is typically to be seen in clear and dramatic cases of 'communication' (prophetic ecstasy). The Spirit's 'completion' of Christ's work is no longer to be seen epistemologically, as a supplement or extension to the teaching of Christ, or even as that which makes it possible to hear and receive the Word. It is, rather, a completion in terms of liberation and transformation: it is *gift*, renewal and life. It is not possible to speak of Spirit in abstraction from the Christian form of life as a whole: Spirit is 'specified' not with reference to any kind of episodic experience but in relation to the human identity of the Christian. The question 'Where, or what, is Holy Spirit?' is not answered (as it might be by Luke) by pointing to prophecy and 'charismata' and saying, 'Spirit is the agency productive of phenomena like this'.

How then is it answered? Perhaps not at all. The theological quest which is preoccupied with identifying the *distinctive* quality or work of the Spirit has so often, as Hanson points out,[46] produced only the most sterile abstractions. And there is at least in eastern Christian thought[47] a sense that the 'face' of the Holy Spirit is not there for us to see. If what we are speaking of is the agency which draws us to the Father by constituting us children, we are evidently speaking of an agency not simply identical with 'Father' or 'Son', or with a sum or amalgam of the two. That perhaps is obvious, or even trivial, but it may be that no more can be said of the Spirit's distinctiveness. The grammar of our talk about the Holy Spirit is not that proper to 'God' as source, ground, terminus of vision and prayer, and so forth, nor that proper to 'God' as the disturbing presence of grace and vulnerability within the world of human relationships as a particular focal story. It is the grammar of 'spirituality' in the fullest sense of that emasculated word, the grammar of the interplay in the human self between the given and the future, between reality as it is and the truth which encompasses it; between Good Friday and Easter. If there can be any sense in which 'Spirit' is a bridge-concept, its work is not to bridge the gap between God and the world or even between the Word and the human soul, but to span the unimaginably greater gulf between suffering and hope, and to do so by creating that form of human subjectivity capable of confronting suffering without illusion but also without despair.

Spirit is the pressure upon us towards Christ's relation with the Father, towards the self secure enough in its rootedness and acceptance in the 'Father', in the source and ground of all, to be 'child', to live vulnerably, as a sign of grace and forgiveness, to decide for the cross of powerlessness.[48] The sign of Spirit is the existence of Christlikeness (being God's child) in the world. And the connection of Spirit with ecclesiology belongs here. We are so used to the rhetoric of the Church as the 'Spirit-filled community' that we have frequently lost a sense of the Church as sign of the Spirit rather than its domicile. The Church signifies (means, points to) the humanity that could be, that could exist in this tension between security and powerlessness, so that it is indeed in one sense *the* place where Spirit is seen. It is 'seen' in prayer and sacrament; that is to say, prayer and sacrament (and I include the reading and preaching of scripture under this head) *name* and interpret the deepest direction and growth of human life as being *in* Christ and *towards* the Father. Baptism and the Eucharist are both sacraments of the inseparability and the tension of suffering and hope. The Byzantine stress on the invocation of the Spirit to consecrate the eucharistic elements – and with them the whole body of believers – vividly points this up:[49] Spirit is active where broken flesh and shed blood become the sign and promise of human wholeness and union with the Father.

Perhaps, too, it is not irrelevant to suggest that some of those experiences associated in the Catholic mystical tradition with maturity in the life of prayer have the same 'signifying' quality.[50] The 'night of faith', the dissolution of tangible mental and emotional securities, in the ascent of contemplative prayer is, for a writer like John of the Cross, part of the way of *illumination*, and a necessary stage before union. Here again, Spirit, the illuminative action of God, can appear where suffering and promise coincide, where death and Godlessness are interpreted in terms of sonship. The relation of this to the early Luther's theology, indeed to the tension between faith and experience which characterizes so much in the Lutheran tradition, may be worth further exploration.[51]

To talk about an entry into the 'Age of the Spirit' is usually nonsense, and often dangerous nonsense. But there may, nonetheless, be aspects of the contemporary consciousness of Western humanity (and I am not equipped to speculate beyond the limits of the West) peculiarly attuned to some such theology of Spirit as I have tried to outline. There are culturally irreversible processes which have indeed obliged us to question certain models of the transcendent in a way which makes concepts of Word and Spirit as 'mediators' very hard to sustain. We can recognize perhaps more clearly the disturbing confusion of theological language in the New Testament under the pressure of the figure of the crucified Messiah: we can accept more readily the breaking of certain kinds of sacral barrier, so that 'Spirit' ceases to be confined to the extraordinary but becomes a qualification of Christian human being. Above all, a theology of Spirit as belonging in the ambience of mortality and secularity, the powerlessness of the cross, refuses to take us away from the *humanum* in its most problematic aspects. Spirit may be a mode of interpreting the world's Godlessness to the world, it is Spirit which takes us out of infantile transcendentalism, uncriticized theism, into the faith of Jesus crucified. The face of Spirit is – as Vladimir Lossky memorably expressed it[52] – the assembly of redeemed human faces in their infinite diversity. Human persons grown to the fullness of their *particular* identities, but sharing in the common divine gift of reconciled life in faith, these are the Spirit's manifestation. The Son is manifest in a single, paradigmatic figure, the Spirit is manifest in the 'translatability' of that into the contingent diversity of history. Freedom in the Spirit is uncircumscribed; and yet it always has the shape of Jesus the Son – another way of expressing Paul's paradoxes of law and liberty. It is Spirit who leads us to 'Godlessness' in order to bring out of us the cry of '*Abba*'; who emancipates us from God to bring us to the Trinity.

Regressive spiritualities are those which seek to restrict the Spirit again to a mediatorial or an episodically inspirational role. They represent the struggle to retain uncriticized theism as one element in some sort of composite religious scheme (Word and Spirit *added* to the Father), and to avoid the critical experience of Godlessness. They will run the risk of making Spirit a refuge from the critical rather than a pressure towards the critical. This essay has been in part an attempt to set out what is involved in some classical and modern theologies of Spirit as interpreter of the Word or agency of inspiration and to question the adequacy of such models for a critical theology. I have, however, no single accessible model to put in their place. The very term 'Spirit' is, as has often been pointed out,[53] a weak and unspecific word, lending itself to much confusion; and this may be taken to underline what I have already called the elusiveness of our subject. Since this is an elusiveness and an unclarity more pervasively present in the NT writings than in some of the more conceptually satisfying schemes of later dogmatics, I do not think we need be unduly disturbed. And after all, if Christian theology is done in the community which lives in Spirit, the problem is no more and no less than the impossibility of seeing one's own face.[54] It may be – as so often in contemporary dogmatics – that we can utter only negations with any confidence. I have not intended to denigrate the charismatic movement and the theologies associated with it: I *have* attempted to question the highly assertive mode of some of these theologies and the (as it appears to me) restrictive assumptions underlying them, the dangers of operating unawares with an only partially Christianized view of transcendence and of divine agency. Yet here again we are brought up against the diversity and unclarity of our NT material: the charismatic may well object to the characteristic preferring of Paul over Luke in most post-Reformation theology. I am painfully aware that this essay has failed to engage directly with this hermeneutical question; but I hope what I have written may suggest some affinities with the hermeneutic expressed by Luther in the words *crux probat omnia*. As we observed at the beginning of this paper, there is a suspicion of pneumatology as something tempted to bypass the cross – not least the cross of twentieth-century experience, religious and secular; here at least our negation can be confident. But a great deal of thinking has still to be done if we are to rescue the theology of Spirit from religiosity and set it to work in the shadow of the contemporary crucifixions of God and the human.

Notes

1 See especially *Charismatic Renewal*, ed. E. D. O'Connor (London: SPCK, 1978); *New Heaven? New Earth?*, S. Tugwell and others (London: DLT, 1976); *A Charismatic Theology*, H. Mühlen (London: Burns and Oates, 1978).

2 Including J. V. Taylor, *The Go-Between God* (London: SCM Press, 1972); C. F. D. Moule, *The Holy Spirit* (London: Mowbrays, 1978); A. M. Ramsey, *Holy Spirit* (London: SPCK, 1977).

3 Austin Farrer, *Saving Belief* (London: Hodder, 1964), pp. 128–9; Moule, *The Holy Spirit*, pp. 50–1. Cf. B. M. G. Reardon, commenting on a paper by H. Cunliffe-Jones in *Theology* (June 1972): 298–301.

4 Though, of course, a pneumatology would have formed part of the completed *Dogmatics*. In addition to the discussion in *Church Dogmatics*, I.1.12, see also IV.2.67 and 68, and IV.3, 72 and 73, especially the exposition in 68.2 of the idea of the Spirit as God making himself 'the basis of our love' (IV.2, trans. G. W. Bromiley; Edinburgh: T. & T. Clarke, 1968, pp. 757–9, 778–9, etc.).

5 The subject is scarcely mentioned in *Gottes Sein ist im Werden* (Tübingen: J. C. B. Mohr/Paul Siebeck, 1964), though it merits a brief section in *Gott als Geheimnis der Welt* (Tübingen: J. C. B. Mohr/Paul Siebeck, 1977), pp. 512–14, 531–4.

6 *Foundations of Christian Faith* (London: DLT, 1978); *On Being a Christian* (London: Collins, 1977). Cf. Küng's *Existiert Gott?* (Munich: R. Piper, 1978), pp. 760–7.

7 *Jesus: An Experiment in Christology* (London: Collins, 1978), see pp. 644–7, 660–1).

8 See especially *The Church in the Power of the Spirit* (London: SCM Press, 1977).

9 See *On Prayer* (London: Geoffrey Chapman, 1961, and SPCK, 1973), pp. 55–67, 150–4; *Herrlichkeit. Eine Theologische Ästhetik*, III.2. Teil II (Einsiedeln: Johannes-Verlag, 1969), section II, *passim*.

10 D. Tracy in *God, Jesus, Spirit*, ed. D. Callahan (New York: Herder, 1969), p. 328.

11 See, for example, Vladimir Lossky, *The Mystical Theology of the Eastern Church* (London and Cambridge, 1957), chs 3, 8 and 9, and *In the Image and Likeness of God* (Crestwood, NY: St Vladimir's Seminary Press, 1974), ch. 4.

12 That is to say, that it leads either to a dyad of Father and Word (as sometimes in Barth and his followers) or to a dyad of transcendent God and immanent Spirit (as in G. W. H. Lampe's recent – and deeply impressive – *God as Spirit* [Oxford: Oxford University Press, 1977]).

13 The question is most interestingly discussed in J. Bowker's *The Religious Imagination and the Sense of God* (Oxford: Oxford University Press, 1978). On the background in Hellenistic Jewish 'Wisdom' speculation, see, e.g., M. Hengel, *Judaism and Hellenism* (London: SCM Press, 1974), vol. 1, pp. 153–75. I must also mention a still unpublished

paper by Professor J. C. O'Neill of Westminster College, Cambridge, on 'The Trinity in the New Testament and Before'.

14   See, for example, chapters IV and V of J. N. D. Kelly, *Early Christian Doctrines*, 5th edn. (London: A. and C. Black, 1977).

15   A term favoured by Professor Lampe in *God as Spirit*.

16   Hermas, *Sim.* [*Similitudes*], V.vi.

17   *Sim.* IX.xii.

18   The Vatican MS of Hermas actually has the gloss 'the Son is the Spirit' in *Sim.* V.v.

19   A commonplace of late classical eclectic philosophy; see, for example, Pseudo-Aristotle, *De mundo*, 6.397b.17–20.

20   *The Attractiveness of God* (London: SPCK, 1973), p. 134.

21   I am assuming that glossolalia is to be regarded not only as a means of praising God but also as a medium of prophecy.

22   *God as Spirit*, 1977.

23   *Church Dogmatics* I.1 (2nd edn., trans. G. W. Bromiley; Edinburgh: T. & T. Clarke, 1975), p. 449.

24   Ibid., p. 454.

25   Ibid., pp. 457–9.

26   Ibid., p. 470.

27   I.2 (Edinburgh: T. & T. Clarke, 1956), p. 239.

28   Ibid., p. 242.

29   Ibid., p. 244.

30   Ibid., p. 249 (compare the discussion of the *filioque* in I.1, pp. 477–87).

31   Ibid., pp. 265ff., 269–79, *passim*.

32   I.1, p. 458.

33   In an essay contributed to *Karl Barth: Studies in his Theological Method*, ed. S. W. Sykes (Oxford: Oxford University Press, 1980).

34   I.1 section 8.2; see esp. pp. 315–33.

35   Ibid., p. 330.

36   See, e.g., E. Trocmé, 'Le Saint-Esprit et l'Eglise d'après le livre des Actes', in *L'Esprit Saint et l'Eglise. Actes du symposium organisé par l'Académie Internationale des Sciences Religieuses* (Paris: Fayard, 1969), especially the discussion on pp. 40–1. Also J. D. G. Dunn, *Jesus and the Spirit* (London: SCM Press, 1977), ch. VII.

37   See, e.g., E. Haenchen's *The Acts of the Apostles* (Oxford: Blackwell, 1971), pp. 92–3, 95.

38   *Church Dogmatics*, I.1, pp. 458–9.

39   Ibid., p. 458.

40   *The Crucified God* (London: SCM Press, 1974), especially pp. 145–53, 240–7.

41   *Suffering* (London: DLT, 1975), pp. 22–8, especially pp. 26–7.

42   On this, see Paul Ricoeur's remarkable paper, 'La paternité: du fantasme au symbole', in *L'Analyse du langage théologique: le nom de Dieu*, ed. E. Castelli and others (Paris: Aubier, 1969), especially pp. 239–42.

43   P. Régamey's work, *Non-violence and the Christian Conscience* (London: DLT, 1966) is worth mentioning in this connection.

44   For an excellent exposition, see ch. 5 of Alan Ecclestone's study of Péguy, *A Staircase for Silence* (London: DLT, 1977).

45   See, e.g., Basil's *De Spiritu Sancto*, Patrologia Graeca (PG) 32, *passim*.

46   Ibid., pp. 131–4.

47   See, e.g., Lossky's *Mystical Theology of the Eastern Church*, pp. 161–2. (referring to Gregory Nazianzen's Fifth Theological Oration, PG 36.161–4) and pp. 172–3.

48 See Schillebeeckx, *Jesus: An Experiment in Christology*, section III, chs 2 and 3: and compare the treatment of 'critical theology' in the same author's earlier essay, *The Understanding of Faith* (London: Sheed and Ward, 1974), ch. 7, sections II and III.

49 See, for example, P. Evdokimov, *L'Orthodoxie* (Neuchâtel: Delachaux et Niestlé, 1965), pp. 249–51.

50 Simon Tugwell, in his book *Did You Receive the Spirit?* (London: DLT, 1972), ch. 10, argues that 'charismatic' prayer and the experiences traditionally associated with the entry into contemplative prayer should be seen as parallel ways of 'discovering' the Spirit. This may be a little oversimplified, but it is valuable and suggestive.

51 I have attempted to discuss this, though only very sketchily, in *The Wound of Knowledge: Christian Spirituality from the New Testament to St John of the Cross* (London: DLT, 1979), chs 7 and 8.

52 *Wound of Knowledge*, p. 173.

53 By Aquinas, for instance, in *Summa Theologiae*, I.xxxvi.1, and II.IIae.xiv.1.

54 And is parallel to the problem of honest theological talk about the resurrection. I am deeply grateful to David Jenkins for illuminating comments on this question; and see his paper, 'The Anguish of Man, the Praise of God and the Repentance of the Church', *Study Encounter* X (4) (1974) (available from the publications office of the World Council of Churches).

5

Church of England Doctrine Commission, "Charismatic Experience"

The charismatic movement features bodily experience of the Holy Spirit within mainstream Christian denominations. Most publications about the charismatic experience fall at two ends of a spectrum: either devotional or sociological. Those books and articles therefore differ in genre from the writings on the Holy Spirit collected here, which belong to the academic genre of theology. Fortunately, we have here an exception to the rule: a study theological and sociological at once, engaging in both fieldwork and doctrinal reflection. The two things ought not, after all, to be at odds: fieldwork should discover indigenous categories, and theology should attend to the sense of the faithful.

Here, the fieldwork discovers that charismatic Christians interpret their experience of the Spirit theologically in two ways. The majority way is linear: the Spirit leads to Christ who leads to the Father. A minority way is more communal: the Spirit initiates the Christian into the relationship between the Father and the Son. The author finds that the first model, which implies steady progress, has more trouble dealing with experiences of difficulty, stasis, regress, or perplexity – even failure, aridity, and depression. The second model makes better sense of those things, familiar from human relationships, and characteristic of human growth. So the essay achieves a nice convergence not only in theological and sociological method, but also in content. It also recapitulates a socio-theological version of the history of Christianity, in which "gifts" are followed by "disciplines," or ascetic authority routinizes charismatic authority. A further merit is that the interviewer seems to have solicited responses to the reflection on prayer and the Spirit in Romans 8, bringing the interview material into conversation with academic interest in that text. By convention, church studies do not name their authors (nor do theologians practice fieldwork), and yet informed readers regard Sarah Coakley as the lead author.

Church of England Doctrine Commission, "Charismatic Experience," in *We Believe in the Holy Spirit* (London: Church House Publications, 1991), pp. 17–36.

Charismatic Experience: Praying 'in the Spirit'

Church of England Doctrine Commission
(Sarah Coakley)

There is little to attract the unbeliever in the traditional, organized church . . .
We have neglected our prayer life; we have stopped listening to God; . . . (yet
people are) hungry and thirsty for God or some form of spiritual reality.
                                                            (David Watson, 1980)

If the Holy Spirit is in you, you will comprehend well enough His action within
you . . . All those who have been baptized in the Holy Spirit have put on Christ
completely; they are children of light and walk in the light which has no decline.
                              (Symeon the New Theologian, early eleventh century)

The charismatic renewal today calls as controversially as did Symeon in his very
different Byzantine milieu for an intense commitment to prayer and the expectation
of specific experiential effects from the invocation of the Holy Spirit. Symeon too
spoke to what he regarded as a tepid generation in the Church; and for him the
blasphemy against the Holy Spirit was precisely the denial that the Spirit could be
vibrantly experienced now, 'divinizing' Christians (to use his eastern terminology),
catching them up into the very life of the Godhead, making them nothing less
than 'sons of God by adoption and grace'. (See Symeon the New Theologian, *The
Discourses*, esp. XXIV, 4).

In a similar way that challenge has been laid at the door of the established churches
and denominations in the last quarter century by the influx of charismatic influence.
And so some hard questions, with which this chapter is concerned, are rightly pressed:
are we truly a praying Church? What (if anything) do we expect of the activity of
the Holy Spirit in prayer? Is the Holy Spirit uniformly and universally present or
only sporadically available? Is indeed a failure to reflect on the Spirit any sign of
the Spirit's absence (or vice versa)? Does the Holy Spirit always guarantee consol-
ing or emotionally satisfying experiences (as the somewhat misleading translation
of Paraclete as 'comforter' could suggest)? And, even more fundamentally, what *is*
an 'experience' of the Holy Spirit? Is it in any clear way distinguishable from an
'experience' of the Father or the Son? And, if not, why should we wish to speak
of the Spirit as a distinct Person at all?

If we are to confront these issues cogently for today, we must surely do so not
just by drawing on scriptural and creedal authority (although these are fundamental
. . .), but by reference precisely to some of the various and rich experiences of the
charismatic constituency in the Church as we find it now. Thus this chapter is largely
based on a number of in-depth interviews with Anglican charismatics from a
particular church which was deemed to be representative of the development of
the movement within the Church of England. The interviews were conducted with
men and women of different ages, social backgrounds and education, all of whom
have, however, been involved in 'renewal' for some lengthy period (between ten

and twenty-five years). They can thus speak with some perspective of time on the phases of development that the movement has undergone in relation to 'prayer in the Spirit', and this at a moment when, self-confessedly, the movement within Anglicanism seems to be facing a crisis of decision and direction which is closely (and interestingly) related to attitudes to prayer. Thus, out of the evidence of contemporary *reportage* emerge theological themes of recurring significance.

The movement within denominational Christianity in general has been said to be in decline: whether this is so in numerical terms is not our concern here, but rather what shifts in understanding may be occurring in relation to our questions about the Spirit and prayer. As a means of comparison in these investigations interviews were also taped with some members of a recent split-off group from the Anglican charismatic church studied, a Fellowship loosely associated with the 'Restoration' movement and now fast making new converts of its own. The members of this group tend to be younger Christians (not necessarily younger in age); they also span an interesting range of class and educational backgrounds: there are professional people here too, and a large gathering of students, but in general the ethos is less middle class than in the Anglican congregation. Manifesting a much purer 'sect'-like form than can be achieved within the episcopal structures of Anglicanism, and also a much more rigorous biblical fundamentalism, this group's maintenance of high levels of prophecy and public tongue-speaking in its worship distinguishes it from what is now the norm in its present Anglican counterpart. Here worship had already become somewhat formalized and sedate before the split-off, and indeed for those who left this was seen as a loss of contact with the Spirit's drive and purpose. The Anglicans have in the meantime reverted to at least the outlines of the ASB's [*Alternative Service Book*] requirements.

Is this a sign of decline and lack of direction in the Anglicans' case (as the Fellowship tends to read it), or rather a new phase of deepening maturity, a distinct pressure of the Spirit towards a new synthesis with tradition (as the Anglican minister reads it)? To answer this, we need to look at the witness of those concerned, and only from there suggest a theological judgement based upon this. What is sure, however, is that we have here a fascinating correlation of sociological and theological factors, different attitudes to the Holy Spirit and prayer being *aligned* with different socially-constituted groupings. To anticipate: the purer 'sect' form, with its rejection of ordained ministry, commitment to egalitarian exercise of 'gifts' (and yet strict refusal of teaching roles to women on fundamentalist grounds), expects high feeling states as the norm in public prayer 'in the Spirit'; whereas the Anglican community, with its self-styled hybrid of 'sect' and 'church'-type organization (the episcopal structure combined with 'elders' and much lay leadership, including some cautious use of women in positions of authority), seems to be moving towards a less sporadic and emotionally dramatic understanding of the Spirit, encouraged by its minister to believe that a new phase of the renewal has been entered, the 'recovery of gifts' being succeeded by the 'recovery of disciplines'. How does this shift of emphasis affect the theological questions with which we are concerned? And what broader theological and historical perspectives may we apply to the divergence between the two groups? We shall look at a number of selected questions in turn.

1. Encountering renewal, 'experiencing' the Spirit

(a) Interviews

It was in questions concerning the initial 'experience' of the Spirit, and the continuing effects of regular prayer 'in the Spirit', that we found least divergence, indeed, negligible divergence, between the two groups. The vexed question of the meaning of 'baptism in the Spirit' . . . was not explicitly raised by the interviewer, and, perhaps significantly, was not an issue for polemicizing by either group. But to the general question, 'How has your prayer changed since you encountered renewal?', there were answers such as, 'There was a sense of new *excitement*', or, 'It was so delightful to find that it was acceptable to be openly *enthusiastic* about God'. 'Affective' (positive emotional) states, then, were universally acknowledged, the sense of a great release of feelings, especially positive feelings of praise and exaltation, that had previously been held back. But even more significant for our question about what characterizes the 'experience' of the Spirit, specifically, was the reiterated remark that people had in a new way found prayer to be a 'two-way relationship', not just a talking at God, but God (the Holy Spirit) already co-operating in one's prayer, energizing it from within, and no less also responding in it, alluring one again, inviting one into a continuing adventure. This was said to be 'the real thing', 'making yourself a channel for the Spirit's work', an intermingling of the human desire for God and the Spirit's interceding to the Father (cf. Rom. 8: 27). With this then came the sense of prayer in the Spirit becoming a uniting thread in one's life, 'an all-encompassing relationship', so that prayer became no longer one activity (or duty) amongst others, but the wellspring of all activities. Thus Paul's injunction 'Pray constantly' (1 Thess. 5: 17) took on a new meaning, as did Jesus' insistence on trust, faith, and confidence in prayer ('Ask, and it will be given you' (Matt. 7: 7)), even though it was admitted that one did not always get what one expected.

(b) Commentary

The actual prayer methods of the people interviewed were enormously varied, as varied as were the people themselves. It was taken for granted that there would be a commitment (indeed an intense commitment) to the usual range of verbal prayers, expressing penitence, praise, petition and intercession; but beyond that most people also made regular and disciplined use of some sort of scriptural meditation. Moreover, it was striking how ingenious and resourceful people had been in working out structured patterns of praying suitable for their own psychological type or mode of life. One husband and wife were somewhat startled to have the interviewer comment that their preferred methods of prayer were almost indistinguishable from (respectively) Luther's 'Simple way to pray' (using each phrase of the Lord's Prayer meditatively in turn), and Ignatius Loyola's 'composition of place' in *The Spiritual Exercises* (thinking one's way imaginatively into a gospel scene). Being of a fundamentalist bent they preferred not to rely on 'tradition', but had painstakingly evolved their own ways.

Likewise, it is worthy of comment that the expected reference to Romans 8: 14–27 (in relation to the crucial experience of the Spirit praying in one) did not in general lead to any clear reflection on the importance of this in *trinitarian* terms. The inter-viewees assumed without question that the Spirit was in some almost inexplicable way experientially distinct from the Son (despite the confusing shifts in Paul's language in Romans 8: 9f.). But the possibility that this experiential starting point might provide some sort of response to those theologians currently challenging the Spirit's distinct personal existence, or otherwise dismantling the doctrine of the Trinity, was far from their minds. In general these controversies had not impinged on them at all (as indeed would be true in most parish contexts). Distant too was any thought that ontological trinitarian reflection might be 'earthed' here, leading perhaps to a reassimilation of the eastern patristic model of 'deification' with which Symeon was familiar – the Spirit *incorporating* one into the life of sonship and so bringing one to the Father.[1] Such categories sounded alien to those of fundamentalist background, although there was a marked, and perhaps unexpected, willingness to consider the possibilities. In short, and doubtless unsurprisingly, there was little knowledge shown of trinitarian controversies in Christian tradition at all, or of where in the history of east/west divergence on this issue the charismatic approach would find its natural allies, if any.

That this is unsurprising, moreover, is a matter in part of our western religious heritage, with its much bemoaned bifurcation of thought and feeling, scholastic theology and piety; and this historical background is worthy of brief (if inevitably over-simplistic) reflection, especially in view of charismatics' much-vaunted claims to a recovery of spiritual 'wholeness'. For not long after Symeon was controver-sially reasserting the significance of the felt apprehension of the Spirit in the east, the west too, though in very different cultural and political circumstances was engaged in an extraordinary shift of consciousness which also evidenced a fresh discovery of 'feeling'. The twelfth century, it has been argued, produced the 'discovery of the individual'; it also witnessed the rise of the age of chivalry, and the complex rituals of courtly love. In the Church's musical life of late twelfth-century France, too, were unleashed strikingly passionate ululations, elongated melismas wound over the traditional plainsong chants. The theological counterpart of all this, one might argue, was Bernard of Clairvaux's fresh assimilation of affective strands in Augustine, which resulted in a new turn to 'feeling' as an indispensable component in spiritual growth. 'Instruction makes us learned', says Bernard, 'but feeling makes us wise'. Moreover he could go on to make startling use of erotic imagery in his construal of the soul's desire for God. He was, after all, addressing young monks in the Cistercian reform who had not been shielded from an adolescence in the world by growing up as child oblates.

Yet if writers in the twelfth century moved to incorporate feeling and body metaphors as positive features in spiritual development, by the fourteenth century there was a discernible, and tragic, disjunction occurring between intellectual, scholastic approaches to God on the one hand, and pietistic feeling-and-body-oriented approaches on the other. This was carried over in a different way into theories of prayer, so that, for instance, 'contemplation' could be construed either as the pure 'intellect' communing with God or, quite differently, as a deliberate shutting down of the mind in favour of the will or 'affectivity'. In a variety of ways piety and theology were being rent apart in the west.

Thus it is a striking irony that, in the fourteenth century, just as Gregory Palamas' defence of 'hesychast' practices was defending the use of the body in prayer and effecting in the east an extraordinary and unexpected *synthesis* of 'affective' and 'intellectual' traditions of prayer in that context, the west was busy driving a wedge between them.

Moreover, we are still in thrall to these disjunctions, as the history of western Christian sectarianism since the late medieval period witnesses. For here it has tended to be the sectarians in *revolt* who have highlighted, sometimes in extreme forms, the significance of 'affective' or 'enthusiastic' prayer-states, and simultaneously claimed the (neglected) Holy Spirit as their own. In this western historical perspective, then, the contemporary charismatic movement calls forth a certain feeling of *déjà vu*: the pietistic emphasis on feeling and bodily response, the sectarian ethos, the claims to direct experience of the Spirit, and an undercurrent of strong anti-intellectualism – all these might be expected to hang together in the western context just described. Even if such western movements are not demonstrably a manifestation of social or economic 'deprivation', then, they may bespeak a more subtle form of 'affective' deprivation in 'church' type western Christianity, a deprivation which goes back to the same divide between 'affectivity' and intellect, spiritual experience and reflective tradition, to which we have just drawn attention and which may be characteristic of western (or at least of North Atlantic) culture as a whole.

What is new in contemporary 'renewal', however, and so vital for our present concern of prayer and the Spirit, is the incorporation of this 'sectarian' constellation of themes *within* established 'church' frameworks, including Anglicanism. Could this in fact provide the possibility of a new *rapprochement* between the disjunct traditions which we have been considering: affective piety on the one hand, and informed reflective theology on the other (the latter rooted as much in an intellectual assessment of *tradition* as of the Bible)? That this tension might be ridden is self-confessedly not the aim of the purer 'sectarian' house-churches currently fast gaining adherents. But that it may be the task implicitly confronting intra-Anglican charismatics, in a new phase of their development, is borne out further by reflection on the specific theme of 'tongues'.

2. The Spirit and 'tongues'

(a) Interviews

Here we can indeed chart a distinct difference of emphasis between the two groups studied. For whereas the Anglican charismatics in the church have now almost ceased to use tongues in public worship (the exception being the occasional, unplanned, and indeed eerily beautiful use of corporate 'singing in tongues'), the Fellowship group deliberately encourages corporate praise in tongues, especially in the often jubilant and noisy introduction to their services, and claims a much greater 'cutting-edge' and 'specificity', too, to their public prophecies. The divergence may partly result from the departure of some of the more 'activist' worshippers from the one group to the other. But there is also, implicitly, a different reading of 1 Cor. 14 in play in the two groups. The Anglicans, curbed in public tongue-speaking to some extent by their minister, after some episodes which were thought to be excessive and unedifying, are now preferring in the main to keep their tongue-speaking as a private 'love-language' *to* God (see v. 2), having found a plethora of tongues and interpretation somewhat repetitive or trite (see v. 19). In contrast the Fellowship is much more anxious to exhibit the 'gifts' in their full range (especially tongues and prophecy, understood as sent from God), and to witness to 'unbelievers' and potential converts (vv. 21ff.). Here, then, is a noticeable difference in opinion over whether the Spirit's presence always is, or should be, publicly or dramatically manifest.

But in fact it is in the private use of tongues that the most interesting material emerged in discussion with the Anglicans. For it was striking, again, how in certain ways their (very diverse) use of tongues converged spontaneously on certain themes from the contemplative traditions of the Church, traditions with which most of them were not in any direct way familiar, and indeed against which their fundamentalist convictions would naturally prejudice them. Thus, whereas the dominical warning against 'vain repetitions' (Matt. 6: 7 AV) made them wary of repetitive or mantric prayer, even of the 'Jesus prayer', they were ready to acknowledge that their 'tongues' often had a repetitive and formalized sound, and could be serving a similar function. Some, indeed, used 'tongues' as a regular discipline of prayer. A memorable example was a charismatic plumber, who often prayed in tongues as he worked alone. ('There are some very prayerfully laid pipes in this area', he remarked).

Similarly, whereas some saw silence in prayer as mainly an absence of thought, or a sign of perplexity, and wished to *fill* such silence with tongues, others could voice the thought that silence could actually be the 'point' or 'end' of tongues, that to which tongues naturally led. (Certainly this could sometimes be witnessed communally in a very sensitive and quiet use of 'singing in tongues' at the evening service, ebbing away into intense stillness and corporate awareness.) Thus, when faced with the charge of the Fellowship group that the Anglicans were losing their 'cutting-edge' in playing down their public use of tongues and prophecy, the minister's response was, 'God is trying to speak to us: *that* should be the feeling.' Others said there had been a certain 'hardness' in some of the more strident public tongues, which had simply 'felt wrong'.

It was the diversity of the application and theological interpretations of private tongues that was most remarkable, however. It was said to be a 'short cut' to God, a direct release of joy or feeling, a way of 'getting out of the way' so that the Spirit could act directly, a prayer for when 'words failed', whether through loss, perplexity or grief, a means of becoming 'like a child' (see Matt. 18: 3), or, used authoritatively, a prayer for warding off danger. While only a few interviewees were familiar with, or happy with, the psychological language of 'releasing the unconscious', or 'exposing one's inner life' to God, all stressed the healing qualities of this prayer, its directness, and its short-circuiting of normal checks and defences. Above all the theme of 'ceding to the Spirit' was stressed, the way in which tongues averted one's normal and natural tendency to 'set the agenda', especially in the areas of counselling and illness. Tongues were found to reach directly to the root of a problem, so that 'if one did not know what to pray for before, one does afterwards' (see Rom. 8: 26). In sum, it was found in the Anglican community that tongues were continuing to be used in diverse and rich ways, in private prayer, in small house groups, and in the semi-private counselling or healing sessions which attended evening communion. But more overt or spectacular usages of tongues in public contexts had become the prerogative of the Fellowship group.

(b) Commentary

The Anglicans, with almost no exception, were emphatic that tongues were 'not the be all and end all', although they admitted they might not have said that a decade ago. They felt that this gift had 'fallen into place', and it was not necessarily for everyone; whereas in the Fellowship it was expected as 'normal' for all 'real Christians', and seemed to be being used in a much more overt and self-conscious way as an (effective) instrument of conversion alongside the other 'gifts'. Only a few interviewees, however, knew anything of the instances of 'tongue-speaking' found in spiritual writers dotted through the tradition. Interestingly here, in writers as contextually diverse as the Desert Fathers and St Teresa, what is noteworthy is how little is made of it: it is simply a natural outflowing of expressiveness in one already deeply committed to prayer. It is recorded of abba Ephraim, for instance, that his prayer was sometimes like 'a well bubbling out of his mouth' (*Apophthegmata Patrum*, Ephraim 2). Over a thousand years later Teresa's autobiography quite passingly refers to a type of prayer in which 'The soul longs to pour out words of praise . . . Many words are then spoken . . . But they are disorderly' (*Life*, ch. 16). And there are many other such scattered examples from the tradition, giving the lie to the suspicion that this gift has been totally dormant since the apostolic age. 'Singing in jubilation', likewise, is seen by Augustine and others as a wholly natural way of letting the Spirit pray in one: for 'this kind of singing (*jubilum*) is a sound which means that the heart is giving birth to something it cannot speak of' (*Sermons on the Psalms*, 32.8).

But again, as we have already intimated, only a few interviewees were beginning to take note of the parallelism in charismatic and contemplative traditions, or to explore the burgeoning popular literature on this theme of the 'recovery of disciplines' from such traditions, although this was clearly being encouraged by the Anglican minister. Once again one felt that the church was at a point of decision: whether to modify its exclusive biblicism, accept a quieter form of worship, and turn to a broader and more intellectual assimilation of tradition; or whether to reassert the more overtly 'enthusiastic' worship of some years previously, and engage consciously in 'power evangelism'. A small minority wanted much more public tongue-speaking to re-emerge (and it is significant that a few of these people left the church during the period of this research); others saw its dangers as 'an excuse not to think' (see 1 Cor. 14: 19). Exactly, however, at the axis of this decision also lie the issues in our last set of themes.

3. Prayer and failure, prayer and aridity, prayer and depression

(a) Interviews

It was in these areas that the greatest ambivalence was found in the interviews, and the ambivalence cut across the two groups. Does 'failure' in prayer, or the common states of dryness ('aridity') and depression when afflicting those who pray, indicate that the Spirit is necessarily inactive or impeded here? Is the Spirit's work in any sense compatible with human failure and weakness?

'Failure' in prayer was confronted movingly in one interview with an Anglican 'elder', a man who for long years had wanted to 'come into tongues'. Repeatedly his friends had prayed for this, but to no avail. The same man's wife was also virtually crippled by back pain; again, repeated prayer had brought little relief. It was poignant to have to ask how he could explain this. His response was that he could only finally 'bow to God's sovereignty'; and in relation to tongues, after great disappointment, he had come to accept, 'I've just got to be me, and that's the Lord's job'. When the interviewer enquired whether such evident humility could not itself be a work of the Spirit, he assented, though there was a sense that this was a new idea. One might juxtapose the thoughts recorded by John Cassian here: 'Wonders and powers are not always necessary, for some are harmful and are not granted to everyone . . . Humility is the queen of all the virtues' (*Conferences*, 15.7).

Attitudes to aridity in prayer were mixed, too. Many of those interviewed felt that joyousness should be the norm (and in the case of one member of the Fellowship group, this was particularly emphatically expressed); but all when pressed admitted to phases of dryness themselves, most explaining them as correlated to stress or other passing human factors. Only one person, interestingly, surmised that dryness might actually be in some circumstances a sign of progress, of the Spirit 'driving one into the desert' to 'sharpen one's thirst' (see Mark 1: 12f.). But no sustained explanation of this was made; there was no reference, for instance, to St John of the Cross' detailed explication of this as the prayer of 'the night of sense', moving one on into 'contemplation', a form of prayer emotionally less satisfying than before, even felt as a 'failure' to pray, and yet characterized by a continuing and restless desire for God.

On depression, however, there was the widest range of response. A minority of people (in both the Fellowship and the Anglican church) felt that depression was largely self-absorption and should be dealt with rapidly and effectively by prayer and exhortation. People in both groups believed in the devil and the demonic but on the whole were not happy with the idea that individual demons caused illness or depression (a view powerfully influential in the area, however, as a result of the 'demonic deliverance' liturgies of a 'healing centre' recently established locally). This sort of particularized personification of evil had been deliberately averted by the minister within the Anglican group. In a particularly interesting interview with a psychiatrist, who is also a member of the Anglican congregation, it was admitted that being a Christian was sometimes a distinct 'risk factor' in depression, because of the possible mood swings from a high affective state into the reverse, the rigorous standards imposed upon the self, and the feelings of further guilt if prayer was not effective in relieving the condition. Often she found the best way through was to set aside theological language altogether, and insist, 'This *isn't* a sin problem; you have a health problem that can be effectively treated with drugs.' It was important, then, that religious people should feel no guilt or shame about accepting medication when needed. The same doctor was, however, wary of saying that the Spirit could in any way be working actively in and through a depression, especially severe psychotic states, although she conceded that 'less severe episodes' could sometimes lead to a 'greater dependence on God'.

In general, then, there was an agreement amongst those interviewed that Christians should not normally be depressed, and that their mood should primarily be characterized by joy. Once again there was only one commentator who strongly urged that to demand the continuous maintenance of a high feeling state was actually 'unbiblical'. 'What of Gethsemane, not to speak of the prophets and the psalms?' The same person distinguished importantly between clinical 'depression' and spiritual 'desolation'. The former he saw as a recognized 'illness', and, just as Jesus had in the gospel stories invariably responded to those who requested healing from sickness, so in this case, too, he believed, the sufferer should rightfully pray to be relieved. In the case of spiritual 'desolation', however (and he admitted depression and desolation might be difficult to disentangle without the discernment of an experienced spiritual guide), one could be confronting the particular activity of the Spirit itself, moving one on into a painful new phase of growth, a sharing in some sense in Christ's own passion.

(b) Commentary

It was clear that here we had reached a theological crux. If the Spirit's activity was deemed in some sense incompatible with 'low' feeling states, then either a necessarily sporadic understanding of the Spirit's activity was in play, or else there was a lurking dualism (as in the questionably orthodox early fifth-century Macarian homilies, where Satan and the Spirit wage war with equal force for the overlordship of the 'heart', the Spirit being associated particularly with the 'feeling of assurance'). But what then of the possibility of genuinely Christ-like dereliction? Could it not be, as von Balthasar has so movingly expressed it in his theology of 'Holy Saturday', that the Spirit may not only on occasion drive one into a sharing of Christ's desolation, but actually be that in God which spans the unimaginable gulf between despair and victory?

Such thoughts about the Spirit are already foreshadowed in the New Testament (e.g. Rom. 8: 11, 17). But they have been spelled out since then with the profoundest practical and psychological insight by spiritual writers as diverse as Diadochus of Photice in the east (fifth century) and John of the Cross in the west (sixteenth century). Diadochus, for whom 'regeneration' in the Spirit is central, speaks of God deliberately 'receding' at times 'in order to educate us', 'to humble the soul's tendency to vanity and self-glory'; through 'feeling ourselves abandoned . . . we become more humble and submit to the glory of God' (*One Hundred Texts*, 89, 69). This is somewhat akin to John of the Cross' first 'night of sense', where prayer seems to lose all its former sweetness. Much more terrible, though, is John's description of the trials and disorientations of the second 'night of spirit', in which God draws so painfully and purgatively *close* that the experience is akin to that of a log being thrown into a devouring fire (*Dark Night*, Bk. II. X). If such as this, then, is truly an implication of Paul's invitation to be compelled by the Spirit into the sharing of Christ's passion, then it has to be said that it is an implication on which so far only a few of those interviewed in our survey had reflected deeply.

Here too, then, it may be that the charismatic movement now faces a dilemma, and one with fundamentally trinitarian implications: is the Spirit only to be a 'triumphalist' Spirit, bearer of joy and positive 'feeling'? Or, if this is Christ's Spirit, breathed out of his scarred body, 'one in being' with Father and Son, must we not allow as much for the fire of purgation (Eliot's 'flames of incandescent terror') as for the refreshment of the comforting dove? William Temple's memorable words are worthy of recollection here:

> When we pray 'Come, Holy Ghost, our souls inspire', we had better know what we are about. He will not carry us to easy triumphs and gratifying successes; . . . He may take us through loneliness, desertion by friends, apparent desertion even by God; that was the way Christ went to the Father . . . He may lead us from the Mount of Transfiguration (if He ever lets us climb it) to the hill that is called the Place of a Skull . . . The soul that is filled with the Spirit must have been purged of all pride or love of ease, all self-complacence and self-reliance; but the soul has found the only real dignity, the only lasting joy. Come then, Great Spirit, come. Convict the world; and convict my timid soul. (*Readings in St John's Gospel*, 16.8–11)

Conclusion

In this chapter we have confronted recurring issues of prayer and desire, prayer and feeling, prayer and pain. The material gleaned from the interviews and participant observation cannot in itself, and without further reflection, solve the hard questions about the nature of the Spirit posed at the beginning of the chapter; but just as 'sect' and 'church' diverge in theology as well as social structure, it is clear that our Anglican community is caught in that tension, and poised in the act of decision between vying theological possibilities. And it may well be, as its minister strongly believes, that it stands on the brink of new, and deeper, perceptions of the Spirit's guidance and intent for the future of the charismatic movement as a whole.

What all the charismatics interviewed shared, however, and what they continue to challenge the Church with, is a deep and impressive commitment to the adventure of prayer, and the call to rediscover an unimpeded participation in that infinite desire of God for God which we call the Spirit, and in which we are drawn into union with Christ. That it is indeed possible to enter into this divine relationship with willing and excited co-operation is what the movement, in all its diversity, testifies to. But it is a participation that can never allow the certainty of attainment or superiority: Bernard of Clairvaux has well said, 'There is no proof of the presence of the Spirit which is more certain than a desire for ever greater grace' (*Second*

Sermon on St Andrew, 4). Indeed, if Bernard is right, we may well reassure those harbouring anxieties about 'sinning against the Holy Spirit', that their very disposition of penitence and concern is an indication of this divine desire in them. . . . Where there *is* prayer, then, and above all that inchoate desire for 'ever greater grace' which destroys all complacency, there indeed is the Spirit already active and effective. Or, as John Chrysostom put it conversely, 'If the Holy Spirit did not exist, we believers would not [even] be able to pray to God' (*Sermons on Pentecost*, 1, 4).

In this sense, then (to return to the hard questions we posed at the outset), *all* prayer is prayer 'in the Spirit';[2] for it is already prompted – however unconsciously in the pray-er – by that divine restlessness that ceaselessly yearns towards the Father. And in this sense, too, a failure to reflect consciously and *theologically* about the Spirit is only a failure if there is also a failure in prayer itself, a failure, that is, to court that flow of divine reciprocity within one, to invite God as Spirit (as Diadochus once put it with a lovely artistic metaphor) to 'paint the divine likeness on the divine image in us' with the 'luminosity of love' (*One Hundred Texts*, 89).

As for our question about the experimental *distinctiveness* of the Spirit in prayer, here is an area where the supposedly remote concerns of early Church trinitarianism are pressingly apposite, and perhaps especially for charismatics. For while charismatics run no danger at all (as others may) of neglecting or relegating the Spirit to metaphysical redundancy, there may be, as we have hinted, a danger of associating particular *sorts* of experience with the Spirit (and possibly others with the Son and Father); and this, as the debates of the fourth century highlighted, may lead either to an implicit tritheism (a belief in three different gods), or else to a sporadic, instrumentalist, and possibly impersonal, vision of the Spirit.

It was precisely to counteract such possibilities that the language of 'one in being' was applied to the Spirit alongside Father and Son. For our experience of the Spirit is an experience of *God*, no less, and whatever divine characteristics are experienced in the Spirit are also the divine characteristics of Father and Son. What then of the *distinctiveness* of the three? Fumbling to express the inexpressible, the late fourth-century Cappadocian Fathers spoke (in what seems to us forbiddingly abstract terms) of the 'internal relations' of the three Persons as being their only distinguishing feature. Their attempted explanations were often abstruse and polemical, and assumed a philosophical framework which we no longer take for granted. But fundamentally they argued from their own profound spiritual experience: if the Spirit was that in God which constantly called and provoked them (most explicitly in prayer) in yearning towards the Father, then it was the Son, in his filial dependence on the Father, with whom they were being united through this life of prayer. In other words, it could not be different *sorts* of 'experience' (in the sense of emotional tonality) that were associated with the three Persons in their one divine flow of activity, but only the particular way they were related to one another internally: Father as source of all, Spirit as divine goad in restless quest for creation's return again to the Father, Son as the divine prototype of that redeemed and transformed creation. The Spirit then was *eternally* active, ceaselessly 'indwelling' the 'saints', to use Pauline language; this was not to deny *particular* goadings of the

Spirit, too, the divine freedom to direct and prompt in special or dramatic ways, as is more characteristic of the Lukan theology of the New Testament.

But why, one must probe further, did the early Fathers need to call the Spirit a distinct Person? In the case of the Son this was obvious: he had been incarnate, had prayed to the Father as clearly distinct from himself. But why should not the Spirit be seen merely as a metaphorical expression for the divine outreach? In the lengthy process of developing a trinitarian theology, was it simply an accident that the Spirit was declared a distinct Person, by a rather simplistic deduction from the threefold structure of the baptismal formula? If we are to understand the real logic of this process of theological evolution and to respond convincingly to the suggestion that we are here dealing only with metaphors, we must continue to explore what it is in the history, language, reflection and experience of the Christian community that has made theology resist such a reduction in the status of the Spirit. And to do this involves, as this chapter has hinted, understanding that area where the experience of charismatics and of contemplatives so significantly converges: in that profound, though often fleeting or obscure, sense of entering in prayer into a 'conversation' *already in play*, a reciprocal divine conversation between Father and Spirit which can finally be reduced neither to divine monologue nor to human self-transcendence. We are dealing here, of course with matters almost inexpressible and thus open to every kind of question about appropriate interpretation. But that there is something irreducible here, which tradition has named 'Spirit', is vividly and freshly testified by the contemporary charismatic movement.

As for the implications of our survey for the relation of the Holy Spirit to 'feelings' – whether pleasurable or painful – this is a matter too, as we have indicated, that calls for deepened trinitarian (and so Christological) reflection. . . . [We would] need to look at some more precise exegetical concerns raised also by the charismatic movement . . . [as well as] whether, and to what degree, the experiences which we claim of the Spirit today can actually be identified within the experiences of the earliest Church of New Testament times.

Notes

1   This approach was pursued systematically in *We Believe in God*, ch. 7.
2   See again Rom. 8: 9ff. for the characteristically Pauline themes of the Spirit's 'indwelling', and of prayer as precisely the prior activity of the Spirit in one. In line too with this generalized interpretation of 'prayer in the Spirit' is Eph. 6: 18: 'Pray *at all times* in the Spirit, with all prayer and supplication'. With this theme of the Spirit's omnipresence should be carefully contrasted Paul's phrase in 1 Cor. 14: 15: 'I will pray with the spirit', in which Paul is commending the openness to God of the *whole person*, both through the reflective mode of prayer, and through prayer as a more direct response to God ('as I am inspired to pray', NEB).

6

Pontifical Council for Promoting Christian Unity, "Vatican Clarification on the Filioque"

The "Filioque" controversy debates whether Christians ought to say, in the Nicene Creed, that the Spirit "proceeds from the Father" full stop, as the creed was adopted in Greek, or whether they may or ought to say further that the Spirit "proceeds from the Father and the Son," where "and the Son" is filioque in Latin. The Greek-speaking East accuses the Latin-derived West of inserting the Filioque unilaterally, and the West defends itself exegetically. The task of the western churches – in my opinion – is how to admit that the Greek-rite Christians are right historically (the West changed the creed) without undermining the theological traditions that derived from the change. The Filioque then becomes a permitted theological opinion which is not church-dividing.[1]

This piece can function in several ways. First, it introduces the Filioque controversy in a way meant to be both substantive and irenic. Second, it exemplifies a genre of theological writing otherwise unrepresented in this volume, that of the careful ecclesial diplomacy of churches in dialogue. The late twentieth century was marked by numerous dialogues among Catholic, Orthodox, and Protestant churches about the theological conflicts that divided them, and they tended to produce position papers and joint statements of this genre. Third, since this is not a consensus statement, but a proposal toward one, it is a useful exercise to follow the discussion and commentary both in the scholarly literature and online.

"The Greek and Latin Traditions Regarding the Procession of the Holy Spirit," *L'Osservatore Romano*, Weekly English Edition, 20 September 1995, pp. 3 and 6. Also published in the *Information Bulletin of the Pontifical Council for Promoting Christian Unity* 89 (1995) II/III, pp. 88–92 and as a short phamphlet, *The Greek and Latin Traditions about the Procession of the Holy Spirit* (London: CTS Publications, 1995). This text is taken from *L'Osservatore Romano*, except that I have transliterated the Greek.

Finally, the document also represents a Catholic genre of high-level publications in the semi-official newspaper *L'Osservatore Romano*, the authorship and authority of which is sometimes hard to evaluate; it calls itself "authentic" and "authoritative," but it is not as if signatures appear at the bottom, or as if the Pontifical Council by itself makes doctrine.[2]

Among its contributions, George Tavard lists these: it acknowledges the unaltered symbol of the First Council of Constantinople as normative for the whole Church in confessing that the Spirit takes his origin from the Father (*ekporeuomenon*), noting that the Catholic Church has never authorized additions to the Greek version of the creed. It notes Greek Fathers who teach that the *ekporeusis* of the Spirit passes "though the Son." It interprets the Filioque as not contradicting the Father as the sole origin of the Spirit. Perhaps most important, it denies that the Latin verb *procedure* properly translates the Greek *ekporeutai*, so that the Latin creed with the Filioque does not contradict the Greek creed without. Finally, it introduces a category of relations "in the manner of the Trinity," which seems to describe a more fluid series of intratrinitarian relations of one Person to the other two, and of which the Filioque becomes just one example.[3] The Clarification opens and closes by invoking God's Spirit of Sonship "who brings human beings into Christ's filial relationship to his Father."

The Greek and Latin Traditions Regarding the Procession of the Holy Spirit

Pontifical Council for Promoting Christian Unity

The Holy Father, in the homily he gave in St Peter Basilica on 29 June in the presence of the Ecumenical Patriarch Bartholomew I, expressed a desire that "the traditional doctrine of the Filioque, *present in the liturgical version of the Latin Credo, [be clarified] in order to highlight its full harmony with what the Ecumenical Council of Constantinople of 381 confesses in its creed: the Father as the source of the whole Trinity, the one origin both of the Son and of the Holy Spirit".*

What is published here is the clarification he has asked for, which has been undertaken by the Pontifical Council for Promoting Christian Unity. It is intended as a contribution to the dialogue which is carried out by the Joint International Commission between the Roman Catholic Church and the Orthodox Church.

In its first report on "The Mystery of the Church and of the Eucharist in the light of the Mystery of the Holy Trinity", unanimously approved in Munich on 6 July 1982, the Joint International Commission for Theological Dialogue between the Roman Catholic Church and the Orthodox Church had mentioned the centuries-old difficulty between the two Churches concerning the eternal origin of the Holy Spirit. Not being able to treat this subject for itself in this first phase of the dialogue, the Commission stated: "Without wishing to resolve yet the difficulties which have arisen between the East and the West concerning the relationship between the Son and the Spirit, we can already say together that this Spirit, which proceeds from the Father (John 15: 26) as the sole source in the Trinity and which has become the Spirit of our sonship (Rom. 8: 15) since he is also the Spirit of the Son (Gal. 4: 6), is communicated to us particularly in the Eucharist by this Son upon whom he reposes in time and in eternity (John 1: 32)" (*Information Service* of the Secretariat for Promoting Christian Unity, n. 49, p. 108, I, 6).

The Catholic Church acknowledges the conciliar, ecumenical, normative and irrevocable value, as expression of the one common faith of the Church and of all Christians, of the Symbol professed in Greek at Constantinople in 381 by the Second Ecumenical Council. No profession of faith peculiar to a particular liturgical tradition can contradict this expression of the faith taught and professed by the undivided Church.

On the basis of John 15: 26, this Symbol confesses the Spirit *"to ek tou Patros ekporeuomenon"* ("who takes his origin from the Father"). The Father alone is the principle without principle (*archē anarchos*) of the two other persons of the Trinity, the sole source (*pēgē*) of the Son and of the Holy Spirit. The Holy Spirit therefore takes his origin from the Father alone (*ek monou tou Patros*) in a principal, proper and immediate manner.[4]

The Greek Fathers and the whole Christian Orient speak, in this regard, of the "Father's monarchy", and the Western tradition, following St Augustine, also confesses that the Holy Spirit takes his origin from the Father "principaliter", that is, as principle (*De Trinitate* XV, 25, 47; PL 42, 1094–1095). In this sense, therefore, the two traditions recognize that the "monarchy of the Father" implies that the Father is the sole Trinitarian Cause (*aitia*) or principle (*principium*) of the Son and of the Holy Spirit.

This origin of the Holy Spirit from the Father alone as principle of the whole Trinity is called *ekporeusis* by Greek tradition, following the Cappadocian Fathers. St Gregory of Nazianzus, the Theologian, in fact, characterizes the Spirit's relationship of origin from the Father by the proper term *ekporeusis*, distinguishing it from that of procession (*to proienai*) which the Spirit has in common with the Son. The Spirit is truly the Spirit proceeding (*proion*) from the Father, not by filiation, for it is not by generation, but by *ekporeusis* (*Discourse* 39, 12; *Sources chrétiennes* 358, p. 175). Even if St Cyril of Alexandria happens at times to apply the verb *ekporeusthai* [to] the Son's relationship of origin from the Father, he never uses it for the relationship of the Spirit to the Son (Cf. *Commentary on St John* X, 2, PG 74, 910 D; *Ep* 55, PG 77, 316 D, etc.). Even for St Cyril, the term *ekporeusis* as distinct from the term "proceed" (*proienai*) can only characterize a relationship of origin to the principle without principle of the Trinity: the Father.

That is why the Orthodox Orient has always refused the formula *to ek tou Patros kai tou Huiou ekporeuomenon* and the Catholic Church has refused the addition *kai tou Huiou* to the formula *to ek tou Patros ekporeuomenon* in the Greek text of the Nicene-Constantinopolitan Symbol, even in its liturgical use by Latins.

The Orthodox Orient does not, however, refuse all eternal relationship between the Son and the Holy Spirit in their origin from the Father. St Gregory of Nazianzus, a great witness to our two traditions, makes this clear in response to Macedonius who was asking: "What then is lacking to the Spirit to be the Son, for if nothing was lacking to him, he would be the Son? – We say that nothing is lacking to him, for nothing is lacking to God; but it is the difference in manifestation, if I may say so, or in the relationship between them (*tēs pros allēla scheseōs diaphoron*) which makes also the difference in what they are called" (*Discourse* 31, 9; *Sources chrétiennes* 250, pp. 290–2).

The Orthodox Orient has, however, given a happy expression to this relationship with the formula *dia tou Huiou ekporeuomenon* (who takes his origin from the Father by or through the Son). St Basil already said of the Holy Spirit: "Through the Son (*dia tou Huiou*), who is one, he is joined to the Father, who is one, and by himself completes the Blessed Trinity" (*Treatise on the Holy Spirit*, XVIII, 45; *Sources chrétiennes* 17 bis, p. 408). St Maximus the Confessor said: "By nature (*phusei*) the Holy Spirit in his being (*kat' ousian*) takes substantially (*ousiodōs*) his origin (*ekporeuomenon*) from the Father through the Son who is begotten (*di' huiou gennēthentos*)" (*Quaestiones ad Thalassium*, LXIII; PG 90, 672 C). We find this again in St John Damascene: "(*ho Patēr*) *aei ēn, echōn ex eautou ton autou logon, kai dia tou logou autou ex eautou to Pneuma autou ekporeuomenon*", in English: "I say that God is always Father since he has always his Word coming from himself, and through his Word, having his Spirit issuing from him" (*Dialogus contra Manichaeos* 5; PG 94, 1512 B, ed. B. Kotter, Berlin 1981, p. 354; cf. PG 94, 848–9 A). This aspect of the Trinitarian mystery was confessed at the seventh Ecumenical council, meeting at Nicaea in 787, by the Patriarch of Constantinople, St Tarasius, who developed the Symbol as follows: *to Pneuma to agion, to kurion kai zōopoion, to ek tou Patros dia tou Huiou ek poreuomenon*" (Mansi XII, 1122 D).

This doctrine all bears witness to the fundamental Trinitarian faith as it was professed together by East and West at the time of the Fathers. It is the basis that must serve for the continuation of the current theological dialogue between Catholic and Orthodox.

The doctrine of the *Filioque* must be understood and presented by the Catholic Church in such a way that it cannot appear to contradict the Monarchy of the Father nor the fact that he is the sole origin (*archē, aitia*) of the *ekporeusis* of the Spirit. The *Filioque* is, in fact, situated in a theological and linguistic context different from that of the affirmation of the sole monarchy of the Father, the one origin of the Son and of the Spirit. Against Arianism, which was still virulent in the West, its purpose was to stress the fact that the Holy Spirit is of the same divine nature as the Son, without calling in question the one monarchy of the Father.

We are presenting here the authentic doctrinal meaning of the *Filioque* on the basis of the Trinitarian faith of the Symbol professed by the second Ecumenical Council at Constantinople. We are giving this authoritative interpretation, while being aware of how inadequate human language is to express the ineffable mystery of the Holy Trinity, one God, a mystery which is beyond our words and our thoughts.

The Catholic Church interprets the *Filioque* with reference to the conciliar and ecumenical, normative and irrevocable value of the confession of faith in the eternal origin of the Holy Spirit, as defined in 381 by the Ecumenical Council of Constantinople in its Symbol. This Symbol only became known and received by Rome on the occasion of the Ecumenical Council of Chalcedon in 451. In the meantime, on the basis of the earlier Latin theological tradition, Fathers of the Church of the West like St Hilary, St Ambrose, St Augustine and St Leo the Great, had confessed that the Holy Spirit proceeds (*procedit*) eternally from the Father and the Son.[5]

Since the Latin Bible (the Vulgate and earlier Latin translations) had translated Jn 15: 26 (*para tou Patros ekporeuetai*) by "*qui a Patre procedit*", the Latins translated the *ek tou Patros ekporeuomenon* of the Symbol of Nicaea-Constantinople by "*ex Patre procedentem*" (Mansi VII, 112 B). In this way, a false equivalence was involuntarily created with regard to the eternal origin of the Spirit between the Oriental theology of the *ekporeusis* and the Latin theology of the *processio*.

The Greek *ekporeusis* signifies only the relationship of origin to the Father alone as the principle without principle of the Trinity. The Latin *processio*, on the contrary, is a more common term, signifying the communication of the consubstantial divinity from the Father to the Son and from the Father, through and with the Son, to the Holy Spirit.[6] In confessing the Holy Spirit "*ex Patre procedentem*", the Latins, therefore, could only suppose an implicit *Filioque* which would later be made explicit in their liturgical version of the Symbol.

In the West, the *Filioque* was confessed from the fifth century through the *Quicumque* (or "*Athanasianum*", DS 75) Symbol, and then by the Councils of Toledo in Visigothic Spain between 589 and 693 (DS 470, 485, 490, 527, 568), to affirm Trinitarian consubstantiality. If these Councils did not perhaps insert it in the Symbol of Nicaea-Constantinople, it is certainly to be found there from the end of the eighth century, as evidenced in the proceedings of the Council of Aquileia-Friuli in 796 (Mansi XIII, 836, Dff.) and that of Aachen of 809 (Mansi XIV, 17). In the ninth century, however, faced with Charlemagne, Pope Leo III, in his anxiety to preserve unity with the Orient in the confession of faith, resisted this development of the Symbol which had spread spontaneously in the West, while safeguarding the truth contained in the *Filioque*. Rome only admitted it in 1014 into the liturgical Latin version of the Creed.

In the Patristic period, an analogous theology had developed in Alexandria, stemming from St Athanasius. As in the Latin tradition, it was expressed by the more common term of procession (*proienai*) indicating the communication of the divinity to the Holy Spirit from the Father and the Son in their consubstantial communion: "The Spirit proceeds (*proeisi*) from the Father and the Son; clearly, he is of the divine substance, proceeding (*proion*) substantially (*ousiodōs*) in it and from it" (St Cyril of Alexandria, *Thesaurus*; PG 75, 585 A).[7]

In the seventh century, the Byzantines were shocked by a confession of faith made by the Pope and including the *Filioque* with reference to the procession of the Holy Spirit; they translated the procession inaccurately by *ekporeusis*. St Maximus the Confessor then wrote a letter from Rome linking together the two approaches – Cappadocian and Latin-Alexandrian – to the eternal origin of the Spirit: the Father is the sole principle without principle (in Greek *aitia*) of the Son and of the Spirit; the Father and the Son are consubstantial source of the procession (*to proienai*) of this same Spirit. "For the procession they [the Romans] brought the witness of the Latin Fathers, as well, of course, as that of St Cyril of Alexandria in his sacred study on the Gospel of St John. On this basis they showed that they themselves do not make the Son Cause (*Aitia*) of the Spirit. They know, indeed, that the Father is the sole Cause of the Son and of the Spirit, of one by generation and of the other by *ekporeusis* – but they explained that the latter comes (*proienai*) through the Son, and they showed in this way the unity and the immutability of the essence" (*Letter to Marinus of Cyprus*, PG 91, 136 A-B). According to St Maximus, echoing Rome, the *Filioque* does not concern the *ekporeusis* of the Spirit issued from the Father as source of the Trinity, but manifests his *proienai* (*processio*) in the consubstantial communion of the Father and the Son, while excluding any possible subordinationist interpretation of the Father's monarchy.

The fact that in Latin and Alexandrian theology the Holy Spirit, proceeds (*proeisi*) from the Father and the Son in their consubstantial communion does not mean that it is the divine essence or substance that proceed in him, but that it is communicated from the Father and the Son who have it in common. This point was confessed as dogma in 1215 by the Fourth Lateran Council: "The substance does not generate, is not begotten, does not proceed; but it is the Father who generates, the Son who is begotten, the Holy Spirit who proceeds: so that there is distinction in persons and unity in nature. Although other (*alius*) is the Father, other the Son, other the Holy Spirit, they are not another reality (*aliud*), but what the Father is the Son is and the Holy Spirit equally; so, according to the orthodox and catholic faith, we believe that they are consubstantial. For the Father, generating eternally the Son, has given to him his substance (. . .) It is clear that, in being born the Son has received the substance of the Father without this substance being in any way diminished, and so the Father and the Son have the same substance. So the Father, the Son and the Holy Spirit, who proceeds from them both, are one same reality" (DS 804–5).

In 1274 the Second Council of Lyons confessed that "the Holy Spirit proceeds eternally from the Father and the Son, not as from two principles but as from one single principle (*tamquam ex uno principio*)" (DS 850). In the light of the Lateran Council, which preceded the Second Council of Lyons, it is clear that it is not the divine essence that can be the "one principle" for the procession of the Holy Spirit. The *Catechism of the Catholic Church* interprets this formula in n. 248 as follows: "The eternal order of the divine persons in their consubstantial communion implies that the Father, as the 'principle without principle' (DS 1331), is the first origin of the Spirit, but also that as Father of the only Son, he is, with the Son, the single principle from which the Spirit proceeds (Second Council of Lyons, DS 850)."

For the Catholic Church, "at the outset the Eastern tradition expresses the Father's character as first origin of the Spirit. By confessing the Spirit as he 'who proceeds from the Father' ('*ek tou Patros ekporeuomenon*' cf. John 15: 26), it affirms that he comes from the Father through the Son. The Western tradition expresses first the consubstantial communion between Father and Son, by saying that the Spirit proceeds from the Father and the Son (*Filioque*). (. . .) This legitimate complementarity, provided it does not become rigid, does not affect the identity of faith in the reality of the same mystery confessed" (*Catechism of the Catholic Church*, n. 248). Being aware of this, the Catholic Church has refused the addition of *kai tou Huiou* to the formula *ek tou Patros ekporeuomenon* of the Symbol of Nicaea-Constantinople in the Churches, even of Latin rite, which use it in Greek. The liturgical use of this original text remains always legitimate in the Catholic Church.

If it is correctly situated, the *Filioque* of the Latin tradition must not lead to a subordination of the Holy Spirit in the Trinity. Even if the Catholic doctrine affirms that the Holy Spirit proceeds from the Father and the Son in the communication of their consubstantial communion, it nonetheless recognizes the reality of the original relationship of the Holy Spirit as person with the Father, a relationship that the Greek Fathers express by the term *ekporeusis*.[8]

In the same way, if in the Trinitarian order the Holy Spirit is consecutive to the relation between the Father and the Son, since he takes his origin from the Father as Father of the only Son,[9] it is in the Spirit that this relationship between the Father and the Son itself attains its Trinitarian perfection. Just as the Father is characterized as Father by the Son he generates, so does the Spirit, by taking his origin from the Father, characterize the Father in the manner of the Trinity in relation to the Son and characterizes the Son in the manner of the Trinity in his relation to the Father: in the fullness of the Trinitarian mystery they are Father and Son in the Holy Spirit.[10]

The Father only generates the Son by breathing (*proballein* in Greek) through him the Holy Spirit and the Son is only begotten by the Father insofar as the spiration (*probolē* in Greek) passes through him. The Father is Father of the One Son only by being for him and through him the origin of the Holy Spirit.[11]

The Spirit does not precede the Son, since the Son characterizes as Father the Father from whom the Spirit takes his origin, according to the Trinitarian order.[12] But the spiration of the Spirit from the Father takes place by and through (the two senses of *dia* in Greek) the generation of the Son, to which it gives its Trinitarian character. It is in this sense that St John Damascene says: "The Holy Spirit is a substantial power contemplated in his own distinct hypostasis, who proceeds from the Father and reposes in the Word" (*De Fide orthodoxa* I, 7; PG 94, 805 B, ed. B. Kotter, Berlin 1973, p. 16; *Dialogus contra Manichaeos* 5; PG 94, 1512 B, ed. B. Kotter, Berlin 1981, p. 354).[13]

What is this Trinitarian character that the person of the Holy Spirit brings to the very relationship between the Father and the Son? It is the original role of the Spirit in the economy with regard to the mission and work of the Son. The Father is love in its source (2 Cor. 13: 13; 1 John 4: 8, 16), the Son is "the Son that he loves" (Col. 1: 14). So a tradition dating back to St Augustine has seen in the Holy Spirit, through whom "God's love has been poured into our hearts" (Rom. 5: 5), love as the eternal Gift of the Father to his "beloved Son" (Mark 1: 11; 9: 7; Luke 20: 13; Eph. 1: 6).[14]

The divine love which has its origin in the Father reposes in "the Son of his love" in order to exist consubstantially through the Son in the person of the Spirit, the Gift of love. This takes into account the fact that, through love, the Holy Spirit orients the whole life of Jesus towards the Father in the fulfilment of his will. The Father sends his Son (Gal. 4: 4) when Mary conceives him through the operation of the Holy Spirit (cf. Luke 1: 35). The Holy Spirit makes Jesus manifest as Son of the Father by resting upon him at Baptism (cf. Luke 3: 21–2; John 1: 33). He drives Jesus into the wilderness (cf. Mark 1: 12). Jesus returns "full of the Holy Spirit" (Luke 4: 1). Then he begins his ministry "in the power of the Spirit" (Luke 4: 14). He is filled with joy in the Spirit, blessing the Father for his gracious will (cf. Luke 10: 21). He chooses his Apostles "through the Holy Spirit" (Acts 1: 2). He casts out demons by the Spirit of God (Matt. 12: 28). He offers himself to the Father "through the eternal Spirit" (Heb. 9: 14). On the Cross he "commits his Spirit" into the Father's hands (Luke 23: 46). "In the Spirit" he descended to the dead (cf. 1 Pet. 3: 19), and by the Spirit he was raised from the dead (cf. Rom. 8: 11) and "designated Son of God in power" (Rom. 1: 4).[15] This role of the Spirit in the inner-most human existence of the Son of God made man derives from an eternal Trinitarian relationship through which the Spirit, in his mystery as Gift of Love, characterizes the relation between the Father, as source of love, and his beloved Son.

The original character of the person of the Spirit as eternal Gift of the Father's love for his beloved Son shows that the Spirit, while coming from the Son in his mission, is the one who brings human beings into Christ's filial relationship to his Father, for this relationship finds only in him its Trinitarian character: "God has sent the Spirit of his Son into our hearts, crying Abba! Father!" (Gal. 4: 6). In the mystery of salvation and in the life of the Church, the Spirit therefore does much more than prolong the work of the Son. In fact, whatever Christ has instituted – Revelation, the Church, the sacraments, the apostolic ministry and its Magisterium – calls for constant invocation (*epiklēsis*) of the Holy Spirit and his action (*energeia*), so that the love that "never ends" (1 Cor. 13: 8) may be made manifest in the communion of the saints with the life of the Trinity.

Notes

1   For an Eastern Orthodox argument, influential in ecumenical dialogues, that the Filioque is theological opinion that need not divide the church, see B. Bolotov, "Thesen über das Filioque," *Revue internationale de théologie* (Berne), vol. 6, no. 24 (Oct.–Dec. 1898): 681–712, and translated more recently into French, "Thèses sur le 'Filioque' par un théologien russe," *Istina* (Boulogne-sur-Seine: Centre d'études) 17 (1972): 261–89.

2   See George H. Tavard, "A Clarification on the *Filioque*," *Anglican Theological Review* 83 (2001): 507–14; here, 508–9.

3   Tavard, "A Clarification," pp. 509–11.

4   These are the terms employed by St Thomas Aquinas in the *Summa Theologica*, Ia, q. 36, a. 3, 1um and 2um.

5   It is Tertullian who lays the foundations for Trinitarian theology in the Latin tradition, on the basis of the substantial communication of the Father to the Son and through the Son to the Holy Spirit: "Christ says of the Spirit: 'He will take from what is mine' (John 16: 14), as he does from the Father. In this way, the connection of the Father to

the Son and of the Son to the Paraclete makes the three cohere one from the other. They who are one sole reality (*unum*) not one alone (*unus*) by reason of the unity of substance and not of numerical singularity" (*Adversus Praxean* [*Against Praxeas*], XXV, 1–2). This communication of the divine consubstantiality in the Trinitarian order he expresses with the verb "procedere" (ibid., II, 6). We find this same theology in St Hilary of Poitiers, who says to the Father: "May I receive your Spirit who takes his being from you through your only Son" (*De Trinitate*, XII; PL 10. 471). He remarks: "If anyone thinks there is a difference between receiving from the Son (John 16: 15) and proceeding (*procedere*) from the Father (John 15: 26), it is certain that it is one and the same thing to receive from the Son and to receive from the Father" (*De Trinitate*, VIII, 20; PL 10. 251 A). It is in this sense of communication of divinity through procession that St Ambrose of Milan is the first to formulate the *Filioque*: "The Holy Spirit, when he proceeds (*procedit*) from the Father and the Son, does not separate himself from the Father and does not separate himself from the Son" (*De Spiritu Sancto*, I, 11, 120; PL 16. 733 A = 762 D). St Augustine, however, takes the precaution of safeguarding the Father's monarchy within the consubstantial communion of the Trinity: "The Holy Spirit proceeds from the Father as principle (*principaliter*) and, through the latter's timeless gift to the Son, from the Father and the Son in communion (*communiter*)" (*De Trinitate*, XV, 25, 47; PL 42. 1095). St Leo, *Sermon* LXXV, 3; PL 54. 402; *Sermon* LXXVI, 2, PL 54. 404.

6 Tertullian uses the verb *procedere* in a sense common to the Word and the Spirit insofar as they receive divinity from the Father: "The Word was not uttered out of something empty and vain, and he does not lack substance, he who proceeded (*processit*) from such a [divine] substance and has made so many [created] substances" (*Adversus Praxean*, VII, 6). St Augustine, following St Ambrose, takes up this more common conception of procession: "All that proceeds is not born, although what is born proceeds" (*Contra Maximinum*, II, 14, 1; PL 42. 770). Much later St Thomas Aquinas remarks that "the divine nature is communicated in every processing that is not *ad extra*" (*Summa Theologica*, a, q. 27, a. 3, 2um). For him, as for all this Latin theology which used the term "procession" for the Son as well as for the Spirit, "generation is a procession which puts the divine person in possession of the divine nature" (ibid., a, q. 43, a. 2, c), for "from all eternity the Son proceeds in order to be God" (ibid.). In the same way, he affirms that "through his procession, the Holy Spirit receives the nature of the Father, as does the Son" (ibid., a, q. 35, a. 2, c). "Of words referring to any kind of origin, the most general is procession. We use it to indicate any origin whatever; we say, for instance, that the line proceeds from the point; that the ray proceeds from the sun, the river from its source, and likewise in all kinds of other cases. Since we admit one or another of these words that evoke origin, we can therefore conclude that the Holy Spirit proceeds from the Son" (ibid., a, q. 36, a. 2, c).

7 St Cyril bears witness here to a Trinitarian doctrine common to the whole school of Alexandria since St Athanasius, who had written: "Just as the Son says: 'All that the Father has is mine' (John 16: 15), so shall we find that, through the Son, it is all also in the Spirit" (*Letters to Serapion*, III, 1, 33; PG 26. 625 B). St Epiphanius of Salamis (*Ancoratus*, VIII; PG 43. 29 C) and Didymus the Blind (Treatise on the Holy Spirit, CLIII; PG 34. 1064 A) link the Father and the Son by the same preposition *ek* in the communication to the Holy Spirit of the consubstantial divinity.

8 "The two relationships of the Son to the Father and of the Holy Spirit to the Father oblige us to place two relationships in the Father, one referring to the Son and the other to the Holy Spirit" (St Thomas Aquinas, *Summa Theologica*, Ia, q. 32, a. 2, c).

9   Cf. *Catechism of the Catholic Church*, n. 248.

10 St Gregory of Nazianzus says that "the Spirit is a middle term (*meson*) between the Unbegotten and the Begotten" (Discourse 31.8, *Sources chrétiennes*, 250, p. 290). Cf. also, in a Thomistic perspective, G. Leblond, "Point of View on the Procession of the Holy Spirit," in *Revue Thomiste* LXXXVI, t. 78 (1978): 293–302.

11 St Cyril of Alexandria says that "the Holy Spirit flows from the Father in the Son (*en tōi Huiōi*)", *Thesaurus*, XXXIV; PG 75. 577 A.

12 St Gregory of Nyssa writes: "The Holy Spirit is said to be of the Father and it is attested that he is of the Son. St Paul says: 'Anyone who does not have the Spirit of Christ does not belong to him' (Rom. 8: 9). So the Spirit who is of God [the Father] is also the Spirit of Christ. However, the Son who is of God [the Father] is not said to be of the Spirit: the consecutive order of the relationship cannot be reversed" (Fragment *In orationem dominicam*, quoted by St John Damascene, PG 46. 1109 BC). And St Maximus affirms in the same way the Trinitarian order when he writes: "Just as the Thought [the Father] is principle of the Word, so is he also of the Spirit through the Word. And, just as one cannot say that the Word is of the voice [of the Breath], so one cannot say that the Word is of the Spirit" (*Quaestiones et dubia*, PG 90. 813 B).

13 St Thomas Aquinas, who knew the *De fide orthodoxa*, sees no opposition between the *Filioque* and this expression of St John Damascene: "To say that the Holy Spirit reposes or dwells in the Son does not exclude his proceeding from the Son; for we say also that the Son dwells in the Father, although he proceeds from the Father" (*Summa Theologica*, a, q. 36, a. 2, 4um).

14 St Thomas Aquinas, following St Augustine, writes: "If we say of the Holy Spirit that he dwells in the Son, it is in the way that the love of one who loves reposes in the loved one" (*SummaTheologica*, Ia, q. 36, a. 2, 4um). This doctrine of the Holy Spirit as love has been harmoniously assumed by St Gregory Palamas into the Greek theology of the *ekporeusis* from the Father alone: "The Spirit of the most high Word is like an ineffable love of the Father for this Word ineffably generated. A love which this same Word and beloved Son of the Father entertains (*chrētai*) towards the Father: but insofar as he has the Spirit coming with him (*sunproelthonta*) from the Father and reposing connaturally in him" (*Capita physica* XXXVI; PG 150, 1144 D-1145 A).

15 Cf. John Paul II, Encyclical *Dominum et Vivificantem*, nn. 18–24, in *Acta Apostolicae Sedis* LXXVIII, 1986, 826–31. Cf. also *Catechism of the Catholic Church*, nn. 438, 689, 690, 695, 727.

7

Stanley Stowers, "Matter and Spirit, or What is Pauline Participation in Christ?"

This article comes from a New Testament scholar using Religious Studies categories to illuminate Paul's account of the Holy Spirit. It is particularly useful in the way that Late Antique accounts of adoption throw light on Paul's metaphors – the very passages that twentieth-century theologians from Adrienne von Speyr to Sarah Coakley have found central. Some readers familiar with theological categories but not with Religious Studies ones may find themselves taken aback by the results of Stowers's refusal to read later categories back into Paul. But, after all, Paul did not have the Cappadocians to go by. And the gain is magnificent: Late Antique theories of kinship, adoption, sonship, and family resemblance yield a set of connections among Father, Son, and Spirit much tighter and more conceptually satisfying than many that followed. That is so for another reason important in this anthology: Stowers's version insists that the Spirit does not make sense apart from bodies, in this case, bodies in familial relationships of generation and adoption. In this essay, the thesis proposed elsewhere in these pages – that the Spirit rests on matter as it rests on the body of the Son – becomes even more concrete, so that the Spirit's connection with matter never stops, but always has farther down to go. A theologian might observe that here the categories of immanence and transcendence of God have not yet come apart, but that more transcendent the Spirit is, the more material it can be.

Stanley Stowers, "What is Pauline Participation in Christ?," in *Redefining First-Century Jewish and Christian Identities*, ed. Fabian E. Udon, *et al.* (Notre Dame, IN: University of Notre Dame Press, 2008).

Matter and Spirit, or What Is Pauline Participation in Christ?

Stanley Stowers

Albert Schweitzer made the classic case for the idea that participation in Christ is the central or most basic or most important element in Paul's thought.[1] But it is due to Ed Sanders' incisive critical reassessment of Schweitzer's position in *Paul and Palestinian Judaism* that the centrality of participation has been widely accepted in New Testament scholarship.[2] Among other things, Schweitzer and Sanders showed decisively that in forming arguments for moral advice, Paul draws these arguments from facts about participation in Christ and not justification by the believer's faith.[3] If there has been wide acceptance of the centrality of participation, the agreement has ended on how to characterize the phenomenon indicated in Paul's discourse. From incomprehensible mystery to a form of corporate personality, the proposals have varied greatly and failed to win wide assent.[4]

Schweitzer's answer was clearer than most. He proposed a historical explanation of sorts for the origins of the idea and a broad cultural context. The context was a rather uniform Jewish eschatology, or as New Testament scholars might say today, apocalypticism, that he posited. Jews, including Paul, held to a series of strict and logically interrelated doctrines about their own age, past ages and the world to come. Paul created the idea of participation in Christ as a solution to the dilemma caused by his belief that the Messiah had come and been raised from the dead well ahead of the end time and its general resurrection. Paul had to make the elect mystically share in the death and resurrection of the Messiah already in this natural age. He writes:

> Paul's conception is that believers in mysterious fashion share the dying and rising again of Christ, and in this way are swept away out of their ordinary mode of existence, and form a special category of humanity. When the Messianic Kingdom dawns, those of them who are still in life are not natural men like others, but men who have in some way passed through death and resurrection along with Christ, and are capable of becoming partakers of the resurrection mode of existence, while other men pass under the dominion of death.[5]

Schweitzer provides a possible conceptual context for the larger problem that confronted Paul, but not for language and discourse of participation itself. That was Paul's pure creation, in his view, a matter of irresistible reasoning from the system of eschatological doctrines that led Paul to invent the language.[6] Schweitzer assures us that Paul came to the idea that believers are in Christ, Christ in them and that they participate in his death and resurrection with the logical reasoning of a genius, but he never tells us how the idea of one person being in another person or sharing in the experiences of another would make sense to Paul or to others in his culture.[7] For all of the celebration of Schweitzer's discovery of Paul's apocalyptic context, there has been little recognition that apocalyptic did not explain – that is, provide a context for – the central idea of participation. We need a discourse or discourses that provide the conditions of intelligibility for the language of participation. Schweitzer's absolute oppositions between Palestinian Judaism and Hellenism and eschatology and Hellenism will not do.[8] What was common sense in the 1920s and 1930s when most Europeans and Americans assumed that supposed racial groups and their fractions had inherently different minds/cultures, and intrinsic and mutually exclusive cultural practices, should not now make sense. In spite of Schweitzer's often admirable liberal values, the antimonies of his constructions belong to his milieu, even if they still frame much New Testament scholarship.

One of his great contributions was the consistency with which he held, against the common liberal understandings of the apostle, that Paul belonged to a milieu that was quite alien to modernity. Schweitzer was certain that Paul's language did require a realistic conception of the supernatural existence that had entered the natural. Participation was a sharing in the corporeality (*Leiblichkeit*) of Christ. He insisted that the language was not symbolic or mere metaphor.[9] Sanders whole-heartedly affirmed this realism even though he did not know how to characterize it. Against Rudolph Bultmann and many others who have proposed that although Paul's language seems to indicate something physical, it has a non-physical refer-ence that is its true meaning, Sanders writes:

> It seems to me best to understand Paul as saying what he meant and meaning what he said: Christians really are one body and Spirit with Christ, the form of this world really is passing away . . . and so on But what does this really mean? How are we to understand it? We seem to lack a category of 'reality' – real participation in Christ, real possession of the Spirit – which lies between naïve cosmological speculation and belief in magical transference on the one hand and a revised self-understanding on the other. I must confess that I do not have a new category of perception to propose here. This does not mean, however, that Paul did not have one. . . . To an appreciable degree, what Paul concretely thought cannot be directly appropriated by Christians today.[10]

Richard Hays has argued on the contrary, both that there is a fitting conception of participation, and that modern Christians can appropriate it. He has recently made a number of proposals about the metaphorical nature and categories of participation, but his most sustained argument has been that participation involves imaginative identification with narratives about Jesus Christ.[11] As he puts it in the sermonic Christian we, "we are caught up into the story of Jesus Christ."[12] Hays glosses Gal. 2: 19–20 where Paul speaks of being crucified with Christ and now living in Christ with: Jesus Christ's "story transforms and absorbs the world."[13] I find it difficult to determine the scope and significance of Hays's claims. Some-times it sounds like what I would call a narrative idealism as when he criticizes realistic readings with the comment that all language is metaphorical.[14]

Hays also chides Bultmann for his demythologizing of this language.[15] I believe that Hays's hermeneutic is just as modernist as Bultmann's. Since, however, it is in part unconscious of its translation from Paul's ancient culture, it lacks the crit-ical reflexivity of Bultmann's approach. Part of the basic structure of modernity, in radical contrast to the ancient world, is the natural/supernatural divide that thinkers like René Descartes created to protect religion from science and science from religion.[16] There is a natural realm of cause and effect in which humans live that is constituted of matter and persistent physical laws that apply equally everywhere. The supernatural, including God and the spiritual, is totally other and constitutes a "realm" to which the principles of the natural realm do not apply. One can only point to this "realm" symbolically and metaphorically. In contrast to this, ancient and medieval thinking had one unified realm consisting of a hierarchy of being or substances, each of which had its own qualitative properties. Anything including God and God's activity could, in principle, be explained in physical terms. This was a holistically interactive cosmos without a neat separation between the symbolic-spiritual and the instrumental-physical.

Thus in modernist thought the spiritual is that which is beyond and in contrast to the physical, substantial and merely natural. But in Paul's world *pneuma* (wind, air, breath, spirit; hereafter pneuma), for example, is a refined, qualitatively higher substance with its own power of movement and intelligence. Paul betrays exactly this kind of physics and cosmology. So for example in 1 Corinthians 15, the substances of the lower and heavenly cosmos vary qualitatively in a grand hierarchy: "Not all flesh is the same flesh, humans have one flesh, but animals another, birds another, and fish another. There are heavenly bodies and earthly bodies, but the glory of the heavenly is one thing and the glory of the earthly is different. The sun has one kind of glory, and the moon another glory, and different glory for the stars, in fact star differs from star in glory."[17] Humans participate in Adam because they share bodies consisting of the same stuff as Adam (15: 42–9). Those in Christ participate in him because they share with him the most sublime kind of pneuma, divine pneuma that he received in being resurrected from the dead. Paul's language here is not metaphorical or at least not only metaphorical in the sense that it does not involve a realistic meaning and reference.

Sanders is right in stressing a realist ontology. It is a reinterpretation into the modernist framework to treat the language of participation as fundamentally metaphorical without the referent of a substantial ontology. Both modern largely anthropological and literary conceptions of myth and modern Christian theology have insisted that myth and theology are about something called meaning in opposition to what is out there. The elaborate modern practices of studying myth and scripture have traded on this opposition and on seeing that the meaning of the text could never include significant notions about the stuff and the processes of the world. Meaning is the realm of religion, literature, art and the humanities; stuff belongs to science and has no meaning.

When Hays dismisses Schweitzer's interpretation as "a crudely literal belief in a shared physical substance between the Messiah and his people," he is overwriting Paul's thought with modernity.[18] The move amounts to unconscious demythologizing. Protestants and European and American Roman Catholics, among others, share a non-human world that is largely disenchanted and "mechanical" – without human-like intelligence and teleology – compared to Paul's world. From the thousand thousands and ten thousand ten thousands of heavenly beings who administer the world for God in Daniel (e.g., 9: 10), and the qualitatively physical principles of purity, pollution and holiness in the Priestly sources, to the aither, pneuma and purposive species essences of Hellenistic and Greco-Roman cultures, the ancient conceptions understood the world to work by the principles of mind (e.g., value, purpose) permeating the cosmos. But New Testament scholars have often assumed that a relative lack of explanation in these terms in some texts meant that Paul, for example, had the scholar's common sense, that is, modern mechanistic under-standing of the world as a background for beliefs about God, Christ, angels and how the supernatural, say in the form of Christ's resurrection, could enter the natural world. The fact that ancient writings do not always refer to these ancient ways of understanding the world should no more be taken to imply modern-like assumptions than my failure to mention atoms, electrons and evolutionary selec-tion should be taken to imply that I hold some non-modern understanding of the world.[19]

Some of those who have tried to describe the logic and origins of Paul's parti-cipationist language have appealed to Paul's or early Christian experience.[20] But I do not view that as an explanation. The conditions for the experiences themselves must be explained rather than treated as originary mysteries. Moreover, Paul does not use our modern language of experience. He does not have an interest in the individual's inner feel for some special event, but on the event itself and its broader significance.

I want to stress three points. First, a hierarchy of qualities of substances is central to the discourse and should not be treated as symbolic for some supposedly deeper theological meaning or existential posture that Paul really meant. Second, the most basic principle by which this thinking with substances works is the logic of contiguity of substances, a matter of extension, identity and contiguousness or lack thereof. Third, these are principles by which Paul reads and constructs narratives about Abraham and his descendents, Adam and his descendents, and Christ and those who are contiguous with him by the logic of patrilineal lineage and physical relat-edness. These are components out of which the language of participation comes.

I can illustrate these points with some brief comments on 1 Cor. 6: 12–20. Paul explains that God will destroy both the stomach and food, but the Lord is "for [or with] the body." God raised the Lord and he will raise those who are mem-bers of Christ. This argument makes sense because there is a contrast between the resurrection body and the human fleshly body. The best commentary on 6: 13–14 is 15: 35–50. Paul follows important strains of Hellenistic thought in treating the human body or bodies in general as like forms that can have various sorts of con-tent.[21] The body that will perish is made of flesh and was probably thought of as concocted out of food grown from the earth. But a better form of the body would consist of divine pneuma. It comes as no surprise then, that in 6: 18 the current body is a temple of this pure or holy pneuma. Paul is clear that a fully pneumatic body will replace the flesh body only at the resurrection (15: 44). So far we have types of stuff, but there is also the contiguity. Those in Christ are members of him. The relation is like the relation of the arm to the rest of the body. The same stuff makes Christ and believers contiguous. Paul means this so realistically that for a believer to be joined to a prostitute in sexual intercourse would be to join her to Christ and create that arm/body relation. On the one hand, Paul explains that the person who is joined to the Lord is one pneuma with him. On the other hand, he cites Gen. 2: 24 to show that in sexual intercourse the partners become one entity: "the two shall become one flesh." Enigmatically, Paul comments that such sexual intercourse is uniquely a sin "against," or more likely, "into" the body.[22] I suggest that he may have in mind the context of the Genesis passage. There, just before the statement about becoming one flesh, Eve is made from one of Adam's bones and she is said to be "bone of his bone and flesh of his flesh." This preceding context makes the "one flesh" statement seem very literal. Man and woman come together so as to share the same substance. Finally, "bone of my bone and flesh of my flesh" is a biblical expression for being a descendant or a relative of someone. This conception of human relatedness by the identity of substance clearly preceded and informed the statement from Genesis. Indeed, I will argue that the basic model for the discourse of participation is that of descendants and relatives sharing the same stuff as ancestors or those to whom they are related.

The reading supposes the subjective genitive construal of *pistis Christou* and related expressions.[23] The reading shows why Paul's focus on what Christ and Abraham did makes sense. In other words, the Pauline letters do not argue that Christ brought a new way to be saved, that is, through the believer's faith, over against the old way of keeping the law. Rather, salvation in an apocalyptic scenario hinges on Abraham's and Christ's faith or faithfulness and not on the believer's faith. Through their actions, God has founded covenants that descendents inherit merely by being born of the chosen lineage.[24] In reading Paul's texts in this way, I would argue, he does not sound as if he were "spiritualizing," religion, but as if he had a genuine investment in Jewish beliefs about kinship and descent that are central to the Hebrew Bible.[25]

In Gal. 3: 7–8 Paul writes, "those who come out of faithfulness are sons of Abraham."[26] I take this to be first of all Abraham's faithfulness in this context. In the Genesis stories, because Abraham believed the unlikely promise that he would have an heir and then acted faithfully so as to have a child, Paul can think of the descendents of Isaac as the lineage of Abraham's faith and of God's promise.[27] Then in Gal. 3: 8–9, "Scripture foreseeing that God would justify the gentiles out of faithfulness, proclaimed the gospel beforehand to Abraham, namely, 'in you (*en soi*) will all the gentiles be blessed.' So that those who come out of [Abraham's] faithfulness are blessed with (*sun*) the faithful Abraham." Paul uses the language of ancient genetics and lineage from the Septuagint to say that the gentiles who are in Christ were blessed when Abraham was blessed because Christ was in Abraham as his seed. Christ was in Abraham at that point and participated in him. He was one with Abraham. I think that the "in Christ" language derives from this logic of descent and genetic participation.[28] Paul may have been just as literal as Hebrews 7 which argues that although he was not yet born, Levi paid ties to Melchizedek because he was in the loins of Abraham as seed when Abraham paid ties to Melchizedek. Paul emphasizes the presence of Christ in Abraham when the promises were given. Thus 3: 16 says, "the promises were pronounced to Abraham and to his Seed."

In Gal. 3: 14, one reads that Christ died "so that the blessing of Abraham might come to the gentiles in Christ Jesus so that we might receive the promise of the spirit through faithfulness." I take this to be the faithfulness of Abraham and Christ.

Nils Dahl long ago suggested that Paul's allusion to Gen. 22: 18 in 3: 14 might be the basis for Paul's "in Christ," expression, at least in some contexts.[29] In 3: 26–7, Paul continues "You are all sons of God in Christ Jesus through [his] faithfulness. For all who have been baptized into Christ have put on Christ." And in 3: 29: "If you are of Christ [participate in Christ], you are the seed of Abraham and heirs according to promise." The logic is this: Abraham and Jesus as blood relatives share the same stuff and the same characteristic of faithfulness to God's promises and are the crucial beginning and end of the God-chosen lineage bearing the promise of blessing. Paul takes the particular blessing promised to the gentiles as the gift of possessing God's pneuma. As Christ participated in Abraham and shared his stuff, so gentiles who come to share the pneuma of Christ in baptism, share in this contiguity back to Abraham and are thus seed of Abraham and co-heirs as they participate in the stuff of Christ. But Christ's spirit is not any normal human pneuma. It is the divine pneuma that brought him back to life on a new level of existence after he allowed himself to die in faithfulness to God's promises.

This interpretation of Galatians 3 allows one to understand why it has been so difficult to fit 3: 28 together with Paul's other statements about women, men, Judeans, non-Judeans, slave and free and make them cohere with modern liberal and rights-based conceptions of equality. Gal. 3: 28 is first of all a denial of a set of ontological differences and an affirmation of an ontological unity. Those in Christ are literally of the same stuff. All share the very same pneuma, Christ's. It would be a wrong turn, however, to in modern fashion separate substance from quality, the spiritual (in the modern sense) from the material. Epictetus illustrates this unity (3.3.22): "When someone has a spell of dizziness, it is not the abilities and the virtues that are thrown into confusion, but the pneuma of which they exist. When the pneuma settles down, the abilities and virtues are settled." Habituated skills and virtues such as courage or self-control are qualities of a person's pneuma. Epictetus acknowledges that because of the substantial nature of these abilities, an external physical force can cause an interruption of normal consciousness that temporarily incapacitates them.[30] It therefore makes perfect sense for Paul to associate pneuma with moral and mental qualities. He goes on to say (Gal. 5: 24, 16–23) that "those who are of Christ have crucified the flesh with its passions and desires" and to oppose the virtues (fruit) of the pneuma, including self-control, with the vices of the flesh. Substances have their qualities and capabilities. Unlike Epictetus's person, Paul's Christ-person has not only ordinary pneuma like all human beings, but also an interpenetration of Christ's pneuma that came directly from God.[31]

Those in Christ are not descendents of Christ, but contemporary kin. As Rom. 8: 29 reveals, Paul thought of them as brothers of Jesus Christ. This perennially vexing passage that has been treated as consisting of references to God's predestination of each person to salvation or damnation and to the lost image of God, actually uses the language of ancient genetics and descent as shown in the dissertation of Caroline Johnson Hodge.[32] Ancient biological thought spoke of the image (*eikon*) of the father being passed on through procreation in a seed from the father. It was widely held that pneuma of the father concentrated in the seed and was the active and organizing force that shaped the matter supplied by the mother in the womb.

Writings of the Hebrew Bible also broadly share in this ancient patrilineal ideology of genetics. Gen. 5: 3 says that "Adam generated a son according to his likeness and according to his image."[33] The Septuagint here uses *eikon* as does Rom. 8: 29. One of the common ideas of patrilineal thought is that all of the seed of all of the descendents are in the ancestor as Hebrews 7, for example, assumes with Levi in Abraham.

In Romans 9 and elsewhere, Paul emphasizes that God plans ahead of time the chosen lineage through which the promises will be passed, and here he correctly reads Genesis. Romans 9: 7–8, for instance, says, " 'In Isaac shall your seed be named,' that is, it is not the children of the flesh that are children of God, but the children of promise are counted as seed." This passage is usually taken to mean that Paul is eliminating descent and spiritualizing (in the modern sense) true religion as the religion of faith in God and his promises. On my reading, he is arguing that mere fleshly descent is not enough.[34] Rather the salvific lineage has to be a line of descent chosen by God for promise. So in Romans 9, he argues that Ishmael and Esau were fleshly descendants of Abraham, but not of the line chosen by God for promise and blessing. God's choosing and empowerment is more important than just flesh. Jeremiah 1: 5 is an example of the language of divine foreknowing and shaping of a chosen agent: "before I formed you in the womb, I knew you, and before you came forth from the womb, I set you apart." Thus Rom. 8: 29–30 is about God shaping the line of salvific participation that would even include gentiles who are grafted in, and not just metaphorically, as a lineage of descendants: "Those whom [God] knew beforehand, he also planned before to be conformed to the image of his son, so that he [Christ] might be the firstborn among many brothers." God has planted the seed of the chosen line in the ancestor from the beginning and this included Christ who carries the image formed by the divine pneuma that all of those baptized into Christ share just as sons share the same image of the father. Ancient readers are likely to have understood that Paul likens the resurrection to a birth. Gentile believers share in that birth by "baptism into Christ" and thus become "seed of Abraham" (Gal. 3: 26–9, cf. Rom. 6: 1–11). Paul stresses this key connection between the salvific line of descent ("seed of David") and God's extension of the line to the gentiles by means of the holy pneuma given to Christ in the resurrection at the very beginning of Romans (1: 1–5).[35] Again, as in Gal. 3: 8, Paul describes this nexus as the good news preached beforehand in the scriptures.

With this logic, other statements in chapter 8 using the language of participation make sense. Earlier, in 8: 9, Paul says, "Anyone who does not have the pneuma of Christ, is not of him." He continues, "But if Christ is in you, though the body is dead because of sin, the pneuma is life because of righteousness."[36] Paul then speaks of the pneuma of him who raised Jesus from the dead dwelling in those who are in Christ. The particular shape of God's pneuma that Jesus received in the resurrection is shared by believers so that Christ can be said to be in them. But since they merely share what belongs first of all to Christ, they can also be said to be "of him" or "in him" just as Christ shared the stuff of Abraham and was in him. One simply cannot understand Paul's idea of participation without recognizing that those who are in or of Christ actually possess as part of them stuff of Christ, a portion of his pneuma. The chapter goes on to speak of them receiving the pneuma of adoption.

That pneuma cooperates with the individual's own "natural" pneuma to certify this adoption as sons of God. As a result, these people are co-heirs and co-sufferers with Christ. Because they possess part of Christ's vital essence endowed by God, they are not only part of the inheriting lineage, but also experience his suffering as they live temporarily still in a flesh or psychic body as he did before his resurrection.

How the pneuma of Christ and the pneuma of the believer relate or intermix is far from clear. It is clear that both maintain their substantial natures and identities in some sense. In 1 Cor. 2: 11–15, the divine pneuma communicates between those in Christ and God:

> the pneuma searches all things, even the depths of God. For what person knows the things of a person except the person's pneuma that is in him. So also no one knows the things of God except the pneuma of God. Now we have not received the pneuma of the world, but the pneuma out of God so that we can understand the things given to us by God.

Romans 8: 16 says that when the readers cry Abba, Father, that "it is the pneuma [of God] itself witnessing together with our pneuma that we are children of God, and if children also heirs of God . . . and fellow heirs with Christ provided that we suffer with him so that we might be glorified with him." The fact that Paul can easily and without caveat (e.g., "I am speaking in a human way") attribute types of pneuma to both God and humans shows that he participates in his ancient culture and Hellenistic thought about pneuma.

The divine pneuma is clearly not a "person" as it becomes in later Christian Trinitarian theology. Paul agreed with the prevailing culture, including philosophers and medical doctors, that pneuma was the vital component of the living person and that there were various kinds and qualities of pneuma in the workings of the world.[37] Sometimes Paul's language makes it sound as if the divine pneuma inhabits the person by a kind of possession so that the natural human pneuma and the divine pneuma are distinct *homunculi* inside of a person. They are separate, but work together. The language of sharing and participation (e.g., *koinonia*), however, may suggest a more "scientific" picture.[38] We learn from the Aristotelian Alexander of Aphrodisias' *de mixtione* (*On the mixture of Physical Bodies*) about the extremely influential Stoic doctrines regarding the mixing of substances that was their basis for picturing a highly interactive cosmos. Philo, Paul's Jewish contemporary, for example, uses the theory in a quite explicit way in interpreting the Septuagint (e.g., *de confusione linguarum* 183–87).[39] In this theory, *krasis* is the type of mixing that occurs in the constitution of the human being as pneuma interpenetrates the whole person.[40] It is not the mere juxtaposition of stuff. Nor is it fusion so that the pneuma and the other substance lose their identities, but the complete extension of active pneuma through passive matter so that each substance retains its identity. Such a theory would facilitate Paul's talk of double identity between Christ and the person in Christ with God's pneuma extending through both the passive matter of the body and the active human pneuma. The person shares all that Christ has experienced and become and yet retains her or his own personal identity. Listen to Paul speaking of himself: "I have been crucified together with Christ. I no longer live, but Christ lives in me. And the life I now live in the flesh, I live in the faithfulness of the son of God who loved me and gave himself up on my behalf" (Gal. 2: 19–20).

Schweitzer, Sanders and others have very clearly shown that Paul's ethical thought, and his language of freedom from sinning and justification depend on his conception of participation.[41] But how does this connection fit my theory that Paul builds participation on notions of participating in founding ancestors by physical descent? What does all of this have to do with faith or faithfulness? It is the very texts where Paul has traditionally been taken to argue his supposedly central concept of justification by the believer's faith and Jesus' atoning death by substitution that Abraham becomes a topic (Romans 4 and Galatians 3). In this tradition, Abraham is taken as a model of how the believer can be saved by faith alone. In my reading, Paul is arguing that non-Jews/Judeans do not have to become Jews/Judeans in order to become right with God by getting into Christ. They do not have to keep the Judean law and are free from its just condemnation of their sin. Gentiles, by participating in Christ and his death and new life, inherit what Abraham and Christ achieved by their faith or faithfulness so that God promised, and now insures, blessings to their descendants. Jews or gentiles born into the line do not earn the status by law-keeping. So, for example, Rom. 4: 15b–17a says, "where there is no law there is no violation. For this reason the promise comes out of [Abraham's and Christ's] faithfulness, so that the promise might be secure, by gift [from God], for all of the seed, not only for those who are of the law, but also for those who are out of the faithfulness of Abraham who is father of us all. As it is written [Gen. 17: 5], 'I have made you the father of many peoples (or gentiles).' "[42] Thus I believe that William Wrede, Schweitzer, Sanders, Krister Stendahl and others are correct when they see justification as in some sense secondary or dependant on participation. But putting this understanding of justification together with the arguments about gentile contiguity in a line of Abraham through Christ provides a reintegration of the supposedly separate discourses. Salvation is effected not by the believer's faith, but by Abraham's and Jesus' faith, and that faith centrally includes faith in (or faithful action in view of) God's promises about blessed lineages consisting of those whom God actively works to make right with him. God's own pneuma conveyed to the ungodly through the death and resurrection of Jesus Christ is the chief instrument of justification. Gentiles "in Christ" are materially improved people who not only have past sins forgiven, but more importantly are empowered and filled with a holy stuff that actively enables obedience to God.

I would like to conclude with a few of many possible reflections on the significance of what I have argued. Ancient Christianity was often eager to get rid of an interest in lineage and birth in its readings of Paul. These had to be rejected as the carnality of the Jews. But it is modernist interpreters who have been most threatened by the hierarchy of substances and physics of contiguity. Descartes still using the language of the scholastics asserted that the medieval cosmos of interactive qualities of substances had to be replaced by an exhaustive dualism of *res extensa* and *res cogitans*. Extension was to be purged of quality, meaning and teleology. Religion had to be limited to mind, culture, the symbolic and separated from any discourse about the material world, cause and effect. A Paul who asserted that true religion was a matter of faith has been a perfect instrument for modernity. The Bible has nothing to say about science, but concerns pure meaning. Paul's message could be made to be about the discontinuity of the physical and the spiritual, matter and meaning. Furthermore, in my view, it is not just as a result of scholarly progress that 20th century scholarship discovered that eschatology is the essence of primitive Christianity. Modernity made the category of time, temporality, triumph over place, space and stuff. Interpretation that focused on narrative has been one means for this triumph in New Testament studies. The story can be rendered with character, plot and so on in a way that leaves behind the ancient baggage of place and stuff with all of its particularity. For moderns, time (e.g., history) has seemed to have an indeterminacy not possessed by the scientific hardness and law-following behavior of stuff, space and place – a refuge for traditional Western understandings of the human and the divine. Because of this, we have lost the sense that part of the meaning for Paul was in the concept and reference to stuff and its particularity.

One example of this departicularizing abstraction, I believe, occurs regarding men, women and gender. The understanding of participation outlined here would reveal the depth, detail and logic of the patriarchal and patrilineal thought that is the raw material for Paul's creative reworkings of biblical stories and commonplace physics and cosmology. The approach, for example, helps us to understand why Paul usually speaks of "sons of God" rather than "children of God." Or why even though language from this tradition in Paul's letters suggests that becoming a son of God is like the birth of a child, that there is no mother, but only a father and sons. If we produce abstracted narratives that have only God, Christ, Christians and unbelievers, then we leave out rich, but troubling conceptions of men, women, slave, free, Jew and gentile, fleshly bodies, and pneumatic bodies. The great irony of this reading is that the ultimate elimination of flesh bodies for pneumatic bodies would seem to eliminate procreation and gender, but the very logic leading to this conclusion derives from a logic of participation in human procreation and kinship.

Notes

1 *The Mysticism of Paul the Apostle* (London: A. and C. Black, 1931).
2 *Paul and Palestinian Judaism* (Philadelphia: Fortress Press, 1977). Acceptance, of course, takes many forms that often attempt to accommodate other soteriological schemes also. An interesting sign of this acceptance is the way that Bart Ehrman's enormously popular introduction to the New Testament (*The New Testament: A Historical Introduction*, 2nd edn. [Oxford and New York: Oxford University Press, 2000] especially pp. 324–28) approaches Paul by comparing two models of salvation, "judicial" and "participationist." One of the most important and creative appreciators of Sanders's revival of participation has been Richard Hays's *The Faith of Jesus Christ: The Narrative Substructure of Galatians 3:1–4:11*, dissertation series, Society of Biblical Literature, 56 (Chico, CA: Scholars Press, 1983; 2nd edn. Grand Rapids, MI: Eerdmans, 2002), on which see below. There are also other distinct scholarly traditions of treating Paul's "mystical" or "corporate" thought, most notably in Roman Catholic

scholarship. A recent conservative evangelical example is Sang Won (Aaron) Son, *Corporate Elements in Pauline Anthropology*, Analecta Biblica 148 (Rome: Pontifical Biblical Institute, 2001).

3   *Mysticism*, pp. 42–3; *Paul and Palestinian Judaism*, pp. 439, 456 and throughout pp. 447–74.

4   Son in *Corporate Elements* provides references to a number of these suggestions or "backgrounds."

5   *Mysticism*, pp. 96–7.

6   For example, he argues (*Mysticism*, p. 38) that Paul created his mysticism out of inferences from beliefs that the early Christians and Palestinian Jews held in common. Thus it was the "personal creation" of Paul, but understandable to others.

7   On Paul's unique logical genius see *Mysticism*, pp. 100, 139–40. A key problem here is not that Schweitzer attributes rationality and intellectual labor to Paul, but that he assumes an unrealistic amount of determinacy in Paul's inferential processes and in reasoning generally.

8   This is not to mention that the fantastic amalgamation that Schweitzer called Hellenism based on the work of scholars in the mode of Richard Reitzenstein holds no credence among scholars of Greek and Roman religion today. For critical discussions of these oppositions, see *Paul Beyond the Judaism/Hellenism Divide*, ed. Troels Engberg-Pedersen (Louisville, KY: Westminster John Knox Press, 2001).

9   *Mysticism*, pp. 15–17, 19, 127–30.

10 *Paul and Palestinian Judaism*, pp. 522–3. Unfortunately, Bultmann brought into the conversation the concepts of magic, transference and cosmological speculation in uncritical, anachronistic and undefined ways that obscure the differences between ancient and modern thought. A critique of such language is beyond the scope of this article. The legitimate point picked up from the language by Sanders is that Paul's letters depict a real and substantial change in those who are in Christ, but such people are still in the flesh and human. For a devastating critique of the scholarly use of the category magic, see Randall Styers, *Making Magic: Religion, Magic and Science in the Modern World* (New York: Oxford University Press, 2004).

11 *Faith of Jesus Christ*. His recent proposals were presented in "What is 'Real Participation in Christ'?: a Dialogue with E. P. Sanders on Pauline Soteriology," an unpublished paper. Hays describes this language as a hermeneutical problem for modern Christian theology and proposes four interpretive categories for the language: familial participation, political/military participation, ecclesial participation and narrative participation. The first two categories consist of metaphorical language, on this interpretation, and the third seems to be a combination of metaphors and a reference to experiences or practices by Paul. The fourth concerns imaginative identification with the stories of Israel and of Jesus. Unfortunately, Hays picks up the red herrings of whether participation is "magical" and "automatic" instead of showing why Paul's language should not be taken realistically (*Faith of Jesus Christ*, pp. 213–15).

12 See especially p. xxix of the introduction to the second edition of *Faith of Jesus Christ* and pp. 210–15. One hopes that the contention of the Bultmann school and others that Paul's anthropological language and faith language refers to the 20th century category of human existence has been put to rest. For any who might linger in such gross anachronism, I recommend Paul Macdonald, *History of the Concept of Mind* (Burlington, VT: Ashgate, 2003) especially p. 100.

13 Hays, *Faith of Jesus Christ*, p. 29.

14 I find it difficult to understand or accept Hays's philosophical position. If one should agree that all language is metaphorical, does that mean that "Bob's arm" does not also refer to the flesh, bone and blood body part of the person Bob? Schweitzer was not claiming that there might not be metaphor involved in the language of participation, but that the language was not *only* metaphorical or figurative with no central reference to substances and objects. This misleading criticism of Schweitzer is clear also in Hays's discussion of him in *Faith of Jesus Christ*, pp. 44–5.

15 Hays, *Faith of Jesus Christ*, pp. 47–52 and R. Bultmann, *Theology of the New Testament*, vol. 1 (New York: Scribner's, 1951), pp. 268–9, 302.

16 For a survey of recent scholarship with bibliography on the ancient, see M. R. Wright, *Cosmology in Antiquity* (London: Routledge, 1995). For a more specialized discussion of some key issues, see *Infinity and Continuity in Ancient and Medieval Thought*, ed. N. Kretzmann (New York: Cornell University Press, 1982). For an accessible comparison with modernity, see Alexandre Koyré, *From the Closed World to the Infinite Universe* (Baltimore: Johns Hopkins University Press, 1957).

17 On the concepts of flesh, body, soul and so forth and the hierarchy of being, see Dale B. Martin, *The Corinthian Body* (New Haven, CT: Yale University Press, 1995), pp. 105–36.

18 Hays, *Faith of Jesus Christ*, p. 451.

19 Just to make sure that I am not misinterpreted, I am not saying that the modern understandings of the world do or should reduce to beliefs in these concepts from the sciences. I am just choosing those examples for the sake of clarity.

20 For one important critique of uses made of the category of religious experience, see Matthew Bagger, *Religious Experience, Justification and History* (Cambridge: Cambridge University Press, 1999).

21 Stoic thought regarding bodies was the most influential, but only one among many kinds of thought that treated the concept in this way. In the Stoic view, for anything to exist it had to have extension and qualities that we would attribute to mass (Stoicorum Veterum Fragmenta [SVF], 2.359, 381, 525). Matter is completely indeterminate and passive. In this creation, it always comes in particular forms that are acted upon by God and the kind of action makes the combination corporeal (e.g., SVF 2.310; Diogenes Laertius 7.134). On Stoic corporealism, see David Hahm, *The Origins of Stoic Cosmology* (Columbus: Ohio State University Press, 1977), pp. 3–28, which needs to be combined with Stoic discussions of the human body and soul. The point is well made by Martin (*Corinthian Body*, pp. 104–36), who cites all kinds of views from different periods including medical sources.

22 Martin (ibid., pp. 177–8) makes the highly plausible suggestion that *eis* in this context means into the body rather than against it.

23 Above all, the subjective genitive is superior to the objective because it allows constructions that read as Greek rather than some bizarre uniquely Pauline language. We can no longer tolerate bloopers like the RSV or NRSV (text) translations of Rom. 3: 26 and 4: 16 (i. e., compare the inconsistent translation of exactly the same construction, *ek pisteos Iesou/Abraam*) and a number of other passages. But in addition to syntax, the subjective genitive also, I believe, makes Paul's thought much more coherent and less like a modern thinker. There is more to be said about the syntax (which needs a book-length monograph) and other issues, but for a reasonably up-to-date discussion of the debate, see Hays, *Faith of Jesus Christ*, pp. 249–97.

24 I am not, of course, denying that the faith of the one who is in Christ is "required" for getting in and baptism, but Paul as in many traditional western interpretations does

not make it involve a transaction between God and individual humans that essentially skips over Abraham, Israel and Christ by, for example, making Christ only an object of faith. On this reading, they actually do the work of salvation through God's spirit. Paul certainly does talk about the *pistis* of the believer in several places.

25   I will be drawing on my earlier work and the 2002 Brown University dissertation by Caroline Johnson Hodge entitled, " 'If Sons, then Heirs': a Study of Kinship and Ethnicity in Paul's Letters." For references to Johnson Hodge's important dissertation, forthcoming in a revised form by Oxford University Press, see the notes throughout. The gist of much of the interpretation is summed up in a passage (p. 246) from my *A Rereading of Romans: Justice, Jews and Gentiles* (New Haven, CT: Yale University Press, 1994):

> The apostle likes this formulation of the promise because it contains the idea of descendants and heirs being incorporated into the ancestor who founded the lineage. Thus the promise was made to Christ, who was present in Abraham together with his fellow adoptees, sons of God by the Spirit. Christ is both a descendant by blood and an adoptee by the Spirit in the resurrection (1: 3–4). Paul's language of "predestination" seems also to come from the logic of patriliny: "Those whom he foreknew he also designated beforehand [cf. *horizein* in 1: 4] to be conformed to the image of his son, in order that he might be the first born of among many brothers" (8: 29). God gives and knows all of the line's offspring because they are already in the founder's seed. Thus Abraham's gentile heirs "in Christ" were already "designated beforehand" in Abraham. Just as each generation passes on and shares the "image" of the ancestor, so also those in Christ are brothers sharing with Christ and each other the image of God the father.

      See also pp. 225, 229–30, 280, 283.

26   On ethnic mythmaking in Galatians see Johnson Hodge, " 'All the Gentiles Shall Be Blessed in You' (Gal. 3: 8): Reading Paul's Gospel in Terms of Ethnicity and Kinship" (an unpublished paper); " 'If Sons, Then Heirs,' " pp. 58–123 and ch. 4 on strategies. On related exegesis of Galatians 3, see *Rereading of Romans*, pp. 201, 221, 225, 229–30.

27   For Paul's and ancient use of *ek* phrases for descent, see Johnson Hodge, "All the Gentiles Shall Be Blessed," pp. 80–3.

28   For Paul's use of *en*, see Johnson Hodge, "All the Gentiles Shall Be Blessed," pp. 107–18 and my *A Rereading*, p. 230.

29   I believe that I first heard this suggestion in one of Dahl's seminars in 1974. For the suggestion, see his *Studies in Paul* (Minneapolis: Augsburg, 1977), p. 131.

30   In other words, a person who is about to pass out from dizziness is in no condition to exercise courage or self-control, but physical interruptions are temporary matters that do not destroy the characteristics of the pneuma.

31   Epictetus' dualism of, for example, the moral will versus the flesh is a purely moral dualism due to his Stoic monism, but Paul's is both a moral and an anthropological dualism.

32   Johnson Hodge, "All the Gentiles Shall Be Blessed," pp. 125–37 and my *A Rereading*, p. 246.

33   According to Gen. 1: 26, God and his divine helpers create the human in their image and likeness. As many scholars have pointed out, in some early context this meant that humans were divine offspring.

34   For a similar reading, see Johnson Hodge, " 'If Sons, Then Heirs,' " pp. 112–17.

35   The attempts to negate the role of the passage in the letter by claiming that it is a "non" or "un-Pauline" quotation are misguided and perhaps examples of Christian and

modernist spiritualizing. First, the corpus of Paul's letters is too small to confidently say that an interest in David as ancestor is un-Pauline. The evidence for Paul's interest in Abraham, for example, rests only on a handful of verses in two letters. Second, the case made here and in the Johnson Hodge dissertation illuminates the web of thought that is a context for an interest in David. Third, even if it were a quotation, Paul's discourse provides no reason to think that he did not, as they say, "mean what he said."

36   According to the argument of Romans, God has overcome the injustice of the gentile bondage to passion and desire, and their related alienation from God, by means of Christ's dying so as to pioneer the new righteous life of the pneuma. Christ will also somehow be a key to the current rebellion of most Jews. All are in the moment of Paul's "now" caught up in the apocalyptic apex of sin that is the prelude to God's salvation of all. I argue for this interpretation in *A Rereading*.

37   On the wide influence of Stoic thought, see the remarks by Samuel Sambursky, *The Physical World of Late Antiquity* (Princeton, NJ: Princeton University Press, 1962), p. 4.

38   I owe the idea that the Stoic *krasis* theory might be involved in Paul's thinking to Caroline Johnson Hodge who first proposed the idea in a 1995 graduate seminar at Brown University. See also " 'If Sons, Then Heirs,' " p. 71.

39   Tertullian also famously uses this theory of mixing to explain Christ's divinity by the interpenetration of God's pneuma.

40   A. A. Long, "Body and Soul in Stoicism," *Stoic Studies* (Berkeley: University of California Press, 1996), pp. 224–49.

41   Another example is Denys Whiteley, *The Theology of St. Paul*, 2nd edn. (Oxford: Blackwell, 1974).

42   " 'If Sons, Then Heirs,' " pp. 90–6.

II
Syriac Resources

8

Ephrem the Syrian,
from Hymn on Virginity, 7

Metaphors of the Holy Spirit often compare it to fluids, substances that flow. We have seen water, wind, breath. Here we have another fluid associated with the Spirit, olive oil. Oil is used to anoint kings, and *Christ*, in Greek, means "anointed," or marked with oil. Anointing with oil is also a feature of baptism in many traditions. From the word "Christ" and the baptismal anointing in the name of the Father, the Son, and the Holy Spirit arises a trinitarian formula in which the Father is the Anointer, the Son the Anointed, and the Spirit the Oil.[1]

In addition to the better-known traditions of maintaining the liturgy in Latin or Greek, a third strain of Christian liturgy was developing in Syriac, a Semitic language closely related to Aramaic, and the language of Christians in the Middle East before the Muslim invasions and of some today from Syria through Iraq and Iran to India. The pre-eminent poet of this tradition was Ephrem the Syrian (d. 373). As Kathleen McVey has written, "oil is symbolic of Christ and the salvation brought by him, not only because he is literally 'the Anointed One' . . . but also due to the natural properties of oil: its healing and strengthening properties, its capacity to provide light, its use with pigments for painting an image, its ability to ease forces in conflict, and even its property of floating on water, as Jesus walked on the water!"[2]

Here Ephrem exploits the properties of oil to depict in paint and reflect from its surface to render concrete the way that the Holy Spirit incorporates the diverse and diversifies the corporate while resting actively on Christ.

Ephrem the Syrian, *Hymns on Virginity*, 7, in Sebastian Brock, *The Harp of the Spirit*, 2nd enlarged edn. (San Bernardino, CA: Borgo Press, 1983), pp. 48–9, 51.

from **Hymn on Virginity, 7**

Ephrem the Syrian

A royal portrait is painted with visible colours,
and with oil that all can see is the hidden portrait of our hidden King portrayed
on those who have been signed . . .
This oil is the dear friend of the Holy Spirit, it serves him,
following him like a disciple. . . .
The hidden seal of the Spirit is imprinted by oil on the bodies
of those who are anointed in baptism: thus they are marked in the baptismal mystery. . . .
The face that gazes on a vessel filled with oil
sees its reflection there, and he who gazes hard sets his spiritual gaze thereon
and sees in its symbols Christ. And as the beauty of Christ is manifold,
so the olive's symbols are manifold.
Christ has many facets, and the oil acts as a mirror to them all:
from whatever angle I look at the oil, Christ looks out at me from it.

Notes

1 In Latin, see Irenaeus of Lyons, *Against Heresies*, 3.18.3, 3.6.1, 3.17.1; in Greek, Basil of Caesarea, *On the Holy Spirit*, 12.28. For Syriac olive imagery, see Robert Murray, *Symbols of Christ and Kingdom: A Study in Early Syriac Tradition*, rev. edn. (Edinburgh: T. & T. Clarke, 2006). For the history of liturgical usages, see Gabriele Winkler, "The Original Meaning of the Prebaptismal Anointing and its Implications," in *Living Water, Sealing Spirit* (Collegeville, MN: Liturgical Press, 1995), pp. 58–81.
2 Kathleen McVey, "Introduction," in *Ephrem the Syrian: Hymns*, Classics of Western Spirituality (New York: Paulist Press, 1989), p. 46, citing Ephrem, *Hymns on Virginity*, 4–7.

9

Isaac of Nineveh, [Eating Love]

This passage provides a good example of a text about the Holy Spirit that goes without mentioning the Holy Spirit. Both the references to "love" and the metaphors of "breath" and "smell" tend to indicate the Spirit. The passage refers only to Christ and not to the Spirit, but it would be a mistake to think the Spirit is absent. Rather, the relations between Christ and the Spirit, and between the Eucharist and the Spirit, make the Spirit tacitly present. Many theological texts require this kind of reading between the lines; well-habituated readers learn to catch the implications that a word-search for "spirit" would leave behind. They exemplify the way the Spirit may be said to hover or float over a text, to scent or perfume it, to be in the air.

[Eating Love]

Isaac of Nineveh

When we have found love, we eat the heavenly bread and we are sustained without labor and without weariness. Heavenly bread is that which has descended from heaven and which gives the world life; this is the food of angels. He who has found love eats Christ at all times and becomes immortal from then onwards. Blessed is he that has eaten from the bread of love which is Jesus. Whoever is fed with love is fed with Christ, who is the all-governing God. John witnesses to this when he says: "God is love." Thus he who lives with love in this creation smells life from God; he breathes here the air of the resurrection. Love is the kingdom of which our Lord spoke, when symbolically he promised the disciples that they would eat in his kingdom: "you shall eat and drink at the table of my kingdom."

Isaac of Nineveh, [Eating Love], in *Mystical Treatises*, trans. A. J. Wensinck (Amsterdam: Koninklijke Akademie von Wetenschappen, 1923), pp. 211–12.

What should they eat, if not love? . . . This is the wine that gladdens the heart of the human being . . . This is the wine which the debauched have drunk and they became chaste, the sinners have drunk and they forgot the paths of stumbling, the drunk and they became fasters, the rich and they became desirous of poverty, the poor and they became rich in hope, the sick and they regained strength, the fools and they became wise.

10

Sebastian Brock, *from* The Holy Spirit in the Syrian Baptismal Tradition

In Ephrem the Syrian and Isaac of Nineveh we have seen two samples of Syriac theology. The selection that follows comes from the single most helpful book that I have read about the Holy Spirit. It is that because it surveys a whole literature; a literature somewhat different from the Greek, Latin, German, and Russian traditions of Protestant, Catholic, and Eastern Orthodox theologies well known in the seminaries, divinity schools, and Ph.D. programs of the West; a literature more devoted to poetry than prose, to hymn, homily, and liturgy than treatise; a literature more concrete in its images and closely related to Hebrew and Aramaic in its vocabulary. The ancient liturgical languages of Christianity were not exhausted by Greek and Latin, but also included Syriac, the Semitic language of the Eastern Mediterranean and Mesopotamia before the Arab invasions of Islam, and, as a liturgical language, still sometimes in use. Separated from Greek and Latin churches by language, political dispute carried forward in theological categories, and the rise of Islam, Syriac-liturgy churches today stretch from Syria, Lebanon, and Israel through Iran and Iraq to Kerala in southwest India, where Brock's book was first printed. Some are allied with Rome, some with Constantinople, some call themselves the Church of the East, but they are here presented as if they shared an orthodoxy. The texts discussed by Brock – the dean of Syriac studies for generations at Oxford – abound in concrete connections with liturgical matter: water, oil, fire, and fragrance all signify the Spirit.

Sebastian P. Brock, *The Holy Spirit in the Syrian Baptismal Tradition*, 2nd rev. and enlarged edn., The Syrian Churches Series, 9, ed. Jacob Vellian (Poona, India: Anita Printers, 1998), pp. 1, 4–11, 27–36. Repr. Piscataway, NJ: Gorgias Press, 2008.

from The Holy Spirit in the Syrian Baptismal Tradition

Sebastian Brock

Introduction

Syriac Christianity is unique in that it represents a genuinely Semitic form of the gospel which itself was preached originally in Aramaic. Although the New Testament itself reached Syriac by way of Greek, the thought forms, imagery, and religious vocabulary of the earliest Syriac writers – above all Aphrahat, Ephrem and the liturgical poets – are purely Semitic and owe little or nothing to the influence of Greek culture. As such, Syriac Christianity can genuinely claim to be an indigenous Asian representative of Christianity, and not a European export. This is not, of course, to deny the very great influence which the Greek speaking church subsequently had on all the Syriac churches, in particular over the period c. AD 400–700;[1] but what is important here is that this Greek element – now thoroughly assimilated as part of the general liturgical and literary heritage of the Syriac churches – is a secondary one.

This double heritage, Semitic and Greek, where the two elements are sometimes kept separate, sometimes fused, lends to Syriac tradition a peculiar richness, the effects of which may be seen in almost all spheres of the life of the Christian community. It is a heritage, moreover, which is common to all four churches which employ, or have in the past employed, Syriac as their liturgical language, the Syrian Orthodox, the Maronite, the Melkite,[2] and the Church of the East. . . .

(2) The Holy Spirit in the Syriac Bible

Although 'Spirit of Holiness' is a term that occurs occasionally in the Old Testament (Ps. 51: 12: Isa. 63: 10–11), alongside the very common 'Spirit of the Lord', it will come as a surprise to many that *ruha d-qudsha*, 'Spirit of Holiness' is quite a frequent term in some Jewish texts, in particular the Palestinian tradition of the Aramaic translations of the Old Testament, or Targumim. Whereas Targum Onkelos, the official Babylonian targum, normally employs the term 'Spirit of Prophecy' (a phrase known to some early Syriac writers too), the earlier Palestinian Targum texts prefer 'Spirit of Holiness'. Thus, for example, at Numbers 27: 18, Joshua is described as 'a man on whom there dwells the Spirit of Holiness from before the Lord'.

The word for 'spirit' or 'wind' happens to be feminine in the Semitic languages, and this of course has had certain consequences for the use of the term *ruha* when applied to the Holy Spirit.[3] Early Syriac writers consistently construe *ruha d-qudsha* as a feminine, and it is clear from a few oft-quoted texts that the Holy Spirit was actually regarded as mother in some circles. This understanding is first found in a quotation preserved by Origen and Jerome from the almost wholly lost Gospel according to the Hebrews:[4]

(Christ speaks) Even so did my mother, the Holy Spirit, take me by one of my hairs and carry me away on the great mountain of Tabor.

In Syriac writers it is rare to find the Holy Spirit described specifically as a 'mother', but there is one well-known passage where this is the case: Aphrahat, in his *Demonstration* 18: 10 'On virginity and marital continence (*Qaddishuta*)', denies that Gen. 2: 24 ('a man shall leave his father and mother . . .') refers to ordinary parents:

> Who is it who leaves father and mother to take a wife? The meaning is as follows: as long as a man has not taken a wife, he loves and reveres God his Father and the Holy Spirit his Mother, and he has no other love. But when a man takes a wife, then he leaves his (true) Father and his Mother.

The same interpretation is found in Greek in the Macarian homilies.[5]

We can see how later generations came to object to this description of the Holy Spirit if we look at one of the beautiful invocations to the Spirit in the *Acts of Thomas*. In §27 Judas Thomas stands by the font and anoints the heads of King Gundaphor and his brother, and his prayer includes, in the Greek (but not the Syriac), the words 'Come, compassionate Mother . . .'. Although Syriac was the original language of the *Acts of Thomas*, the surviving texts in this language have undergone a little expurgation, and the phrase 'compassionate Mother' has been dropped as unsuitable, and so survives only in the Greek translation which has received less attention from later editors.

As we shall discover below, the verb *rahhef*, 'to hover', is frequently used of the action of the Holy Spirit, derived from Gen. 1: 2 and Deut. 32: 11. That this is essentially a feminine action in the eyes of Syriac writers can be clearly seen from two comparatively late writers who compare the Holy Spirit to a mother. Sahdona,[6] writing about 600, speaks of the man 'who has been held worthy of the hovering of the all holy Spirit, who, like a mother, hovers over us as she gives sanctification, and through her hovering over us, we are made worthy of sonship'. Nearly three centuries later Moshe bar Kepha[7] describes in a homily how the Holy Spirit 'hovered over John the Baptist and brought him up like a compassionate mother'.

Although we shall find many pointers to the feminine character of the Holy Spirit in the baptismal texts, the actual title 'mother' does not, to my knowledge, occur, and the nearest we come to it is in a baptismal *qolo* [hymn][8] beginning 'stretch out your wings, o holy church, and receive the perfect sheep to whom the Holy Spirit has *given birth* in the baptismal water . . .'

For the majority of the writers, however, it would be unwise to stress their consciousness of the femininity of the Spirit. Moreover it should be remembered that *Logos*, the Word, was also rendered by a feminine Syriac word, *melta*, and in the Old Syriac version of St. John's Gospel it is still construed as a feminine (in the Peshitta [standard Syriac translation of the Bible] however, and in later Syriac writers generally, *melta*, 'Word', is always treated as a masculine). It is in fact quite likely that the existence in second and third century Mesopotamia of a number of pagan triads consisting of father, mother and son (e.g. at Palmyra, Hatra), may have acted, as a deterrent against the development of this sort of imagery in ecclesiastical circles.

From the late fourth, and especially fifth, century onwards, under Greek influence, *ruha*, '(Holy) Spirit', came to be construed as a masculine. In the biblical translations the process has begun in the Peshitta New Testament (though in many places a feminine verb is left), to be completed in a consistent way in the Harklean (and probably already in the Philoxenian) version. In non-biblical texts we find examples of the feminine lingering on into the early centuries of the Islamic period, surviving especially in liturgical texts. For some reason the feminine adjective *qaddishta*, however, tends to be avoided, while a feminine verb after *ruha d-qudsha* is much more likely to survive. On occasions one finds *ruha* construed as both feminine and masculine in the same sentence; and in poets like Jacob of Serugh it seems to be considerations of versification that mainly govern the choice.

Actually it is Jacob of Serugh, together with a number of Syrian Orthodox contemporaries, who preserves one of the rare instances of piece of fundamental exegesis which does seem to be governed by considerations of the gender of *ruha*. In a homily on the Annunciation he stresses on several occasions that the 'Spirit' and 'Power' of Gabriel's greeting in Luke 1: 35 ('The Holy Spirit shall come upon you and the power of the Most High shall overshadow you') are not synonymous, as is commonly assumed to be the case. The Spirit, according to Jacob, came first and his role was to cleanse, while the Power was the Word.[9]

> It was necessary for the Holy Spirit to come before the Only-Begotten; for it was the Spirit, and then the Power, that dwelt in the pure Virgin.

A little below, the 'Power' is again defined:[10]

> The Power of the Most High that is the child from on high: he is Christ, the Power of the Father, as is written.

The same concept is found in both Severus and Philoxenus[11] as well as in other Syrian Orthodox writers, and still features in the *Fenqitho* [collection of propers of fixed feasts].[12] In origin the exegesis would appear to go back to the difficulties that were felt to arise in the verse if the Spirit is regarded as feminine; this can be seen from a remark to be found in the Coptic Gospel of Philip, a work of the second century with Syrian affinities:

> Some have said that Mary conceived of the Holy Spirit. They are wrong, and they do not realize what they are saying, for when did a woman ever conceive of a woman? (§17)

In the biblical texts, and especially in the Old Testament, 'Spirit' is used very often in the sense of an impersonal force, but for the most part the Fathers do not take into account the difference between the impersonal and personal uses of the term 'spirit' in the Bible, and Theodore of Mopsuestia was exceptional in this respect, in that he denied that the Old Testament showed any knowledge of a distinct person or hypostasis of the Spirit.[13] Theodore's historically-minded view, taken over by some East Syrian writers, to some extent anticipates that of modern scholarship.

The other Fathers, however, looked at the matter differently: what the writers of the Old Testament books themselves understood by the term 'spirit' was only of secondary importance to them, since in their view the Church is able to interpret what these writers say in the light of revelation of the Holy Spirit in the New Testament; thus they feel justified in reading back this newly-gained knowledge into the Old Testament. This deeper understanding is on a completely different plane from the purely historical understanding, and should not be confused with it.

Because of this outlook it will be important to look at the activities of the Spirit in the Old, as well as in the New Testament, since the biblical evidence is format-ive in many areas of phraseology and imagery. In the following pages the Peshitta is used throughout, and the Hebrew and Greek are only mentioned when these differ in any notable way.

In the Old Testament the verbs most commonly found where 'spirit' is the sub-ject are as follows:

(1) 'reside upon': Num.11: 26; 2 Kings 2: 15; 2 Chr. 15: 1, 20: 14; Isaiah 11: 2 ('rest and reside upon'; the Hebrew and Greek only have one verb).
(2) 'be upon': Num. 24: 2; Judges 11: 29; 1 Sam. 19: 20, 23.
(3) 'put on': Judges 6: 34 (Greek 'empower'); 1 Chr. 12: 19; 2 Chr. 24: 20.
(4) 'take': 1 Kings 18: 12; 2 Kings 2: 16 (Greek 'find'); Ezra 3: 12, 8: 3, 11: 1 and 24.
(5) 'lead': Ps. 143: 10; Isaiah 63: 14.
(6) 'hover' (*rahhef*): Gen. 1: 2.

Although it only occurs once in connection with the Spirit in both Hebrew and Syriac, the verb *rahhef*, 'hover' is perhaps the most important word of all, for it has become, together with *agen* ('overshadow', taken from the New Testament), a technical term for the action of the Holy Spirit in Syriac writers. The verb is actually quite common in the Peshitta Old Testament (in contrast to the Hebrew), and it trans-lates the Hebrew 'have pity or compassion on' in several places (e.g. Isaiah 27: 11, 30: 18; Jer. 13: 14). The noun *ruhhafa is* also used a number of times, always trans-lating Hebrew words for 'mercy, pity' (e.g. Prov. 3: 22; Isaiah 63: 9). In one passage, Zech. 12: 10, it is specifically associated with 'Spirit': 'spirit of *ruhhafa* and mercy'.

Looking next at passages where 'spirit' is the object of a verb, the most import-ant words are the following:

(1) 'give': Num. 11: 29; Isaiah 42: 1; Ezek. 11: 19.
(2) 'fill with': Exod. 28: 3, 31: 3, 35: 31.
(3) 'pour out': Isaiah 44: 3; Joel 2: 28; Zech. 12: 10.
(4) 'send': Ps. 104: 30; Isaiah 48: 16.
(5) 'partake of': Ps. 51: 11.

In the New Testament, the Old Testament phraseology of Isaiah 11: 2 ('rest upon') is picked up in 1 Peter 4: 14, but apart from this there are a number of new verbs used of the Spirit's activity: the Spirit 'comes'[14] (Luke 1: 35; Acts 1: 8, 19: 16), is upon (Luke 2: 25; cp. Gen. 41: 38 'is in'), 'descends' (Matt. 3: 16, Mark 1: 10; Luke 3: 22, John 1: 32); 'breathes' (John 3: 8), 'dwells in' (Rom. 8: 9, 11; 2 Tim. 1: 14), and above all 'overshadows' (*agen*). This last term, which is hard to translate exactly, has evidently become a technical term for the Spirit's activity from an early date in the Syriac-speaking church, for it is used to render a number of different Greek verbs: thus it translates *episkiazo* 'overshadow', in the Annunciation message of Luke 1: 35, and the same verb again at Acts 5: 15; it translates *epipipto*, 'fall upon', twice used of the Spirit in Acts 10: 44 and 11: 15. With subjects other than 'Spirit' *agen* renders *skenoo* and derivatives in John 1: 14 (where the word is subject), Acts 2: 26, and 2 Cor. 12: 9 (where the 'power of Christ' is subject).

The term *agen* in fact has its background in the Peshitta Old Testament and the Targumim,[15] but never in context of the 'spirit'. In the narrative of Sinai theophany God tells Moses, 'I will cause my hand to overshadow (*agen*) you until I have passed by' (Exod. 33: 22). The Hebrew verb which *agen* translates here is *skk*, 'hedge in, protect'; in the light of the etymologically related word *gnuna*, 'bridal chamber', it is interesting that the Syriac translators have evidently associated the Hebrew verb *sakak* with *sukkah*, 'canopy, tabernacle, or booth,' used in the Jewish wedding ceremony (compare also the Peshitta at Job 1: 10, 3: 23).

Elsewhere *agen* always translates Hebrew verbs meaning 'protect' (e.g., 2 Kings 19: 34; Isaiah 31: 5; cp. also Wisdom 5: 16). In the Old Testament texts the 'Lord' is always subject of the verb, and it is only in writings or the intertestamental period that we find a shift in usage: in Wisdom 19: 8 the Lord's 'hand' is subject (developed from passages such as Exod. 33: 22, and Ps. 138: 8, 'cause your hand to overshadow me, Lord'); in Ben Sira 23: 18d the subject is 'shade', while in IV Ezra 7: 122 it is 'the glory of the Most High' which will 'overshadow those who have lived in chastity'.

Seeing that *agen*, 'overshadow', has become a technical term in Syriac, it is very possible that the non-biblical Greek word *epiphoitao*, itself frequently used of the Spirit's activity in liturgical and patristic Greek texts, is in fact a rendering of *agen* which originated in a bilingual, Syriac-Greek-speaking area. Certainly the converse is found, for *epiphoitao* occurs in the epiclesis of the Greek Anaphora of St. James, and in the Syriac eucharistic epicleses modelled on this anaphora this verb is rendered either by *agen* or *rahhef* (or derivative nouns).

There is one important New Testament passage, however, where *agen* is not used; this is in the Transfiguration narrative, where the Greek *episkiazo is* rendered by *atel*, 'give shadow', in Matt. 17: 5 = Mark 9: 7 = Luke 9: 34.

Turning to transitive verbs where the Spirit is subject, we find 'seize' (Acts 8: 39), 'teach' (Luke 12: 12; John 14: 26), 'comfort' (Acts 9: 31 where the Peshitta uses a noun rather than a verb), 'search out' (1 Cor. 2: 10), 'give life to' (2 Cor. 3: 6), 'announce, make known' (John 16: 13f. with different verbs in the Old Syriac and Peshitta; Heb. 9: 8), 'testify' (Acts 20: 23; Heb. 10: 15) and 'lead' (John 16: 13; cp. Mark 4: 1; Luke 4: 1). Only the last of these has its basis in the Old Testament.

Where the Spirit is the object of a verb, however, the Old Testament provides the model for 'give' (Luke 11: 13 etc.), 'send' John 14: 26; Gal. 4: 6), and 'pour out' (Acts 2: 17–18; Tit. 3: 5). New verbs are 'receive' (John 20: 22), 'quench' (1 Thess. 5: 19) and 'grieve' (Eph. 4: 30).

Finally two negative points should be made: the verb *shken*, 'reside', is only used of birds in the Syriac New Testament (Matt. 16: 37 Old Syriac; Mark 4: 32 Peshitta). In view of the importance of this verb – and especially the noun Shekina[16] – in Jewish literature, this is not without interest. Secondly, it should be noted that the Johannine name for the Spirit, *parakletos*, is simply transliterated in the Syriac Gospels; in earlier Syriac writers the term is not at all common (perhaps due to the fact that Mani had appropriated it to himself).

The Syriac Bible serves as the source for most of the phraseology employed by the later liturgical texts in connection with the activities of the spirit. Besides *rahhef* and *agen*, three other verbs with biblical antecedents would seem to be particularly characteristic of Syriac tradition: come, rest and reside on. One group of verbs, however, stands out as having no obvious biblical origin: in early Syriac tradition the Holy Spirit 'mixes' or 'mingles'[17] in with the baptismal water, the bread and the wine, and the baptized themselves. To quote but a single example, according to Ephrem, Christ came to baptism 'in order to mix (*da-nmazzeg*) the invisible Spirit in with the visible water.'[18]

The symbols of the Spirit

In the early Christian writers three symbols of the Holy Spirit stand out: fire, dove and the oil. Of these by far the most prominent and important in Syriac tradition is that of fire.

(1) The Holy Spirit as fire

In the 73rd of his *Hymns on Faith* Ephrem provides, as an illustration of the Trinity, the example of the sun: the sun corresponds to the Father, the light to the Son, and the heat to the Spirit (Hymns *De fide* 73.1). The analogy is particularly helpful, in Ephrem's eyes, in the way it helps to explain the penetration of the Holy Spirit into the created world:

> The might of the Spirit's heat resides
> in everything, with everything,
> yet it is wholly with the One
> and is not cut off from the Radiance,
> being mixed in it, nor from the Sun,
> being mingled with it.
>> (H. Fid. 74, 3–4)

The Holy Spirit as fire above all consecrates:

> In fire is the symbol of the Spirit,
> it is a type of the Holy Spirit
> who is mixed in the baptismal water
> so that it may be for absolution,
> and in the bread,
> that it may be an offering.
>> (H. Fid. 40.10)

The consecrating fire of the Holy Spirit has its origins in the Old Testament, where, besides such passages as Isaiah 6, the descent of fire on a sacrifice is seen as the sign of its acceptance (e.g. 2 Chr. 7: 1). This was a concept that was much extended in post-biblical Judaism and in early Christianity. In the Targum to the Song of Songs 5: 1 God is represented as saying that, as a sign of his acceptance of Solomon's sacrifice in the Temple (2 Chr. 7: 1), 'I sent fire from heaven and so I consumed the whole offerings and the sacred sacrifice.' Theodosius, the Jewish Greek translator of the Old Testament, rendered Gen. 4: 4 with the words 'and God *burnt up* Abel's offering', thus providing an explanation of how Abel knew that his sacrifice had been accepted. Aphrahat, in his *Demonstration* 4 on Prayer, lists the Old Testament instances of the descent of fire to assure his correspondent that 'when Abel and Cain offered up their offerings both together, living fire, which was doing service before God, came down and licked up Abel's pure sacrifice, but did not touch Cain's because it was impure' (*Dem.* 4.2).

The Holy Spirit as 'fire' thus has two aspects: the fire is a sign of acceptance of a sacrifice, and at the same time it also consecrates it. In the case of the coming of the Holy Spirit on to the baptismal oil and water the former aspect is of course not applicable, but at the Eucharist both aspects are very much present.

The consecrating role of the fire can be seen very well in the Syriac *Acts of John*: the Apostle prays over the baptismal oil and 'immediately flaming fire was there over the oil, without the oil itself burning.[19] Fire *over* the baptismal water was seen by Constantine, according to Jacob of Serugh's poem on his baptism.[20] More frequently, however, the water itself is described as going up in flames; this goes back to an ancient tradition that the Jordan went up in flames at Christ's own baptism.[21] In the case of Christ's own baptism it is of course Christ himself who effects this, not the Holy Spirit (though Jacob speaks of 'the Spirit of Christ' going ahead and heating the water); in Christian baptism, however, it is the Holy Spirit who sets aflame the water. Thus in the long list of exorcisms common to the Maronite service and the Syrian Orthodox one attributed to Timothy we find: 'the Father rejoices, the Son exults, the Spirit hovers; the baptismal water is set aflame with fire and the Spirit . . .'.

At the Eucharist the descent of the Holy Spirit as fire at the epiclesis similarly consecrates the bread and wine; as a poem by Balai, on the consecration of a church at Qenneshrin, puts it: 'the priests stands, he kindles fire (i.e., by uttering the epiclesis), he takes bread, but gives forth the Body, he receives wine, but distributes the Blood.'[22]

The 'fire' of the Holy Spirit is also imparted to the baptized in the Eucharist, thus effecting a continuing process of sanctification in them. Ephrem's tenth *Hymn on Faith is* worth quoting at length in this context:

> In your Bread there is hidden the Spirit who is not consumed,
> in your Wine there dwells the Fire that is not drunk:
> the Spirit is in your Bread, the Fire in your Wine,
> a manifest wonder, which our lips have received.
>
> When the Lord came down to earth to mortal men
> he created them again in a new creation, like angels,

> mingling Fire and Spirit within them,
> so that in a hidden manner they might be of Fire and Spirit.
>
> The Seraph could not touch the fire's coal with his fingers,
> but just brought it close to Isaiah's mouth:
> the Seraph did not hold it, Isaiah did not consume it,
> but us our Lord has allowed to do both.
>
> To the angels who are spiritual Abraham brought
> food for the body, and they ate. The new miracle
> is that our mighty Lord has given to bodily man
> Fire and Spirit to eat and drink.
>
> Fire descended in wrath and consumed sinners,
> the Fire of mercy descended and dwelt in the bread.
> Instead of that fire which consumed mankind,
> you have consumed Fire in the Bread and you come to life.
> Fire descended and consumed Elijah's sacrifices,
> the Fire of mercies has become a living sacrifice for us:
> Fire consumed the oblation,
> and we, Lord, have consumed your Fire in your oblation.
>
> (H. Fid. 10. 8–13)

Fire, like water, is an ambiguous symbol – it can also be destructive. But in the case of the Holy Spirit as fire, what is destroyed is only what is impure or evil:

> Your Bread slays the Greedy one who had made us his food,
> your cup destroys Death who had swallowed us up.
>
> We have eaten you, O Lord, we have drunken you –
> not that we would consume you up, but through you we shall be saved.
>
> (H. Fid. 10. 18)

Or

> When Moses signed and anointed
>   the sons of the Levite Aaron,
> fire consumed their bodies,
>   fire preserved their clothes.
> Blessed are you, my brothers,
>   for the fire of mercy has come down,
> utterly devouring your sins,
>   purifying and sanctifying your bodies.
>
> (*Hymns on Epiphany* 3.10)

Narsai adapts the same idea to the font:[23]

> As though in a furnace the priest recasts bodies in the baptismal water; and as in a fire he consumes the weeds of mortality . . . by the heat of the Spirit he purges away the rust of body and soul.

We are not far here from the eschatological imagery of the 'river of fire'.[24]

In many passages the concept of the Holy Spirit as fire is tied up with the image of the pearl, much beloved by Syriac writers. According to ancient mythology, when lightning strikes the mussel in the sea, the mussel opens as a direct result of this conjunction of disparate elements, fire and water.[25] In his famous set of five poems on the Pearl,[26] Ephrem meditates on the many analogies with the Incarnation that the pearl offers: Christ the Pearl is born through the coming of the Fire of the Holy Spirit upon Mary the mussel. From an early date the consecrated Eucharistic elements also came to acquire the technical name of 'pearls.' 'Christ gave us pearls, his Body and holy Blood', says Ephrem in his *memra* on the Sinful Woman.[27] Here again it is the descent of the 'Fire' at the epiclesis which has given rise to the terminology. As Jacob of Serugh puts in his *Homily on Ezekiel's Chariot*, in the context of the cherubs' 'coals of fire':[28]

> It is not the priest who is authorized to sacrifice the Only-Begotten
> or to raise up that sacrifice for sinners to the Father's presence:
> rather, the Holy Spirit goes forth from the Father
> and descends, overshadows and resides in the bread,
> making it the Body, and making it treasured pearls
> to adorn the souls that are betrothed by him.

As a final example to illustrate the activities of the 'Fire of the Spirit' we may quote a fine passage of Sahdona, where he compares prayer to a sacrifice:[29]

> The beginning of our prayer should be watchful and alert, and with suffering of heart we should let streams of tears pour down our cheeks. The whole of our service should be completed according to the will of God, so that it may be without spot and acceptable to him. Then the Lord will be pleased with us and take pleasure in our offering; smelling the sweet scent of the pure whole-offering of our heart he will send the fire of his Spirit and consume our sacrificial offerings, raising up our mind with them in the flame to heaven, and we shall see the Lord, our delight, without perishing, as the stillness of his revelation falls upon us and the hidden things of his knowledge are depicted in us. The spiritual joy settles in our heart, together with hidden mysteries which cannot readily be described in words for the simple. In this way we should make our bodies a living, holy and acceptable sacrifice that is pleasing to God in our rational service.

(2) The Holy Spirit as a dove

At Christ's baptism the Holy Spirit descended in the *likeness* of a dove, and on the basis of this episode the dove has, from at least the fifth century on, been a regular symbol of the Holy Spirit in Christian art.[30] In the sixth century, however, both Severus and Philoxenus objected to the use of this symbolism in the fashion for making 'eucharistic doves'; their objection did not stem (as has sometimes been supposed) from iconoclast tendencies, but from the pagan associations of the dove in the pre-Christian cult centred at Mabbugh.[31] It is perhaps because of such pagan connotations that 'dove' symbolism is not so prominent in Syriac writers as it is in those of other Christian traditions.

There is, however, one early text where the image of the dove is prominent, the 24th of the Odes of Solomon which opens:

> The dove flew over the head of our Lord Christ
> for he was her head;
> she sang above him
> and her voice was heard . . .

The scene of this very obscure poem is certainly Christ's baptism, but it is not clear whether the dove is used as a symbol of the Holy Spirit, or whether the author did not yet know the Gospel accounts and was simply using the bird as a recognition motif.[32]

It is possible that the vocabulary of 'flying', very frequently found in connection with the activities of the Spirit, derives from the imagery of the Holy Spirit as a dove, but then it could just as well have had its origin in the use of the verb *rahhef* 'hover' in Gen. 1: 2, or the phrase 'wings of the Spirit/wind' in Ps. 104: 3, both passages frequently alluded to by Syriac writers. (The Gospel accounts of Christ's baptism do not use 'fly', only 'come down').

Passages such as the following,[33] where the Holy Spirit is described straightforwardly as a dove, seem to be exceptional:

> Come, my brethren, let us go and see that Tree planted by the streams of water, whose leaves never fall. In its summit the heavenly Eagle makes its nest, in its branches, the Dove the Holy Spirit; its roots pour forth the water of baptism, into which sinners go down to be baptized, and come up pure.

On the whole Syriac writers prefer to use 'dove' imagery in quite a different context, and derived from another biblical passage, Song of Songs 6: 8: it is Mary who is the dove, and she bears the heavenly Eagle,[34] the 'Ancient of Days' (Dan. 7: 9), as in the following beautiful stanza:[35]

> A young dove, she carried
> the Eagle, the Ancient of days,
> singing praise as she carried him
> in her lovely songs:
> 'O my Son most rich, in a tiny nest
> you have chosen to grow; melodious harp,
> you are silent like a child, please let me sing to you
> with the lyre whose chords stir the Cherubim;
> pray let me speak to you.'

Later poets, such as Jacob of Serugh,[36] take up this imagery of Mary as the dove, and develop it in many different ways.

There would seem, then, to be tendency in most Syrian writers to move away from seeing the dove as a symbol of the Holy Spirit, and to transfer the imagery to Mary. This can already be observed in Ephrem's typological treatment of the dove at Christ's baptism, which he sees as prefigured by Noah's dove (Gen. 8: 9–11), the bearer of the olive leaf:

> The ark marked out by its course the sign of its preserver,
> the cross of its steersman, and the wood of its sailor
> who has come to fashion for us a church in the water of baptism:
> with the three-fold name he rescues those who in her live;
> in the place of the dove, the Spirit ministers her anointing
> and the mystery of her salvation. Praises to her Saviour.
>
> (H. Fid. 49. 4)

Although Noah's dove here serves as a type of the Holy Spirit in Christian baptism, Ephrem also implies an element of contrast; in another poem he shifts away from this altogether, and prefers to see Noah's dove as 'related to Mary'[37] instead:

> The dove gave comfort to Noah in the flood, and related to the dove is Mary
> [John 12: 3–5]:
> instead of a leaf, she depicted symbolically the death of the Son by means of fine oil;
> in the alabaster vase that she poured over him, she emptied out on him a treasury
> of types:
> at that moment the symbols of oil found their home in Christ,
> and oil, that treasurer of symbols, handed over the symbols to the Lord of symbols.
> Creation conceived the symbols of him, but Mary conceived his actual limbs.
>
> (Hymns on Virginity 6–7)

In that Noah's dove brings an olive branch, it is also understood as conveying olive oil; as one of the Epiphany hymns ascribed to Ephrem puts it, more directly:

> The olive leaf arrived
>   carrying the symbol of anointing;
> those in the ark rejoiced at its coming
>   for it brought the message of salvation.
> You [sc. the baptized] too rejoiced at the coming
>   of this holy oil;
> your bodies laden with guilt were joyful,
>   for it brought the same message of salvation.
>
> (H. Epiph. 3: 8)

This brings us to our next point.

(3) The Holy Spirit and olive oil/myron

Olive oil is very closely associated with the Holy Spirit in the Syriac literature, but this is because oil was understood as the ideal 'conductor' for the power of the Spirit, rather than as an actual symbol of the Spirit.[38] As Ephrem puts it:

> This oil is the dear friend of the Holy Spirit, it serves him, following him like a disciple. (H. Virg. 7.6. 1–2)

Thanks to the play on words available in Syriac, the olive oil *(meshha)* is much more commonly understood as a symbol of Christ *(meshha* 'the anointed') in our texts;[39] as Ephrem puts it later on in the same poem:

From whatever angle I look at the oil, Christ looks out at me from it. (*H. Virg.* 7.14.6)

There is, however, another important biblical passage which associates the Spirit with oil and anointing, Isaiah 61: 1. The Septuagint version, which is quoted in Luke 4: 18 (cp. Acts 10: 38), reads 'The Spirit of the Lord is upon me, wherefore he has anointed me'; here the Spirit is the subject of the verb 'anointed', but this is not the case in either the original Hebrew or in the Peshitta Old Testament, which have 'wherefore the Lord has anointed me'.

In the later baptismal commentaries it is stated that 'the holy Mar Severus says in one of his writings that the myron typifies the Holy Spirit.'[40] The source for this statement is Severus' letter to John the soldier or 'Roman', where he speaks of 'perfecting' Arians who are received into the orthodox church and says that they are 'imprinted with myron and that 'we thus indicate that the Holy Spirit, whose type this imprint is, is the perfecter of the gift that is given by baptism'. Characteristically the Syriac commentators prefer to see the myron as symbolizing Christ, rather than the Holy Spirit.

Notes

1 As a matter of fact this Greek element was itself largely the product of the bilingual Greek-Aramaic/Syriac culture of Syria-Palestine: in liturgy and hymnography, as well as in art and architecture, Syria-Palestine appears to have been one of the most creative areas of the late antique world.

2 Syriac was used (often, since the 11th century, alongside Arabic) in Melkite liturgical texts up to the 15th or 16th century.

3 The Holy Spirit of course also inherits much imagery from the feminine figure of Wisdom, popular in post-exilic Judaism.

4 E. Henneke and W. Schneemelcher, *New Testament Apocrypha* (London: Lutterworth Press, 1963), vol. I, p. 164.

5 See R. Murray, *Symbols of Church and Kingdom: A Study in Early Syriac Tradition* (Cambridge: Cambridge University Press, 1975), p. 318 (and in general on this subject, pp. 142–50, 312–20). In the *Didascalia* (§9; ed. Lagarde, p. 36) the deacons are said to represent Christ, but the deaconesses the Holy Spirit.

6 André de Halleux, ed., Martyrius (Sahdona), *Oeuvres Spirituelles*, 2 vols. (Louvain: Secrétariat du Corpus SCO, 1960), vol. 1, p. 32.

7 Nurse, ed., *American Journal of Semitic Languages and Literature* 26 (1909/10), p. 95.

8 Homs edn. of Severus, p. 43.

9 Paul Bedjan, ed., *Homilies* in *S. Martyrii qui et Sahdona quae supersunt* (Paris, 1902), p. 631 (cp. pp. 642, 682, 733).

10 Ibid., p. 632.

11 E.g. Severus, *Philalethes*, ed. and trans. R. Hespel (Louvain: L. Durbecq, 1952), p. 132; Philoxenus, *De Trinitate et Incarnatione*, ed. A. A. Vaschalde (Paris: E Typographeo Reipublicae, 1907), p. 95; *Letter to the Monks of Senun* (ed. A. de Halleux), p. 60.

12 E.g. *Fenqitho=Breviarium iuxta Ritum Ecclesiae Antiochenae Syrorum* (Mosul, 1886–96), IV, p. 872a.

13 *Commentary on Haggai*, PG [Patrologia Graeca] 66, col. 486.

14 In the Hebrew Old Testament the Spirit *'comes* on me' in Ezek. 3: 24, but the Peshitta translates by 'enters in'.

15 E.g. Targum Exodus 12: 13 'I will overshadow (protect) you with my Memra'. The verb is understood as being etymologically related to Hebrew *magen* 'shield'.

16 In some (late?) East Syrian liturgical texts the corresponding form *shkinta* is quite often found. The verb is occasionally used in epiclesis, e.g. *Liturgia sanctorum apostolorum Adaei et Maris* (Urmia: Press of the Archbishop of Canterbury's Mission, 1890), p. 68 (oil).

17 *Mazzeg, hlat* (e.g. Urmia, p. 67 [oil]). The only possible biblical source seems to be Isaiah 19: 14. Syriac writers also frequently speak of the baptized being 'mingled' in the flock (e.g. *Acts of Thomas* 156: 'mingle them in your sheep' and often in the *ordines* themselves), for which compare Gen. 30: 40. The verbs are also used of the union of the divine and human natures of Christ (as *sunkerannumi* in some early Greek writers), though later on this language fell into disrepute.

18 *Sermo de Domino Nostro* §55.

19 William Wright, ed., *Apochryphal Acts of the Apostles* (London: Williams and Norgate, 1871), p. 42, cp. p. 58 (repr. Amsterdam: Philo Press, 1968).

20 A. L. Frothingham, ed., Jacob of Serug, *L'omelia di Giacomo di Sarûg sul battesimo di Costantino imperatore* (Rome: Accademia nazionale dei Lincei, 1882), pp. 235–6.

21 See especially C. M. Edsman, *Le Baptême de feu* (Uppsala: Almovist & Wiksells, 1940), pp. 182–90.

22 J. J. Overbeck, ed., *S. Ephraemi Syri, Rabulae episcopi Edesseni, Balaei aliorumque opera selecta* (Oxford: Clarendon Press, 1865), p. 252.

23 A. Mingana, ed. and trans., *Narsai Doctoris Syri homilae et carmina* (Mosul, 1905), I, p. 343 (repr. Piscataway, NJ: Gorgias Press, 2007).

24 On which see Edsman, *Le Baptême*, pp. 57–63.

25 Cp. ibid., pp. 190–9.

26 Hymns *de Fide*, 81–5.

27 *Sermones*, II.iv. 9–10.

28 Bedjan, ed., *Homilies*, IV, p. 597.

29 de Halleux, ed., Martyrius, III, p. 7.

30 Among Syriac illuminated manuscripts, see for example the illustration of Pentecost in the Rabula Gospels of AD 586 (J. Leroy, *Les manuscripts syriaques à peintures* [Paris, 1964], II, plate 34; cp. plate 73.4, Annunciation in Vat. Syr. 559). In the (late) Targum to the Song of Songs, the turtle-dove of 2: 12 becomes the 'Holy Spirit of salvation'.

31 Cp. my 'Iconoclasm and Monophysites', in *Iconoclasm*, ed. A. Bryer and J. Herrin (Birmingham: Centre for Byzantine Studies, 1977), p. 54.

32 So S. Gero, 'The Spirit as Dove at the Baptism of Jesus', *Novum Testamentum* 18 (1976), pp. 17–35.

33 *Fenqitho*, III, pp. 259b–60a (Lilyo [right office] on Epiphany).

34 Here of course the Son, in contrast to the extract just cited. Christ as an 'eagle' is quite common in Syriac writers, e.g. Ephrem, *H. Eccl.* (*Hymns on the Church*), 1.3.4; *Sermones*, II.iv.58; *H. Nativ.* (*Hymns on the Nativity*), 4.3; Cyrillona (ed. G. Bickell [Munich: J. Kösel, 1912]), p. 573; Jacob of Serugh (ed. Bedjan), II, p. 675, *Homilies*, p. 767; *Fenqitho*, II, p. 102b, etc.

35 T. J. Lamy, ed., *Sancti Ephraem Syri Hymni et Sermones*, 4 vols. (Mallines: H. Dassein, 1886), II, col. 543 (Hymns on Mary).

36 E.g. Bedjan, ed., *Homilies*, p. 742 (Mary the dove visits Elizabeth the eagle); p. 767 (mankind is the dove, Christ the eagle), in Overbeck, *S. Ephraemi Syri*, p. 396 (the Church

is the dove). Gregory of Nyssa in his commentary to Song of Songs 6: 8 describes the Holy Spirit at Christ's baptism as 'the Mother of the chosen dove (i.e. the Church)'.

37 Ephrem here as elsewhere fuses the two Mary's together (for this feature see Murray, *Symbols*, pp. 146–8, 329–35).

38 Note, however, the anonymous East Syrian commentator (ed. Connolly), II, p. 104: 'The horn of oil represents the Holy Spirit'; and Isho'yahb I (J. B. Chabot, ed., in *Synodicon Orientale* [Paris: Imprimerie Nationale, 1902]), pp. 186–445: 'the holy oil of anointing symbolizes the garment of sonship and of incorruption, and is the promise of the anointing that comes from the Holy Spirit', Timothy II, *On the Sacraments* III (Vat. Syr. 150). Likewise Daniel of Tella comments on Ps. 23: 5 ('my head with oil'): 'by the "head" he means the mind which receives the gifts of the Holy Spirit at baptism: with the baptismal anointing there enters into the soul the divine draught which makes it drunk'; and on Ps. 45:.8 he comments: 'the "oil" is the Holy Spirit who came down upon our Lord in the Jordan' (Harvard syr. 75, f. 76, 109).

39 Christ is also the olive, the source of oil: cp. Murray, *Symbols*, pp. 322–4.

40 E.g., Moshe bar Kepha, *On Myron*, 13.

III
Early Greek Resources

11

Cyril of Jerusalem, from Catechetical Oration 16

One of the remarkable things about this oration is its personalizing use of "Living Water" imagery for the Spirit. Several fluids – water, wind, oil, even fire – prevail among apparently impersonal metaphors for the Spirit. Biblical images of water can even lead to entire trinities: "Source" for the Father, "Wellspring" for the Son, and "Living Water" for the Spirit.[1] The image of water for the Spirit is particularly appropriate in the context of baptism, and their title suggests that Cyril has directed these orations to catechumens, those who are being instructed in Christianity for baptism. If water images for the Spirit are not to be merely pieces of theological engineering, they will need to go beyond hydraulics to invest the metaphor with personal force. The water must describe a kind of personal action. That is the case here. For the water produces both biological diversity in creation, and personal diversity among Christians. Here Cyril has hit on a pattern of language that renders the recipients of the Spirit more distinctive, more individual, more personal, even more odd, by having received the common Spirit. Here the baptismal Spirit follows the eucharistic pattern, that it incorporates the diverse, and diversifies the corporate. Cyril portrays the fruits of the Spirit, like those nourished by water, as unimaginably particular and various. The Spirit, you might say, varies and distinguishes.

Excerpt from Cyril of Jerusalem, *Catechetical Orations*, in *A Select Library of the Nicene and Post-Nicene Fathers of the Christian Church*, Second Series, ed. Philip Schaff et al., in several editions, vol. 7.

from Lecture XVI: "On the Article, and in One Holy Ghost, the Comforter, which Spake in the Prophets"

Cyril, Archbishop of Jerusalem

1 Corinthians xii. 1, 4: Now concerning spiritual gifts, brethren, I would not have you ignorant. . . . Now there are diversities of gifts, but the same Spirit.

1.   Spiritual in truth is the grace we need, in order to discourse concerning the Holy Spirit; not that we may speak what is worthy of Him, for this is impossible, but that by speaking the words of the divine Scriptures, we may run our course without danger. For a truly fearful thing is written in the Gospels, where Christ has plainly said, *Whosoever shall speak a word against the Holy Ghost, it shall not be forgiven him, neither in this world, nor in that which is to come.*[2] And there is often fear, lest a man should receive this condemnation, through speaking what He ought not concerning Him, either from ignorance, or from supposed reverence. The Judge of quick and dead, Jesus Christ, declared that he hath no forgiveness; if therefore any man offend, what hope has he?

2.   It must therefore belong to Jesus Christ's grace itself to grant both to us to speak without deficiency, and to you to hear with discretion; for discretion is needful not to them only who speak, but also to them that hear, lest they hear one thing, and misconceive another in their mind. Let us then speak concerning the Holy Ghost nothing but what is written; and whatsoever is not written, let us not busy ourselves about it. The Holy Ghost Himself spake the Scriptures; He has also spoken concerning Himself as much as He pleased, or as much as we could receive. Let us therefore speak those things which He has said; for whatsoever He has not said, we dare not say.

3.   There is One Only Holy Ghost, the Comforter; and as there is One God the Father, and no second Father; – and as there is One Only-begotten Son and Word of God, who hath no brother; – so is there One Only Holy Ghost, and no second spirit equal in honour to Him. Now the Holy Ghost is a Power most mighty, a Being divine and unsearchable; for He is living and intelligent, a sanctifying principle of all things made by God through Christ. He it is who illuminates the souls of the just; He was in the Prophets, He was also in the Apostles in the New Testament. Abhorred be they who dare to separate the operation of the Holy Ghost! There is One God, the Father, Lord of the Old and of the New Testament; and One Lord, Jesus Christ, who was prophesied of in the Old Testament, and came in the New; and One Holy Ghost, who through the Prophets preached of Christ, and when Christ was come, descended, and manifested Him.

4.   Let no one therefore separate the Old from the New Testament; let no one say that the Spirit in the former is one, and in the latter another; since thus he offends against the Holy Ghost Himself, who with the Father and the Son together is honoured, and at the time of Holy Baptism is included with them in the Holy

Trinity. For the Only-begotten Son of God said plainly to the Apostles, *Go ye, and make disciples of all the nations, baptizing them into the name of the Father, and of the Son, and of the Holy Ghost.*³ Our hope is in Father, and Son, and Holy Ghost. We preach not three Gods; let the Marcionites be silenced; but with the Holy Ghost through One Son, we preach One God. The Faith is indivisible; the worship inseparable. We neither separate the Holy Trinity, like some; nor do we as Sabellius work confusion. But we know according to godliness One Father, who sent His Son to be our Saviour; we know One Son, who promised that He would send the Comforter from the Father; we know the Holy Ghost, who spake in the Prophets, and who on the day of Pentecost descended on the Apostles in the form of fiery tongues, here, in Jerusalem, in the Upper Church of the Apostles; for in all things the choicest privileges are with us. Here Christ came down from heaven; here the Holy Ghost came down from heaven. And in truth it were most fitting, that as we discourse concerning Christ and Golgotha here in Golgotha, so also we should speak concerning the Holy Ghost in the Upper Church; yet since He who descended there jointly partakes of the glory of Him who was crucified here, we here speak concerning Him also who descended there: for their worship is indivisible.

11   . . . [L]et us return to the divine Scriptures, and let us *drink waters out of our own cisterns* [that is, the holy Fathers], *and out of our own springing wells.*⁴ Drink we of *living water, springing up into everlasting life;*⁵ but this spake the Saviour *of the Spirit, which they that believe on Him should receive.*⁶ For observe what He says, *He that believeth on Me* (not simply this, but), *as the Scripture hath said* (thus He hath sent thee back to the Old Testament), *out of his belly shall flow rivers of living water*, not rivers perceived by sense, and merely watering the earth with its thorns and trees, but bringing souls to the light. And in another place He says, *But the water that I shall give him, shall be in him a well of living water springing up into everlasting life*, – a new kind of water, living and springing up, springing up unto them who are worthy.

12.   And why did He call the grace of the Spirit water? Because by water all things subsist; because water brings forth grass and living things; because the water of the showers comes down from heaven; because it comes down one in form, but works in many forms. For one fountain watereth the whole of Paradise, and one and the same rain comes down upon all the world, yet it becomes white in the lily; and red in the rose; and purple in violets and hyacinths; and different and varied in each several kind; so it is one in the palm-tree, and another in the vine, and all in all things; and yet is one in nature, not diverse from itself; for the rain does not change itself, and come down first as one thing, then as another, but adapting itself to the constitution of each thing which receives it, it becomes to each what is suitable.⁷ Thus also the Holy Ghost, being one, and of one nature, and indivisible, divides to each His grace, *according as He will:*⁸ and as the dry tree, after partaking of water, puts forth shoots, so also the soul in sin, when it has been through repentance made worthy of the Holy Ghost, brings forth clusters of righteousness. And though He is One in nature, yet many are the virtues which by the will of God and in the Name of Christ He works. For He employs the tongue of one man for wisdom; the soul of another He enlightens by Prophecy; to another He gives

power to drive away devils; to another He gives to interpret the divine Scriptures. He strengthens one man's self-command; He teaches another the way to give alms; another He teaches to fast and discipline himself; another He teaches to despise the things of the body; another He trains for martyrdom: diverse in different men, yet not diverse from Himself, as it is written, *But the manifestation of the Spirit is given to every man to profit withal. For to one is given through the Spirit the word of wisdom; and to another the word of knowledge according to the same Spirit; to another faith; in the same Spirit; and to another gifts of healing; in the same Spirit; and to another workings of miracles; and to another prophecy; and to another discernings of spirits; and to another divers kinds of tongues; and to another the interpretation of tongues: but all these worketh that one and the same Spirit, dividing to every man severally as He will.*[9]

22.   Great indeed, and all-powerful in gifts, and wonderful, is the Holy Ghost. Consider, how many of you are now sitting here, how many souls of us are present. He is working suitably for each, and being present in the midst, beholds the temper of each, beholds also his reasoning and his conscience, and what we say, and think, and believe. Great indeed is what I have now said, and yet is it small. For consider, I pray, with mind enlightened by Him, how many Christians there are in all this diocese, and how many in the whole province of Palestine, and carry forward thy mind from this province, to the whole Roman Empire; and after this, consider the whole world; races of Persians; and nations of Indians, Goths and Sarmatians, Gauls and Spaniards, and Moors, Libyans and Ethiopians, and the rest for whom we have no names; for of many of the nations not even the names have reached us. Consider, I pray, of each nation, Bishops, Presbyters, Deacons, Solitaries, Virgins, and laity besides; and then behold their great Protector, and the Dispenser of their gifts; – how throughout the world He gives to one chastity, to another perpetual virginity, to another almsgiving, to another voluntary poverty, to another power of repelling hostile spirits. And as the light, with one touch of its radiance sheds brightness on all things, so also the Holy Ghost enlightens those who have eyes; for if any from blindness is not vouchsafed His grace, let him not blame the Spirit, but his own unbelief.

24.   He preached concerning Christ in the Prophets; He wrought in the Apostles; He to this day seals the soul in Baptism. And the Father indeed gives to the Son; and the Son shares with the Holy Ghost. For it is Jesus Himself, not I, who says, *All things are delivered unto Me of My Father;*[10] and of the Holy Ghost He says, *When He, the Spirit of Truth, shall come, and the rest . . . He shall glorify Me; for He shall receive of mine, and shall shew it unto you.*[11] The Father through the Son, with the Holy Ghost, is the giver of all grace; the gifts of the Father are none other than those of the Son, and those of the Holy Ghost; for there is one Salvation, one Power, one Faith; One God, the Father; One Lord, His only-begotten Son; One Holy Ghost, the Comforter. And it is enough for us to know these things; but inquire not curiously into His nature or substance:[12] for had it been written, we would have spoken of it; what is not written, let us not venture on; it is sufficient for our salvation to know, that there is Father, and Son, and Holy Ghost.

Notes

1 This is the proposal of David Cunningham, *These Three Are One: The Practice of Trinitarian Theology* (Oxford: Blackwell, 1997), p. 72 and throughout.
2 Matt. xii. 32.
3 Matt. xxviii. 19.
4 Prov. v. 15.
5 John iv. 14, quoted more fully at the end of the section.
6 John vii. 38, 39.
7 Compare a similar passage on rain in *Catechetical Orations*, ix. 9, 10.
8 1 Cor. xii. 11.
9 1 Cor. xii. 7–11.
10 Matt. xi. 27.
11 John xvi. 13, 14.
12 In regard to the caution with which St. Cyril here speaks, we must remember that the heresy of Macedonius had not yet given occasion to the formal discussion and determination of the "nature and substance" of the Holy Ghost.

12

Athanasius of Alexandria, from Orations against the Arians

This passage is less important for the content of what it says, than for the *pattern* of how it says it. The pattern is trinitarian: determinedly, deliberately, resolutely so. Athanasius makes constant, repeated, insistent reference to Father, Son, and Spirit. The drumbeat of the pattern would be repetitious in the sense of dull only if its intention were to convey information. Rather it seeks to practice a discipline. Disciplines are meant to be repeated. This discipline beats out a trinitarian ostinato because it seeks, as percussion instruments do, to make the beat infectious, to leave it ringing consciously or unconsciously in the ear. Athanasius seeks to play, finally, not the instrument of the text but the mind of the listener. He seeks to form it too into a trinitarian pattern. The reader comes away feeling if not thinking that patterns naming only one or two of the three Persons are somehow incomplete. They come to sound wrong. Athanasius conveys the reader into a trinitarian as into a musical space, one that outlasts the reading of the text. The language includes the reader in a realm or community or soundstage that she cannot leave behind, but follows and surrounds her after she finishes a text not yet finished with her.

Consider this pregnant line: "As Thou hast given Me to bear this body, grant to them Thy Spirit." The speaker is Jesus; the one he addresses, the Father; the one he speaks of, the Spirit. One short sentence implicates all three persons of the Trinity: Father, Son, and Spirit. But that's not all. Jesus also speaks in one clause of his human body and in the next of "them," other human beings with bodies. The sentence not only tags all three members of the Trinity, but looks to the inclusion of human beings within its embrace. The means of inclusion in the

Excerpt from Athanasius of Alexandria, *Orations Against the Arians*, in *A Select Library of the Nicene and Post-Nicene Fathers of the Christian Church*, Second Series, ed. Philip Schaff et al., in several editions, vol. 5.

Trinity is the incarnation, God's taking up humanity in the Word. Athanasius famously encapsulates that elsewhere by saying that God became human, that human beings might become divine (*On the Incarnation of the World*, ch. 54). Here he makes the blessed exchange more concrete. The body refers humanity to the incarnation; the Holy Spirit refers divinity to the Trinity. It is as if Athanasius had here recast the blessed exchange like this: the Son bears a human body, that those with bodies might bear his Spirit.

The famous version, whereby the Word is humanified, that the human being might be divinized, can sound like an automatic or physical exchange. But this text makes the blessed exchange personal, makes it indeed part of the interaction and opening up of a community. The Son *bids* the Father to *give* the Spirit, manifesting the Trinity as a community of petition, gift, gratitude, and further gift – a community, that is, of prayer. Both the incarnation of the Son, and the gift of the Spirit, appear here not as unilateral actions by one of the Trinitarian Persons, but as appropriated actions of the Trinity in counsel together, or at prayer. Without saying so, this request of the Son transposes Romans 8: 11 into a Johannine key. There as here one sentence identifies all three members of the Trinity by their relation to the Son. There as here the Spirit correlates somehow with the human body. There as here the Trinity is at prayer; there as here the human being is incorporated somehow into it, as there the Spirit prays with and here the Son prays for us. There as here we see a great inclusion whereby the Trinity opens up to take human beings into its exchange of gift and gratitude.

from Orations against the Arians, III

Athanasius of Alexandria

Chapter XXV

22.   The Word then has the real and true identity of nature with the Father; but to us it is given to imitate it, as has been said; for He immediately adds, 'I in them and Thou in Me; that they may be made perfect in one.' Here at length the Lord asks something greater and more perfect for us; for it is plain that the Word has come to be in us, for He has put on our body. 'And Thou Father in Me' [John 17: 21]; 'for I am Thy Word, and since Thou art in Me, because I am Thy Word, and I in them because of the body, and because of Thee the salvation of men is perfected in Me, therefore I ask that they also may become one, according to the body that is in Me and according to its perfection; that they too may become perfect, having oneness with It, and having become one in It; that, as if all were carried by Me, all may be one body and one spirit, and may grow up unto a perfect man.'[1] For we all, partaking of the Same, become one body, having the one Lord in ourselves. The passage then having this meaning, still more plainly is refuted the heterodoxy of Christ's enemies. I repeat it; if He had said simply and absolutely 'that they may be one in Thee,' or 'that they and I may be one in Thee,'

God's enemies had had some plea, though a shameless one; but in fact He has not spoken simply, but, 'As Thou, Father, in Me, and I in Thee, that they may be all one.' Moreover, using the word 'as,' He signifies those who become distantly as He is in the Father; distantly not in place but in nature; for in place nothing is far from God, but in nature only all things are far from Him. And, as I said before, whose uses the particle 'as' implies, not identity, nor equality, but a pattern of the matter in question, viewed in a certain respect.

23.   Indeed we may learn also from the Saviour Himself, when He says, 'For as Jonah was three days and three nights in the whale's belly, so shall the Son of man be three days and three nights in the heart of the earth.'[2] For Jonah was not as the Saviour, nor did Jonah go down to Hades; nor was the whale Hades; nor did Jonah, when swallowed up, bring up those who had before been swallowed by the whale, but he alone came forth, when the whale was bidden. Therefore there is no identity nor equality signified in the term 'as,' but one thing and another; and it shews a certain kind of parallel in the case of Jonah, on account of the three days. In like manner then we too, when the Lord says 'as,' neither become as the Son in the Father, nor as the Father is in the Son. For we become one as the Father and the Son in mind and agreement of spirit, and the Saviour will be as Jonah in the earth; but as the Saviour is not Jonah, nor, as he was swallowed up, so did the Saviour descend into Hades, but it is but a parallel, in like manner, if we too become one, as the Son in the Father, we shall not be as the Son, nor equal to Him; for He and we are but parallel. For on this account is the word 'as' applied to us; since things differing from others in nature, become as they, when viewed in a certain relation. Wherefore the Son Himself, simply and without any condition is in the Father; for this attribute He has by nature; but for us, to whom it is not natural, there is needed an image and example, that He may say of us, 'As Thou in Me, and I in Thee.' 'And when they shall be so perfected,' He says, 'then the world knows that Thou hast sent Me, for unless I had come and borne this their body, no one of them had been perfected, but one and all had remained corruptible. Work Thou then in them, O Father, and as Thou hast given to Me to bear this, grant to them Thy Spirit, that they too in It may become one, and may be perfected in Me. For their perfecting shews that Thy Word has sojourned among them; and the world seeing them perfect and full of God, will believe altogether that Thou hast sent Me, and I have sojourned here. For whence is this their perfecting, but that I, Thy Word, having borne their body, and become man, have perfected the work, which Thou gavest Me, O Father? And the work is perfected, because men, redeemed from sin, no longer remain dead, but being deified, have in each other, by looking at Me, the bond of charity.'

24.   We then, by way of giving a rude view of the expressions in this passage, have been led into many words, but blessed John will shew from his Epistle the sense of the words, concisely and much more perfectly than we can. And he will both disprove the interpretation of these irreligious men, and will teach how we become in God and God in us; and how again we become One in Him, and how far the Son differs in nature from us, and will stop the Arians from any longer thinking that they shall be as the Son, lest they hear it said to them, 'Thou art a man and not God,' and 'Stretch not thyself, being poor, beside a rich man.'[3] John

then thus writes; 'Hereby know we that we dwell in Him and He in us, because He hath given us of His Spirit.'⁴ Therefore because of the grace of the Spirit which has been given to us, in Him we come to be, and He in us; and since it is the Spirit of God, therefore through His becoming in us, reasonably are we, as having the Spirit, considered to be in God and thus is God in us. Not then as the Son in the Father, so also we become in the Father; for the Son does not merely partake the Spirit, that therefore He too may be in the Father; nor does He receive the Spirit, but rather He supplies It Himself to all; and the Spirit does not unite the Word to the Father, but rather the Spirit receives from the Word. And the Son is in the Father, as His own Word and Radiance; but we, apart from the Spirit, are strange and distant from God, and by the participation of the Spirit we are knit into the Godhead; so that our being in the Father is not ours, but is the Spirit's which is in us and abides in us, while by the true confession we preserve it in us, John again saying, 'Whosoever shall confess that Jesus is the Son of God, God dwelleth in him and he in God.'⁵ What then is our likeness and equality, to the Son? Rather, are not the Arians confuted on every side? And especially by John, that the Son is in the Father in one way, and we become in Him in another, and that neither we shall ever be as He, nor is the Word as we; except they shall dare, as commonly, so now to say, that the Son also by participation of the Spirit and by improvement of conduct came to be Himself also in the Father. But here again is an excess of irreligion, even in admitting the thought. For He, as has been said, gives to the Spirit, and whatever the Spirit hath, He hath from the Word.

25. The Saviour, then, saying of us, 'As Thou, Father, art in Me, and I in Thee, that they too may be one in Us,' does not signify that we were to have identity with Him; for this was shewn from the instance of Jonah; but it is a request to the Father, as John has written, that the Spirit should be vouchsafed through Him to those who believe through whom we are found to be in God, and in this respect to be conjoined in Him. For since the Word is in the Father, and the Spirit is given from the Word, He wills that we should receive the Spirit, that, when we receive It, thus having the Spirit of the Word which is in the Father, we too may be found on account of the Spirit to become One in the Word, and through Him in the Father. And if He say, 'as we,' this again is only a request that such grace of the Spirit as is given to the disciples may be without failure or revocation. For what the Word has by nature, as I said, in the Father, that He wishes to be given to us through the Spirit irrevocably; which the Apostle knowing, said, 'Who shall separate us from the love of Christ?' for 'the gifts of God' and 'grace of His calling are without repentance.'⁶ It is the Spirit then which is in God, and not we viewed in our own selves; and as we are sons and gods because of the Word in us, so we shall be in the Son and in the Father, and we shall be accounted to have become one in Son and in Father, because that that Spirit is in us, which is in the Word which is in the Father. When then a man falls from the Spirit for any wickedness, if he repent upon his fall, the grace remains irrevocably to such as are willing; otherwise he who has fallen is no longer in God (because that Holy Spirit and Paraclete which is in God has deserted him), but the sinner shall be in him to whom he has subjected himself, as took place in Saul's instance; for the Spirit of God departed from

him and an evil spirit was afflicting him.[7] God's enemies hearing this ought to be henceforth abashed, and no longer to feign themselves equal to God. But they neither understand (for 'the irreligious,' he saith, 'does not understand knowledge'[8]) nor endure religious words, but find them heavy even to hear.

Notes

1   See Eph. iv. 13.
2   Matt. xii. 40.
3   Ez. xxviii. 2; Prov. xxiii. 4, LXX [Septuagint].
4   1 John iv. 13.
5   1 John iv. 15.
6   Rom. viii. 35; see xi. 29.
7   1 Sam. xvi. 14.
8   Prov. xxix. 7.

13

Basil of Caesarea,
from On the Holy Spirit

This famous treatise argues that the Holy Spirit is God without explicitly drawing that conclusion, because the Bible does not say "The Holy Spirit is God" in so many words. It exemplifies, therefore, a soft-pedaling theological argument for precisely the most important sorts of conclusions: it leads the reader to conclude for him- or herself what the author believes and urges but modestly does not state. This is not false modesty, but a rhetorical strategy of great power, because it leaves the reader – or the Spirit – free to participate in the argument by drawing the conclusion or not. In this case, the strategy succeeded, and Basil is credited with the argument that he implied.

Basil is writing in an argumentative context that heightens the difficulty of his project, because the divinity of the Holy Spirit is not the only thing in dispute. The divinity of Jesus is still insecure. So Basil executes a pincer movement. If he aligns the Holy Spirit with the Father and the Son, the argument in favor of the divinity of the Spirit will enclose and secure the divinity of the Son. The three – Father, Son, and Spirit – hang together. The advantage of that strategy is twofold. One, all of the parties on all sides have been baptized into the name of the Three, so they can't separate the Three (argues Basil) without denying their own baptism. Two, the beginning of the argument for the Spirit's divinity is the end of the argument over the Son's. Offense is the best defense.

Now, the baptismal argument does have a disadvantage, from a contemporary point of view. It focuses attention on two matters. On the logic of salvation, which is all to Basil's good: if the Holy Spirit saves you, the Holy Spirit must be God. But it also focuses attention on the specific words that relate Father, Son, and Spirit in biblical and baptismal formulas: on conjunctions and prepositions.

Excerpt from Basil of Caesarea, *On the Holy Spirit*, in *A Select Library of the Nicene and Post-Nicene Fathers of the Christian Church*, Second Series, ed. Philip Schaff et al., in several editions, vol. 8.

Basil's labor over "and," "with," "by," "through," and other words of relation –
omitted here – has bored generations of students ever since. Could a writer bore
his audience on purpose? Perhaps, if he bores them with the arguments of his
opponents. Then those arguments won't bear repeating any more. All the more
so if Basil's own arguments lodge in the memory because they explain salvation
itself. Just if readers come to say, "enough with those pesky prepositions!" then
Basil wins, because what remains is the impression that Father, Son, and Spirit
belong together, no matter what. Here the reader's impatience is the rhetorician's
gain. Basil's prepositional arguments succeed like a filibuster, where boring
the audience hurts opponents more. Rendering prepositions petty, Basil throws
salvation into grander relief. If readers remember only that the Holy Spirit brings
salvation with the Father and the Son, then Basil has closed his case – and left
worries about the Son far behind.

from On the Holy Spirit

Basil of Caesarea

Chapter XV

36.   Through the Holy Spirit comes our restoration to paradise, our ascension into
the kingdom of heaven, our return to the adoption of sons, our liberty to call God
our Father, our being made partakers of the grace of Christ, our being called children of light, our sharing in eternal glory, and, in a word, our being brought into
a state of all "fulness of blessing,"[1] both in this world and in the world to come,
of all the good gifts that are in store for us, by promise whereof, through faith,
beholding the reflection of their grace as though they were already present, we await
the full enjoyment. If such is the earnest, what the perfection? If such the first fruits,
what the complete fulfilment? Furthermore, from this too may be apprehended the
difference between the grace that comes from the Spirit and the baptism by water:
in that John indeed baptized with water, but our Lord Jesus Christ by the Holy
Ghost. "I indeed," he says, "baptize you with water unto repentance; but he that
cometh after me is mightier than I, whose shoes I am not worthy to bear: he shall
baptize you with the Holy Ghost and with fire."[2] Here He calls the trial at the
judgment the baptism of fire, as the apostle says, "The fire shall try every man's
work, of what sort it is."[3] And again, "The day shall declare it, because it shall be
revealed by fire."[4] And ere now there have been some who in their championship
of true religion have undergone the death for Christ's sake, not in mere similitude,
but in actual fact, and so have needed none of the outward signs of water for their
salvation, because they were baptized in their own blood. Thus I write not to dis-
parage the baptism by water, but to overthrow the arguments of those who exalt
themselves against the Spirit; who confound things that are distinct from one another,
and compare those which admit of no comparison.

Chapter XVI

37.   Let us then revert to the point raised from the outset, that in all things the Holy Spirit is inseparable and wholly incapable of being parted from the Father and the Son. St. Paul, in the passage about the gift of tongues, writes to the Corinthians, "If ye all prophesy and there come in one that believeth not, or one unlearned, he is convinced of all, he is judged of all; and thus are the secrets of the heart made manifest; and so falling down on his face he will worship God and report that God is in you of a truth."[5] If then God is known to be in the prophets by the prophesying that is acting according to the distribution of the gifts of the Spirit, let our adversaries consider what kind of place they will attribute to the Holy Spirit. Let them say whether it is more proper to rank Him with God or to thrust Him forth to the place of the creature. Peter's words to Sapphira, "How is it that ye have agreed together to tempt the Spirit of the Lord? Ye have not lied unto men, but unto God,"[6] show that sins against the Holy Spirit and against God are the same; and thus you might learn that in every operation the Spirit is closely conjoined with, and inseparable from, the Father and the Son. God works the differences of operations, and the Lord the diversities of administrations, but all the while the Holy Spirit is present too of His own will, dispensing distribution of the gifts according to each recipient's worth. For, it is said, "there are diversities of gifts, but the same Spirit; and differences of administrations, but the same Lord; and there are diversities of operations, but it is the same God which worketh all in all."[7] "But all these," it is said, "worketh that one and the self-same Spirit, dividing to every man severally as He will."[8] It must not however be supposed because in this passage the apostle names in the first place the Spirit, in the second the Son, and in the third God the Father, that therefore their rank is reversed. The apostle has only started in accordance with our habits of thought; for when we receive gifts, the first that occurs to us is the distributor, next we think of the sender, and then we lift our thoughts to the fountain and cause of the boons.

38.   Moreover, from the things created at the beginning may be learnt the fellowship of the Spirit with the Father and the Son. . . . [I]n the creation bethink thee first, I pray thee, of the original cause of all things that are made, the Father; of the creative cause, the Son; of the perfecting cause, the Spirit; so that the ministering spirits subsist by the will of the Father, are brought into being by the operation of the Son, and perfected by the presence of the Spirit. . . . For the first principle of existing things is One, creating through the Son and perfecting through the Spirit. The operation of the Father who worketh all in all is not imperfect, neither is the creating work of the Son incomplete if not perfected by the Spirit. The Father, who creates by His sole will, could not stand in any need of the Son, but nevertheless He wills through the Son; nor could the Son, who works according to the likeness of the Father, need co-operation, but the Son too wills to make perfect through the Spirit. "For by the word of the Lord were the heavens made, and all the host of them by the breath [the Spirit] of His mouth."[9] The Word then is not a mere significant impression on the air, borne by the organs of speech; nor is the Spirit

of His mouth a vapour, emitted by the organs of respiration; but the Word is He who "was with God in the beginning" and "was God,"[10] and the Spirit of the mouth of God is "the Spirit of truth which proceedeth from the Father."[11] You are therefore to perceive three, the Lord who gives the order, the Word who creates, and the Spirit who confirms. And what other thing could confirmation be than the perfecting according to holiness? This perfecting expresses the confirmation's firmness, unchangeableness, and fixity in good. But there is no sanctification without the Spirit. . . . For how are angels to cry "Glory to God in the highest"[12] without being empowered by the Spirit? For "No man can say that Jesus is the Lord but by the Holy Ghost, and no man speaking by the Spirit of God calleth Jesus accursed"[13]. . . .

39.   But when we speak of the dispensations made for man by our great God and Saviour Jesus Christ,[14] who will gainsay their having been accomplished through the grace of the Spirit? Whether you wish to examine ancient evidence; – the blessings of the patriarchs, the succour given through the legislation, the types, the prophecies, the valorous feats in war, the signs wrought through just men; – or on the other hand the things done in the dispensation of the coming of our Lord in the flesh; – all is through the Spirit. In the first place He was made an unction, and being inseparably present was with the very flesh of the Lord, according to that which is written, "Upon whom thou shalt see the Spirit descending and remaining on Him, the same is"[15] "my beloved Son;"[16] and "Jesus of Nazareth" whom "God anointed with the Holy Ghost."[17] After this every operation was wrought with the co-operation of the Spirit. He was present when the Lord was being tempted by the devil; for, it is said, "Jesus was led up of the Spirit into the wilderness to be tempted."[18] He was inseparably with Him while working His wonderful works;[19] for, it is said, "If I by the Spirit of God cast out devils."[20] And He did not leave Him when He had risen from the dead; for when renewing man, and, by breathing on the face of the disciples,[21] restoring the grace, that came of the inbreathing of God, which man had lost, what did the Lord say? "Receive ye the Holy Ghost: whose soever sins ye remit, they are remitted unto them; and whose soever ye retain, they are retained."[22] And is it not plain and incontestable that the ordering of the Church is effected through the Spirit? For He gave, it is said, "in the church, first Apostles, secondarily prophets, thirdly teachers, after that miracles, then gifts of healing, helps, governments, diversities of tongues,"[23] for this order is ordained in accordance with the division of the gifts that are of the Spirit.[24]

Chapter XVIII

47.   And when, by means of the power that enlightens us, we fix our eyes on the beauty of the image of the invisible God, and through the image are led up to the supreme beauty of the spectacle of the archetype, then, I ween, is with us inseparably the Spirit of knowledge, in Himself bestowing on them that love the vision of the truth the power of beholding the Image, not making the exhibition from without, but in Himself leading on to the full knowledge. "No man knoweth the Father save the Son."[25] And so "no man can say that Jesus is the Lord but by the Holy Ghost."[26] For it is not said through the Spirit, but by the Spirit, and "God is a

spirit, and they that worship Him must worship Him in spirit and in truth,"[27] as it is written "in thy light shall we see light,"[28] namely by the illumination of the Spirit, "the true light which lighteth every man that cometh into the world."[29] It results that in Himself He shows the glory of the Only-begotten, and on true worshippers He in Himself bestows the knowledge of God. Thus the way of the knowledge of God lies from One Spirit through the One Son to the One Father, and conversely the natural Goodness and the inherent Holiness and the royal Dignity extend from the Father through the Only-begotten to the Spirit. Thus there is both acknowledgment of the hypostases and the true dogma of the Monarchy is not lost. . . .

Chapter XIX

Against those who assert that the Spirit ought not to be glorified

48. "Be it so," it is rejoined, "but glory is by no means so absolutely due to the Spirit as to require His exaltation by us in doxologies." Whence then could we get our demonstrations of the dignity of the Spirit, "passing all understanding,"[30] if His communion with the Father and the Son were not reckoned by our opponents as good for testimony of His rank? It is, at all events, possible for us to arrive to a certain extent at intelligent apprehension of the sublimity of His nature and of His unapproachable power, by looking at the meaning of His title, and at the magnitude of His operations, and by His good gifts bestowed on us or rather on all creation. He is called Spirit, as "God is a Spirit,"[31] and "the breath of our nostrils, the anointed of the Lord."[32] He is called holy,[33] as the Father is holy, and the Son is holy, for to the creature holiness was brought in from without, but to the Spirit holiness is the fulfilment of nature, and it is for this reason that He is described not as being sanctified, but as sanctifying. He is called good,[34] as the Father is good, and He who was begotten of the Good is good, and to the Spirit His goodness is essence. He is called upright,[35] as "the Lord is upright,"[36] in that He is Himself truth,[37] and is Himself Righteousness,[38] having no divergence nor leaning to one side or to the other, on account of the immutability of His substance. He is called Paraclete, like the Only-begotten, as He Himself says, "I will ask the Father, and He will give you another comforter."[39] Thus names are borne by the Spirit in common with the Father and the Son, and He gets these titles from His natural and close relationship. From what other source could they be derived? Again He is called royal,[40] Spirit of truth,[41] and Spirit of wisdom.[42] "The Spirit of God," it is said "hath made me,"[43] and God filled Bezaleel with "the divine Spirit of wisdom and understanding and knowledge."[44] Such names as these are super-eminent and mighty, but they do not transcend His glory.

49. And His operations, what are they? For majesty ineffable, and for numbers innumerable. How shall we form a conception of what extends beyond the ages? What were His operations before that creation whereof we can conceive? How great the grace which He conferred on creation? What the power exercised by Him over the ages to come? He existed; He pre-existed; He co-existed with the Father and the Son before the ages. It follows that, even if you can conceive of anything beyond the ages, you will find the Spirit yet further above and beyond. And if you think

of the creation, the powers of the heavens were established by the Spirit,[45] the establishment being understood to refer to disability to fall away from good. For it is from the Spirit that the powers derive their close relationship to God, their inability to change to evil, and their continuance in blessedness. Is it Christ's advent? The Spirit is forerunner. Is there the incarnate presence? The Spirit is inseparable. Working of miracles, and gifts of healing are through the Holy Spirit. Demons were driven out by the Spirit of God. The devil was brought to naught by the presence of the Spirit. Remission of sins was by the gift of the Spirit, for "ye were washed, ye were sanctified . . . in the name of the Lord Jesus Christ, and in the holy Spirit of our God."[46] There is close relationship with God through the Spirit, for "God hath sent forth the Spirit of His Son into your hearts, crying Abba, Father."[47] The resurrection from the dead is effected by the operation of the Spirit, for "Thou sendest forth thy spirit, they are created; and Thou renewest the face of the earth."[48] If here creation may be taken to mean the bringing of the departed to life again, how mighty is not the operation of the Spirit, Who is to us the dispenser of the life that follows on the resurrection, and attunes our souls to the spiritual life beyond? Or if here by creation is meant the change to a better condition of those who in this life have fallen into sin (for it is so understood according to the usage of Scripture, as in the words of Paul "if any man be in Christ he is a new creature"[49]), the renewal which takes place in this life, and the transmutation from our earthly and sensuous life to the heavenly conversation which takes place in us through the Spirit, then our souls are exalted to the highest pitch of admiration. With these thoughts before us are we to be afraid of going beyond due bounds in the extravagance of the honour we pay? Shall we not rather fear lest, even though we seem to give Him the highest names which the thoughts of man can conceive or man's tongue utter, we let our thoughts about Him fall too low?

It is the Spirit which says, as the Lord says, "Get thee down, and go with them, doubting nothing: for I have sent them."[50] Are these the words of an inferior, or of one in dread? "Separate me Barnabas and Saul for the work whereunto I have called them."[51] Does a slave speak thus? And Isaiah, "The Lord God and His Spirit hath sent me,"[52] and "the Spirit came down from the Lord and guided them."[53] And pray do not again understand by this guidance some humble service, for the Word witnesses that it was the work of God; – "Thou leddest thy people," it is said "like a flock,"[54] and "Thou that leadest Joseph like a flock,"[55] and "He led them on safely, so that they feared not."[56] Thus when you hear that when the Comforter is come, He will put you in remembrance, and "guide you into all truth"[57] do not misrepresent the meaning.

Notes

1 Rom. xv. 29.
2 Matt. iii. 11.
3 1 Cor. iii. 13.

4 Ibid.
5 1 Cor. xiv. 24, 25.
6 Acts v. 9 and 4. "Thou hast not lied," said to Ananias, interpolated into the rebuke of Sapphira.
7 1 Cor. xiii. 4, 5, 6.
8 1 Cor. xii. 11.
9 Ps. xxxiii. 6.
10 John i. 1.
11 John xv. 26.
12 Luke ii. 14.
13 1 Cor. xii. 3.
14 Titus ii. 13.
15 John i. 33.
16 Matt. iii. 17.
17 Acts x. 38.
18 Matt. iv. 1.
19 *Dunamis*, rendered "wonderful works" in Matt. vii. 22; "mighty works" in Matt. xi. 20, Mark vi. 14, and Luke x. 13; and "miracles" in Acts ii. 22, xix. 11, and Gal. iii. v.
20 Matt. xii. 28.
21 Gen. ii. 7.
22 John xx. 22, 23.
23 1 Cor. xii. 28.
24 cf. 1 Cor. xii. 11.
25 Matt. xi. 27.
26 1 Cor. xii. 3.
27 John iv. 24.
28 Ps. xxxvi. 9.
29 John i. 9.
30 Phil. iv. 7.
31 John iv. 24.
32 Lam. iv. 20. *Sic* in AV and RV, the reference being to Zedekiah. cf. Jer. xxxix. 5.
33 1 John i. 20.
34 Ps. cxliii. 10.
35 Ps. li. 10.
36 Ps. xcii. 15.
37 John xiv. 17; xv. 26; xvi. 13; 1 John v. 6.
38 2 Cor. iii. 8, 9.
39 John xiv. 16.
40 Ps. li. 12, lxx.
41 John xv. 26, etc.
42 Isa. xi. 2.
43 Job xxxiii. 4.
44 Exod. xxxi. 3, LXX [Septuagint].
45 cf. Ps. xxxiii. 6.
46 1 Cor. vi. 11, RV.
47 Gal. iv. 6.
48 Ps. civ. 30.
49 2 Cor. v. 17.

50   Acts x. 20.
51   Acts xiii. 2.
52   Isa. xlviii. 16.
53   Isa. lxiii. 14, LXX.
54   Ps. lxxvii. 20.
55   Ps. lxxx. 1.
56   Ps. lxxviii. 53.
57   John xvi. 13. cf. xiv. 26.

14

Gregory of Nazianzus,
from On Holy Baptism

This sermon is important for treating baptism as "Gift" with a capital G, that is, as the occasion of the Gift of the Spirit. In the following remarkable passage, the Gift ramifies throughout the entire Christian religion, rendering it quietly Spirit-centered. As you will read below in context,

> And as Christ the Giver of it is called by many various names, so too is this Gift . . . We call it, the Gift, the Grace, Baptism, Unction, Illumination, the Clothing of Immortality, the Laver of Regeneration, the Seal, and everything that is honorable. We call it the Gift, because it is given to us in return for nothing on our part; Grace, because it is conferred even on debtors; Baptism, because sin is buried with it in the water; Unction, as Priestly and Royal, for such were they who were anointed; Illumination, because of its splendour; Clothing, because it hides our shame; the Laver, because it washes us; the Seal because it preserves us, and is moreover the indication of Dominion. In it the heavens rejoice; it is glorified by the Angels, because of its kindred splendour. It is the image of the heavenly bliss. We long indeed to sing out its praises, but we cannot worthily do so.

"Gift" is also one of the primary names of the Holy Spirit, as "Word" is one of the primary names of the Son. *Usually*, Christianity – as the name indicates – is a religion constructed from relationships among manifestations of the body of Christ. In the incarnation, God the Word himself takes on the body of Christ. In the Church, the believers become the body of Christ. In the Eucharist, the bread and wine become the body of Christ. At the resurrection, the redeemed become the body of Christ. The body of Christ is – in this construction of Christianity – the center that holds it all together. Both theology and social science would agree on that; theology would call the series of relationships "analogy," and sociology

Excerpt from Gregory of Nazianzus, *On Holy Baptism*, in *A Select Library of the Nicene and Post-Nicene Fathers of the Christian Church*, Second Series, ed. Philip Schaff et al., in several editions, vol. 7.

would call it "totemism," but they are pointing to the same Christ-centered feature of the religion.

Usually, I said – but not here. *This* passage constructs Christianity as a series of relationships among gifts, that is, among manifestations of the Holy Spirit. In this passage, Christianity becomes a religion of the Spirit. In this passage, the Spirit unites a theology of deification and the materiality of the sacraments, leaving nothing untouched. As I wrote elsewhere:

> Just as Christ centers a series in which Jesus is the body of Christ and the believer is the body of Christ, until the body of Christ is the body of God, so too the Gift centers a series in which baptism is the Gift and the Holy Spirit is the Gift, the community is the Gift and the neighbor is the Gift, until by the Gift the believer becomes [united with] God.[1]

In the sermon as a whole, Gregory takes for grated a theology of deification, that is, a theology that identifies the undisputed benefits of the saved in heaven – sinlessness, understanding, immortality – with divine characteristics. It is divine to be holy, to enjoy complete understanding, to have everlasting life; therefore the human being is deified. No one who uses that term ascribes to the human being *trinitarian* characteristics: to be God by nature, to create worlds, to reverse the relation of dependence of creature on Creator. But they do want to praise God's goodness is raising human beings to fellowship with God. That communion or participation – in Greek *koinonia* – belongs especially to the Spirit, and baptism marks its ritual beginning.

Gregory knows that the Spirit works before and without baptism. And yet the association with something paraphysical – light – is very strong. The passage shows another feature of robust Spirit-talk: it does not float free of embodied realities, but accompanies them. Note how physical substances touch the body: water washes it, the seal marks it, oil anoints it, clothing envelopes it, light enlightens and illuminates it at every point. It is no paradox that Gregory's account of the Gift reaches both "high" and "low," up to God and down to body. Rather the body is where the Spirit settles and what it uses, how it accompanies human beings and befriends them. In doing that, the Spirit does not so much make a contrast to Christ's incarnation as do the same thing in a new way, befriending again and anew the body of Christ in many and various ways.

from Oration 40: On Holy Baptism

Gregory of Nazianzus

Preached at Constantinople January 6, 381, being the day following the delivery of that on the Holy Lights.

I.   Yesterday we kept high Festival on the illustrious Day of the Holy Lights; for it was fitting that rejoicings should be kept for our Salvation, and that far more than for weddings and birthdays, and namedays, and house-warmings, and registrations of children, and anniversaries, and all the other festivities that men observe for their earthly friends. And now today let us discourse briefly concerning Baptism, and the benefits which accrue to us therefrom, even though our discourse yesterday spoke of it cursorily; partly because the time pressed us hard, and partly because the sermon had to avoid tediousness. For too great length in a sermon is as much an enemy to people's ears, as too much food is to their bodies . . . It will be worth your while to apply your minds to what we say, and to receive our discourse on so important a subject not perfunctorily, but with ready mind, since to know the power of this Sacrament is itself Enlightenment.[2]

II.   The Word recognizes three Births for us; namely, the natural birth, that of Baptism, and that of the Resurrection. Of these the first is by night, and is servile, and involves passion; but the second is by day, and is destructive of passion, cutting off all the veil[3] that is derived from birth, and leading on to the higher life; and the third is more terrible and shorter, bringing together in a moment all mankind, to stand before its Creator, and to give an account of its service and conversation here; whether it has followed the flesh, or whether it has mounted up with the spirit, and worshipped the grace of its new creation. My Lord Jesus Christ has showed that He honoured all these births in His own Person; the first, by that first and quickening Inbreathing;[4] the second by His Incarnation and the Baptism wherewith He Himself was baptized; and the third by the Resurrection of which He was the Firstfruits; condescending, as He became the Firstborn[5] among many brethren, so also to become the Firstborn from the dead.[6]

III.   Concerning two of these births, the first and the last, we have not to speak on the present occasion. Let us discourse upon the second, which is now necessary for us, and which gives its name to the Feast of the Lights. Illumination [i.e., baptism] is the splendour of souls, the conversion of the life, the question put to the Godward conscience.[7] It is the aid to our weakness, the renunciation of the flesh, the following of the Spirit, the fellowship of the Word, the improvement of the creature, the overwhelming of sin, the participation of light, the dissolution of darkness. It is the carriage to God, the dying with Christ, the perfecting of the mind, the bulwark of Faith, the key of the Kingdom of heaven, the change of life, the removal of slavery, the loosing of chains, the remodelling of the whole man. Why should I go into further detail? Illumination is the greatest and most magnificent of the Gifts of God. For just as we speak of the Holy of Holies, and the Song of Songs, as more comprehensive and more excellent than others, so is this called Illumination, as being more holy than any other illumination which we possess.

IV.   And as Christ the Giver of it is called by many various names, so too is this Gift, whether it is from the exceeding gladness of its nature (as those who are very fond of a thing take pleasure in using its name), or that the great variety of its benefits has reacted for us upon its names. We call it, the Gift, the Grace, Baptism, Unction, Illumination, the Clothing of Immortality, the Laver of Regeneration, the Seal, and everything that is honorable. We call it the Gift, because it is given to us in return for nothing on our part; Grace, because it is conferred even on debtors; Baptism, because sin is buried with it in the water; Unction, as Priestly and Royal, for such were they who were anointed; Illumination, because of its splendour; Clothing, because it hides our shame; the Laver, because it washes us; the Seal because it preserves us, and is moreover the indication of Dominion. In it the heavens rejoice; it is glorified by the Angels, because of its kindred splendour. It is the image of the heavenly bliss. We long indeed to sing out its praises, but we cannot worthily do so.

V.   God is Light:[8] the highest, the unapproachable, the ineffable, That can neither be conceived in the mind nor uttered with the lips,[9] That giveth life to every reasoning creature.[10] He is in the world of thought, what the sun is in the world of sense; presenting Himself to our minds in proportion as we are cleansed; and loved in proportion as He is presented to our mind; and again, conceived in proportion as we love Him; Himself contemplating and comprehending Himself, and pouring Himself out upon what is external to Him. That Light, I mean, which is contemplated in the Father and the Son and the Holy Ghost, Whose riches is Their unity of nature, and the one outleaping of Their brightness. A second Light is the Angel, a kind of outflow or communication of that first Light, drawing its illumination from its inclination and obedience thereto; and I know not whether its illumination is distributed according to the order of its state, or whether its order is due to the respective measures of its illumination. A third Light is man; a light which is visible to external objects. For they call Man light[11] because of the faculty of speech in us. And the name is applied again to those of us who are more like God, and who approach God more nearly than others. I also acknowledge another light, by which the primeval darkness was driven away or pierced. It was the first of all the visible creation to be called into existence; and it irradiates the whole universe, the circling orbit of the stars, and all the heavenly beacon fires.

VI.   Light was also the firstborn commandment given to the firstborn man (for the commandment of the Law is a lamp and a light;[12] and again, because Thy judgments are a light upon the earth);[13] although the envious darkness crept in and wrought wickedness. And a light typical and proportionate to those who were its subjects was the written law, adumbrating the truth and the sacrament of the great Light, for Moses' face was made glorious by it.[14] And, to mention more Lights – it was Light that appeared out of Fire to Moses, when it burned the bush indeed, but did not consume it,[15] to shew its nature and to declare the power that was in it. And it was Light that was in the pillar of fire that led Israel and tamed the wilderness.[16] It was Light that carried up Elias in the car of fire,[17] and yet did not burn him as it carried him. It was Light that shone round the Shepherds[18] when the Eternal Light was mingled with the temporal. It was Light that was the beauty of the Star that went before to Bethlehem to guide the Wise Men's way,[19] and to be the escort of the Light That is above us, when He came amongst us. Light was That Godhead Which was shewn upon the Mount to the disciples – and a little too strong for their eyes.[20] Light was That Vision which blazed out upon Paul,[21] and by wounding his eyes healed the darkness of his soul. Light is also the brilliancy of heaven to those who have been purified here, when the righteous shall shine forth as the Sun,[22] and God shall stand in the midst of them,[23] gods and kings, deciding and distinguishing the ranks of the Blessedness of heaven. Light beside these in a special sense is the illumination of Baptism of which we are now speaking; for it contains a great and marvellous sacrament of our salvation.

XXXVIII.   Let us cleanse every member, Brethren, let us purify every sense; let nothing in us be imperfect or of our first birth; let us leave nothing unilluminated. Let us enlighten our eyes,[24] that we may look straight on, and not bear in ourselves any harlot idol through curious and busy sight; for even though we might not worship lust, yet our soul would be defiled. If there be beam or mote,[25] let us purge it away, that we may be able to see those of others also. Let us be enlightened in our ears; let us be enlightened in our tongue, that we may hearken what the Lord God will speak,[26] and that He may cause[27] us to hear His loving-kindness in the morning, and that we may be made to hear of joy and gladness,[28] spoken into godly ears, that we may not be a sharp sword, nor a whetted razor,[29] nor turn under our tongue labour and toil,[30] but that we may speak the Wisdom of God in a mystery, even the hidden Wisdom,[31] reverencing the fiery tongues.[32] Let us be healed also in the smell, that we be not effeminate; and be sprinkled with dust instead of sweet perfumes,[33] but may smell the Ointment that was poured out for us,[34] spiritually receiving it; and so formed and transformed by it, that from us too a sweet odour may be smelled. Let us cleanse our touch, our taste, our throat, not touching them over gently, nor delighting in smooth things, but handling them as is worthy of Him, the Word That was made flesh for us; and so far following the example of Thomas,[35] not pampering them with dainties and sauces, those brethren of a more baleful pampering, but tasting and learning that the Lord is good,[36] with the better and abiding taste; and not for a short while refreshing that baneful and thankless dust, which lets pass and does not hold that which is given to it; but delighting it with the words which are sweeter than honey.[37]

XLIV   . . . If it be thus, and according to this teaching that you come to Baptism, lo I will not refrain my lips,[38] lo I lend my hands to the Spirit; let us hasten your salvation. The Spirit is eager, the Consecrator is ready, the Gift is prepared. But if you still halt and will not receive the perfectness of the Godhead, go and look for someone else to baptize – or rather to drown you: I have no time to cut the Godhead, and to make you dead in the moment of your regeneration, that you should have neither the Gift nor the Hope of Grace, but should in so short a time make shipwreck of your salvation. For whatever you may subtract from the Deity of the Three, you will have overthrown the whole, and destroyed your own being made perfect.

XLVI.   But one thing more I preach unto you. The Station in which you shall presently stand after your Baptism before the Great Sanctuary [Bema] is a foretype of the future glory. The Psalmody with which you will be received is a prelude to the Psalmody of Heaven; the lamps which you will kindle are a Sacrament of the illumination there with which we shall meet the Bridegroom, shining and virgin souls, with the lamps of our faith shining, not sleeping through our carelessness, that we may not miss Him that we look for if He come unexpectedly; nor yet unfed, and without oil, and destitute of good works, that we be not cast out of the Bridechamber. For I see how pitiable is such a case. He will come when the cry demands the meeting, and they who are prudent shall meet Him, with their light shining and its food abundant, but the others seeking for oil too late from those who possess it. And

He will come with speed, and the former shall go in with Him, but the latter shall be shut out, having wasted in preparations the time of entrance; and they shall weep sore when all too late they learn the penalty of their slothfulness, when the Bridechamber can no longer be entered by them for all their entreaties, for they have shut it against themselves by their sin, following in another fashion the example of those who missed the Wedding feast[39] with which the good Father feasts the good Bridegroom; one on account of a newly wedded wife; another of a newly purchased field; another of a yoke of oxen; which he and they acquired to their misfortune, since for the sake of the little they lose the great. For none are there of the disdainful, nor of the slothful, nor of those who are clothed in filthy rags and not in the Wedding garment even though here they may have thought themselves worthy of wearing the bright robe there, and secretly intruded themselves, deceiving themselves with vain hopes. And then, What? When we have entered, then the Bridegroom knows what He will teach us, and how He will converse with the souls that have come in with Him. He will converse with them, I think in teaching things more perfect and more pure. Of which may we all, both Teachers and Taught, have share, in the Same Christ our Lord, to Whom be the Glory and the Empire, for ever and ever. Amen.

Gregory Nazianzus, *from* On Pentecost

In this oration, Gregory constantly implies that the Holy Spirit is God, because the Holy Spirit does what God alone can do. And the primary God-alone act the Holy Spirit performs here is to *save*. Thus Gregory puts opponents in a bind: deny the deity of the Holy Spirit, and you put your own salvation at stake, because if it isn't God saving you, then who is? This argument so characterizes Gregory that one author has called it "Nazianzene logic."[40] The inference "if it saves you, it must be God" makes a transcendental argument: God creates the possibility of salvation. Such an argument only becomes more compelling, when one conceives salvation as deification. Then the Holy Spirit must count as God, since the Holy Spirit imparts God's qualities. God's qualities include those that even traditions unfamiliar with talk of deification see as salvation's benefits: everlasting life, complete understanding, (comm)union with God, holiness. For Gregory, salvation makes no sense, unless the Holy Spirit (with the Father and the Son) is God.

from Oration 41: *On Pentecost*

Gregory of Nazianzus

V.   We are keeping the feast of Pentecost and of the Coming of the Spirit, and the appointed time of the Promise, and the fulfilment of our hope. And how great, how august, is the Mystery. The dispensations of the Body of Christ are ended; or rather, what belongs to His Bodily Advent (for I hesitate to say the Dispensation of His Body, as long as no discourse persuades me that it is better to have put off the body[41]), and that of the Spirit is beginning. And what were the things pertaining

Excerpt from Gregory of Nazianzus, *On Pentecost*, in *A Select Library of the Nicene and Post-Nicene Fathers of the Christian Church*, Second Series, ed. Philip Schaff et al., in several editions, vol. 7.

to the Christ? The Virgin, the Birth, the Manger, the Swaddling, the Angels glorifying Him, the Shepherds running to Him, the course of the Star, the Magi worshipping Him and bringing Gifts, Herod's murder of the children, the Flight of Jesus into Egypt, the Return from Egypt, the Circumcision, the Baptism, the Witness from Heaven, the Temptation, the Stoning for our sake (because He had to be given as an Example to us of enduring affliction for the Word), the Betrayal, the Nailing, the Burial, the Resurrection, the Ascension; and of these even now He suffers many dishonours at the hands of the enemies of Christ; and He bears them, for He is longsuffering. But from those who love Him He receives all that is honourable. And He defers, as in the former case His wrath, so in ours His kindness; in their case perhaps to give them the grace of repentance, and in ours to test our love; whether we do not faint in our tribulations[42] and conflicts for the true Religion, as was from of old the order of His Divine Economy, and of his unsearchable judgments, with which He orders wisely all that concerns us. Such are the mysteries of Christ. And what follows we shall see to be more glorious; and may we too be seen. As to the things of the Spirit, may the Spirit be with me, and grant me speech as much as I desire; or if not that, yet as is in due proportion to the season. Anyhow He will be with me as my Lord; not in servile guise, nor awaiting a command, as some think.[43] For He bloweth where He wills and on whom He wills, and to what extent He wills.[44] Thus we are inspired both to think and to speak of the Spirit.

VI.   They who reduce the Holy Spirit to the rank of a creature are blasphemers and wicked servants, and worst of the wicked. For it is the part of wicked servants to despise Lordship, and to rebel against dominion, and to make That which is free their fellow-servant. But they who deem Him God are inspired by God and are illustrious in their mind; and they who go further and *call* Him so, if to well disposed hearers are exalted; if to the low, are not reserved enough, for they commit pearls to clay, and the noise of thunder to weak ears, and the sun to feeble eyes, and solid food to those who are still using milk;[45] whereas they ought to lead them little by little up to what lies beyond them, and to bring them up to the higher truths; adding light to light, and supplying truth upon truth. Therefore we will leave the more mature discourse, for which the time has not yet come, and will speak with them as follows.

VII.   If, my friends, you will not acknowledge the Holy Spirit to be uncreated, nor yet eternal, clearly such a state of mind is due to the contrary spirit – forgive me, if in my zeal I speak somewhat over boldly. If, however, you are sound enough to escape this evident impiety, and to place outside of slavery Him Who gives freedom to yourselves, then see for yourselves with the help of the Holy Ghost and of us what follows. For I am persuaded that you are to some extent partakers of Him, so that I will go into the question with you as kindred souls. Either shew me some mean between lordship and servitude, that I may there place the rank of the Spirit; or, if you shrink from imputing servitude to Him, there is no doubt of the rank in which you must place the object of your search. But you are dissatisfied with the syllables, and you stumble at the word, and it is to you a stone of stumbling and a rock of offence;[46] for so is Christ to some minds. It is only human after all. Let us meet one another in a spiritual manner; let us be full rather of brotherly than of self love. Grant us the Power of the Godhead, and we will give up to you the use of the Name. Confess the Nature in other words for which you have greater reverence, and we will heal you as infirm people, filching from you some matters in which you delight. For it is shameful, yes, shameful and utterly illogical, when you are sound in soul, to draw petty distinctions about the sound, and to hide the Treasure, as if you envied it to others, or were afraid lest you should sanctify your own tongue too. But it is even more shameful for us to be in the state of which we accuse you, and, while condemning your petty distinctions of words to make petty distinctions of letters.

VIII.   Confess, my friends, the Trinity to be of One Godhead; or if you will, of One Nature; and we will pray the Spirit to give you this word God. He will give it to you, I well know, inasmuch as He has already granted you the first portion and the second;[47] and especially if that about which we are contending is some spiritual cowardice, and not the devil's objection. Yet more clearly and concisely, let me say, do not you call us to account for our loftier word (for envy has nothing to do with this ascent), and we will not find fault with what you have been able to attain, until by another road you are brought up to the same resting place. For we are not seeking victory, but to gain brethren, by whose separation from us we are torn. This we concede to you in whom we do find something of vital truth, who are sound as to the Son. We admire your life, but we do not altogether approve your doctrine. Ye who have the things of the Spirit, receive Himself in addition, that ye may not only strive, but strive lawfully,[48] which is the condition of your crown. May this reward of your conversation be granted you, that you may confess the Spirit perfectly and proclaim with us, aye and before us, all that is His due. Yes, and I will venture even more on your behalf; I will even utter the Apostle's wish. So much do I cling to you, and so much do I revere your array, and the colour of your continence, and those sacred assemblies, and the august Virginity, and purification, and the Psalmody that lasts all night[49] and your love of the poor, and of the brethren, and of strangers, that I could consent to be Anathema from Christ, and even to suffer something as one condemned, if only you might stand beside us, and we might glorify the Trinity together. For of the others why should I speak, seeing they are clearly dead (and it is the part of Christ alone to raise them, Who quickeneth the dead by His own Power), and are unhappily separated in place as they are bound together by their doctrine; and who quarrel among themselves as much as a pair of squinting eyes in looking at the same object, and differ with one another, not in sight but in position – if indeed we may charge them only with squinting, and not with utter blindness. And now that I have to some extent laid down your position, come, let us return again to the subject of the Spirit, and I think you will follow me now.

IX.   The Holy Ghost, then, always existed, and exists, and always will exist. He neither had a beginning, nor will He have an end; but He was everlastingly ranged with and numbered with the Father and the Son. For it was not ever fitting that either the Son should be wanting to the Father, or the Spirit to the Son. For then Deity would be shorn of Its Glory in its greatest respect, for It would seem to have arrived at the consummation of perfection as if by an afterthought. Therefore He

was ever being partaken, but not partaking; perfecting, not being perfected; sanctifying, not being sanctified; deifying, not being deified; Himself ever the same with Himself, and with Those with Whom He is ranged; invisible, eternal, incomprehensible,
unchangeable, without quality, without quantity, without form, impalpable, self-
moving, eternally moving, with free-will, self-powerful, all-powerful (even though all
that is of the Spirit is referable to the First Cause, just as is all that is of the Only-
begotten); Life and Lifegiver; Light and Lightgiver; absolute Good, and Spring of
Goodness; the Right, the Princely Spirit; the Lord, the Sender, the Separator; Builder
of His own Temple; leading, working as He wills; distributing His own Gifts; the Spirit
of Adoption, of Truth, of Wisdom, of Understanding, of Knowledge, of Godliness, of
Counsel, of Fear (which are ascribed to Him[50]) by Whom the Father is known and
the Son is glorified; and by Whom alone He is known; one class, one service, worship,
power, perfection, sanctification. Why make a long discourse of it? All that the Father
hath the Son hath also, except the being Unbegotten; and all that the Son hath the
Spirit hath also, except the Generation. And these two matters do not divide the
Substance, as I understand it, but rather are divisions within the Substance.[51]

XI.   He wrought first in the heavenly and angelic powers, and such as are first
after God and around God. For from no other source flows their perfection and
their brightness, and the difficulty or impossibility of moving them to sin, but from
the Holy Ghost. And next, in the Patriarchs and Prophets, of whom the former saw
Visions of God, or knew Him, and the latter also foreknew the future, having their
master part moulded by the Spirit, and being associated with events that were yet
future as if present, for such is the power of the Spirit. And next in the Disciples
of Christ (for I omit to mention Christ Himself, in Whom He dwelt, not as energizing but as accompanying His Equal), and that in three ways, as they were able to
receive Him, and on three occasions; before Christ was glorified by the Passion, and
after He was glorified by the Resurrection; and after His Ascension, or Restoration,
or whatever we ought to call it, to Heaven. Now the first of these manifests Him
– the healing of the sick and casting out of evil spirits, which could not be apart
from the Spirit; and so does that breathing upon them after the Resurrection, which
was clearly a divine inspiration; and so too the present distribution of the fiery
tongues, which we are now commemorating. But the first manifested Him indistinctly, the second more expressly, this present one more perfectly, since He is no
longer present only in energy, but as we may say, substantially, associating with us
and dwelling in us. For it was fitting that as the Son had lived with us in bodily form
– so the Spirit too should appear in bodily form; and that after Christ had returned
to His own place, He should have come down to us – *Coming* because He is the
Lord; *Sent*, because He is not a rival God. For such words no less manifest the
Unanimity than they mark the separate Individuality.

XII.   And therefore He came after Christ, that a Comforter should not be lacking
unto us; but *Another* Comforter, that you might acknowledge His co-equality. For
this word Another marks an Alter Ego, a name of equal Lordship, not of inequality.
For Another is not said, I know, of different kinds, but of things consubstantial.
And He came in the form of Tongues because of His close relation to the Word. And
they were of Fire, perhaps because of His purifying Power (for our Scripture knows

of a purifying fire, as any one who wishes can find out), or else because of His Substance. For one God is a consuming Fire, and a Fire[52] burning up the ungodly;[53] though you may again pick a quarrel over these words, being brought into difficulty by the Consubstantiality. And the tongues were cloven, because of the diversity of Gifts; and they sat to signify His Royalty and Rest among the Saints, and because the Cherubim are the Throne of God. And it took place in an Upper Chamber (I hope I am not seeming to anyone over-tedious), because those who should receive it were to ascend and be raised above the earth; for also certain upper chambers[54] are covered with Divine Waters,[55] by which the praises of God are sung. And Jesus Himself in an Upper Chamber gave the Communion of the Sacrament to those who were being initiated into the higher Mysteries, that thereby might be shewn on the one hand that God must come down to us, as I know He did of old to Moses; and on the other that we must go up to Him, and that so there should come to pass a Communion of God with men, by a coalescing of the dignity. For as long as either remains on its own footing, the One in His Glory the other in his lowliness, so long the Goodness of God cannot mingle with us, and His loving-kindness is incommunicable, and there is a great gulf between, which cannot be crossed; and which separates not only the Rich Man from Lazarus and Abraham's Bosom which he longs for, but also the created and changing natures from that which is eternal and immutable.

XIV. This Spirit shares with the Son in working both the Creation and the Resurrection, as you may be shewn by this Scripture; By the Word of the Lord were the heavens made, and all the power of them by the breath of His Mouth;[56] and this, The Spirit of God that made me, and the Breath of the Almighty that teacheth me;[57] and again, Thou shalt send forth Thy Spirit and they shall be created, and Thou shalt renew the face of the earth.[58] And He is the Author of spiritual regeneration. Here is your proof: – None can see or enter into the Kingdom, except he be born again of the Spirit,[59] and be cleansed from the first birth, which is a mystery of the night, by a remoulding of the day and of the Light, by which every one singly is created anew. This Spirit, for He is most wise and most loving,[60] if He takes possession of a shepherd makes him a Psalmist, subduing evil spirits by his song,[61] and proclaims him King; if he possess a goatherd and scraper of sycamore fruit,[62] He makes him a Prophet. Call to mind David and Amos. If He possess a goodly youth, He makes him a Judge of Elders,[63] even beyond his years, as Daniel testifies, who conquered the lions in their den.[64] If He takes possession of Fishermen, He makes them catch the whole world in the nets of Christ, taking them up in the meshes of the Word. Look at Peter and Andrew and the Sons of Thunder, thundering the things of the Spirit. If of Publicans, He makes gain of them for discipleship, and makes them merchants of souls; witness Matthew, yesterday a Publican, today an Evangelist. If of zealous persecutors, He changes the current of their zeal, and makes them Pauls instead of Sauls, and as full of piety as He found them of wickedness. And He is the Spirit of Meekness, and yet is provoked by those who sin. Let us therefore make proof of Him as gentle, not as wrathful, by confessing His Dignity; and let us not desire to see Him implacably wrathful. He too it is who has made me today a bold herald to you; – if without rest to myself, God be thanked; but if with risk, thanks to Him nevertheless; in the one case, that He may spare those that hate us; in the other, that He may consecrate us, in receiving this reward of our preaching of the Gospel, to be made perfect by blood.

XVIII.   These questions have been examined before by the studious, and perhaps not without occasion; and whatever else any one may contribute at the present day, he will be joined with us. But now it is our duty to dissolve this Assembly, for enough has been said. But the Festival is never to be put an end to; but kept now indeed with our bodies; but a little later on altogether spiritually *there*, where we shall see the reasons of these things more purely and clearly, in the Word Himself, and God, and our Lord Jesus Christ, the True Festival and Rejoicing of the Saved – to Whom be the glory and the worship, with the Father and the Holy Ghost, now and for ever. Amen.

Notes

1   Eugene F. Rogers, *After the Spirit: A Constructive Pneumatology from Resources Outside the Modern West* (Grand Rapids, MI: Eerdmans, 2005), p. 144.
2   Enlightenment (*photismos*) is one of the most ancient names for Holy Baptism: the name, in fact, which S. Gregory uses throughout this Oration, and which his Latin translator almost invariably renders by Baptismus.
3   This veil is original Sin, by which the soul is darkened and as it were covered.
4   Gen. ii. 7.
5   Rom. viii. 29.
6   Col. i. 18.
7   This is the literal version of the passage, which is somewhat loosely quoted from 1 Peter iii. 21.
8   1 John i. 5.
9   1 Tim. vi. 16.
10   John i. 9.
11   *Phos* (masc.) is a common poetical word for Man. 11 Prov. vi. 23.
12   Prov. vi. 23.
13   Ps. cxix. 105.
14   Exod. xxxiv. 30.
15   Exod. iii. 2.
16   Exod. xiii. 21.
17   2 Kings ii. 11.
18   Luke ii. 9.
19   Matt. ii. 9.
20   Luke ix. 32, 34.
21   Acts ix. 3.
22   Matt. xiii. 43.
23   Wisd. iii. 7.
24   Prov. iv. 25.
25   Matt. vii. 2.
26   Ps. lxxxv. 8.
27   Ps. cxliii. 8.

28 Ps. li. 8.
29 Ps. lvii. 4; lii. 2.
30 Ps. x. 7.
31 1 Cor. ii. 7.
32 Acts ii. 3.
33 Isa. iii. 34.
34 Canticles i. 3.
35 John xx. 28.
36 Ps. xxxiv. 8.
37 Ps. cxix. 103.
38 Ps. xl. 9.
39 Luke xiv. 16, etc.
40 Kevin Hector uses the phrase in this sense in "The Mediation of Christ's Normative Spirit: a Constructive Reading of Schleiermacher's Pneumatology," *Modern Theology* 24 (2008): 1–22, on pp. 3, 19 n. 10. An earlier use in a similar sense appears in Najeeb G. Awad, "Between Subordination and Koinonia: Toward a New Reading of Cappadocian Theology," *Modern Theology* 23 (2007): 181–204, on p. 203, n. 72.
41 S. Gregory makes this explanation because there were certain heretics who taught that our Lord at His Ascension laid aside His Humanity. It is said that this was held by certain Manicheans, who based their idea on Ps. xix. 4, where the LXX [Septuagint] and Vulgate read, "He hath set His Tabernacle in the Sun."
42 Eph. iii. 13.
43 The reference is to the Macedonians or Pneumatomachi, followers of Macedonius, Patriarch of Constantinople, who had passed from extreme or Anomoean Arianism to Semi-Arianism, and was forcibly intruded on the See by order of Constantius in 343, but was afterwards deposed. After his deposition he broached the heresy known by his name, denying the Deity of the Holy Ghost; some of its adherents, with Macedonius himself, maintaining Him to be a mere creature; others stopping short of this; and others calling Him a creature and servant of the Son. The heresy was formally condemned in the Ecumenical Council of Constantinople in 381.
44 John iii. 8.
45 Heb. v. 12.
46 Isa. viii. 14; Rom. ix. 33; 1 Pet. ii. 8.
47 I.e., inasmuch as He has granted you a right faith in the Consubstantiality and Unity of the Trinity, I am sure He will in time grant you the grace also to call Him by the Name of God.
48 2 Tim. ii. 5.
49 The Constantinopolitan followers of Macedonius at the period were noted for their strict asceticism. The attempt to revive the Night Office among the secular Clergy of the Diocese brought great odium on S. John Chrysostom a few years later.
50 I.e., by Isaiah.
51 Job xxxviii. 4, Ps. v. 10, xxxvi, cxxxix. 7–15, cxlii, Isa. xi. 1–3, xlviii. 16, Mal. iii. 6, Wisd. i. 2, John i. 14, iii. 24, xv. 26, xvi. 14, 15, Acts xiii. 2, Rom. iv. 17, xv. 16, 19, 1 Cor. ii. 10, Heb. ix. 14.
52 Heb. xii. 20.
53 Deut. iv. 24.
54 Ps. civ. 3.
55 Ps. cxlviii. 4.

56   Ps. xxxiii. 6.
57   Job xxxiii. 4.
58   Ps. civ. 30.
59   John iii. 3.
60   Wisd. i. 6.
61   1 Sam. xvi. 23.
62   Amos vii. 14.
63   Susannah.
64   Dan. vi. 22.

IV
Latin Resources

15

Augustine of Hippo, Homily on the First Epistle of John

In trinitarian thought, Augustine is identified with the "psychological" analogy for the Trinity. The several versions that Augustine tries out in his *De Trinitate*, "On the Trinity," circle around the triad memory, reason, and will for Father, Son, and Holy Spirit. The analogy makes the oneness of God as easy to see as the oneness of a human mind. The threeness is also easy to see. In Augustine's analogies, we can see both that God's action is indivisible toward the outside (if my memory, reason, or will does something, then no one else does it but I), and that the characteristic roles of the three are distinguishable from one another only among themselves (forgetting is different from not wanting).

Critics find a number of problems with the analogy – as with any others. First, the distinction among the three makes sense in *human* terms primarily in the breech. That is, human beings distinguish memory, reason, and will in our own minds primarily when we want to blame one faculty rather than another for some failure. "I forgot!" "I didn't see!" "But I didn't want to!" are distinct excuses, but when things work well, the unified I takes credit ("Of course I was there for you"). Second, as that objection points up, the analogy seems to rely on human psychology to an alarming extent, although Augustine protects himself against that. Third, the analogy implies that one can see into the inner psychology of God, as if God had an inside and an outside like ours, which raises questions about God's reliability. What if God is really different "inside," and only pretending or acting in the way that we observe? Of course, all these questions can be answered by switching analogies, just as the problems with other analogies can be addressed by switching to this one. In the end, all the analogies break down. They work, not if the mind seizes God, but if God seizes the mind. Only the God-seized mind, Augustine concludes, can analogize God.

Augustine of Hippo, *Homilies on the First Epistle of John*, no. 7, in *A Select Library of the Nicene and Post-Nicene Fathers of the Christian Church*, First Series, ed. Philip Schaff et al., in several editions, vol. 7.

In the following selection, therefore, we do not see the analogy worked out in an attempt to reach completeness or to answer objections. This homily belongs to a different genre than conceptual exposition. Rather, it is a sermon about love. Love is, of course, the form that will takes when will is good. But here we see the difference it makes that God is love, the Holy Spirit is love, and human beings are to love God and one another. In this homily, Augustine keeps readers from worrying about whether he or they have got the Trinity right, by showing how it looks when the Trinity has them right – when they love with the love of God. Robert Jenson has (like Peter Lombard in the Middle Ages) posed the question whether the Holy Spirit only *bestows* the love of God and neighbor on human beings as some other thing, or whether the Holy Spirit gives its very *self* as the love of God and neighbor.[1] Augustine shows the second, more audacious view here in action. If you want to see the Holy Spirit, serve your neighbor.

Homily VII, on 1 John iv. 4–12

Augustine of Hippo

"Now are ye of God, little children, and have overcome him: because greater is He that is in you, than he that is in this world. They are of the world: therefore speak they of the world, and the world heareth them. We are of God: he that knoweth God heareth us; he that is not of God heareth not us. From this know we the spirit of truth, and [the spirit] of error. Dearly beloved, let us love one another: for love is of God; and every one that loveth is born of God, and knoweth God. He that loveth not knoweth not God; for God is love. In this was manifested the love of God in us, that God sent His only-begotten Son into this world, that we may live through Him. Herein is love, not that we loved, but that He loved us, and sent His Son to be the Atoner for our sins. Dearly beloved, if God so loved us, we ought also to love one another. No man hath seen God at any time" [1 John 4: 4–12a].

1. So is this world to all the faithful seeking their own country, as was the desert to the people Israel. They wandered indeed as yet, and were seeking their own country: but with God for their guide they could not wander astray. Their way was God's bidding. For where they went about during forty years, the journey itself is made up of a very few stations, and is known to all. They were retarded because they were in training, not because they were forsaken. That therefore which God promiseth us is ineffable sweetness and a good,[2] as the Scripture saith, and as ye have often heard by us rehearsed, which "eye hath not seen, nor ear heard, neither hath entered into the heart of man."[3] But by temporal labors we are exercised, and by temptations of this present life are trained. Howbeit, if ye would not die of thirst in this wilderness, drink charity. It is the fountain which God has been pleased to place here that we faint not in the way: and we shall more abundantly drink thereof, when we are come to our own land. The Gospel has just been read; now to speak

of the very words with which the lesson ended, what other thing heard ye but concerning charity? For we have made an agreement with our God in prayer, that if we would that He should forgive us our sins, we also should forgive the sins which may have been committed against us.[4] Now that which forgiveth is none other than charity. Take away charity from the heart; hatred possesseth it, it knows not how to forgive. Let charity be there, and she fearlessly forgiveth, not being straitened. And this whole epistle which we have undertaken to expound to you, see whether it commendeth aught else than this one thing, charity. Nor need we fear lest by much speaking thereof it come to be hateful. For what is there to love, if charity come to be hateful? It is by charity that other things come to be rightly loved; then how must itself be loved! Let not that then which ought never to depart from the heart, depart from the tongue.

2. "Now," saith he, "are ye of God little children, and have overcome him:"[5] whom but Antichrist? For above he had said, "Whosoever unmaketh Jesus Christ and denieth that He is come in the flesh is not of God." Now we expounded, if ye remember, that all those who violate charity deny Jesus Christ to have come in the flesh. For Jesus had no need to come but because of charity: as indeed the charity we are commending is that which the Lord Himself commendeth in the Gospel, "Greater love than this can no man have, that a man lay down his life for his friends."[6] How was it possible for the Son of God to lay down His life for us without putting on flesh in which He might die? Whosoever therefore violates charity, let him say what he will with his tongue, his life denies that Christ is come in the flesh; and this is an antichrist, wherever he may be, whithersoever he have come in. But what saith the apostle to them who are citizens of that country for which we sigh? "Ye have overcome him." And whereby have they overcome? "Because greater is He that is in you, than he that is in this world." Lest they should attribute the victory to their own strength, and by arrogance of pride should be overcome, (for whomsoever the devil makes proud, he overcomes,) wishing them to keep humility, what saith he? "Ye have overcome him." Every man now, at hearing this saying, "Ye have overcome," lifts up the head, lifts up the neck, wishes himself to be praised. Do not extol thyself; see who it is that in thee hath overcome. Why hast thou overcome? "Because greater is He that is in you, than he that is in the world." Be humble, bear thy Lord; be thou the beast for Him to sit on. Good is it for thee that He should rule, and He guide. For if thou have not Him to sit on thee, thou mayest lift up the neck, mayest strike out the heels: but woe to thee without a ruler, for this liberty sendeth thee among the wild beasts to be devoured!

3. "These are of the world."[7] Who? The antichrists. Ye have already heard who they be. And if ye be not such, ye know them, but whosoever is such, knows not. "These are of the world: therefore speak they of the world, and the world heareth them." Who are they that "speak of the world"? Mark who are against charity. Behold, ye have heard the Lord saying, "If ye forgive men their trespasses, your heavenly Father will forgive you also your trespasses. But if ye forgive not men their trespasses, neither will your Father forgive your trespasses."[8] It is the sentence of Truth: or if it be not Truth that speaks, gainsay it. If thou art a Christian and believest Christ,

He hath said, "I am the truth." This sentence is true, is firm. Now hear men that "speak of the world." "And wilt thou not avenge thyself? And wilt thou let him say that he has done this to thee? Nay: let him feel that he has to do with a man." Every day are such things said, They that say such things, "of the world speak they, and the world heareth them." None say such things but those that love the world, and by none are such things heard but by those who love the world. And ye have heard that to love the world and neglect charity is to deny that Jesus came in the flesh. Or say if the Lord Himself in the flesh did that? if, being buffeted, He willed to be avenged? if, hanging on the cross, He did not say, "Father, forgive them, for they know not what they do"?[9] But if He threatened not, who had power; why dost thou threaten, why art thou inflated with anger, who art under power of another? He died because it was His will to die, yet He threatened not; thou knowest not when thou shalt die, and dost thou threaten?

4.   "We are of God."[10] Let us see why; see whether it be for any other thing than charity. "We are of God: he that knoweth God heareth us; he that is not of God heareth not us. Hereby know we the spirit of truth, and of error": namely by this, that he that heareth us hath the spirit of truth; he that heareth not us, hath the spirit of error. Let us see what he adviseth, and let us choose rather to hear him advising in the spirit of truth, and not antichrists, not lovers of the world, not the world. If we are born of God, "beloved,"[11] he goes on – see above from what: "We are of God: he that knoweth God heareth us; he that is not of God heareth not us. Hereby know we the spirit of truth, and of error": aye, now, he makes us eagerly attentive: to be told that he who knows God, hears; but he who knows not, hears not; and that this is the discerning between the spirit of truth and the spirit of error: well then, let us see what he is about to advise; in what we must hear him – "Beloved, let us love one another."[12] Why? because a man adviseth? "Because love is of God." Much hath he commended love, in that he hath said, "Is of God": but he is going to say more; let us eagerly hear. At present he hath said, "Love is of God; and every one that loveth is born of God, and knoweth God. He that loveth not knoweth not God."[13] Why? "For God is love" [Love is God].[14] What more could be said, brethren? If nothing were said in praise of love throughout the pages of this epistle, if nothing whatever throughout the other pages of the Scriptures, and this one only thing were all we were told by the voice of the Spirit of God, "For Love is God"; nothing more ought we to require.

5.   Now see that to act against love is to act against God. Let no man say, "I sin against man when I do not love my brother (mark it!), and sin against man is a thing to be taken easily; only let me not sin against God." How sinnest thou not against God, when thou sinnest against love? "Love is God." Do "we" say this? If we said, "Love is God," haply some one of you might be offended and say, What hath he said? What meant he to say, that "Love is God"? God "gave" love, as a gift God bestowed love. "Love is of God: Love *is* God." Look, here have ye, brethren, the Scriptures of God: this epistle is canonical; throughout all nations it is recited, it is held by the authority of the whole earth, it hath edified the whole earth. Thou art here told by the Spirit of God, "Love is God." Now if thou dare, go against God, and refuse to love thy brother!

6.   In what sense then was it said a while ago, "Love is of God;" and now, "Love *is* God?" For God is Father and Son and Holy Ghost: the Son, God of God, the Holy Ghost, God of God; and these three, one God, not three Gods. If the Son be God, and the Holy Ghost God, and that person loveth in whom dwelleth the Holy Ghost: therefore "Love is God;" but "*is* God," because "Of God." For thou hast both in the epistle; both, "Love is of God," and, "Love is God." Of the Father alone the Scripture hath it not to say, that He is "of God": but when thou hearest that expression, "Of God," either the Son is meant, or the Holy Ghost. Because while the apostle saith, "The love of God is shed abroad in our hearts by the Holy Spirit which is given unto us":[15] let us understand that He who subsisteth in love is the Holy Ghost. For it is even this Holy Spirit, whom the bad cannot receive, even He is that Fountain of which the Scripture saith, "Let the fountain of thy water be thine own, and let no stranger partake with thee."[16] For all who love not God, are strangers, are antichrists. And though they come to the churches, they cannot be numbered among the children of God; not to them belongeth that Fountain of life. To have baptism is possible even for a bad man; to have prophecy is possible even for a bad man. We find that king Saul had prophecy: he was persecuting holy David, yet was he filled with the spirit of prophecy, and began to prophesy.[17] To receive the sacrament of the body and blood of the Lord is possible even for a bad man: for of such it is said, "He that eateth and drinketh unworthily, eateth and drinketh judgment to himself."[18] To have the name of Christ is possible even for a bad man; i.e., even a bad man can be called a Christian: as they of whom it is said, "They polluted the name of their God."[19] I say, to have all these sacraments is possible even for a bad man; but to have charity, and to be a bad man, is not possible. This then is the peculiar gift, this the "Fountain" that is singly one's "own." To drink of this the Spirit of God exhorteth you, to drink of Himself the Spirit of God exhorteth you.

7.   "In this was manifested the love of God in us."[20] Behold, in order that we may love God, we have exhortation. Could we love Him, unless He first loved us? If we were slow to love, let us not be slow to love in return. He first loved us; not even so do we love. He loved the unrighteous, but He did away the unrighteousness: He loved the unrighteous, but not unto unrighteousness did He gather them together: He loved the sick, but He visited them to make them whole. "Love," then, "is God." "In this was manifested the love of God in us, because that God sent His only-begotten Son into the world, that we may live through Him." As the Lord Himself saith: "Greater love than this can no man have, that a man lay down his life for his friends":[21] and there was proved the love of Christ towards us, in that He died for us: how is the love of the Father towards us proved? In that He "sent His only Son" to die for us: so also the apostle Paul saith: "He that spared not His own Son, but delivered Him up for us all, how hath He not with Him also freely given us all things?"[22] Behold the Father delivered up Christ; Judas delivered Him up; does it not seem as if the thing done were of the same sort? Judas is "*traditor*," one that delivered up [or, a traitor]: is God the Father that? God forbid! sayest thou. I do not say it, but the apostle saith, "He that spared not His own Son, but '*tradidit Eum*' delivered Him up for us all." Both the Father delivered

Him up, and He delivered up Himself. The same apostle saith: "Who loved me, and delivered Himself up for me."[23] If the Father delivered up the Son; and the Son delivered up Himself, what has Judas done? There was a "*traditio*" (delivering up) by the Father; there was a "*traditio*" by the Son; there was a "*traditio*" by Judas: the thing done is the same, but what is it that distinguishes the Father delivering up the Son, the Son delivering up Himself, and Judas the disciple delivering up his Master? This: that the Father and the Son did it in love, but Judas did this in treacherous betrayal. Ye see that not what the man does is the thing to be considered; but with what mind and will he does it. We find God the Father in the same deed in which we find Judas; the Father we bless, Judas we detest. Why do we bless the Father, and detest Judas? We bless charity, detest iniquity. How great a good was conferred upon mankind by the delivering up of Christ! Had Judas this in his thoughts, that therefore he delivered Him up? God had in His thoughts our salvation by which we were redeemed; Judas had in his thoughts the price for which he sold the Lord. The Son Himself had in His thoughts the price He gave for us, Judas in his the price he received to sell Him. The diverse intention therefore makes the things done diverse. Though the thing be one, yet if we measure it by the diverse intentions, we find the one a thing to be loved, the other to be condemned; the one we find a thing to be glorified, the other to be detested. Such is the force of charity. See that it alone discriminates, it alone distinguishes the doings of men.

8. This we have said in the case where the things done are similar. In the case where they are diverse, we find a man by charity made fierce; and by iniquity made winningly gentle. A father beats a boy, and a boy-stealer [kidnapper] caresses. If thou name the two things, blows and caresses, who would not choose the caresses, and decline the blows? If thou mark the persons, it is charity that beats, iniquity that caresses. See what we are insisting upon; that the deeds of men are only discerned by the root of charity. For many things may be done that have a good appearance, and yet proceed not from the root of charity. For thorns also have flowers: some actions truly seem rough, seem savage; howbeit they are done for discipline at the bidding of charity. Once for all, then, a short precept is given thee: Love, and do what thou wilt: whether thou hold thy peace, through love hold thy peace; whether thou cry out, through love cry out; whether thou correct, through love correct; whether thou spare, through love do thou spare: let the root of love be within, of this root can nothing spring but what is good.

9. "In this is love – in this was manifested the love of God toward us, because that God sent his only-begotten Son into this world, that we may live through Him. – In this is love, not that we loved God, but that He loved us":[24] we did not love Him first: for to this end loved He us, that we may love Him: "And sent His Son to be the Atoner for our sins: "*litatorem*," i.e., one that sacrifices. He sacrificed for our sins. Where did He find the sacrifice? Where did He find the victim which he would offer pure? Other He found none; His own self He offered. "Beloved, if God so loved us we ought also to love one another.[25] Peter," saith He, "lovest thou me?" And he said, "I love." "Feed my sheep."

10. "No man hath seen God at any time:"[26] He is a thing invisible; not with the eye but with the heart must He be sought. But just as if we wished to see the

sun, we should purge the eye of the body; wishing to see God, let us purge the eye by which God can be seen. Where is this eye? Hear the Gospel: "Blessed are the pure in heart, for they shall see God."[27] But let no man imagine God to himself according to the lust of his eyes. For so he makes unto himself either a huge form, or a certain incalculable magnitude which, like the light which he sees with the bodily eyes, he makes extend through all directions; field after field of space he gives it all the bigness he can; or, he represents to himself like as it were an old man of venerable form. None of these things do thou imagine. There is something thou mayest imagine, if thou wouldest see God; "God is love." What sort of face hath love? what form hath it? what stature? what feet? what hands hath it? no man can say. And yet it hath feet, for these carry men to church: it hath hands; for these reach forth to the poor: it hath eyes; for thereby we consider the needy: "Blessed is the man," it is said, "who considereth the needy and the poor."[28] It hath ears, of which the Lord saith, "He that hath ears to hear let him hear."[29] These are not members distinct by place, but with the understanding he that hath charity sees the whole at once. Inhabit, and thou shalt be inhabited; dwell, and thou shalt be dwelt in. For how say you, my brethren? who loves what he does not see? Now why, when charity is praised, do ye lift up your hands, make acclaim, praise? What have I shown you? What I produced, was it a gleam of colors? What I propounded, was it gold and silver? Have I dug out jewels from hid treasures? What of this sort have I shown to your eyes? Is my face changed while I speak? I am in the flesh; I am in the same form in which I came forth to you; ye are in the same form in which ye came hither: charity is praised, and ye shout applause. Certainly ye see nothing. But as it pleases you when ye praise, so let it please you that ye may keep it in your heart. For mark well what I say brethren; I exhort you all, as God enables me, unto a great treasure. If there were shown you a beautiful little vase, embossed, inlaid with gold, curiously wrought, and it charmed your eyes, and drew towards it the eager desire of your heart, and you were pleased with the hand of the artificer, and the weight of the silver, and the splendor of the metal; would not each one of you say, "O, if I had that vase!" And to no purpose ye would say it, for it would not rest with you to have it. Or if one should wish to have it, he might think of stealing it from another's house. Charity is praised to you; if it please you, have it, possess it: no need that ye should rob any man, no need that ye should think of buying it; it is to be had freely, without cost. Take it, clasp it; there is nothing sweeter. If such it be when it is but spoken of, what must it be when one has it?

11. If any of you perchance wish to keep charity, brethren, above all things do not imagine it to be an abject and sluggish thing; nor that charity is to be preserved by a sort of gentleness, nay not gentleness, but tameness and listlessness.[30] Not so is it preserved. Do not imagine that thou then lovest thy servant when thou dost not beat him, or that thou then lovest thy son when thou givest him not discipline, or that thou then lovest thy neighbor when thou dost not rebuke him: this is not charity, but mere feebleness. Let charity be fervent to correct, to amend: but if there be good manners, let them delight thee; if bad, let them be amended, let them be corrected. Love not in the man his error, but the man: for the man God made, the error the man himself made. Love that which God made, love not that which the

man himself made. When thou lovest that, thou takest away this: when thou esteemest that, thou amendest this. But even if thou be severe at any time, let it be because of love, for correction. For this cause was charity betokened by the Dove which descended upon the Lord.[31] That likeness of a dove, the likeness in which came the Holy Ghost, by whom charity should be shed forth into us: wherefore was this? The dove hath no gall: yet with beak and wings she fights for her young; hers is a fierceness without bitterness. And so does also a father; when he chastises his son, for discipline he chastises him. As I said, the kidnapper, in order that he may sell, inveigles the child with bitter endearments; a father, that he may correct, does without gall chastise. Such be ye to all men. See here, brethren, a great lesson, a great rule: each one of you has children, or wishes to have; or if he has altogether determined to have no children after the flesh, at least spiritually he desires to have children: – what father does not correct his son? what son does not his father discipline? And yet he seems to be fierce with him. It is the fierceness of love, the fierceness of charity: a sort of fierceness without gall after the manner of the dove, not of the raven. Whence it came into my mind, my brethren, to tell you, that those violaters of charity are they that have made the schism: as they hate charity itself, so they hate also the dove. But the dove convicts them: it comes forth from heaven, the heavens open, and it abideth on the head of the Lord. Wherefore this? That John may hear, "This is He that baptizeth."[32] Away, ye robbers; away, ye invaders of the possession of Christ! On your own possessions, where ye will needs be lords, ye have dared to fix the titles of the great Owner. He recognizes His own titles; He vindicates to Himself His own possession. He does not cancel the titles, but enters in and takes possession. So in one that comes to the Catholic Church, his baptism is not cancelled, that the title of the commander[33] be not cancelled: but what is done in the Catholic Church? The title is acknowledged; the Owner enters in under His own titles, where the robber was entering in under titles not his own.

Notes

1   Robert W. Jenson, *Systematic Theology* (New York: Oxford University Press, 1997), vol. 1, pp. 148–9.
2   Isa. lxiv. 4.
3   1 Cor. ii. 9.
4   Matt. vi. 12.
5   1 John iv. 4.
6   John xv. 13.
7   1 John iv. 5.
8   Matt. vi. 14, 15.
9   Luke xxiii. 34.
10   1 John iv. 6.
11   1 John iv. 7.
12   1 John iv. 7.
13   1 John iv. 7, 8.

14　*Deus dilectio est*: Augustine here expounds it, "Love is God"; it is "of God" and "is God" (as "the Word was *with* God and *was* God"); this is clear from sec. 6 and Homily viii. 14, "For He has not hesitated to say, *Deus charitas est*, Charity is God." In the theological exposition *de Trin.* xv. 27, he takes it in the usual sense, "God is Love" (as "God is Spirit"). In the Greek the proposition is not convertible, *agape* being marked as the predicate by the absence of the article while *theos* has it: *ho theos agape estin*.

15　Rom. v. 5.

16　Prov. v. 16.

17　1 Sam. xix.

18　1 Cor. xi. 29.

19　 Ezek. 36: 20.

20　1 John iv. 9.

21　John xv. 13.

22　Rom. viii. 32.

23　Gal. ii. 20.

24　1 John iv. 9, 10.

25　1 John iv. 11.

26　1 John iv. 12.

27　Matt. v. 8.

28　Ps. xli. 1.

29　Luke viii. 8.

30　Epistles cliii. 17, c. litt. Petil. [Against the Letters of Petilianus], ii. 67: Sermons clxxi. 5.

31　Hom. in Ev. vi. p. 82; Matt. iii. 16.

32　John i. 33.

33　"Captain of their salvation." Heb. ii. 10.

16

Veni Spiritus Hymns

Two Latin hymns, one ninth-century and one twelfth-century, collect many of the Holy Spirit tropes characteristic of western liturgies and continue to be popular in Catholic and Protestant worship. Both hymns open with the imperative "Come!" "*Veni, Creator Spiritus*" (Come, Creator Spirit) functions as a hymn of election and anointing: it marks the ordination of priests, the crowning of monarchs, and the entrance of cardinals into the Sistine Chapel to elect a new pope, and it appears at the vespers of Pentecost. "*Veni, Sancte Spiritus*" (Come, Holy Spirit), called "the Golden Sequence," accompanies the gospel procession at Pentecost and functions therefore as a prayer for illumination. It enjoys attributions variously to King Robert II of France, Stephen Langton the Archbishop of Canterbury, and Pope Innocent III. Both hymns boast many translations and settings.

Veni, Creator Spiritus	*Veni, Creator Spiritus*
ninth century, att. Rabanus Maurus	paraphrase by John Dryden

Veni, Creator Spiritus
mentes tuorum visita
Imple superna gratia
quae tu creasti pectora.

Creator Spirit, by whose aid
The world's foundations first were laid,
Come visit every pious mind.
Come pour thy joys on human kind;
From sin and sorrow set us free,
And make thy temples worthy thee.

Qui Paraclitus diceris,
Donum Dei Altissimi,
fons vivus, ignis, caritas,
et spiritualis unctio.

O source of uncreated light
The Father's promised Paraclete!
Thrice holy fount, thrice holy fire
Our hearts with heavenly love inspire;
Come, and thy sacred unction bring,
To sanctify us while we sing.

Tu septiformis munere,
dextrae Dei tu digitus;
tu rite promissum Patris,
sermone ditans guttura.

Plenteous of grace, descend from high,
Rich in thy seven-fold energy!
Thou strength of his almighty hand
Whose power does heaven and earth
command!
Proceeding Spirit, our defence,
Who dost the gifts of tongues dispense,
And crown'st thy gift with eloquence!

Accende lumen sensibus,
infunde amorem cordibus,
infirma nostri corporis,
virtute firmans perpeti.

Refine and purge our earthly parts;
But, O, inflame and fire our hearts!
Our frailties help, our vice control,
Submit the senses to the soul;
And when rebellious they are grown,
Then lay thy hand and hold 'em down.

Hostem repellas longius,
pacemque duces protinus,
ductore sic te praevio,
vitemus omne noxium.

Chase from our minds the infernal foe,
And peace, the fruit of love, bestow;
And, lest our feet should step astray,
Protect and guide us on the way.

Per te sciamus da Patrem,
noscamus atque Filium,
te utriusque Spiritum
credamus omni tempore.

Make us eternal truths receive,
And practise all that we believe;
Give us thyself, that we may see
The Father and the Son by thee.

Sit laus Patri cum Filio,
Sancto simul Paraclito:
nobisque mittat Filius
charisma Sancti Spiritus.

Amen

Immortal honour, endless fame,
Attend the Almighty Father's name;
The Saviour Son be glorified,
Who for lost man's redemption died;
And equal adoration be,
Eternal Paraclete, to thee.

Veni, Sancte Spiritus

twelfth century

Veni, Sancte Spiritus

translation by John Mason Neale

Veni, Sancte Spiritus,
et emitte caelitus
lucis tuae radium.

Come, thou holy Paraclete,
and from thy celestial seat
send thy light and brilliancy.

Veni, pater pauperum,
veni, dator munerum
veni, lumen cordium.

Father of the poor, draw near;
giver of all gifts, be here;
come, the soul's true radiancy.

Consolator optime,
dulcis hospes animae,
dulce refrigerium.

Come, of comforters the best,
of the soul the sweetest guest,
come in toil refreshingly.

In labore requies,
in aestu temperies
in fletu solatium.

Thou in labor rest most sweet,
thou art shadow from the heat,
comfort in adversity.

O lux beatissima,
reple cordis intima
tuorum fidelium.

Sine tuo numine,
nihil est in homine,
nihil est innoxium.

Lava quod est sordidum,
riga quod est aridum,
sana quod est saucium.

Flecte quod est rigidum,
fove quod est frigidum,
rege quod est devium.

Da tuis fidelibus,
in te confidentibus,
sacrum septenarium.

Da virtutis meritum,
da salutis exitum,
da perenne gaudium,

Amen, Alleluia

O thou Light, most pure and blest,
shine within the inmost breast
of thy faithful company.

Where thou art not, man hath nought;
every holy deed and thought
comes from thy Divinity.

What is soilèd, make thou pure;
what is wounded, work its cure;
what is parchèd, fructify.

What is rigid, gently bend;
what is frozen, warmly tend;
strengthen what goes erringly.

Fill thy faithful who confide
in thy power to guard and guide,
with thy sevenfold mystery.

Here thy grace and virtue send;
grant salvation in the end,
and in heaven felicity.

Plate 1. Some Christian exegetes have read the three visitors to Abraham in Genesis 18 as the members of the Trinity. God and human beings share a feast together, figuring the Last Supper, the Eucharist, and the heavenly feast – all occasions on which the members of the Trinity and human beings exchange hospitality. To indicate that the Three are one and beyond gender, they typically bear the same, androgynous face.

Icon with the Hospitality of Abraham. Benaki Museum, Athens, Greece.

Photo Credit: Scala / Art Resource, NY

Plate 2. This image shows in schematic fashion the Spirit resting on the Son and joining the Son with the Father even in the Crucifixion. Twentieth-century theologians will, much later, interpret Romans 8 to think of the Holy Spirit as reuniting Father and Son after death – incorporating other human beings into that movement.

Master of the Berthold Sacramentary, thirteenth century: *The Trinity*, from a missal, Germany (Abbey of Weingarten), *ca.*1200–32. M.710, f.132v. The Pierpont Morgan Library, New York.

Photo Credit: The Pierpont Morgan Library / Art Resource, New York

Plate 3. At the very top of the Altieri chapel in San Francesco a Ripa in Rome, the Holy Spirit as a dove hovers among rays of gilded light. At the bottom, the blessed Ludovica Albertoni lies dying in the rapture of union with God. As in Romans 8, the Holy Spirit presides over an experience of "groaning too deep for words," at once erotic and divine – both indicate union with a loving other. As in Romans 8, the Spirit catches up the human being in an experience of weakness that recalls the death – and therefore the resurrection – of Christ. Bernini suggests supernatural movement in the upward billowing of the cloth, union in the gesture of the hand on the heart, and Christ in the disposition of the figure as in that of Michelangelo's *Pietà*. (See Shelley Perlove, *Bernini and the Idealization of Death: The Blessed Ludovica Albertoni and the Altieri Chapel* (University Park, PA and London: Pennsylvania State University Press, 1990). These features suggest the tendency of the Spirit to excite and orchestrate human experience, to hover over and deploy matter, and to reunite Christ and the Father – therefore also the believer participant in Christ – in death.

    Gian Lorenzo Bernini (1598–1680): *Beata Ludovica Albertoni.* San Francesco a Ripa, Rome. Photo Credit: Biblioteca Herziana

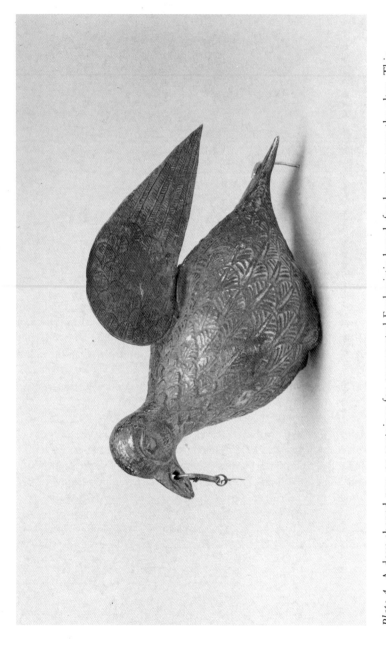

Plate 4. A dove-shaped pyx, or container for consecrated Eucharistic bread, for hanging over the altar. This example indicates the tendency to associate the Holy Spirit with material objects, centrally the body of Christ (in the bread). Like the Spirit, this dove can hover over the people. Like the Spirit consecrating the host, it can descend over the altar. Like the Spirit, it can distribute gift's and sacraments.

Hanging silver dove, probably a pyx (container for consecrated bread), sixth to seventh century, early Byzantine, North Syrian, made in Attarouthi. The Metropolitan Museum of Art, New York.

Photo Credit: Image copyright © The Metropolitan Museum of Art / Art Resource, New York

17

Rupert of Deutz, [The Holy Spirit Hovers over Baptism]

In this short passage, Rupert (1075–1129), abbot of the Benedictine abbey at Deutz near Cologne comments on the scriptural readings at baptism, asking why the creation story is read. He explains it in terms of the hovering of the Spirit over the waters of creation, the womb, and the font – terms that make the most of the image of the Holy Spirit as a hovering or brooding bird. The passive metaphor of "being" born again here becomes active: the Holy Spirit re-bears or even re-hatches the believer in the waters of baptism. It is unclear whether a translator should use "he" or "she" for the Spirit as the metaphor becomes more concretely feminine. Rupert even adds a grammatically feminine appositive – *bonitas*, goodness – to the grammatically masculine *Spiritus*, with the result that succeeding pronouns share a masculine and a feminine antecedent. At the beginning of the passage, we find Rupert playing on the senses of the Vulgate's *ferebatur*, according to which the Spirit at creation "was carrying itself" over the waters, "was bearing itself up," used of birds for flying or hovering – a verb used in the active also for carrying young, bearing children, and being pregnant. The waters of creation imply the waters of a womb, from which creation knits together under the influence of its mother's warmth, an implication spelled out for Christ in the womb of Mary. In the middle of the passage the Spirit becomes explicitly a bird – presumably female – incubating her eggs, and by the end of the passage the Spirit is the "Mother" of believers. I have here rendered the Spirit in feminine pronouns because no masculine images compete or interfere. In other medieval

Rupert of Deutz, *De divinis officiis*, book 7, ed. Hrabanus Haacke, Corpus christianorum continuatio medievalis, vol. 7 (Turnhout: Brepols, 1967), pp. 225–8. I owe my attention to this passage to Wanda Zemler-Cizewski, " 'The Lord, the Giver of Life': A Reflection on the Theology of the Holy Spirit in the Twelfth Century," *Anglican Theological Review* 83 (2001), pp. 547–56. While this translation is my own, it was inspired and influenced by Cizewski's exposition and partial translation, pp. 552–3.

contexts, the Father has a womb and the Son has breasts while retaining the gendered designations "Father" and "Son." Here we may see less gender-bending, since no masculine images appear in the vicinity. The question belongs to the general difficulty in using human language to speak of God at all: how to render a figure who is both beyond gender and its source.

[The Holy Spirit Hovers over Baptism]

Rupert of Deutz

[In the rite of baptism are] readings and passages pertaining to the sacrament of baptism at the present day. At the beginning, readings pertaining to this sacrament from the Old Testament to the New are read, and similarly hymns drawn from them are sung. For it is difficult to enumerate how familiarly and how frequently the Holy Spirit was revered even before the coming of Christ, mostly with respect to water, and by mystical things said and done to prefigure grace to the baptized. . . . The reading that comes first is from the book of Genesis, "In the beginning God created heaven and earth" [Gen. 1: 1]. Perhaps someone will ask what that has to do with the sacrament of baptism. . . . Briefly . . . it brings forward clear testimony to the baptism of Christ because it reads "And the Spirit of God was hovering over the waters" [Gen. 1: 2], and simultaneously it proclaims for the first time and repeatedly an evident oracle of the divine name in which we are baptized, that is, of the Holy Trinity. For it says, "In the beginning God created the heavens and the earth," by which we are to understand no other beginning than the Son. . . . For "the beginning" is "the Son." By the Son, God made the heavens and the earth. "Everything was made by Him," as John the Evangelist tells it, "and without him was not anything made that was made" [John 1: 3]. For, without any doubt, in the word "God," the Father is to be understood, and, in the word "beginning," the Son is to be understood. Indeed, when it says: "In the beginning God made the heavens and the earth," it then adds, "and the Spirit of God was hovering over the waters," who is the third Person in the Trinity.

Then in the same reading, "Let us make the human being to our own image and likeness" [Gen. 1: 26]. . . . Now the Holy Spirit was hovering over the waters so that the likeness of God, which had been abolished by sin, should be restored by the regenerating grace of baptism. . . . Therefore, in order that we might be able to recover the likeness to God, which we lost by our own will, the goodness of God, the Holy Spirit, came down to a place we could easily reach, while She was hovering over the waters which have been made ready, asking of us only willingness and taking care of everything else for free. For She created even the water that flowed out from the dead body of Christ, since She caused the body of Christ itself to grow together from the water of our nature by Her own incubating warmth, as we have it in the Creed, "and He was incarnate by the Holy Spirit," or in the Gospel, "for what is born in her is of the Holy Spirit" [Matt. 1: 20], and who in the creation of the world, as it is written in the present reading, "was hovering over the waters," like a bird, as Jerome says, animating her eggs by her heat. Now the same one bears herself over the waters of baptism, so that, brooding them all together, she might re-bear those coming under her favor into true life, spreading her wings and lifting them up, and even carrying them on her back. And if it is necessary that she approach any more closely to anyone, that is, if anyone should be kept from the waters, and wanting to reach them should not be able to – as the centurion Cornelius was shut out by Jews prohibiting Gentiles from receiving, to say nothing of the many baptized who, confessing Christ under persecution, were not able to reach the waters, kept away by prisons and shackled with chains – if then it should be necessary for some reason of that sort then at length the Mother, the Grace of God, who extends her wings beyond the nest of the waters, flies forth to her own, as the Holy Spirit swooped down upon all who were listening to the word when Peter was preaching, and were speaking in tongues and magnifying God.

18

Guerric of Igny, Fourth Sermon for Palm Sunday

Modern American evangelicalism makes much of "having" or "letting Jesus into your heart." Medieval Cistercians made something rather different of it. Medieval Cistercian monks "conceived" Jesus within themselves, like Mary. As at the Annunciation, that conception was the work of the Holy Spirit. The monk was thus biologically male and religiously female, in order to give birth to Christ in his heart. But that's not all. The relation of inside and outside, for the Cistercians, worked both ways: not only did the believer conceive Jesus within him or herself, but the believer also hid himself in the safe places *within* Jesus – within the wound in his side, which is the Church. This sermon rings the changes on Song of Songs 2: 14, which speaks of nesting in the cleft of the rock. The one nesting is at once the Holy Spirit penetrating the rocky heart of the believer, and the believer nesting in the wounds of Jesus. These changes bend gender in several ways: The male monk – like the human being generally – is thought on the pattern of Mary, and is told to conceive and give birth to Christ. Christ, similarly, accepts the believer into himself, whether maternally or homoerotically, it is hard to say. Sexual and birth metaphors abound. Guerric crafts them with great deliberation and subtlety: why not both?

The ellipses marking the cuts in this sermon bring initial passages about the Holy Spirit closer together with later passages about the dove. Unlike elsewhere in this volume, these cuts are not innocent. In the sermon as a whole, Guerric takes the passage about raising up children from the rocks of the ground in an ugly, supersessionist, anti-Semitic direction. I deliberated about leaving it in so as not to bowdlerize or cover up. I imagined teaching opportunities and essay assignments on whether the anti-Semitism was really separable from the pneumatology or not. In the end I remembered that space was finite, and I had not cut good passages from other texts to let ugly ones stand here.[1]

Guerric of Igny, Sermon 32, Fourth Sermon for Palm Sunday, in *Liturgical Sermons*, trans. by the monks at Mount Saint Bernard Abbey (Kalamazoo, MI: Cistercian Publications, 2006), vol. 2, pp. 73–9.

Sermon 32: Fourth Sermon for Palm Sunday

Guerric of Igny

"HOSANNA TO THE SON OF DAVID."[2] This is the voice of exultation and salvation,[3] the voice of gladness and devotion, the voice of faith and love, rejoicing in the arrival of the Savior and proclaiming with a Prophet's gladness the joy of redemption long desired. "Hosanna to the Son of David," says David's family; salvation belongs to him who has been made of David's seed that he may save those who are of David's faith. Praise the Lord, you sons, praise the name of the Lord. Say: "May the name of the Lord be blessed."[4] May he be blessed who comes in the name of the Lord."[5] From the mouth of these you have brought forth, O Father, the praise of your Son, so as to destroy by the uncorrupted witness of simple innocence the enemy and the avenger[6] the Pharisee and the High Priest. He is not the avenger of God's law, as iniquity has lied to itself;[7] he is rather the avenger of his own envy and fury. But his mischief shall return upon his own head, and upon his own pate shall his iniquity come down."[8] "God, be not silent in my praise," says the Son to the Father," for the mouth of the sinner and the mouth of the deceiver is opened against me."[9] The Father cannot deny the Son anything; the Father's voice, often heard from heaven, did not keep silent the Son's praise.[10] Creation did not keep it silent, in so many signs and prodigies confessing him as the author of nature. The angels bore him witness, devils confessed him, the ranks of the prophets and of the apostles sang of him, answering one another with harmonious voice. This finally is perfect praise, which cannot be repressed by little ones who know nothing of flattery and cannot dissimulate what the Spirit suggests.

For what could be more obvious than the fact that that age neither said nor did of itself things so new and so unaccustomed? The Holy Spirit according to his wont bore witness to the Son by speaking through the mouths of the simple.

2.   Surely the Holy Spirit, aware of Christ's works, aware, that is, of what Christ's coming would cause, aware of the joy and the salvation which his passion would bring forth, stirred up prophetic joys in the hearts of the innocent. For foretelling to the world the gladness of redemption he made his own the ministry of simple minds. It was to these that the Spirit spoke, calling "those who are not as if they were,"[11] when through his prophet he foretold what today has taken place. He gave the command then, and now they have been created.[12] "Exult," he says, "exult greatly, daughter of Sion; be jubilant, daughter of Jerusalem. Behold your king shall come to you, just and a Savior; poor he will be and seated upon an ass!"[13] Now, he says: "Exult greatly, you who hitherto were in sadness; now satiate yourself, if indeed you can be satiated, with unspeakable joy, which satiates desire in such a way as to cause greater and happier hunger. Let your mouth and your tongue be filled with exultation,[14] and if neither mouth nor tongue can contain it, let jubilation pour forth with the overflow of your affections. Be jubilant, daughter of Jerusalem; for blessed is the people which is acquainted with jubilation."[15] Truly blessed is the people which knows and understands that today it must rejoice unspeakably, when the Savior has come to it who

was promised and awaited from the beginning of the ages. Blessed is the people which go to meet him today with all the eagerness of devotion, crying at once with heart and voice: "Blessed is he who comes in the name of the Lord."[16] For in this the Son has been blessed by the Father, that he who blesses is filled with blessings,[17] not with one, but with many. The blessing which a man lends to the Lord on interest, returns upon his head with manifold interest.

Woe to the sinful nation, the worthless seed, the criminal sons,[18] to whom that terrible complaint of the Lord applies: "I have not lent nor have I borrowed, yet all of them curse me, says the Lord."[19] . . .

3.   Yet I am afraid, my brethren, that perhaps these lukewarm and faithless times are the object of the Lord's complaint: "I have not lent nor have I borrowed"; because grace is offered and is not welcomed, work is promised its reward and scarcely anyone works to obtain the reward. The Lord lends when he distributes talents in his servants,[20] bestowing skill in speaking or the grace of any office for a man's benefit. But the generous man, who has compassion and lends,[21] is the one who lends to the Lord – as Scripture says: "He lends to the Lord who shows compassion to his neighbor."[22] Indeed whoever does anything in the hope of a reward from God lends to the Lord, so that he can say: "I know in whom I have trusted.[23] I know who it was that said: 'If you spend anything further I will pay you back when I return!' "[24] We either lend him nothing or are so timid and cold about it that we treat him as an untrustworthy debtor or one who has not the wherewithal to pay us back.

. . . "I tell you," he says, "that if these are silent, the stones will cry out,[25] for God will not keep my praise silent."[26] So indeed it is: "If these are silent, the stones will cry out," for at the time of the passion these were silent, but the stones cried out when in witness to and praise of the dying Christ the rocks were split and tombs were opened."[27] . . . The stones cry out from which he who is powerful has raised up sons to Abraham.[28] "Give praise," the Prophet says, "you that dwell on the rock; from the summit of the mountains they shall cry out."[29] Behold today in the clefts of the rock, in the hollows of the wall,[30] the voice of the dove echoes, crying out and saying: "Hosanna to the Son of David. Blessed is he who comes in the name of the Lord."[31]

5.   Blessed is he who, in order that I might be able to build a nest in the clefts of the rock,[32] allowed his hands, feet and side to be pierced and opened himself to me wholly that I might enter "the place of his wonderful tent"[33] and be protected in its recesses.[34] The rock is a convenient refuge for the badgers,[35] but it is also a welcome dwelling-place for the doves. These clefts, so many open wounds all over his body, offer pardon to the guilty and bestow grace on the just. Indeed it is a safe dwelling-place, my brethren, and a tower of strength in the face of the enemy,[36] to linger in the wounds of Christ, the Lord, by devout and constant meditation. By faith in the Crucified and love of him a man keeps his soul safe from the heat of the flesh, from the turmoil of the world, from the attacks of the devil. The protection this tent affords surpasses all the world's glory. It is a shade from the heat by day, a refuge and a shelter from the storm and the rain,[37] so that by day the sun shall not scorch you with prosperity,[38] nor the storm move you with adversity.

Go into the rock, then, man; hide in the dug ground.[39] Make the Crucified your hiding place. He is the rock, he is the ground, he who is God and man. He is the cleft rock, the dug ground, for "they have dug my hands and my feet."[40] Hide in the dug ground from the fear of the Lord,[41] that is, from him fly to him, from the judge to the Redeemer, from the tribunal to the Cross, from the just One to the Merciful, from him who will strike the earth with the rod of his mouth[42] to him who inebriates the earth with the drops of his blood, from him who will kill the godless with the breath of his lips[43] to him who with the blood of his wounds gives life to the dead. Rather do not fly only to him but into him, go into the clefts of the rock, hide in dug ground, hide yourself in the very hands that were cleft, in the side that was dug. For what is the wound in Christ's side but a door in the side of the Ark for those who are to be saved from the flood?[44] But the one was a figure, the other is very truth, in which not only is mortal life preserved but immortal life is recovered. For in his loving kindness and his compassion he opened his side in order that the blood of the wound might give you life, the warmth of his body revive you, the breath of his heart flow into you as if through a free and open passage. There you will lie hidden in safety until wickedness passes by.[45] There you will certainly not freeze, since in the bowels of Christ charity does not grow cold. There you will abound in delights.[46] There you will overflow with joys, at least then when your mortality and that of all the members of his body have been swallowed up by the life of the Head.

6.   Rightly then the dove of Christ, Christ's fair one, for whom his wounds have provided clefts so safe, so good for the building of a nest, sings his praises every-where today with rejoicing. From the remembrance or the imitation of his passion, from meditation on his wounds, a pleasing voice sounds in the ears of the Bridegroom[47] as if from the clefts of the rock. Now you, my brethren, have built your nests the more deeply within the clefts of the rock the more secretly you live in Christ and your life is hidden with Christ in God,[48] so it is for you surely to see that the more tranquil and protected your life is, the sweeter your devotion is, especially today when the recurrence of the anniversary and the performance of the liturgy make us present as it were at the festival joy with which he was welcomed into Jerusalem. Blessed is he who comes as king in the name of the Lord.[49] To him be blessing, kingship and empire, who rules as God over all things, blessed for ever and ever.[50] Amen.

Notes

1   For more on Christian supersessionism, or the teaching that the Church has superseded Israel – now officially rejected by Catholics and mainline Protestants – see Kendall Soulen, *The God of Israel and Christian Theology* (Minneapolis: Fortress Press, 1996).
2   Matt. 21: 9. This is the text, of course, which marks out most characteristically the celebration of Palm Sunday as such.
3   Ps. 117: 15.
4   Ps. 112: 1f.
5   Ps. 117: 26.
6   Ps. 8: 3.
7   Ps. 26: 12.

8　Ps. 7: 17.

9　Ps. 108: 2.

10　Luke 3: 22; 9: 35; John 12: 28.

11　Rom. 4: 17.

12　Ps. 148: 5.

13　Zech. 9: 9.

14　Ps. 125: 2.

15　Ps. 88: 16.

16　John 12: 13.

17　Cf. Gen. 21: 29.

18　Isa. 1: 4.

19　Jer. 15: 10f.

20　Cf. Matt. 25: 14ff.

21　Ps. 111: 5.

22　Prov. 19: 17; Sir. 29: 1.

23　2 Tim. 1: 12.

24　Luke 10: 35.

25　Luke 19: 40.

26　Ps. 108: 2.

27　Matt. 27: 51.

28　Luke 3: 8.

29　Isa. 42: 11.

30　S. of S. 2: 14.

31　Matt. 21: 9.

32　S. of S. 2: 14. Bernard of Clairvaux in his commentary on the Song of Songs (Sermon 61: 7f.) also sees the "clefts of the rock" as the wounds of Christ the Savior, a place of refuge for sinful man; *The Works of Bernard of Clairvaux*, vol. 11, trans. K. Walsh, Cistercian Fathers Series, 31 (Spencer, MA: Cistercian Publications, 1971–80).

33　Ps. 41: 5.

34　Ps. 26: 5.

35　Ps. 103: 18.

36　Ps. 60: 4.

37　Isa. 4: 6.

38　Ps. 120: 6.

39　Isa. 2: 10.

40　Ps. 21: 17.

41　Isa. 2: 10.

42　Isa. 11: 4.

43　Ibid.

44　Gen. 6f. Guerric must have learned this interpretation from Saint Augustine, *Commentary on John*, Tract 120, no. 1; Corpus Christianorum Latinorum, 36: 661 or possibly from the Venerable Bede, *Hexaemeron*, book 2; Patrologia Latina, 91: 90A.

45　Ps. 56: 2.

46　S. of S. 8: 5.

47　S. of S. 2: 14.

48　Col. 3: 3.

49　Luke 19: 38.

50　Rom. 9: 5.

19

Thomas Aquinas,
from Summa Theologica

The following selections from Thomas Aquinas describe two halves of a single movement by which the Trinity brings creatures to itself. The first selection describes the movement from God's side. It comes from a section called "the mission of the Persons," by which God the Father sends God the Son and God the Holy Spirit to human beings. The Father sends the Son to become incarnate in a human being so that human beings may know God. The Father sends the Spirit to indwell the human heart so that human beings may love God. Those missions activate two inseparable aspects of God's image in human beings: human beings resemble God in directing their acts toward an end or goal, and that ability requires knowing the end and desiring the goal. The Son demonstrates the goal of life with God to be known, and the Spirit displays the goal of life with God to be desired. Those missions bring God's very presence in the human being. The Son brings God to indwell the human being as the known in the knower; the Spirit brings God to indwell the human being as the beloved in the lover. No static picture, the image of God in the human being partakes of God's constant movement: the image is to develop over time by intentional action. It is to grow. In the mission of the Persons, God induces – engages – attracts the growth of the image toward greater likeness with God.

The second selection describes God's drawing the human being into God from the human side. It comes from a section or tractate on grace, describing the transformation the Holy Spirit works in the heart. God transforms the heart, or grows the image, both internally and externally. Externally, God provides structures or parameters, called law, within which stress on the image aids rather than undermines growth. Internally, the Holy Spirit habituates the human being

Excerpt from Thomas Aquinas, *Summa Theologica*, trans. by the Fathers of the English Dominican Province (New York: Benziger Brothers, 1947–8).

to desire the good by laying down tracks or stable dispositions to act, starting in the heart. Internal and external aspects of God's guidance work together to grow the human being into a freedom like God's, not arbitrary but powerful in seeking the good. Law is a structure that liberates for the good, and habit a disposition that practices the good. The tractate on grace unifies the two under the Holy Spirit, for the Spirit writes the law on the heart. The Spirit works both from the outside and most internally – more internally than we work on ourselves, because the Spirit draws and excites our deepest desires.

The tractate on grace displays a vision of freedom that differs from most modern ones. Modern versions of freedom tend to suppose that more choices are always better, and that the freedom of other agents competes with our own. Choices, on this view, are finite, and if I have more, then you have less. Modern versions of freedom come at your expense and extend even to bad choices.

Thomas Aquinas has a more hopeful view. He regards choice as a way of seeking the good by reason. Good choices alone make free; bad choices enslave. Freedom is not ambivalent: it comes with a direction; it seeks the good. The good, in God, is infinite. If God does more, I can do more. The best way to increase my freedom is to tap into God's infinite supply. So God's freedom and human freedom do not compete. They are not rivals. Rather, they co-operate. Divine and human freedom relate not inversely, but directly. Aquinas would have reservations about the popular saying "God must increase, I must decrease." He would prefer to say that God doesn't need increasing, and I increase precisely in God. Grace, then, increases my participation in God and therefore my freedom. Because grace divinely increases my participation *in God*, it is the work – even the indwelling – of the Holy Spirit in me. Because grace increases "my" participation in God, the Holy Spirit does not leave me out, but involves, engages, activates me more, making me more myself and more free. For that reason, Aquinas will even speak of grace as a "quality" in the human being, not to domesticate grace, but to indicate the reliability of God's commitment to the human.

A word about how to read this. Thomas's questions build in controversy; they encapsulate disputes. Each query – called an "article" – begins with the arguments of his opponents, called "objections," which he does not accept, beginning "It would seem" (but it does not really). The dispute pivots on one authority that Thomas finds persuasive, called the *sed contra*, beginning "on the contrary." He attempts to settle the dispute with his own argument in the section called the "body," "corpus," or "response" of the article, beginning, "I answer that . . ." Finally, he goes back and offers "replies" to the objections in the same sequence. Readers find that this order takes some getting used to. Thomas begins with views he *does not hold*, pivots on a citation of authority in the *sed contra*, gives his own position in the middle, and answers his opponents at the end. (Thomas has here actually simplified the medieval disputed question, which boasted *two* sets of objections for the response to navigate.) Readers new to this may prefer to see first why and how Thomas has made up his mind, reading the *sed contra* and the body of the article, and only then the first objection with its reply, the second objection with its reply, and so on.

from Summa Theologica

Thomas Aquinas

Part I, question 43

Article 3. Whether the invisible mission of the divine person is only according to the gift of sanctifying grace?

Objection 1. It would seem that the invisible mission of the divine person is not only according to the gift of sanctifying grace. For the sending of a divine person means that He is given. Hence if the divine person is sent only according to the gift of sanctifying grace, the divine person Himself will not be given, but only His gifts; and this is the error of those who say that the Holy Ghost is not given, but that His gifts are given.

Objection 2. Further, this preposition, "according to," denotes the habitude of some cause. But the divine person is the cause why the gift of sanctifying grace is possessed, and not conversely, according to Rom. 5: 5, "the charity of God is poured forth in our hearts by the Holy Ghost, Who is given to us." Therefore it is improperly said that the divine person is sent according to the gift of sanctifying grace.

Objection 3. Further, Augustine says (*de Trin.* iv, 20) that "the Son, when temporally perceived by the mind, is sent." But the Son is known not only by sanctifying grace, but also by gratuitous grace, as by faith and knowledge. Therefore the divine person is not sent only according to the gift of sanctifying grace.

Objection 4. Further, Rabanus says that the Holy Ghost was given to the apostles for the working of miracles. This, however, is not a gift of sanctifying grace, but a gratuitous grace. Therefore the divine person is not given only according to the gift of sanctifying grace.

On the contrary, Augustine says (*de Trin.* iii, 4) that "the Holy Ghost proceeds temporally for the creature's sanctification." But mission is a temporal procession. Since then the creature's sanctification is by sanctifying grace, it follows that the mission of the divine person is only by sanctifying grace.

I answer that, The divine person is fittingly sent in the sense that He exists newly in any one; and He is given as possessed by anyone; and neither of these is otherwise than by sanctifying grace.

For God is in all things by His essence, power and presence, according to His one common mode, as the cause existing in the effects which participate in His goodness. Above and beyond this common mode, however, there is one special mode belonging to the rational nature wherein God is said to be present as the object known is in the knower, and the beloved in the lover. And since the rational creature by its operation of knowledge and love attains to God Himself, according to this special mode God is said not only to exist in the rational creature but also to dwell therein as in His own temple. So no other effect can be put down as the reason why the divine person is in the rational creature in a new mode, except sanctifying grace. Hence, the divine person is sent, and proceeds temporally only according to sanctifying grace.

Again, we are said to possess only what we can freely use or enjoy: and to have the power of enjoying the divine person can only be according to sanctifying grace. And yet the Holy Ghost is possessed by man, and dwells within him, in the very gift itself of sanctifying grace. Hence the Holy Ghost Himself is given and sent.

Reply to Objection 1. By the gift of sanctifying grace the rational creature is perfected so that it can freely use not only the created gift itself, but enjoy also the divine person Himself; and so the invisible mission takes place according to the gift of sanctifying grace; and yet the divine person Himself is given.

Reply to Objection 2. Sanctifying grace disposes the soul to possess the divine person; and this is signified when it is said that the Holy Ghost is given according to the gift of grace. Nevertheless the gift itself of grace is from the Holy Ghost; which is meant by the words, "the charity of God is poured forth in our hearts by the Holy Ghost."

Reply to Objection 3. Although the Son can be known by us according to other effects, yet neither does He dwell in us, nor is He possessed by us according to those effects.

Reply to Objection 4. The working of miracles manifests sanctifying grace as also does the gift of prophecy and any other gratuitous graces. Hence gratuitous grace is called the "manifestation of the Spirit" (1 Cor. 12: 7). So the Holy Ghost is said to be given to the apostles for the working of miracles, because sanctifying grace was given to them with the outward sign. Were the sign only of sanctifying grace given to them without the grace itself, it would not be simply said that the Holy Ghost was given, except with some qualifying term; just as we read of certain ones receiving the gift of the spirit of prophecy, or of miracles, as having from the Holy Ghost the power of prophesying or of working miracles.

Article 6. Whether the invisible mission is to all who participate grace?

Objection 1. It would seem that the invisible mission is not to all who participate grace. For the Fathers of the Old Testament had their share of grace. Yet to them was made no invisible mission; for it is said (John 7: 39): "The Spirit was not yet given, because Jesus was not yet glorified." Therefore the invisible mission is not to all partakers in grace.

Objection 2. Further, progress in virtue is only by grace. But the invisible mission is not according to progress in virtue; because progress in virtue is continuous, since charity ever increases or decreases; and thus the mission would be continuous. Therefore the invisible mission is not to all who share in grace.

Objection 3. Further, Christ and the blessed have fullness of grace. But mission is not to them, for mission implies distance, whereas Christ, as man, and all the blessed are perfectly united to God. Therefore the invisible mission is not to all sharers in grace.

Objection 4. Further, the Sacraments of the New Law contain grace, and it is not said that the invisible mission is sent to them. Therefore the invisible mission is not to all that have grace.

On the contrary, According to Augustine (*de Trin.* iii, 4; xv, 27), the invisible mission is for the creature's sanctification. Now every creature that has grace is sanctified. Therefore the invisible mission is to every such creature.

I answer that, As above stated (3, 4, 5), mission in its very meaning implies that he who is sent either begins to exist where he was not before, as occurs to creatures; or begins to exist where he was before, but in a new way, in which sense mission is ascribed to the divine persons. Thus, mission as regards the one to whom it is sent implies two things, the indwelling of grace, and a certain renewal by grace. Thus the invisible mission is sent to all in whom are to be found these two conditions.

Reply to Objection 1. The invisible mission was directed to the Old Testament Fathers, as appears from what Augustine says (*de Trin.* iv, 20), that the invisible mission of the Son "is in man and with men. This was done in former times with the Fathers and the Prophets." Thus the words, "the Spirit was not yet given," are to be applied to that giving accompanied with a visible sign which took place on the day of Pentecost.

Reply to Objection 2. The invisible mission takes place also as regards progress in virtue or increase of grace. Hence Augustine says (*de Trin.* iv, 20), that "the Son is sent to each one when He is known and perceived by anyone, so far as He can be known and perceived according to the capacity of the soul, whether journeying towards God, or united perfectly to Him." Such invisible mission, however, chiefly occurs as regards anyone's proficiency in the performance of a new act, or in the acquisition of a new state of grace; as, for example, the proficiency in reference to the gift of miracles or of prophecy, or in the fervor of charity leading a man to expose himself to the danger of martyrdom, or to renounce his possessions, or to undertake any arduous work.

Reply to Objection 3. The invisible mission is directed to the blessed at the very beginning of their beatitude. The invisible mission is made to them subsequently, not by "intensity" of grace, but by the further revelation of mysteries; which goes on till the day of judgment. Such an increase is by the "extension" of grace, because it extends to a greater number of objects. To Christ the invisible mission was sent at the first moment of His conception; but not afterwards, since from the beginning of His conception He was filled with all wisdom and grace.

Reply to Objection 4. Grace resides instrumentally in the sacraments of the New Law, as the form of a thing designed resides in the instruments of the art designing, according to a process flowing from the agent to the passive object. But mission is only spoken of as directed to its term. Hence the mission of the divine person is not sent to the sacraments, but to those who receive grace through the sacraments.

First part of the Second Part, question 106

Article 1. Whether the New Law is a written law?

Objection 1. It would seem that the New Law is a written law. For the New Law is just the same as the Gospel. But the Gospel is set forth in writing, according to John 20: 31: "But these are written that you may believe." Therefore the New Law is a written law.

Objection 2. Further, the law that is instilled in the heart is the natural law, according to Rom. 2: 14, 15: "(The Gentiles) do by nature those things that are of the law . . . who have [Vulg.: 'show'] the work of the law written in their hearts." If therefore the law of the Gospel were instilled in our hearts, it would not be distinct from the law of nature.

Objection 3. Further, the law of the Gospel is proper to those who are in the state of the New Testament. But the law that is instilled in the heart is common to those who are in the New Testament and to those who are in the Old Testament: for it is written (Wisdom 7: 27) that Divine Wisdom "through nations conveyeth herself into holy souls, she maketh the friends of God and prophets." Therefore the New Law is not instilled in our hearts.

On the contrary, The New Law is the law of the New Testament. But the law of the New Testament is instilled in our hearts. For the Apostle, quoting the authority of Jeremias 31: 31, 33: "Behold the days shall come, saith the Lord; and I will perfect unto the house of Israel, and unto the house of Judah, a new testament," says, explaining what this statement is (Heb. 8: 8, 10): "For this is the testament which I will make to the house of Israel . . . by giving [Vulg.: 'I will give'] My laws into their mind, and in their heart will I write them." Therefore the New Law is instilled in our hearts.

I answer that, "Each thing appears to be that which preponderates in it," as the Philosopher states (*Ethics*, ix, 8). Now that which is preponderant in the law of the New Testament, and whereon all its efficacy is based, is the grace of the Holy Ghost, which is given through faith in Christ. Consequently the New Law is chiefly the grace itself of the Holy Ghost, which is given to those who believe in Christ. This is manifestly stated by the Apostle who says (Rom. 3: 27): "Where is . . . thy boasting? It is excluded. By what law? Of works? No, but by the law of faith": for he calls the grace itself of faith "a law." And still more clearly it is written (Rom. 8: 2): "The law of the spirit of life, in Christ Jesus, hath delivered me from the law of sin and of death." Hence Augustine says (*De Spiritu et Littera* [*On the Spirit and the Letter*], xxiv) that "as the law of deeds was written on tables of stone, so is the law of faith inscribed on the hearts of the faithful": and elsewhere, in the same book (xxi): "What else are the Divine laws written by God Himself on our hearts, but the very presence of His Holy Spirit?"

Nevertheless the New Law contains certain things that dispose us to receive the grace of the Holy Ghost, and pertaining to the use of that grace: such things are of secondary importance, so to speak, in the New Law; and the faithful need to be instructed concerning them, both by word and writing, both as to what they should believe and as to what they should do. Consequently we must say that the New Law is in the first place a law that is inscribed on our hearts, but that secondarily it is a written law.

Reply to Objection 1. The Gospel writings contain only such things as pertain to the grace of the Holy Ghost, either by disposing us thereto, or by directing us to the use thereof. Thus with regard to the intellect, the Gospel contains certain matters pertaining to the manifestation of Christ's Godhead or humanity, which dispose us by means of faith through which we receive the grace of the Holy Ghost: and with regard to the affections, it contains matters touching the contempt of the world, whereby man is rendered fit to receive the grace of the Holy Ghost: for "the world," i.e. worldly men, "cannot receive" the Holy Ghost (John 14: 17). As to the use of spiritual grace, this consists in works of virtue to which the writings of the New Testament exhort men in divers ways.

Reply to Objection 2. There are two ways in which a thing may be instilled into man. First, through being part of his nature, and thus the natural law is instilled into man. Secondly, a thing is instilled into man by being, as it were, added on to his nature by a gift of grace. In this way the New Law is instilled into man, not only by indicating to him what he should do, but also by helping him to accomplish it.

Reply to Objection 3. No man ever had the grace of the Holy Ghost except through faith in Christ either explicit or implicit: and by faith in Christ man belongs to the New Testament. Consequently whoever had the law of grace instilled into them belonged to the New Testament.

Article 2. Whether the New Law justifies?

Objection 1. It would seem that the New Law does not justify. For no man is justified unless he obeys God's law, according to Heb. 5: 9: "He," i.e. Christ, "became to all that obey Him the cause of eternal salvation." But the Gospel does not always cause men to believe in it: for it is written (Rom. 10: 16): "All do not obey the Gospel." Therefore the New Law does not justify.

Objection 2. Further, the Apostle proves in his epistle to the Romans that the Old Law did not justify, because transgression increased at its advent: for it is stated (Rom. 4: 15): "The Law worketh wrath: for where there is no law, neither is there transgression." But much more did the New Law increase transgression: since he who sins after the giving of the New Law deserves greater punishment, according to Heb. 10: 28, 29: "A man making void the Law of Moses dieth without any mercy under two or three witnesses. How much more, do you think, he deserveth worse punishments, who hath trodden underfoot the Son of God," etc.? Therefore the New Law, like the Old Law, does not justify.

Objection 3. Further, justification is an effect proper to God, according to Rom. 8: 33: "God that justifieth." But the Old Law was from God just as the New Law. Therefore the New Law does not justify any more than the Old Law.

On the contrary, The Apostle says (Rom. 1: 16): "I am not ashamed of the Gospel: for it is in the power of God unto salvation to everyone that believeth." But there is no salvation but to those who are justified. Therefore the Law of the Gospel justifies.

I answer that, As stated above (1), there is a twofold element in the Law of the Gospel. There is the chief element, viz. the grace of the Holy Ghost bestowed inwardly. And as to this, the New Law justifies. Hence Augustine says (*De Spir. et Lit.,* xvii): "There," i.e. in the Old Testament, "the Law was set forth in an outward fashion, that the ungodly might be afraid"; "here," i.e. in the New Testament, "it is given in an inward manner, that they may be justified." The other element of the Evangelical Law is secondary: namely, the teachings of faith, and those commandments which direct human affections and human actions. And as to this, the New Law does not justify. Hence the Apostle says (2 Cor. 3: 6) "The letter killeth, but the spirit quickeneth": and Augustine explains this (*De Spir. et Lit.*, xiv, xvii) by saying that the letter denotes any writing external to man, even that of the moral precepts such as are contained in the Gospel. Wherefore the letter, even of the Gospel, would kill, unless there were the inward presence of the healing grace of faith.

Reply to Objection 1. This argument holds true of the New Law, not as to its principal, but as to its secondary element: i.e., as to the dogmas and precepts outwardly put before man either in words or in writing.

Reply to Objection 2. Although the grace of the New Testament helps man to avoid sin, yet it does not so confirm man in good that he cannot sin: for this belongs to the state of glory. Hence if a man sin after receiving the grace of the New Testament, he deserves greater punishment, as being ungrateful for greater benefits, and as not using the help given to him. And this is why the New Law is not said to "work wrath": because as far as it is concerned it gives man sufficient help to avoid sin.

Reply to Objection 3. The same God gave both the New and the Old Law, but in different ways. For He gave the Old Law written on tables of stone: whereas He gave the New Law written "in the fleshly tables of the heart," as the Apostle expresses it (2 Cor. 3: 3). Wherefore, as Augustine says (*De Spir. et Lit.*, xviii), "the Apostle calls this letter which is written outside man, a ministration of death and a ministration of condemnation: whereas he calls the other letter, i.e., the Law of the New Testament, the ministration of the spirit and the ministration of justice: because through the gift of the Spirit we work justice, and are delivered from the condemnation due to transgression."

V
German Resources

20

Martin Luther,
from "The Last Words of
David"

A strange title, you might think, for a treatise on the Holy Spirit. Martin Luther
(1483–1546), instigator (despite himself) of the break between Protestants and
Catholics at the Reformation, here perseveres uninterruptedly in the medieval Christian
practice of interpreting the Hebrew Bible to find Christ and Trinity at every turn.
The Reformation located its disputes over grace outside of trinitarian doctrine.
While skeptical readers will find a good deal of eisegesis, or reading things in,
as well as *ad hominem* attacks on Luther's critics, Luther also makes several more
constructive moves. First, Luther finds what you might call a hermeneutical Trinity,
or a Trinity implied in the very reading of a canonical text. Wherever the text
mentions God, Luther finds the Three Persons: "God" is the Father; God's Word,
in the text, implies the speaking of the Son; and God's engagement of a human
author or reader – here supposed to be David – implies the Holy Spirit.
Trinitarian expositions of revelation often require something like that. Furthermore,
Luther treats the three as Speaker, Word, and Inspirer in a particularly "Lutheran"
way. The Triune God is the promising God. God is the Promiser, the Promise,
and the Witness or Pledge.

Luther begins with words attributed to David in II Samuel but – counting David
as a prophet – races through parallel examples in other prophets until he finally
finds himself in the New Testament, where he treats the account of Christ's
baptism in the gospel of John as a trinitarian epiphany or self-display. In the
baptism of Christ, as Luther reads it, the Trinity makes visible the dynamics that
Luther claims to overhear in other texts. The Father speaks audibly, rather than
by implication. The Son presents himself bodily, rather than verbally. The
Spirit alights on the human being externally, rather than internally. The baptism

Martin Luther, Treatise on the Last Words of David, in *Luther's Works,* vol. 15, ed. and trans. Jaroslav
Pelikan and Hilton C. Oswald (St Louis, MO: Concordia Publishing, 1972), pp. 276, 280, 289–90,
301–9, 310–12, 315–16.

vindicates, Luther thinks, his procedure of exegesis. It also occasions a clear and down-to-earth catechesis on the grammar of trinitarian language as modeled in the so-called Athanasian Creed and according to the rule that while the Three are distinguishable among themselves, their acts toward creation are indivisible.

from The Last Words of David

Martin Luther

"These are the last words of David, the oracle of David, the son of Jesse, the oracle of the man who is assured of the Messiah of the God of Jacob, the sweet psalmist of Israel: 'The Spirit of the Lord has spoken by me, His Word is upon my tongue. The God of Israel has talked to me, the Rock of Israel has spoken; He who rules justly over men, He who rules in the fear of God.'" [2 Samuel 23: 1–3 as it appears in *Luther's Works*, with Luther's comments.]

Now we have three speakers. Above, David remarks that the Spirit of the Lord has spoken through his tongue. There the Person of the Holy Spirit is clearly indicated to us Christians. Whatever Turks, Jews, and other ungodly persons believe we disregard. Thus we have heard that Scripture and our Creed ascribe to the Holy Spirit the external working, as He physically speaks to us, baptizes us, and reigns over us though the prophets, apostles, and ministers of the church. Therefore these words of David are also those of the Holy Spirit, which He speaks with David's tongue regarding two other Speakers. What does he say of these? First of all he speaks of the God of Israel and says that He has spoken to David, that is, has given him a promise. Which Person of the Godhead this Speaker is we Christians know from the Gospel of John. It is the Father who said in the beginning (Gen. 1: 3): "Let there be light." And His Word is the Person of the Son, through which Word "all things were made" (John 1: 3). The same Son the Spirit by the mouth of David here calls *"Rock"* of Israel and *just ruler among mankind*. He, too, speaks, that is, the Holy Spirit introduces the Rock of Israel to let Him speak too. Thus all three Persons speak, and yet there is but one Speaker, one Promiser, one Promise, just as there is but one God.

. . .

Here [in 2 Sam. 7: 11–16 and 1 Chr. 17: 10–14] we again find the three Persons of the Godhead: first the Holy Spirit, who speaks by the prophet Nathan. We heard before that Holy Scripture is spoken by the Holy Spirit in keeping with the words of David: *The Spirit of the Lord has spoken by me*. In like manner He speaks by all prophets. The Holy Spirit, furthermore, introduces the Person of the Father when He says: "The Lord declares to you." And immediately after that He presents the Person of the Son, saying that *the Lord will build you a house*. And yet it is but one God and Lord who speaks through Nathan, makes an announcement to David, and builds his house. All three are but one Speaker, one Announcer, one Builder. It is immaterial whether or not everybody's reason discerns these three Persons in Scripture. I am well aware how the saucy prigs who make bold to instruct the Holy Spirit make annotations here and in similar passages.

Wherever in Scripture you find God speaking about God, as if there were two persons, you may boldly assume that three Persons of the Godhead are there indicated. . . .

. . .

In Isa. 60: 19–20 we read in like manner: "The sun shall be no more your light by day, nor for brightness shall the moon give light to you by night; but the Lord will be your everlasting Light, and your God will be your Glory. Your sun shall no more go down, nor your moon withdraw itself; for the Lord will be your everlasting Light, and your days of mourning shall be ended." Here it is clearly stated that the Lord and our God Himself will be our everlasting Light. Here the one Lord speaks about the other. Indeed, in the entire chapter it is not Isaiah who is speaking but the Lord. It is He who says: "The Lord will be your everlasting Light." Who is the Lord who speaks these words? Without a doubt, God the Father. Who is the Lord of whom He says: "The Lord will be your everlasting Light"? Without a doubt, God the Son, Jesus Christ. For here we find the great name of God, Jehovah, which our Bibles print with capital letters, LORD, in contradistinction to the other names. Who is it who speaks these words by the tongue of Isaiah? Without a doubt, God the Holy Spirit, who speaks by the prophets, introducing the Person of the Father, who, in turn, speaks of the eternal Light, that is, of His Son, Jesus of Nazareth, the Son of David and of Mary.

. . .

This is how David read and understood Moses [i.e., the account of creation in Genesis 1] when he wrote in Ps. 33: 6: "By the Word of the Lord the heavens were made, and all their host by the Breath of His mouth." He says that the heavens and all that is in and on them are "made." My dear man, made out of what? Out of nothing. By what? By God's Word and the Breath of His mouth. Does not David's speech here coincide with that of Moses? Does he not wish to say with practically the same words that God said, "Let there be the heaven," and the heaven came into being? But if the heaven that all that is therein came into being and was made by God's Speech, or Word, then the earth with all that is therein indubitably also came into being and was made by the same Word. Now, the Word is not the heaven nor the earth, nor anything that is in them, nor anything that is made together with these by the Word. Therefore it must be God Himself, and, at the same time, a Person apart from the Speaker, who makes all things through the Word, united in one indivisible essence of divine power, might, and effect. But if we have the Word, it is easy to discover the third Person in David's speech: "All their host by the Breath of His mouth."

The author uses the word "made" only once, saying: "By the Word of the Lord the heavens were made, and all their host by the Breath of His mouth." He mentions three distinct Persons, namely, the Lord, His Word, and His Breath; and yet he does not set up more than one Creator, without any differentiation. All things are made. By whom, by one Creator, who is Lord, Word, and Breath. The Lord does not do His own work separately, the Word does not do His own work separately, and the Breath does not do His own work separately. All three distinct Persons are but one Creator of the work of each. And each one's work is that of all three Persons as that of one Creator and Master. For as the Lord creates the heavens, the Word creates the same and no different heavens, and the Breath creates the same and no different heavens. It is one essence that creates, and it is one creation that all three Persons create. And again, just as the Lord creates the host of the heavens by His Spirit (as the text says "And all their host by the Breath of His mouth") thus the Breath creates the same and no other host of the heavens, and the Word creates the same and no other host of the heavens.

Therefore a Christian must here take careful note not to mingle the Persons into one Person nor to divide and separate the one divine in essence into three Persons, as Athanasius sings in his Creed. For if I ascribe to each Person a distinct external work in creation and exclude the other two Persons from this, then I have divided the one Godhead and have fashioned three gods or creators. And that is wrong. Again, if I do not ascribe to each Person within the Godhead, or outside and beyond creation, a special distinction not appropriate to the other two, then I have mingled the Persons into one Person. And that is also wrong. Here the rule of St. Augustine is pertinent: "The works of the Trinity toward the outside are not divisible."[1] The works performed by God outside the Godhead must not be divided, that is, one must not separate the Persons with regard to the works and ascribe to each its distinct external work; but one must distinguish the Person within the Godhead and yet ascribe, externally, each work to all three without distinction.

Let me illustrate this with an example. The Father is my God and Creator and yours, who created you and me. This same work, your creation and mine, was also performed by the Son, who is also my God and Creator and yours, just as the Father is. Likewise, the Holy Spirit created the selfsame work, that is, you and me, and He is my God and Creator and yours as well as the Father and the Son. This notwithstanding, there are not three gods and creators, but one God and Creator of us both. With this creed I guard against the heresy of Arius and his ilk, to keep me from dividing the one divine essence into three gods or creators and to help me retain in the true Christian faith no more than the one God and Creator of all creatures.

On the other hand, when I go beyond and outside of creation or the creature and move into the internal, incomprehensible essence of divine nature, I find that Holy Scripture teaches me – for reason counts for nought in this sphere – that the Father is a different and distinct nature [Person] from the Son in the one indivisible and eternal Godhead. The difference is that He is the Father and does not derive His Godhead from the Son or anyone else. The Son is a Person distinct from the Father in the same, one paternal Godhead. The difference is that He is the Son and that He does not have the Godhead from Himself, nor from anyone else but the

Father, since he was born of the Father from eternity. The Holy Spirit is a Person distinct from the Father and the Son in the same, one Godhead. The difference is that He is the Holy Spirit, who eternally proceeds both from the Father and from the Son, and who does not have the Godhead from Himself nor from anyone else but from both the Father and the Son, and all of this from eternity to eternity. With this belief I guard against the heresy of Sabellius and his ilk, of Jews, Mohammed, and all others who presume to be smarter than God Himself. Thus I refrain from jumbling the Persons together into one Person, but I retain, according to the true Christian belief, three distinct Persons in the one divine and eternal essence, all three of which are, over against us and all creatures, one God, Creator and Worker of all things.

. . .

When St. John baptized our Lord in the Jordan, heaven opened and the Holy Spirit descended physically in the form of a dove, and the Father's voice was heard to say: "This is My beloved Son; with whom I am well pleased" [cf. Luke 3: 22, 2 Peter 1: 17]. Here we find a dove, a creature which not only the Holy Spirit but also the Father and the Son had created. As I was saying: "The works of the Trinity to the outside are not divisible," whatever is a creature has been created by God the Father, the Son, and the Holy Spirit as one God. Still the dove is called only Holy Spirit, or, as Luke says, it was only the Holy Spirit, who descended in the form of a dove. And the Christian Creed would by no means tolerate that you say of the dove: That is God the Father, or: That is God the Son. No, you must say: That is God the Holy Spirit, although God the Father, the Son, and the Holy Spirit are but one God. You may say very correctly of the dove: That is God, and there is no God beyond that one. And yet it would be incorrect for you to say: That is God the Father; that is God the Son. You must say: That is God the Holy Spirit.

In like manner, the voice that says "This is My beloved Son, etc." is a creature created not only by the Father but also by the Son and the Holy Spirit. As I was saying: "The works of the Trinity, etc." Outside the Godhead all creatures are created equally by all three Persons as by one God, and over against the creature all three Persons are one God. And again, with regard to the three Persons the creature is but one work and not three works. And yet this voice is called, and is, none but the Father's. As a Christian you cannot say of the voice: That is God the Holy Spirit or that is God the Son. No, you must say: That is God the Father, although God the Holy Spirit and God the Son and God the Father are but one God. You may say very correctly of this voice: That is God, and there is no God beyond that. But it would be incorrect to say: That is God the Son or God the Holy Spirit. No, you must say: That is God the Father.

Of Christ's humanity we say similarly: It is a real creature created by the Father, the Son, and the Holy Spirit. We would not permit the Creed to state that the Father alone or the Son alone or the Holy Spirit alone created this creature, or humanity; this is "an indivisible work of the Trinity," a work which all three Persons created as one God and Creator of one and the same work. Thus the angel Gabriel says to the Virgin Mary in Luke 1: 35: "The Holy Spirit will come upon you, and the power of the Most High will overshadow you." "Not only the Holy Spirit," says he, "will come upon you but also the Most High, that is, the Father will overshadow you with His power, that is, with His Son, or Word. And 'the Child to be born of you' will be called the Son of the Most High." Thus the entire Trinity is present here as one Creator and has created and made the one work, the humanity. And yet it was only the Person of the Son that united with the human nature and became incarnate, not the Father nor the Holy Spirit.

Of this Man you cannot say: That is God the Father or that is God the Holy Spirit; but you must say: That is God the Son, although God the Father, the Son, and the Holy Spirit are one God, and although you can say very correctly of the Man: That is God, and there is no other god beside Him. And yet it would be incorrect to say: That is God the Father or God the Holy Spirit. No, you must say: That is God the Son, as St. Paul declares in Col. 2: 9: "For in Him the whole full-ness of deity dwells bodily." And yet the Father and the Holy Spirit are not thereby deprived of their Godhead but are one God together with the Son and Man Christ. Here you observe how the three Persons are to be believed as distinct within the Godhead and are not to be jumbled together into one Person and that, for all of that, the divine essence is not to be divided to make three gods. Viewed from without, from the point of view of the creature, there is but one Creator, so com-pletely one that even the creature forms which the three Persons individually take are the single work of all three Persons of the one God.

To make such a profound matter somewhat intelligible, the doctors, particularly Bonaventure, adduce a crude illustration.[2] If, for example, three young women would take a dress and put it on one of their number and this one would also take part in clothing herself with this dress, then one could say that all three were dressing her; and yet only one is being attired in the dress and not the other two. Similarly we must understand here that all three Persons, as one God, created the one humanity, clothed the Son in this, and united it with His person, so that only the Son became man, and not the Father or the Holy Spirit. In the same way, we should think also of the dove which the Person of the Holy Spirit adopted and of the voice which the Person of the Father adopted; also the fiery tongues on the Day of Pentecost, in which the Person of the Holy Spirit was revealed; also the wind and whatever else is preached in Christendom or in Holy Scripture about the operation of the Holy Spirit.

Here one might reasonably ask: Why, then, do we say, or rather, why does Holy Scripture teach us to say: "I believe in God the Father, Creator of heaven and earth," and not to mention also the Son as Creator? Also, why do we say: "I believe in Jesus Christ, who was conceived by the Holy Ghost?" Also, why do we say that the Holy Spirit quickens us and that he spoke by the prophets? Here the peculiar and distinctive works are being assigned externally to each Person by way of differ-entiation. This is perhaps too subtle too for simple Christians who want to adhere to their plain faith that God the Father, the Son, and the Holy Spirit are one God, etc. However, it is necessary to discourse on this subject in Christendom and to learn to understand it in order to withstand the devil and his heretics. In the first place, it is certain that God wants to be known by us, here on earth by faith, yonder by sight, that He is one God and yet three Persons. And according to John

17: 3, this is our everlasting life. To this end He gave us His Word and Holy Scripture, attested with great miracles and signs. We must learn from it. To attain that knowledge of God, it is surely necessary that He Himself instruct us, that He reveal Himself and appear to us. By ourselves we could not ascend into heaven and discover what God is or how His divine essence is constituted. Well, for this purpose He employs visible elements in His creation, as Scripture teaches us, so that we may comprehend this; for invisible creatures do not make an impression on our senses.

Accordingly, you must view the creature in two different ways; in the first place, as a creature, or work, per se, absolutely, created or made in this or that way by God. In that sense all creatures are God's work, that is, the single work of all three Persons without distinction. This we have already heard. For in that respect they manifest no distinctive revelation of the three Persons, since they are all the same single work of the three Persons as of the one God. Secondly, you must view the creature not per se, absolutely, but relatively, according to each one's function, as God uses them toward us. Here God takes His creature, which all three Persons as one God have created, and uses it as an image, or form, or figure, in which He reveals Himself and in which He appears. Here distinctive images, forms, and revelation of the three separate Persons come into being. Thus God employs the dove to become an image, or revelation, of the Holy Spirit. This is a distinctive image, which does not portray the Father or the Son but only the Holy Spirit. The Father, the Son, and the Holy Spirit want the dove to depict and reveal distinctively only the person of the Holy Spirit, to assure us that God's one essence is definitely three separate Persons from eternity. That is why Luke 3: 22 states: "The Holy Spirit descended upon Him in bodily form, as a dove."

In the same way, we say of the Son that He is revealed to us in His humanity, or, as St. Paul says in Phil. 2: 7, "taking the form of a servant, being born in the likeness of men." And this form, or humanity, is not the image, or revelation, of the Father or of the Holy Ghost, although it is the same single creation of all three, Father, Son, and Holy Spirit, but it is the peculiar and special form and revelation of the Son alone. For thus it has pleased God, that is, Father, Son, and Holy Spirit, that the Son should be revealed to and recognized by humankind in this form, or figure, of humanity as a Person apart from the Father and the Holy Spirit in one eternal essence of divine nature. In like manner we should profess that the Father was revealed to us in the voice. This form, or figure, is not a revelation of the Son or of the Holy Spirit but only of the Father who in that distinctive form wants to manifest Himself to us as a Person distinct from the Son and the Holy Spirit in one, indivisible divine essence.

You may also choose a crude example illustrating this from grammar. When the priest baptizes or absolves, he uses the word: "In the name of the Father and of the Son and of the Holy Spirit." All of these words in our mouth are the creation and work of God (as we and all that we have are), and not one word is distinctively only that of the Father, or of the Son, or of the Holy Spirit, but it is the work of all three Persons, the single creation of the one God. However, in accordance with this interpretation, or revelation, you must not say that the words "of the Father" signify all three Persons, but specifically only the Father, and the words "of the

Son" specifically only the Son, and the words "of the Holy Spirit" specifically only the Holy Spirit – all in one Godhead. Thus these words, or their interpretation, reveal to us that there are three distinct Persons in the one Godhead. For the priest does not say: "In the names," as of many, or as though each Person had a special name and essence. No, he says, "In the name," as in the name of one being and yet three distinct Persons.

Accordingly, you observe that the creature must be considered in a twofold manner, as a reality and as a symbol, that it is something per se, created by God, and that it is also used to signify or teach something else, something that is not of itself. Smoke is a reality, a thing per se and at the same time a sign of something else, something which is not but which it indicates and reveals, namely, fire. St. Augustine comments at length on this in *On Christian Doctrine*.[3] But here in this sublime subject it means more. For the humanity of Christ is not a mere sign or a mere figure, as the dove and the voice also are not empty figures or images. No, the humanity in which God's Son is distinctively revealed is complete, it is united with God in one Person, which will sit eternally at the right hand of God, as was promised to David in 1 Chr. 17: 12 above. The dove is a figure assumed for a time by the Holy Spirit to reveal Himself, but it was not united with Him forever. No, He again shed this form, as angels, too, adopt human form, appear in it, and later again abandon it. The same is true of God the Father. There is no promise involved that it should be so forever, but it is a temporary revelation.

When we confess in the children's Creed:[4] "I believe in God the Father Almighty, Creator of heaven and earth," we do not mean to imply that only the Person of the Father is the almighty Creator and Father. No, the Son is likewise almighty, Creator, and Father. And the Holy Spirit is likewise almighty, Creator, and Father. And yet there are not three almighty creators and fathers but only one almighty Creator and Father of heaven and earth and of us all. Similarly, the Father is our Savior and Redeemer, the Son is our Savior and Redeemer, and the Holy Spirit is our Savior and Redeemer, and yet there are not three saviors and redeemers, but only one Savior and Redeemer. Likewise, the Father is our God, the Son is our God, and the Holy Spirit is our God, and yet there are not three gods, but only one God. Likewise, the Holy Ghost sanctifies Christendom, so does the Father, so does the Son, and still there are not three sanctifiers, but only one Sanctifier, etc. "The works of the Trinity to the outside are not divisible."

. . .

Beyond this internal distinction of the Persons, there is also the external difference, in which the Son and the Holy Spirit are revealed. The Son is revealed in the humanity, for the Son alone became human. He alone was conceived by the Holy Spirit, was born of the Virgin Mary, suffered and died for us, as our Creed informs us. However it is also correct to say that God died for us, for the Son is God, and there is no other God but only more Persons in the same Godhead. Only the Holy Spirit was diversely revealed in the fiery tongues, in the gifts, in the variety of languages and miraculous signs, etc., although the humanity was created by all three

Persons, and the fiery tongues and the gifts of the Holy Spirit are the creation and work of all three Persons, as we have heard sufficiently for the present. We have precious books on this subject by St. Augustine, Hilary, and Cyril at our disposal. And this article of faith remained pure in the papacy and among the scholastic theologians, and we have no quarrel with them on that score.

Some people worry and wonder whether they are addressing the Person of the Father or the Divine Essence when they pray the Lord's Prayer. It is not at all surprising that strange thoughts come to a person in this extremely mysterious and incomprehensible article of faith and that occasionally one of these goes away and a word miscarries. But wherever the basis of faith remains intact, such splinters, chips, or straws will not harm us. But the foundation of faith, as we have heard, is this, that you believe that there are three Persons in the one Godhead and that each person is the same, one, perfect God, in other words, the Persons are not intermingled and the essence is not divided but the distinction of Persons and the unity of the essence is preserved. For it is this mystery, of which, as we read in 1 Peter 1: 12, the angels cannot behold and wonder their fill in all eternity and about which they are in bliss through all eternity. And if they were able to satisfy their longing, their happiness would end too. We, too, shall behold this, and it will make us eternally blissful, as the Lord says in John 17: 3: "And this is eternal life, that they know Thee the only true God, and Jesus Christ, whom Thou hast sent." In the meantime, faith must cling to the Word, for reason cannot do otherwise than assert that it is impossible and contradictory that there should be three Persons, each one perfect God, and yet not more than one God; that only the Son is Man; that he who has the Father and the Son will surely learn to know the Holy Spirit from the Father and the Son.

You have heard earlier that the Father is the God and Father of us all, that the Son is the God and Father of us all, that the Holy Spirit is the God and Father of us all, and that, for all of that, not more than one God is our Father. For the essence is undivided, therefore no matter which Person you may mention, you have named the one true God in three Persons, since each Person is the same, one, perfect God. In this you cannot err or go wrong. For Jesus Christ is no other God or Father or Creator than the Father or the Holy Spirit, even though He is a different Person. The same is true of the Father and of the Holy Spirit. Hence it would not only be incorrect but also impossible and futile for you to restrict the name "Father" to the Person of God the Father and to the exclusion of the Son and the Holy Spirit; for that would be dividing the Divine Essence and eliminating the Son and the Holy Spirit. That is out of the question. For according to such a manner of personal paternity, the Father has no more than one Son, and the Son has no more than one Father. He is not such a Father to you, and you are not such a Son to Him. No, this is the only-begotten Son of the Father from eternity, as Ps. 2: 7 says: "The Lord said to Me, 'You are My Son, today I have begotten you.'" But you are a temporal son of all three Persons, of one God, and may be 30, 40, or 50 years of age, depending upon the time of your birth and baptism.

As the works of the Trinity to the outside are indivisible, so the worship of the Trinity from the outside is indivisible. Whatever God does to the creature is done by all three Persons without distinction. For there is one Divine Essence of all three Persons, and what we or the creature do to each Person of the Godhead we do to the one God and to all three Persons without distinction. In relation to us He is one God; within Himself He is distinctive in three Persons. Thus Christ Himself says to in John 14: 9–10: "Philip, he who has seen Me has seen the Father; how can you say, 'Show us the Father'? Do you not believe that I am in the Father and the Father in Me?" And in John 10: 30: "I and the Father are one." We mean to say: "One entity, one essence, one God, one Lord."

. . .

. . . For the three distinct Persons are one God, Creator and Father of the world. And each Person is the same complete, one God, Creator and Father of all the world. And when you call upon Jesus Christ, saying: "My dear Lord God, my Creator and Father, Jesus Christ, one, eternal God!" you need have no concern that the Father and the Holy Spirit are resentful on that account, but you may know that you immediately call upon all three Persons and the one God, no matter which Person you may address.

Notes

1 Cf. Augustine, *De Trinitate*, II, v. 9.
2 Neither the Weimar editors nor [the editors of *Luther's Works*] have succeeded in identifying this reference to Bonaventure.
3 Augustine, *Christian Doctrine*, I, 2.
4 "Children's Creed" was Luther's term for the Apostles' Creed.

21

Hans Urs von Balthasar, from Mysterium Paschale

Hans von Balthasar (1905–88) is now best known as the theologian of the Descent into Hell. Theologians can be typed according to which part of the life of Jesus – and which corresponding day of the liturgical calendar – they find most salient in accounting for salvation. You might find that the Incarnation and birth of Christ most important, and propose a Christmas theology; or find the Resurrection most important, and stress Easter, or the Crucifixion the most important, and stress Good Friday. Von Balthasar brings out the Descent into Hell on Holy Saturday, the day between Good Friday and Easter. That is the both the Son's farthest remove from the Father, and at the same time his closest way back to him: the road back to the Father leads through hell, encompassing all of human sin and suffering within the trinitarian embrace.

By implication it is the Spirit that stretches to accommodate the distance of the Son from the Father when one is in hell and the other in heaven – and brings them back, a divine rubber band, at the Resurrection. "Only if the Spirit, as *vinculum amoris* [chain of love] between the Father and the Son, can re-relate Father and Son in their estrangement in the Descent, can the unity of the Revealed and the Revealer be maintained." But that line is not quite by von Balthasar: it is by Aidan Nichols in the Introduction to *Mysterium Paschale* (p. 7). It is a both a frustration and a strength of Balthasar's exposition that he sticks close to biblical and historical materials, and suggests more than he asserts. What follows is von Balthasar's account of the Spirit's role in that re-relation at the Resurrection.

Hans Urs von Balthasar, *Mysterium Paschale: The Mystery of Easter*, trans. with an Introduction by Aidan Nichols (Grand Rapids, MI: Eerdmans, 1990), pp. 203, 210–12.

from **Mysterium Paschale**

Hans Urs von Balthasar

The Resurrection of the dead Son is consistently ascribed to the action of the Father, and in the closest possible connexion with the Resurrection there is presented to us the outpouring of the divine Spirit. Only because 'God has sent the Spirit of his Son into our hearts' (Galatians 4: 6) does the objective event become something that touches our own existence. . . . [I]t is in the strength of the Spirit of God, his *pneuma*, that the Resurrection of Jesus Christ is accomplished, as Romans 8: 11 and 1 Peter 3: 18 indicate. In this powerful, transfiguring action of his Spirit, God shows himself so much, and so definitively, the God who raises the dead that participial or relative forms – 'he who raised Christ Jesus from the dead' (Romans 8: 11; 2 Corinthians 4: 14; Galatians 1: 1; Ephesians 1: 20; Colossians 2: 12) – become, as J. Schniewind once remarked, God's 'honorific names'.[1]

· · ·

Lastly, the Resurrection of the Son is the revelation of the *Spirit*. To see this as it originally was, it is best not to begin from the temporal division into periods found in the Acts of the Apostles, where the Easter event and that of the Ascension are separated by an interval of forty days and the Ascension is made into a pre-supposition for the sending of the Spirit at Pentecost. If we leave the question of the forty days provisionally to one side, the Lucan idea[2] of how the Son, ascending to the Father, receives from him for the first time the promised Spirit so as to him pour forth upon the Church (Acts 2: 33; 1: 4ff.) can take on a theologically deeper meaning – especially if we relate this event to the promise of the departing Lord in the Fourth Gospel. He must depart so that the Spirit may come (John 16: 7); he will ask the Father (that means, of course, when he is exalted) to send to the disciples another Paraclete, who will abide with them for ever (14: 16), and, more than that, will himself send this Spirit from the Father (15: 26; cf. Luke 24: 49). If one holds together these aspects of the Johannine teaching with the message of Luke then what transpires is the reunion with the Father of the Son who was sent to the world, and to the Cross, a reunion which takes place after the complete fulfilment of his mission (John 19: 30). In the tones of speculative theology we might say that the reunion of the Father and the Son (in his human nature) as a single principle of aspiration (in the economy) appears as the condition for the sending forth of the Spirit to the Church and to the redeemed world. Luke offers his own interpretation of this idea by extending the temporal and festal cycle, spacing out his material in a way which is at once pedagogical but also, certainly, cultic in character. John, on the other hand, in no less essentially theological a manner, compresses Easter, the Ascension and Pentecost so that they inter-penetrate one another. As early as the evening of Easter Day, the Risen One, as John presents him, breathes out the Spirit upon the Church (20: 22), which is not to deny that

John knows, at least by allusion, the 'ascending to the Father' (20: 17) which precedes the breathing forth of that Spirit. Even Luke, in Acts 2: 33, in no way implies
that Jesus had to await the Ascension in order himself to 'receive from the Father
the promise of the Holy Spirit': what is at stake here is a promise made by Jesus to
his disciples, a promise whose content is meant for them (Luke 24: 49): in other words,
the great promise of the prophet Joel that the Spirit will be poured out eschatologically 'upon all flesh' (Acts 2: 17). What was essential in Luke's eyes is that:

> one can only receive the Spirit from Jesus, just as, in general, one can only participate
> in the present epoch of saving history which is the time of the Spirit on the condition
> that one shares, by the Spirit, in the time of Jesus.[3]

Paul's contribution here was decisive in that, for him, all the problems concerning the lapse of time between the Resurrection and the sending of the Spirit fall
away, since he sees the two events in the closest possible unity. We have already
noted that the Father raises the Son by his Spirit (Romans 8: 11), and that the terms
dynamis [power], *doxa* [glory], and *pneuma* [spirit], which alternate as principles
of resurrection, are to a considerable degree interchangeable. But the Spirit is
not only the instrument of the Resurrection. He is also the milieu in which the
Resurrection takes place: *zōopoiēstheis de pneumati*, 'he who was made alive in
the Spirit' (1 Peter 3: 18); *edikaiōthē en pneumati*, 'he was vindicated in the Spirit'
(1 Timothy 3: 16; cf. Romans 1: 4). This milieu is not, however, one which Christ
enters as into an environment strange to him. Rather is it an inheritance that belongs
to him, since he is beforehand, as 'second Adam', the *pneuma zōopoioun*, 'life-giving
Spirit' (1 Corinthians 15: 45); rises again as *sōma pneumatikon*, 'a spiritual body'
(1 Corinthians 15: 44); and is wholly identified with the realm of the Spirit ('The
Lord is the Spirit', 2 Corinthians 3: 17). Whoever wishes to live in the Lord must
live in the Spirit and by him (Galatians 5: 16, 22 and 25). John puts into words
the same idea when he makes the earthly Jesus one to whom the Father gives
the Spirit 'without measure' (John 3: 34) and (as the true 'rock in the desert') the
dispenser *par excellence* of water and the Spirit (7: 38). Yet the rock must first be
struck by the lance of the Passion before he can pour out, with his blood, this
water (and that Spirit) which before his glorification is only promised (7: 39; 4: 10
and 14), but which afterwards is both the foundation and the testimony – in
the unity of the Spirit with the water and the blood – of the faith of the Church
(1 John 5: 6ff.; John 3: 5 and 8). When Jesus on the Cross gives over his *pneuma*,
he also, doubtless, breathes forth the Spirit who is sent on mission, 'given without measure' (*pneuma aiōnion*, Hebrews 9: 14) – the Spirit whom the Father, in
raising Jesus returns to him as in the highest possible manner personally his own,
but who is henceforth also the divine Spirit, identical with *dynamis* and *doxa* and
now made known openly to the world (Romans 1: 4).

This explains why for Paul, as for the author of the Acts of the Apostles, and
indeed 'for the witness of all the New Testament writers',[4] the action of the Holy
Spirit, manifesting himself in the Church, remains the real proof of Christ's risen
being. For that Resurrection was nothing less than Christ's taking possession of

God's Spirit and power, access to which he had promised to those who believe in him. Luke for his part provides for the Church, aware as she is of her living possession of the Spirit, a central moment of a cultic kind, and one capable of being dated – namely, the event of Pentecost. Such possession of the Spirit is expressed not only in the continuation of the 'signs and wonders' on whose basis Jesus had been 'attested . . . by God' (Acts 2: 22), but also in the inner dispositions of the community: its prayer, its living faith, its brotherliness of common life, concern for the needy and so forth.[5] Last but not least to be mentioned among these indices of the ownership of the Spirit comes: being found worthy to share in the sufferings of Christ, something only possible through the inner incorporation of believers into the realm of Christ and the Spirit.[6]

The decisive revelation of the mystery of the Trinity is not, therefore, something which precedes the *Mysterium Paschale* [paschal mystery] itself.[7]

Notes

1 H. Schlier, *Über die Auferstehung Jesu Christi* (Einsiedeln: Johannes-Verlag, 1968), p. 21.

2 E. Lohse, 'Die Bedeutung des Pfingstberichtes im Rahmen des lukanischen Geschichtswerkes', *Evangelische Theologie* 13 (1953), pp. 422–36.

3 U. Wilckens, *Die Missionsreden der Apostelgeschichte. Form- und Traditionsgeschichtliche Untersuchungen*, 2nd edn. (Neukirchen: Neukirchener Verlag, 1963), p. 95.

4 P. Seidensticker, *Die Auferstehung Jesu in der Botschaft der Evangelisten* (Stuttgart: Katholisones Bibelwerk, 1967), p. 24.

5 Ibid., pp. 100–1.

6 The extended and coherent account of the healing miracle in Jesus' name at the Beautiful Gate, the courageous testifying before the Great Council ('filled with the Holy Spirit', Acts 4: 8), the prayer of the community 'in the Spirit' (4: 31), the whipping of the apostles who suffered 'dishonour for the Name' (5: 41) and the stoning of Stephen, successively develop different aspects of the presence of the Spirit.

7 The anticipated dating of the revelation of the Trinity in Luke 1: 28, 31 and 35, indicates a post-paschal composition: A Resch, *Das Kindheits-evangelium nach Lukas und Matthäus* (Leipzig: Hinrichs, 1897); R. Laurentin, *Structure et théologie de Luc I–II* (Paris: Gabalda, 1957).

22

Jürgen Moltmann, from The Trinity and the Kingdom

Jürgen Moltmann (b. 1926) combines several tendencies in twentieth-century Christian thought: the tendency to define God through God's history with the world, following Hegel; the tendency to emphasize God's suffering with humanity; the tendency to treat the Trinity as a social unity. As with all careful thinkers, Moltmann has answers to the questions that those tendencies raise. Does God engage with the world because God needs to experience it, as Hegel sometimes suggests, or out of a self-commitment to it? Does God's suffering with humanity trap God and humanity in the same boat, so that God cannot stand enough apart from the world to save it? Does the quasi-social interaction of the Persons of the Trinity undermine God's unity?[1] On the contrary, Moltmann has reasons to answer "no" to all those questions.

Critics point out that traditional ways of handling God's suffering with humanity divided things up like this: God does suffer, in the Person of the Son. "One of the Trinity has died for us," Cyril of Alexandria proclaims. Cyril states the matter in the tightest of paradoxes: "Impassibly God suffers," meaning: it is no part of divinity to suffer, but God chooses solidarity with us.[2] In the traditional understanding, the Father and the Spirit are not the subjects of the suffering. The idea that the Father suffers is even the heresy of patripassianism. Why should opponents of patripassianism want to preserve the Father from suffering? Because freedom from suffering is part of the salvation that they think Christ returns us to the Father to receive. If the *Father* does not enjoy freedom from suffering, then, they think, there is no hope for us. Critics of this tradition find opposition to the suffering Father a Greek, unbiblical idea; opponents of the suffering Father reply that the character of the Father is not, in the New Testament, a sentimental, human figure but the creator of the world. The parables, on the other hand, do depict the Father in human terms. And so on.

Jürgen Moltmann, *The Trinity and the Kingdom*, trans. Margaret Kohl (Minneapolis: Fortress Press, 1993), pp. 64, 81–3, 88–90, 94, 104–5.

How much this debate affects the Holy Spirit is an interesting question.[3] Here, the Spirit mediates between the Father in heaven and the Son on the Cross, at the point where the Son cries, "My God, my God, why have you forsaken me?" (Mark 15: 34, Matt. 27: 46). The Spirit enacts his role as bond of love between the Father and the Son in empowering and glorifying their common cause to join and save the lost, precisely at the cross, when that purpose drives them farthest apart. The Spirit rejoins Father and Son at the Resurrection. And the Spirit initiates other human beings into the trinitarian society in the Church and in the communion of the saints.

from **The Trinity and the Kingdom**

Jürgen Moltmann

The New Testament talks about God by proclaiming in narrative the relationships of the Father, the Son and the Spirit, which are relationships of fellowship and are open to the world. . . .

The surrender of the Son

. . . The Father forsakes the Son 'for us' – that is to say, in order to become the God and Father of the forsaken. The Father 'delivers up' the Son in order through him to become the Father of those who have been delivered up (Rom. 1: 18ff.). The Son is given over to death in order that he may become the brother and saviour of the condemned and the cursed.

The Son suffers death in this forsakenness. The Father suffers the death of the Son. So the pain of the Father corresponds to the death of the Son. And when in this descent into hell the Son loses the Father, then in this judgment the Father also loses the Son. Here the innermost life of the Trinity is at stake. Here the communicating love of the Father turns into infinite pain over the sacrifice of the Son. Here the responding love of the Son becomes infinite suffering over his repulsion and rejection by the Father. What happens on Golgotha reaches into the innermost depths of the Godhead, putting its impress on the trinitarian life in eternity.

But according to Galatians 2: 20, the Son was not only given up by the Father. He also 'gave himself for me.' . . .

. . . Theologically this means an inner conformity between the will of the surrendered Son and the surrendering will of the Father. That is what the Gethsemane story is about too. But this profound community of will arises at precisely the point when the Son is furthest divided from the Father, and the Father from the Son,[4] in the accursed death on the cross, in 'the dark night' of that death. On the cross the Father and the Son are so deeply separated that their relationship breaks off. Jesus died 'without God' – godlessly. Yet on the cross the Father and the Son are at the same time so much one that they represent a single surrendering movement. 'He who has seen the Son has seen the Father.' The Epistle to the Hebrews expresses this by saying that Christ offered himself to God 'through the eternal Spirit (*dia pneumatos aioniou*) (9: 14). The surrender through the Father and the offering of the Son take place 'through the Spirit.' The Holy Spirit is therefore the link in the separation. He is the link joining the bond between the Father and the Son, with their separation.

. . .

To put it in trinitarian terms – the Father lets his Son sacrifice himself through the Spirit.[5] 'The Father is crucifying love, the Son is crucified love, and the Holy Spirit is the unvanquishable power of the cross.'[6] The cross is at the centre of the Trinity.

. . .

If finally, we ask by what means the Father raised the Son from the death to which he delivered him up, then we come face to face with the activity of the Holy Spirit: He was raised through the creative *Spirit* (Rom. 1: 4; 8: 11; 1 Peter 3: 18; 1 Tim. 3: 16). He was raised through *the glory of the Father* (Rom. 6: 4). He was raised through *the power of God* (1 Cor. 6: 14). God's power, God's glory and the divine Spirit are used synonymously here. They are the name for something which is not the Father, and not the Son either, but which is a third divine subject in the history of Jesus, the Son.

. . .

Where was Jesus raised *to?* . . . Jesus is risen into the innermost being of God himself. He has been exalted into the divine origin of the Holy Spirit. That is the trinitarian centre. That is why God's glory is manifested through him in this world. That is why in this present history he is the Lord of the divine kingdom. That is why in this present time he is the 'life-giving spirit' (1 Cor. 15: 45), sending the Spirit upon the disciples, and the energies of the Spirit upon the church, and through the church 'on all flesh'.

Here our interest is concentrated particularly on the relationship of the risen Son to the quickening Spirit. Whereas in the sending, in the surrender and in the resurrection, the Spirit acts on Christ, and Christ lives from the works of the creative Spirit, now the relationship is reversed: the risen Christ sends the Spirit; he is himself present in the life-giving Spirit; and through the Spirit's energies – the charismata – he acts on men and women. The Spirit witnesses to Christ, and whoever confesses Christ as his Lord does so in the power of the Spirit who creates life from the dead. That is why after Easter the Spirit is called 'the Spirit of sonship' (Rom. 8: 15), 'the Spirit of faith' (2 Cor. 4: 13), or the 'Spirit of Christ': 'Where the Spirit of the Lord is, there is freedom' (2 Cor. 3: 17). The Spirit proceeds from the Father and is now 'sent' by the Son (John 15: 26). Through his resurrection the Son is evidently so near to the Father, and so much in the Father, that he participates in the sending of the Spirit out of its divine origin. Whereas the sending, the surrender and the resurrection of Christ were the works of the life-giving Spirit, so now the sending and outpouring of the Spirit who makes all things new becomes a work of the Son.

Here it cannot be forgotten that in the whole of the New Testament the Spirit is understood eschatologically. He is the power of the new creation. He is the power of the resurrection. He is the earnest and pledge of glory. His present efficacy is the rebirth of men and women. His future goal is the raising up of the kingdom of glory. His activity is experienced inwardly, in the heart; but it points ahead into what is outward and public. He lays hold on the soul, but will only find rest when he 'gives life to mortal bodies' (Rom. 8: 11).

What form of the Trinity do we encounter here?

- The Father raises the dead Son through the life-giving Spirit;
- the Father enthrones the Son, as the Lord of his kingdom;
- the risen Son sends the creative Spirit from the Father, to renew heaven and earth.

Whereas until his resurrection we were able to perceive in the history of Jesus the sequence: *Father–Spirit–Son,* we now encounter the sequence *Father–Son–Spirit.* What does this mean?

It means that in the sending of the Spirit the Trinity is an open Trinity. Through the sending of the creative Spirit, the trinitarian history of God becomes a history that is open to the world, open to men and women, and open to the future. Through the experience of the life-giving Spirit in faith, in baptism, and in the fellowship of believers, people are integrated into the history of the Trinity. Through the Spirit of Christ they not only become participators in the eschatological history of the new creation. Through the Spirit of the Son they also become at the same time participants in the trinitarian history of God himself. That is the profounder reason why acknowledgment of the Trinity was developed in the context of baptism first of all.[7]

The explicitly 'triadical' formulations in the New Testament are without exception baptismal formulations (Matt. 28: 19). Didache 7.1 stipulates baptism in the name of the Father, the Son and the Spirit. All the acknowledgments of the Trinity that follow are baptismal ones. That is to say, trinitarian theology is baptismal theology. It has to be, because the history of the Son and the creative Spirit of God which the New Testament relates is not a completed history. It is an inviting, eschatological history that is open in a forward-looking direction. Through baptism people are absorbed into it. The doctrine of the Trinity has baptism as its original *Sitz im Leben* – its situation in life.

Which form of the Trinity do we encounter in baptism?

- In baptism we encounter the divine Trinity as the eschatological history of God which is open in a forward-looking direction.

- The *unity* of the Father, the Son and the Spirit is hence an *open* unity, not a closed one.
- It is open for *unification* with believers, with humankind, and with the whole creation.

. . . Father, Son and Spirit do not only combine or work together according to a single pattern. In the sending, in the surrender, and in the resurrection, the Father is the actor, the Son the receiver, and the Spirit the means through which the Father acts on his Son and the Son receives the Father.

In the lordship of the Son and the diffusion of the creative Spirit, the Son together with the Father are the actors. The Spirit takes his sending from the Son, just as he takes his issue from the Father.

In eschatology, finally, the Son is the actor, he transfers the kingdom to the Father; he subjects himself to the Father. But in eschatology the Spirit is the actor equally: he glorifies the Father through the praise of all created beings who have been liberated by Christ's rule. The Father is the One who receives. He receives his kingdom from the Son; he receives his glory from the Spirit.

. . .

The New Testament writings do not only witness to the experience of salvation in Christ, and to faith in Christ as the mediator of creation; they also testify to the experience of the Holy Spirit, and the hope that through him *the world will be transfigured*, transformed into God's world, which means into God's own home.[8] This hope is expressed in continually new visions of *the indwelling of God* in this new world. The experience of the Spirit is expressed in words quite distinct from those describing creation and God's 'works' in history. The words used for the Spirit are 'outpouring', 'flowing', and so forth. The Spirit is 'poured out' on all flesh in the Last Days (Joel 2: 28ff.; Acts 2: 16ff.), and then old and young, men and women, all alike, will have dreams and visions. Through the Holy Spirit the love of God is 'poured out' into our hearts, Paul says when he is talking about believers (Rom. 5: 5). People are 'born' anew of the Spirit (John 3: 3, 5f.). The charismata, the gifts and energies of the Spirit in the new fellowship, will not be 'created'; as fruits of *charis*, the gift of the Spirit itself, they will be 'effected' (1 Cor. 12). These are the divine energies which already quicken life now, in the present, because they are the energies of the new creation of all things.

A new *divine presence* is experienced in the experience of the Spirit. God does not simply confront his creation as creator. He is not merely, as the incarnate One, the representative and advocate for men and women. In the Spirit God dwells in the human being himself. The experience of the Spirit is therefore the experience of the Shekinah, the divine indwelling. The Shekinah is a divine presence which was otherwise only experienced in the Temple, in worship on the Lord's day. But now men and women themselves, in their own bodies, already become the temple of the Holy Spirit (1 Cor. 6: 13–20). In the end, however, the new heaven and the new earth will become the 'temple' of God's indwelling. The whole world will become God's home. Through the indwelling of the Spirit, people and churches are already glorified *in the body*, now, in the present. But then the whole creation will be transfigured through the indwelling of God's glory. Consequently the hope which is kindled by the experience of the indwelling Spirit gathers in the future, with pantheistic visions. Everything ends with God's being 'all in all' (1 Cor. 15: 28 AV). *God in the world* and *the world in God* – that is what is meant by the glorifying of the world through the Spirit. That is *the home of the Trinity*. If the world is transformed and glorified into this through the Holy Spirit, then creation can only be conceived of in trinitarian terms, if it is to be understood in Christian terms at all.

Notes

1 For a careful critique of some social doctrines, see Karen Kilby, "Perichoresis and Projection: Problems with Social Doctrines of the *Trinity*," *New Blackfriars* 81 (2000), pp. 432–45.
2 See Cyril of Alexandria, "3rd Letter to Nestorius," in *Select Letters of Cyril of Alexandria*, ed. Lionel Wickam (Oxford: Oxford University Press, 1983); Second Council of Constantinople, "Anathema 10," in *Documents of the Christian Church*, 3rd edn., ed. Henry Bettenson and Chris Maunder (Oxford: Oxford University Press, 1999), p. 101. For a recent defense of the classical view, see Thomas Weinandy, *Does God Suffer?* (Edinburgh: T. & T. Clarke; Notre Dame, IN: University of Notre Dame Press, 2000).
3 For more, see Lyle Dabney, *Die Kenosis des Geistes* (Neukirchen-Vluyn: Neukirchener Verlag, 1997).
4 Cf. also further reflections in H. Mühlen, *Die Veränderlichkeit Gottes als Horizont einer zukünftigen Christologie*, 2nd edn. (Münster: Aschendorff, 1976).
5 So already B. Steffen, *Das Dogma vom Kreuz. Beitrag zu einer staurozentrischen Theologie* (Gütersloh: Bertelsmann, 1920), p. 152.
6 This astonishing sentence comes from Patriarch Philareth of Moscow; quoted in P. Evdokimov, *Christus im russischen Denken* (Trier: Paulinus-Verlag, 1977), pp. 64 and 227.
7 O. Weber, *Grundlagen der Dogmatik*, 2nd edn. (Neukirchen: Neukirchener Verlag, 1957), vol. I, pp. 419ff: Heilsgeschen und Trinitätslehre ('The Event of Salvation and the Doctrine of the Trinity').
8 I am here picking up ideas which I expressed most recently in 'Theology of Mystical Experience,' in *Experiences of God* (English translation: London: SCM Press; Philadelphia: Fortress Press, 1980), pp. 55ff.

VI
Russian and Romanian Resources

23

Pavel Florensky, from "The Comforter," in The Pillar and Ground of the Truth

Twentieth-century Russian Orthodox theology flowed in two main streams, sophiological and neo-Patristic, both found among exiles in Paris. Sergei Bulgakov founded the sophiological stream; it was innovative and conversant with the German Enlightenment and Idealism – with Kant, Hegel, Marx, and Schelling – and was interested in philosophy, politics, and economics as well as theology. Vladimir Lossky, Paul Evdokimov, and (in Romania) Dumitru Staniloae founded the neo-patristic stream that, like Protestant neo-Orthodoxy (Barth) and Catholic Nouvelle Theologie (Henri de Lubac, Marie-Dominique Chenu) revived and returned to earlier authoritative texts. Pavel Florensky, who stayed in Russia and died young, originated *both* sophiological and neo-Patristic streams. Not only did he recover Patristic sources, but he developed "Sophia," or Holy Wisdom, in a way that no one found unorthodox. Not only did he work with nineteenth-century German philosophy, but he also studied the writings of the American pragmatist Charles Peirce (which no other Eastern Orthodox theologian has considered, before or since). And he influenced not only Russian theology and philosophy but poetry and aesthetics – and later, American studies of sexuality and gender (his chapter "Friendship" is in *The Pillar and Ground of the Truth*).

At the beginning of this volume, Robert Jenson rehearsed the twentieth-century's repeated alarms over Spirit-reticence. Florensky anticipated all twentieth-century worries about the spirit when *The Pillar and Ground of the Truth* first appeared in Russian in 1914. None of the later critics read it. Florensky's diagnosis reaches both much earlier – he finds a reticence about the Spirit since the patristic period – and more widely: he finds a reticence about the Spirit also among mystics, ascetics, spiritual writers, and even in the liturgy. But his tone is

Pavel Florensky, "The Comforter," in *The Pillar and Ground of the Truth*, trans. Boris Jakim (Princeton, NJ: Princeton University Press, 1997), pp. 80–3, 85–99, 101–5.

entirely different. Florensky does not sound alarmed. He sounds bemused. Perhaps, he suggests, reticence about the Spirit is just as it should be. Spirit-enthusiasts are trying to bring in the Kingdom. Whether one agrees with that assessment or not, the tone of confident unconcern is a marvelous change.

A further passage, too technical to reproduce here, deserves notice. In an earlier chapter, called "Doubt," Florensky asks, Why three? and speculates on an answer. Although he permits himself the word "prove," he takes care (like Anselm!) to maintain an apophatic moment: to insist that "I ask; I do not affirm," that "If I am asked about grounds, I will curl up in myself like a snail."[1] The "proof" remains a thought-experiment. It ends with a Peircean assertion that "Truth is the contemplation of Oneself through Another in a Third," so that the Subject of the Truth, or God, must be threefold to be stable (or "absolute"). For the same reason, Florensky writes the book itself in the form of letters to an unnamed friend. If the account of threefoldness is a bit sterile, the practice (in letter form) is of the purplest, and here it leads to something substantial: a sketch of deification, or of salvation as inclusion in the divine life:

> But more than three? Yes, there can be more than three – through the acceptance of new hypostases into the interior of the life of the Three. But these new hypostases are not members which support the Subject of the Truth, and therefore they are not inwardly necessary for this Subject's absoluteness. They are conditional hypostases, which can be but do not have to be in the Subject of the Truth. Therefore, they cannot be called hypostases in the strict sense, and it is better to call them deified persons. (p. 380)

Trinitarian speculation becomes soteriology as the Trinity shows hospitality to human beings as guests – not founders of the feast to rival Father, Son, and Spirit – but guests in their common life, their *koinonia*. "Thou preparest a table before me . . . my cup overflows . . . I shall dwell in the house of the Lord forever" (Ps. 23: 5–6).

from Letter Five: The Comforter

Pavel Florensky

Do you remember, my gentle one, our long walks in the forest, the forest of dying August? The silvery trunks of the birches stood like stately palms, and their gold-green tops, as though exuding blood, pressed against the crimson and purple aspens. And above the surface of the earth, the branches of a hazel grove spread like green gauze. There was a holy hush of solemnity beneath the vaults of this temple.

My far and yet eternally near Friend, do you remember our intimate conversations? The Holy Spirit and religious antinomies – that, it appears, is what interested us most. And finding ourselves in this solemn grove, we walked at sunset through the cornfield, became drunk with the flaming west, and rejoiced that the question was becoming clear, that we had come independently to the same answer. Then our thoughts flowed out in streams flaming like the vault of heaven, and we grasped each other's thoughts almost before they were spoken. The roots of our hair tingled with an inspired, cold, yet flaming rapture. Shivers ran up our spines.

My brother, you who shared one soul with me, do you remember the reeds over the black backwater? We stood in silence at the precipitous bank, and listened to the mysterious evening rustlings. An ineffably exultant mystery grew in our souls, but we were silent about it, speaking to each other by silence. That was then.

But now it is winter outside. I work at a lamp, and the evening light in the window seems blue and majestic like Death. And I, as if before my death, review all that has passed, and am again agitated by an unearthly joy. But there is nothing for me to gather now that I am alone. I now write down my poor fragmentary thoughts for you. Nevertheless, I write: so many hopes are connected with the question of the Holy Spirit that I will attempt to write something in your memory. Let the pages of this letter be the dried flowers of that autumn.

Knowledge of the Truth, i.e., of the consubstantiality of the Holy Trinity, is achieved by the grace of the Holy Spirit. The entire ascetic life, i.e., life in the Truth, is directed by the Holy Spirit. The third Hypostasis of the Holy Trinity is, as it were, the closest, the most open for the ascetic of Truth. It is this Hypostasis, "the Spirit of Truth" (John 16: 13), that bears witness in the very soul of the ascetic to the Lord, i.e., to *consubstantiality*. It is this Hypostasis that "shall teach . . . what . . . to say" (Luke 12: 12) to all who stand outside the Spirit and therefore persecute the Lord, i.e., the idea of consubstantiality. Nevertheless, knowledge of the Spirit as the Comforter, the joy of the Comforter makes golden only the highest points of sorrow. Just as the roses of the sun that has become fatigued in the course of the day smile on the snowy peaks of the Caucasus. Only at the end of the path of thorns can we see the rosy clouds of purified creation and the snowy-white radiance of holy, transfigured flesh.

Only at the end. It is thus in the personal life of each of us. It is also thus in the integral life of mankind. Before it stepped out with firm foot on the way of salvation, mankind was supported by the Lord. Then all sorrows were forgotten. But the sorrows were already there in embryo; they were being prepared. "Can the children of the bridechamber mourn, as long as the bridegroom is with them? But the days will come, when the bridegroom shall be taken from them, and then shall they fast" (Matt. 9: 15).

It is true that, at the beginning of the ascetic way, the Bride will meet one with a gentle kiss. It is true that apostolic Christianity trembled with the fullness of joy. But this kiss, this joy, is only a betrothal. It is given in view of the long way, the many torments – not because we are worthy of it but to give us courage.

The miraculous moment flashed blindingly, and then it apparently was no more. The Lord left the earth and all that with His light He had overcome – directly, visibly – on the earth. He is with us, but not in a human, earthly manner. It is the same way in personal life, at the beginning of the ascetic way, when great ineffable joy fills our soul without our having deserved or expected it. That joy – like the Most Pure Body and Precious Blood of Christ, which are given to us for nourishment and sustenance – is given "in betrothal to the future Kingdom," in betrothal to the spiritualization and illumination of the whole being.[2]

That, I repeat, is how it is at the beginning of the way. Infinitely joyous is this beginning. It is so unutterably good then that, remembering the sweet parting, mankind finds the strength to overcome obstacles even in the memory of the fleeting vision. With dreams of the bliss of first love, the ascetic chases away the black thoughts of everyday toil, and the boredom and melancholy of gray, everyday life.

But in general, on the average, under ordinary circumstances, both the personal life of a Christian (apart from its highest ascents) and the everyday life of the Church (except for the elect of heaven) know but little, dimly, and confusedly the Holy Spirit as a Person. Connected with this is insufficient and inconstant knowledge of the heavenly nature of Creation.

It could not be otherwise. Knowledge of the Holy Spirit would give perfect spirituality, perfect deification to all Creation, perfect illumination. Then history would end; the fullness of time would be achieved; in the whole world. Time would be no longer. Let me repeat, this is the fulfillment that the Mystery-Contemplating Eagle, St. John, was deemed worthy of seeing: "And the angel which I saw stand upon the sea and upon the earth lifted up his hand to heaven. And sware by him that liveth for ever and ever, who created heaven, and the things that therein are, and the earth, and the things that therein are, and the sea, and the things which are therein, that there should be time no longer. But in the days of the voice of the seventh angel, when he shall begin to sound, the mystery of God should be finished, as he hath declared to his servants the prophets" (Rev. 10: 5–7). That is what will be at the limit of history, when the Comforter is revealed.

But as long as history continues, only moments and instants of illumination by the Spirit are possible. The Comforter is known only at certain moments and instants by certain individuals, who then rise above time into Eternity: "There is no time for them," and history ends for them. The fullness of the acquisition of the Spirit is inaccessible to the faithful as a whole. It is also inaccessible to an individual believer, within the limits of his life. Christ's victory over Death and Corruption is not yet assimilated by Creation, not wholly assimilated. Thus, knowledge is not perfect. Just as the holy, incorruptible relics of ascetics are pledges of the victory over Death, i.e., manifestations of the Spirit in fleshly nature, so holy spiritual illuminations are pledges of the victory over rationality, i.e., manifestations of the Spirit in psychic nature. But to the extent there is no resurrection, to that extent there is no perfect illumination of the mind by the Holy Spirit. To assert that perfect knowledge or perfect purification of the flesh has been achieved is imposture, the imposture of Simon Magus, Manes, Montanus, the Khlysts,[3] and thousands of other false bearers of the spirit, who have lied and are lying about the Spirit. This is that perversion of man's nature which is called *prel'shchenie* or *prelest'* (tempting illusion or spiritual error).[4]

Yes, the Holy Spirit operates in the Church. But knowledge of the Spirit has always been only a pledge or a reward – at special moments or in exceptional people; and it will be thus until time ends. That is why, when reading the Church literature, one cannot fail to notice a certain phenomenon, which at first seems strange but then, in the light of previous considerations, reveals its internal necessity. That is, all the holy fathers and mystical philosophers speak of the importance of the idea of the Spirit in the Christian worldview but hardly any of them gives a clear and precise explanation of anything. It is clear that the holy fathers know something. But it is even clearer that this knowledge is so deeply buried, so unutterable, that they do not have the power to clothe it in precise words. This applies chiefly to dogmatists, for they are the ones who have to speak decisively and to the heart of the matter. And it is they who turn out to be almost mute, or clearly confused. Let us recall, from the 2nd century, the "binitarian system" of Hermas and the author of the Second Pseudo-Clementine Epistle to the Corinthians. In both places, the Holy Spirit is directly confused with the Church. Or let us recall Tertullian's system, where the Spirit is so poorly distinguished from the Word that He is almost identified with the Latter and is often named instead of Him.[5]

. . .

To be sure, debates go on and various affirmations are made concerning the Holy Spirit. But they all have a formal and schematic character. They all differ from corresponding affirmations about the Son and the Father in the same way that pencil sketches differ from a painted canvas. Whereas the hypostatic being of the Father and the Son is apprehended by every nerve of the spiritual organism; whereas heresy with regard to the Father and the Son is organically and immediately unacceptable, unacceptable by the very heart of one's being; whereas the nature of the Father and the Son is disclosed in crystal-clear, geometrically harmonious formulas, which have a religiously axiomatic character – the doctrine of the Holy Spirit is noticed not at all or almost not at all, but is disclosed in a derivative or roundabout manner, as a rational theorem, according to the schema: "Since such-and-such is said about the Son, it follows that we are compelled to say such-and-such about the Spirit."

For a believer the truthfulness of propositions about the Son is immediately evident. But the truthfulness of propositions about the Spirit is clarified in a roundabout way, is established through the formal correctness of the intermediate arguments. The proofs and justifications of logology could and did turn out to be naive, insufficient, and preliminary structures, whereas the very building of dogmatics rested on the great word *homoousios*, which was immediately true for consciousness, for life according to faith in Jesus Christ.

The consubstantiality of the Word for spiritual people was given from the experience of life, and these people recognized and confessed consubstantiality, despite the weak argumentation and the proofs to the contrary. The argumentation in the doctrine of the Word was no more than an appendix. But, in the doctrine of the Holy Spirit, argumentation was almost everything, and without it the dogma lost its persuasiveness. That which Origen, adamantine in other respects, says about the being and origin of the Holy Spirit is a doctrine thought up *ad hoc*, a deliberate sophistry, created so as not to come into conflict with Church tradition. In essence, for Origen, if it were possible, it would have been much more natural and convenient to remain completely silent about the Holy Spirit.

. . .

Basil the Great gazed at the consubstantiality of the Holy Spirit with his peripheral vision, whereas his direct vision was focused on the consubstantiality of the Son. A willing and free confession and defense of the Son inevitably drew him into an involuntary and inevitable confession and defense of the Spirit.

Let us repeat, this is not an accident of the history of theology but the inexorable order in the fulfillment of the hours and seasons, a necessary and inevitable definition given to the relatively indistinct revelation of the Spirit as a Hypostasis, a deficiency of life itself. Our assertion is easy to prove. For where is the immediate expression of spiritual experience? Where is spiritual experience least processed? In prayers and hymns, in the liturgy. The liturgy is the most significant and essential function of the life of the body of the Church. The witness of the liturgy is the most reliable witness. But, let us ask, where should we first look for an indication of the place that was occupied by the Holy Spirit in the minds and hearts of the members of the early Church compared with the other Hypostases? Of course, at the point where the very celebration was directed toward the glorification of all three Hypostases.

The service of the Day of the Trinity should give us a decisive indication of how much the hypostatic character of the Holy Spirit was something apprehended in living Church experience, and not just a theorem of dogmatic theology. And this indication is all the more precious to us because the main part of the Office of the Pentecost[6] (by this I mean the three solemn prayers of genuflection) was composed, most probably, around the time of Basil the Great. What do we find there? The first prayer with genuflection begins with the words: "Lord most pure, incorruptible, without beginning, unfathomable, invisible, unsearchable, immutable, invincible, immeasurable, never desiring evil; who alone has immortality, who lives in unapproachable light, who has created heaven and earth, and the sea, and all things there; who answers men's petitions even before being asked. We pray to You and we beseech You, Lord Who loves man, Father of our Lord and God and Savior Jesus Christ . . ." This is obviously addressed to God the Father.

The second prayer of genuflection is addressed to the Son: "Lord Jesus Christ, our God, who gave Your peace to men and the gift of the Most Holy Spirit when You were still with us in life. As an inalienable inheritance You always bestow it upon the faithful . . ."

Finally, the third prayer, which occupies in the office a place that precisely corresponds to that of the two previous prayers, i.e., which is their liturgical analogue, opens with the address: "Eternally flowing, living, and illuminating Source, consubstantial with the Father, enabling Power, You Who wonderfully accomplished the economy of human salvation . . ."

But to Whom precisely is this prayer addressed? What comes next? According to the meaning of the feast itself (the Day of the "Trinity"!), according to the liturgical place of this third prayer, and finally, according to the epithets it uses for the Person to Whom it is addressed, it is natural to expect the following continuation: "O Holy Spirit" or "Comforter" or "King of Truth" or some other name of the Third Hypostasis of the Holy Trinity. This expectation is so natural that, in listening to this prayer, one inevitably hears something like this and remains convinced that it is addressed to the Holy Spirit. But this is not in fact the case. Here is the immediate continuation of this prayer which we interrupted: "O Christ our God; You Who have broken the indestructible chains of death and the unbreakable bonds of hell, and trampled a multitude of evil spirits; Who have given Yourself for us as an immaculate sacrifice . . ." and so on. Everything here is addressed to the Lord Jesus Christ, and in no wise to the Holy Spirit.

An age of stereotypical, more or less widespread doctrines, when the dogma of the Holy Spirit was fixed in word only in passing and only insofar as the economic activity of the Spirit was linked to the that of the Father and the Son, was followed by an age in which concepts found for the Son were applied to the Holy Spirit. But it is remarkable that the personal character of the Third Hypostasis was still represented only formally, by the word *ekporeusis*, "procession." However, no concrete content was attached to this word.

And thus it continued. The theological recipe existing then spoke of the Spirit in the same way the Word was spoken of. That is, it created, in essence, a shadowgraph of the Word. This recipe reigned, in one way or another, in orthodox circles, although at the same time in the deserts of the Thebaid and Palestine the Spirit revealed Himself to individual saints, those almost superhuman peaks of the Church. And through these saints, through their souls and through their bodies, the Spirit revealed Himself to those who surrounded them. Meanwhile, unorthodox circles fell into obvious false-teaching when they attempted to know the Comforter by force, forcibly to imprison Him the Spirit of Freedom, in a cage of philosophical concepts. Instead of the Spirit, they captured illusory, pseudo–mystical experiences of the soul, which was submerged in the dark underground of the world and grasped after dark powers as if they were angels of light. This demonstrated once again that, outside of ascesis and discipline, the Spirit was and is known only negatively.

Mystics of later ages, who always had a lively interest in pneumatology, were not in a better position. Distinguishing in words the Hypostases of the Spirit and the Son, in the last analysis, these mystics usually equated these hypostases in practice. This was because they attributed to the Holy Spirit everything that had been said about the Son, and also confused the Spirit with Sophia.[7]

But in what does the personal character of the Holy Spirit consist? There has been too much discussion of this but too little has been said. Basil the Great[8] admits that "the mode of procession remains inexplicable" and therefore he makes no attempt to clarify it. It is noteworthy that the famous defender of Orthodoxy against Catholic leanings, against attempts to rationalize dogma and to explain forcibly as a philosopheme that which is not subject to philosophy, namely, Mark of Ephesus . . . writes to "Orthodox Christians": ". . . We, together with St. John of Damascus and all the holy fathers, *do not know the difference between birth and procession.* By contrast, they distinguish with St. Thomas and the Latins two kinds of origin:

immediate and mediate."[9] This testimony is not unique; one could cite many such affirmations. Let me mention only St. Gregory of Nyssa, who spoke of "the unfathomability of the procession of the Holy Spirit."[10]

When theosophical speculation did not have recourse to the Catholic *Filioque*, that naive product of excessive piety and half-baked theology, this speculation either did not completely spell out or became entangled in the difference between birth and procession. Is it worth mentioning "names"? Let us leave them in peace. Let the inventors of various theories about the Holy Spirit sleep peacefully beneath the earth until the day when all these questions will resolve themselves without our efforts. It would be too naive to seek the cause of this two-thousand-year-old failure to spell out the difference between birth and procession in the insufficient perspicacity of theologians. And can it be a question of perspicacity when we are dealing with faith? "*Ex nihilo nihil*," more than to anything else, applies to theology, an *empirical* science.[11] If now there are no perfect perceptions of the Holy Spirit as a Hypostasis, if there are no personal pneumatophanies, with the exception of extraordinary cases and where exceptional people are involved, it is not possible to derive the formulas, for the formulas grow in the soil of a common, everyday Church life, in a field of common, constant phenomena, and not in connection with singular points of spiritual life. Of course, in the Holy Church everything is a miracle: sacrament is a miracle; the prayer of the blessing of water is a miracle; every icon is a miracle; every hymn is a miracle. Yes, everything is a miracle in the Church, for everything in its life is full of grace and God's grace is precisely the only thing that is worthy of the name "miracle." But all this is a constant miracle. But there are even rarer currents in the Church, "miracles" in the more customary sense of the word. And the rarer they are, the farther they are from verbal expression. It is not possible to create formulas for such miracles, for every formula is a formula of repeatability. Except for certain separate moments when the believers were jointly (and this is the key!) in the Holy Spirit or began to be in Him, this being in the Holy Spirit did not become an ordinary current of life.

But in those communities where the experience of the Spirit was proclaimed as the norm, there inevitably arose a sectarianism of the khlyst type, the term "khlyst" taken broadly to mean any pseudo-spiritual, pseudo-mystical, psychical (not spiritual) excitement of a group of enthusiasts.

Let us carefully examine the patristic writings, particularly the ascetic ones, where spiritual life is depicted most clearly. Here we see a typical phenomenon: Little is said of the Father; rather more is said of the Son of God; but the Holy Spirit is discussed most of all. But, despite this, one cannot get away from the impression that the Son of God as an independent Hypostasis is known very clearly by the saintly ascetics; and that He is so close to their consciousness that He even somewhat obscures the Father. They also know about the Father, but about the Holy Spirit as a Hypostasis they know little, almost nothing. If, by their indecisiveness or silence, the dogmatist fathers show their inner uncertainty concerning the question of the Holy Spirit, their insufficient knowledge of the Spirit as a Hypostasis, the ascetic fathers by their copious words reveal the same state of consciousness even more clearly. For them the Holy Spirit is, in the practical, the life sense, the "Spirit of Christ," the "Spirit of God," a kind of sanctifying and purifying impersonal power of God. After all, it is not by chance that, later, instead of the Holy Spirit, the fathers began unnoticeably and gradually to speak of "grace," i.e., of something completely impersonal. What is usually known is not the Holy Spirit but His grace-giving energies, His powers, His acts and activities. "Spirit," "spiritual," "spirit-bearing," "spirituality," and so forth appear everywhere in the patristic writings. But it is seen from these writings that these words refer to the special states of a believer, states produced by God, but that they do not (or virtually do not) refer to the personal, independent being of the Third Hypostasis of the Holy Trinity. In essence, the holy fathers speak much not about the Holy Spirit but about a holy spirit, and it is difficult to make a demarcation and to distinguish when they speak of the Spirit from when they speak of the spirit. The overall impression is that, from the Spirit, through the Spirit, there is an unnoticeable transition here to the spirit. At best, an inference is drawn from the spirit of God to the Spirit. True, our spirituality comes from the Spirit, just as our sonhood in relation to God comes from the Son and our creative personality comes from the Father. But is it possible that anyone reading the writings of the holy fathers could be uncertain (even if he keeps this uncertainty to himself) as to whether a particular passage is talking about the Son or a son, the Creator or a creator?

Furthermore, wishing to prove the consubstantiality of the Spirit with the Father and the Son, the fathers equated the sin-purifying activity of the Holy Spirit with the activity of the Son.[12] Thus, for the holy fathers there was no clear boundary even as regards the perception of the grace-giving acts of the Holy Spirit and the Son. Here, Macarius the Great differs little from St. Isaac the Syrian and John Climacus differs little from St. Ephrem the Syrian. Of course, I am making the matter cruder and simpler than it actually was. My picture is drawn not with fine pencil strokes but with rough brush strokes. What I say here is, of course, incomplete. Unquestionably, features of another knowledge, the personal perception of the Holy Spirit, sometimes emerge. But these features are preliminary and incomplete. However, it would be ridiculous to see in this incompleteness a personal defect of the saints, a defect attributable to some deficiency of profundity or purity. Out of the dark abyss of the centuries, out of the fog of history, the holy fathers shine for us like living, incorruptible stars, like the God-seeing eyes of the Church.

But the time has not yet come, and even those radiant eyes could not see Him by Whom all creation will be gladdened and comforted. The fullness of time had not come then, just as it has not yet come now. The fathers felt a longing and waited. In the same way, the righteous in the Old Testament awaited knowledge of the Son of God. The entire life of pre-Christian antiquity – religion, science, art, social life, even personal attitudes – was based entirely on a revelation of the Father, on an experiencing of the Father, the Creator of all things, on a conscious or half-forgotten Covenant with Him. Pre-Christian antiquity's entire understanding of life and the world was the development of a single category, the category of fatherhood, birth, generation, however it is called. And to clarify the unclear features of their knowledge is just as impossible as it is to develop an underexposed photographic plate; and if one were to keep this plate in the developer past a certain time, the whole image would only become "veiled," would be covered with a gray shroud, as it were. In the same way, thought that wishes without holiness to perceive the Spirit is "veiled." By the way, that is precisely what happens to people of the "new consciousness."[13]

As the End of History approaches, new, hitherto almost unseen, rosy rays of the coming Unfading Day appear on the cupolas of the Holy Church. Symeon the New Theologian is the first to speak in new tones, differently from the ancient ascetic fathers. In our own Russian Church these tones "play" like the rising sun on the Feast of Feasts.[14] St. Seraphim of Sarov and the great fathers of the Optina Hermitage"[15] (the elders Lev, Leonid, Makarii, and especially Amvrosii) concentrate in themselves, as in a fiery focus, the people's holiness. They are saints who, in part, are no longer monks in the narrow sense. Through them, as through a telescope, one sees Him Who comes. There is a new, special apocalyptic tenor here. Only the blind cannot see this. It would be frivolous or mad not to follow them but rather to walk past them, for that would be to strive willfully to truncate the eternally predetermined course of world history. This would be to reject the words of the Lord Jesus: "Which of you by taking thought can add one cubit unto his stature?" (Matt. 6: 27; also see Luke 12: 25).

But pay attention: Our entire understanding of life, our entire science (I speak not of theological science but of science in general, the scientific spirit) is based on the idea of Logos, on the idea of God the Word. This holds true not only for science but even for the whole of life itself, for the whole structure of our soul. We conceive of everything under the category of the law, the measure of harmony. This idea of logism,[16] an idea that is often distorted to the point of unrecognizability, is the basic nerve of everything that is alive and genuine in our mental, moral, and aesthetic life. The one universal, all-embracing "Law" of the World, the hypostatic Name of the Father, Divine Providence, without the will of Which a hair does not fall from our heads, Which makes "the lilies of the field" (Matt. 6: 28) grow and feeds "the birds of the air" (Matt. 6: 26), God, Who depletes Himself by His creation of the world and by economy – that is the religious presupposition of our science, and outside of this presupposition, more or less abstractly formulated, there is no science. The "uniformity of the laws of nature" – that is the postulate without which all science is empty sophistry.[17] But this postulate can he made a psychological reality only by faith in That Word about Which St. John prophesies in the first verses of his paschal Gospel: "In the beginning was the Word, and the Word was with God, and the Word was God. The same was in the beginning with God. All things were made by him; and without him was not anything made that was made. In him was life; and the life was the light of men. And the light shineth in darkness; and the darkness comprehended it not" (John 1: 1–5). Those are the "foundations of science."[18] And if we reject them, a cruel revenge is inevitable: the fall of a science that is built on shifting and engulfing sands.

What science has discovered is the lawfulness of the world, the orderliness and harmony of the world, the cosmos of creation. This law of the universe, this World number, this harmony of the spheres that is given to creaturely being is rooted wholly in God the Word, in the personal character of the Son, and in the gifts proper to Him.

But everything that rests not on this character, everything that is connected with the express gifts of the Holy Spirit, is not subject to knowledge by our science, the science of the Logos taken in isolation. Inspiration, creativity, freedom, ascesis, beauty, the value of the flesh, religion, and much else – all this is felt only indistinctly, is described only rarely, is established as being present, but stands outside the methods and means of scientific research, for the fundamental presupposition of such methods and means is, of course, the presupposition of connectedness, the pre-supposition of continuity, gradualness. In its existing form, the idea of lawfulness is completely inapplicable to all this. There is discontinuity here, and discontinuity goes beyond the limits of our science, does not jibe with the fundamental ideas of the contemporary worldview but destroys this worldview. It may be that the latest investigations and trends[19] in the domain of the idea of discontinuity hint precisely at the same nearness of the End.

A one-sided knowledge of the First Hypostasis created the religion and life of antiquity, antiquity's "substantial," organic worldview, according to which people thought that a metaphysical cause directly produces its phenomenal effect.

A one-sided knowledge of the Second Hypostasis produced the religion and life of modernity, its "lawful" logical worldview, in accordance with which phenomena are ordered according to their ideal form.

Finally, the free striving toward beauty, the love of the Goal – these are the deviations from scientism that typologically predict an immortal life and a holy, resurrected flesh. Holy fasts are the first fruits of the illumination of the body; holy relics, which we kiss, are glimmers of resurrection; holy sacraments are sources of deification. These are the pledges and betrothals of the future kingdom. But this kingdom comes (for individuals) and will come (for society) only when the Comforter as a Hypostasis is known and will be known, and when the Triunity that illuminates the soul is perceived and will be perceived by this knowledge:

> By the Holy Spirit every soul is made alive
> And is elevated by purity.
> It is illuminated by the Triunity
> in sacred mystery."[20]

The holy, hoary mysteriousness of ancient science; the moral, serious rigor of the new science; finally, the joyous, light, winged inspiration of the future "gay science."[21]

My winged one! On paper I sketch thoughts that I feel more than I can express. It is as if some sort of fabric, some sort of body composed of the finest stellar rays is being woven in the world's foundations; something is awaited. Something is lacking. My soul – wishing to be liberated and to be with Christ – longs for some-thing. And something will come: "It doth not yet appear what we shall be" (1 John 3: 2). And the more acutely one feels what is being prepared, the closer and more intimate will the connection with the Mother Church become, and the easier and simpler it will be to endure out of love for Her the dirt that is cast upon Her. What will be will be in Her and through Her, not otherwise. With quiet joy I await what will be, and *Nunc dimittis* is being chanted and resounds in my tranquil heart for days at a time. When that which is awaited comes, when the Great Easter of the world is revealed, all human disputes will end. I do not know whether this will happen soon, or whether it will be necessary to wait for millions of years, but my heart is at peace, because hope already brings to it that which is awaited. Absolutely foreign to me is the desire of people of the "new religious consciousness"[22] to acquire forcibly, as it were, the Holy Spirit. Desiring to destroy the "times or seasons" (Acts 1: 7), they stop seeing what is before their very eyes, what is given to them, and what they do not know or understand inwardly. Chasing everything, they lose that which exists now, and greater than which we are now not in a state to acquire, for our heart is not yet pure, the heart of creation is not yet pure, and, impure, it would be consumed in fire from nearness to the Most Pure. Let tranquility return to them (at least for a brief time), and then perhaps they will see, these men of false knowledge, that they have no real ground beneath their feet, that they are uttering empty words, and are themselves beginning to believe these words. What is happening is similar to what happened to Leo Tolstoy: he created the scheme (!) of a graceless, imaginary ecclesiality. Then he smashed it, which, of course, he was able to do without difficulty. And, satisfied with the victory over a chimera produced by his utterly rationalistic, self-assertive mind, he abandoned grace-giving, even if contaminated, soil and went into a desert of "good" words, which he himself has not learned to manage, but only tempts others with. For ecclesiality is so beautiful that one who participates in it cannot even aesthetically, as a matter of taste, tolerate the unbearable smell of conceits of Tolstoy's kind. Can one imagine anything more tasteless than to write one's own "fifth gospel"?[23]

Nevertheless, a true idea lies at the base of Tolstoyism, as well as at the base of the "new consciousness." Consider if only the fact that the ancients prayed to the Father, but that in the course of our entire epoch people pray mainly to the Son. But people pray to the Spirit (if they pray to Him at all) for the most part in expectation of Him, rather than having Him face to face. They pray more in longing for the Comforter than rejoicing in Him before the Father in the Son. I know that many passages can be found that affirm the opposite. I myself can supply them. But I speak of what is typical, although it is almost unprovable, I write "letters" to you instead of composing an "article" precisely because I am afraid of asserting but prefer to ask. What appears typical to me is expectation and hope, but only meek and tranquil expectation and hope.

. . .

To be sure, some passages of the Apostle Paul's Epistles reveal the hypostatic being of the Holy Spirit to the consciousness as in a lightning flash. "As many as are led by the Spirit of God," testifies the Apostle of the Gentiles, "they are the sons of God." "Ye have received the Spirit of adoption, whereby we cry, Abba, Father. The Spirit itself beareth witness with our spirit, that we are the children of

God" (Rom. 8: 14–16). Further: "And because ye are sons, God hath sent forth the Spirit of his Son into your hearts, crying, Abba, Father" (Gal. 4: 6). Also: "The Spirit also helpeth our infirmities: for we know not what we should pray for as we ought: but the Spirit itself maketh intercession for us with groanings which cannot be uttered" (Rom. 8: 26). Indisputably, this "intercession" of the Holy Spirit for us, these "groanings which cannot be uttered," these cries of the Comforter, these "Abba, Fathers," were known to the Apostles, as well as to saintly men and women. But it is just as indisputable that these glimmers, these instants and points of spiritual fullness, these flashes of total knowledge have heretofore remained something special, something accessible only to exceptional people at exceptional times – something like the messianic visions of the Old Testament. Just as there were Christ-bearers before Christ, so there are Spirit-bearers before the full descent of the Spirit. These ancient righteous men and women "all died in faith, not having received the promises, but having seen them afar off, and were persuaded of them, and embraced them, and confessed that they were strangers and pilgrims on the earth. For they that say such things declare plainly that they seek a country" (Heb. 11: 13–14). Such also were the ancient Christians before Christ: "Who through faith subdued kingdoms, wrought righteousness, obtained promises, stopped the mouths of lions, quenched the violence of fire, escaped the edge of the sword, out of weakness were made strong, waxed valiant in fight, turned to flight the armies of the aliens. Women received their dead raised to life again: and others were tortured, not accepting deliverance; that they might obtain a better resurrection: And others had trial of cruel mockings and scourgings, yea, moreover of bonds and imprisonment. They were stoned, they were sawn asunder, were tempted, were slain with the sword; they wandered about in sheepskins and goatskins; being destitute, afflicted, tormented; (Of whom the world was not worthy:) they wandered in deserts, and in mountains, and in dens and caves of the earth. And these all, having obtained a good report through faith, received not the promise: God having provided some better thing for us, that they without us should not be made perfect" (Heb. 11: 33–40).

The knowledge of Christ trembled before them; they almost touched Christ. They saw their salvation in their hope (cf. Rom. 8: 24). But the "times or the seasons" (Acts 1: 7) had to be fulfilled for hope to be realized and for the invisible to become visible. They knew how to wait and be patient: "Hope that is seen is not hope: for what a man seeth, why doth he yet hope for? But if we hope for that we see not, then do we with patience wait for it" (Rom. 8: 24–5). They, great and holy, did not see Christ, in order "that they without us should not be made perfect." But they almost knew Him – at special times and by the purest minds. At such times their faces trembled with eternal life: this is the Spirit-Dove that had brushed their hearts with its snow-white wing. Just as the perception of God the Word trembled before the fathers and the prophets, so the knowledge of the Holy Spirit trembles before the saints of our time, almost touches them. But, here too, the fullness of time has not yet come; here too, the highest peaks of mankind must wait so "that they without us should not be made perfect." *Their* hearts have been purified. Their temple has been swept and put in order so as to receive the Comforter. But *our* hearts are full of filth. And here the higher wait for the lower, the seeing wait for the blind, the holy wait for the sinful, the living wait for the dead, the spiritual wait for the fleshly, those who run ahead and even anticipate wait for those who are inert and lag behind. Only at rare moments is the curtain of the future pulled open before them.

"That they without us should not be made perfect." This explains why, despite their profundity, teachings of the Holy Spirit that have appeared in the history of the Church somehow have not received any response and have remained solitary. In addition, those aspects of Christian life which refer specifically to the Holy Spirit, i.e., Christian freedom, filiation, creativity, and spirituality, were falsified or distorted by various heretics who willfully desired to bring these aspects to premature life. People of the "new religious consciousness," from the 1st century to the 20th century inclusive, have always betrayed themselves by their works, for the rose bushes planted by them have always brought forth thorns and thistles. The "new consciousness" has always turned out to be not above the Church, as it has claimed to be, but against the Church and against Christ, anti-Church and anti-Christ. Anyone who possesses the Spirit to the same degree that the saints possessed Him clearly sees how insane it is to pretend to more. But in all ages it has been too easy for people who are utterly unspiritual to fall into self-delusion and to replace real spirituality with their subjectively human, psychic creativity, and then with demoniacal hallucination. Frenzy and enthusiasm, dreamy prophetism and somber exaltation were taken to be rejoicing in the Holy Spirit. Meanwhile, sin, left to itself, acquired "freedom." The search for the "two infinities" began, and beyond this search was the submergence into the "two abysses": into the upper abyss of gnostic theory and into the lower abyss of khlyst practice. And it was this that was passed off as the fullness of the life full of grace. Let me repeat, parallel to all of Church history there stretches the thread of this pseudo-religious consciousness that has always passed itself off as "new."[24]

. . .

St. Gregory of Nazianzus affirms the gradualness of the historical manifestation of the Spirit; but it is necessary to consider yet another aspect: the discontinuity of the meta-historical revelation of the Spirit. Just like the Kingdom of God, the Spirit has both a gradual historical manifestation and a discontinuously historical manifestation, which are irreducible one to the other. Otherwise, it is incomprehensible how the final state, the illumination of creation, the expulsion of death, in a word, the "future age" could be distinguished from the preliminary state of the waiting, from "this age," in which death still reigns.

The ideas of the Kingdom of God and of the Holy Spirit resemble each other formally. But this resemblance is not only formal. In its general idea, the doctrine of the Holy Spirit as the Kingdom of the Father unquestionably has its roots in the Gospel, and it gets its verbal justification in the Apostle Paul: "The kingdom of God is righteousness, and peace, and joy in the Holy Spirit" (Rom. 14: 17) – *En Pneumati Agiōi*, "in" or "of the Holy Spirit," i.e., in the righteousness, peace, and joy produced by the Holy Spirit. The subjective state of righteousness, peace, and joy produced by the Holy Spirit is that same Kingdom of God which is "within" us (Luke 17: 21), the barely noticeable mustard seed of faith sown in the soul. But growing and showing itself above the field of what is mine and only mine, above the domain of subjectivity, the sprout of the seed of faith becomes objective, cosmic, universal. Liturgy and the sacraments are the outward manifestations of the Kingdom of God in Church life. The working of miracles and contemplative insights reveal the same Kingdom in the personal lives of the saints. And all of us daily summon the Fullness of the acquisition of this Kingdom, the Holy Spirit. For, according to St. Gregory of Nyssa, the Lord's Prayer in Matthew 6: 10 and that in the old Luke 11: 12 were read differently in a significant way, a difference in reading that does not exist in the modern text. These were the readings:

"Our Father . . . Thy kingdom come (*elthetē hē basileia sou*)" (Matt. 6: 10 and the modern Luke 11: 12).

"Our Father . . . Thy Holy Spirit come down upon us and purify us (*eltheto to hagion Pneuma sou eph hēmas, kai katharisatō hēmzas*)" (the old Luke 11: 12).

By comparing these variants of the passage from Luke, Gregory of Nyssa deduces that the terms "Holy Spirit" and "Kingdom of God" have the same meaning, i.e., that "the Holy Spirit is the Kingdom (*Pneuma to hagion basileia estin*)." Then, basing his discussion on this conclusion, St. Gregory develops a remarkable doctrine of the Spirit as "the Kingdom of the Father and the Anointment of the Son."[25]

The Kingdom presupposes a king. This king is the Father, and therefore the royal majesty of the Father Himself resides in the Holy Spirit. Moreover, the Son, who is begotten before the foundation of the world by the Father and is consubstantial with Him, acquires from all eternity in the Holy Spirit the royal glory belonging to the Father. The Spirit crowns the Son with glory. This is the anointing activity of the Spirit, and if in relation to the Father the Spirit is the Kingdom, then in relation to the Son, He is Anointment, Chrism. Gregory of Nyssa verifies this conclusion by an analysis of the messianic psalm: "God, thy God hath anointed thee with the oil of gladness above thy fellows" (Ps. 45: 7; cf. Heb. 1: 9). The Anointing One is the Father; the Anointed One is the Son; the Anointment or the Anointing Oil of Joy is the Holy Spirit.[26]

The anointing oil has always been a symbol of joy, and the Holy Spirit has always been the Comforter, the Paraclete, the Bringer of Joy. He is the True Chrism, the Chrism of chrisms, the Chrism that relieves the pain of the wounded, torn, broken heart.

Therefore the very name Christ (*Christos, Meshiah*; Messiah = the Anointed One) contains an indication of the trinity of Hypostases in Divinity. "The confession of this name," says Gregory, "contains the teaching of the Holy Trinity, because to this name Each of the Persons in Whom we believe is respectively expressed."[27] "In this name we recognize the Anointing One, the Anointed One, and the One through Whom He is anointed."[28] The anointing relation of the Spirit to the Son is even more explicit in the Apostle Paul's speech to Cornelius: "God anointed Jesus of Nazareth with the Holy Spirit and with power" (Acts 10: 38).[29] By virtue of this anointment He is Christ and King from the foundation, is "eternally clothed with the royal glory of the Spirit, which constitutes His anointment."[30]

Thus, if previously the interrelationship of the Hypostases was defined through love, through the giving of oneself, through the intra-Divine self-depletion of the Hypostases, through eternal humility and kenosis, now, on the contrary, it is defined as eternal restoration and affirmation of One by Another, as glorification and kingship. "Eternally glorious is the Father, Who existed before all ages; the glory of the Father is the everlasting Son [the Father in giving Himself to the Son finds in Him His own glory] just as the glory of the Son is the Spirit of Christ."[31]

The *first* aspect, examined above, of the intra-Divine life consists in the mutual exchange of tragic, sacrificial love, in mutual self-depletion, impoverishment, and humiliation of the Hypostases. The *second* aspect, which we are examining now, is the reverse current as it were, one that we – who have not acquired the Spirit and who know closely only the Sacrificial God – cannot know at all clearly. For creatures there has not yet begun the restoration and the glory, whose revelation they are awaiting, groaning and travailing in pain (cf. Rom. 8: 19–23). In the supratemporal order of the life of the Trinity eternal is this aspect of *answering love*, triumphant love, glorifying the Loving One and restoring Him, this transfer of glory from Hypostasis to Hypostasis. "The Son is glorified by the Spirit, the Son glorifies the Father; conversely, the Son receives glory from the Father, and the Only Begotten One becomes the glory of the Spirit, because what glorifies the Father if not the true glory of the Only Begotten One, and what glorifies the Son if not the majesty of the Spirit?"[32] Thus, the Holy Spirit is *Khrisma basileias,* the Anointment of the Kingdom; He is *Axiōma basileias*, the Royal Dignity. But these names are applicable to Him for His activity within the Trinity. He is not a sign of Divine being, not a dignity and not an attribute of Divinity, but a "living, substantial, and personal kingdom (*basileia de zōsa kai ousiades kai enupustatos Pneuma to hagion*)."[33] The Holy Spirit is also a Person Who by His unconditional activity, as the Third Person of the Holy Trinity, is to be the Kingdom of the Father and the Anointment of the Son.

A similar doctrine of the anointing activity of the Spirit was developed by St. Irenaeus of Lyons.[34] But without stopping to examine this teaching, I will move on to St. Maximus the Confessor.

According to Maximus,[35] the first words of the Lord's Prayer "contain an indication of the Father, of the name of the Father, and of the Father's Kingdom, so that, from the very beginning [of the prayer], we learn to honor the Trinity, to invoke it, and to worship it. For the Name of God the Father, Who abides essentially and hypostatically, is the Only Begotten Son of the Father. Whereas the Kingdom of God the Father, which abides essentially and hypostatically, is the Holy Spirit. For what Matthew calls the Kingdom here another evangelist calls the Spirit, saying: 'Let Thy Holy Spirit come and purify us.' For the Father has this Name not as newly acquired, and the Kingdom is understood by us not as a quality perceived in Him. Because He never began to be, He does not begin to be Father and King. But, always existent, He always is Father and Son, without having a beginning to His being or a beginning to His being Father and King. If he is always Existent and is always Father and King, then the Son and the Holy Spirit always co-exist with the Father substantially and hypostatically; They exist from Him and in Him naturally, above cause and word, but They came into being not after Him, not according to the law of causality, not later. For the relationship of the Persons of Divinity has the force of joint being and does not permit one to think that Some of Those found in this relationship were after Others."

That is what St. Maximus the Confessor teaches.

Around the Holy Spirit all the uncertainties, difficulties, and torments of our life are crystallized. And all our hopes are in the revelation of the Holy Spirit. Let us pray together for the appearance of the Holy Spirit. Together, let us invoke Him with the mystical invocation of Symeon the New Theologian:

"Come, true light. Come, eternal life. Come, hidden mystery. Come, nameless treasure. Come, ineffable thing. Come, person who flees human comprehension. Come, ceaseless courage. Come, true hope of all who are being saved. Come, resurrection of the dead. Come, powerful one. You do everything always. You transform and change with a single gesture of the hand. Come, fully invisible, untouchable, impalpable. Come, you who always remain unmoving, though you hourly move and come to us, who lie in the underworld, though you yourself live above the heavens. Come, name most desired and encountered more than anything. But to say about you what you are or to know what you are, we are absolutely forbidden. Come, eternal joy. Come, unfading wreath. Come, purple of our great God and Sovereign. Come, girdle, like a crystal transparent and studded with precious stones. Come, unapproachable refuge. Come, the king's purple and the right hand of holy majesty. Come! My poor soul has needed and needs you. Come, alone to alone, for I am alone, as you see. Come! You have isolated me and made me alone on the earth. Come! You have become my need, and made it so that I have need of you, of you who are accessible to no one. Come, my breath and life. Come, the comfort of my contemptible soul. Come, my joy, glory, and unceasing consolation. I give thanks to you because here, amid turbulence, change, and dizzying motion, you have become a spirit one with me; and though you are God above all, you have become for me all in all.

"Ineffable drink! You can never be taken away, and you ceaselessly pour yourself into the lips of my soul, and copiously flow in the source of my heart. Shining garment, which burns demons. Purifying sacrifice! You bathe me with unceasing holy tears, copiously shed from your presence among those to whom you come. I give thanks to you, because for me you have become an unfading day and a sun on this side of its setting. You have nowhere to hide yourself, and with your glory you fill universes. You have never hidden yourself from anyone, but we ourselves always hide from you, until we wish to come to you. For where can you hide, if there is no place where you can rest? Or why would you hide yourself, you who do not despise anyone, do not fear anyone? Create now out of me a tabernacle for yourself, meek Lord, and live in me, and until my death do not leave, do not separate yourself from me, your servant, so that I too, at my death and after my death, will abide in you and reign with you, God Who reigns over everything.

"Remain, Lord, and do not leave me alone, so that when my enemies come, who constantly seek to devour my soul, they will find you in me, and run away for good and not defeat me, because they will see you, stronger than all, inside, dwelling in the mansion of my humble soul. Truly, just as you remembered me, Lord, when I was in the world, and when without my knowledge you yourself chose me, and separated me from the world, and placed me before the face of your glory, so even now protect me through your unchanging, perfectly stable abiding in me, so that every day, contemplating you, I, mortal one, may live, so that, possessing you, I, poor one, may always be rich. This way, I would be more powerful than any king; and partaking of you and drinking you, and hourly being clothed in you, I would enjoy unutterable blessed delight. Since you are every good and every adornment and every delight, and to you belongs the glory of the holy and consubstantial Trinity, which is glorified in the Father, the Son, and the Holy Spirit, and is known and honored by the whole community of the faithful now and always and for ever and ever. Amen."[36]

Amen. Amen. Amen.

Notes

1   P. 31.

2   "In betrothal to the future life and kingdom (*eis ararabōna tēs mellousēs zōēs kai baileias*)" (St. John of Damascus, 5th Prayer before Holy Communion; the 6th prayer in the Greek *Sunekdemos*).

3   Khlysts were members of an ascetic and ecstatic sect that originated in Russia in the 17th century or earlier. These schismatics held that God becomes incarnate in many "christs" through their suffering. Khlysts and kblystovstvo ("khlysthood") have come to connote frenzied religious ecstasy. [Translator's note.]

4   "*Prelest'* is the soul's passional tendency to falsehood on the basis of pride" (Archimandrite, later Bishop, Ignatius Brianchaninov, *O molitve Iisusovoi* [On the Prayer of Jesus], *The Works of Bishop Ignatius*, Saint Petersburg, 1865, vol. 1, p. 130).

5   Tertullian, *Adversus Praxeam*, 26; Patrologia Latina, vol. 2. Let me cite as an example: *Hic spiritus Dei erit Sermo. Sicut enim Johanno dicente* (John 1:14): *Sermo caro factus est, spiritum quoque intelligimus in mentione sermonis . . . nam spiritus substantia est sermonis et sermo orperatio spiritus*," etc. Tertullian teaches that the Holy Spirit becomes an independent hypostasis separate from the Word only from the moment of the Pentecost (*De oratione*, 25), and, opposing the Divinity of Christ to His Humanity, His flesh, he calls His Divinity the Spirit of performing miracles, whereas the flesh experienced hunger, thirst, and miseries (*De carne Christi*).

6   *Bol'shoi Trebnik Dopolnitel'nyi*, ch. 78: The office of the Holy Pentecost, edition of the Kiev-Pech. Lavra, 1875, ch. 215, nos. 218, 219. It was Prof. V. Popov who drew my attention to this asymmetry of the office.

7   See Letter 10, "Sophia," in *The Pillar and Ground of the Truth*.

8   "The mode of the procession remains inexplicable (*tou de tropou tēs huparxeōs arretou phulassomenon*)" (Basil the Great, *On the Holy Spirit*; PG [Patrologia Graeca], vol. 32, col. 152 B). However, a certain hint at an actual "deduction" of the procession, made by Athanasius the Great is repeated more definitely by Basil: "Why is the Holy Spirit not the Son of the Son? Not because He is from God not through the Son, but so that the Trinity not be considered as infinite multiplicity, that it not be considered to have sons from sons as it is with people. To speak of a son from the Son would be to lead people who hear this to the idea of multiplicity in the Trinity of God. For it

would be easy to conclude that from the son was born another son, and that from this other son yet another was born, and so on, until one gets a multiplicity [that is, an infinite multiplicity] . . ." *Refutation of Eunomius' Pleading*, V; PG, vol. 29, col. 732 B, 734 B.

9 *The Unpublished Works of Mark of Ephesus*, trans. Avraam Norov from the manuscript at the Paris Imperial Library, Saint Petersburg, 1860, p. 27 (= *Khris. Cht.*, 1861).

10 Gregory of Nyssa, *Catechistic Discourse*, III; PG, vol. 45, col. 171. Cf. Gregory of Nazianzus: To the question, "What is procession?" he answers decisively: "We cannot even see what is beneath our very feet; far be it from us to try to plumb the depths and to judge about ineffable and inexpressible nature" (*Theological Oration*, 5; PG, vol. 36, col. 141).

11 Corderius, publisher of the works of Dionysius the Areopagite, calls mysticism "*sapientia experimentalis*" – empirical wisdom.

12 For example, Gregory of Nyssa, *Against Eunomius*, II, col. 559. Also by the same author: *On the Lord's Prayer*, III; PG, vol. 44, col. 1157–60.

13 The "new [religious] consciousness" was a worldview that appeared in Russia at the beginning of the 20th century. Heavily influenced by Vladimir Solovyov this worldview was allied with the Symbolist movement in poetry and art. The "new religious consciousness" movement was deliberately opposed to historical Christianity; it yearned for new revelations, attempted to create a religiously based social utopia, but, at the same time, was full of eschatological expectations. The two leading adepts of this movement were Dmitrii Merezhkovsky (1865–1940) and Nikolai Berdiaev (1874–1948). [Translator's note, truncated.]

14 An allusion to a folk belief.

15 The Optina Pustyn' hermitage was the center of the great flowering of *starchestvo* in nineteenth-century Russia. The *startsy* Leonid (1769–1841), Makarii (1788–1860), and Amvrosii (1812–91) made Optina Pustyn' famous throughout Russia, drew crowds of the faithful, who asked their counsel. Such figures as Dostoevsky, Tolstoy, the Slavophile Ivan Kireevsky, and Konstantin Leontyev were drawn to Optina and its *startsy*. Optina Pustyn' is accurately depicted in the monastery described in *The Brothers Karamazov*. The spiritual blossoming at Optina ended soon after the Russian Revolution. [Translator's note.]

16 I use "logism," as derived from *Logos*, after V. F. Ern, *Bor'ba za Logos* [The Battle for Logos], Moscow, 1911, pp. 72–119. This author, together with certain ideas of V. S. Solovyov, Prince S. N. Trubetskoy, and N. A. Berdiaev, clarifies the positive side of logism. By contrast, the books of V. V. Rozanov powerfully attack the Manichaean/monistic currents parasitic on logism. They expose the abstractness, deadness, and emptiness of the verbalism that in many minds and hearts has replaced communion with the Word. Although Rozanov does not wish to distinguish *abusus* from *usus*, the reader, by making such a distinction, can draw much that is useful from his critique.

17 John Stuart Mill, *The System of Logic*.

18 An allusion to the celebrated book of the inventor of the "logic machine," William Stanley Jevons.

19 These works are most advanced in the domain of the formal investigation of the idea of discontinuity, i.e., in mathematics and in logistic. Their number is so great that there is no possibility of presenting a bibliography here; such a bibliography has been given in my special work ["The idea of discontinuity as an element of a worldview"], which is as yet only in manuscript. [Long discussion omitted.]

20   Gradual sung before the Gospel in the matins office.

21   An allusion to a work by Nietzsche.

22   The main representatives of the "new religious consciousness" are D. S. Merezhkovsky, Z. N. Gippius, and D. Filosofov. In different senses and to different degrees, Andrey Belyi (B. N. Bugaev), N. A. Berdiaev, and others are associated or have been associated with this "consciousness."

23   Leo Tolstoy was not embarrassed even at Optina Pustyn' to speak of "My Gospel." A colorful tale of this kind about his meeting with K. N. Leontyev is included in Erast Vytorsky's book, *Istoricheskoe opisanie Kozel'skoi Optinoi pustyni* [Historical description of the Optina Pustyn' of Kozelsk], Trinity-St. Sergius Lavra, 1902, p. 128.

24   Simon Magus, the Nicolaites, all sorts of Gnostics, the Montanists, the Templars, spiritualists, etc.

25   Here, I expound Gregory of Nyssa's doctrine of the Kingdom of the Father and the Anointment of the Son according to Nesmelov, *Dogmaticheskaia sistema Grigoriia Nisskago* [The Dogmatic System of Gregory of Nyssa], Kazan', 1889, pp. 279–83.

26   Gregory of Nyssa, *Against Apollinarius*, 52; PG, vol. 45, col. 1249 D–1251 A.

27   Ibid., col. 1249 B.

28   Ibid., col. 1249 D–1252 A.

29   Cf. "The Spirit of the Lord will rest upon him" (Isa. 11: 2); "The Spirit of the Lord God is upon me" (Isa. 61: 1 – Luke 4: 18).

30   Gregory of Nyssa, *Against Apollinarius*, 53; PG, vol. 45, col. 1252 C.

31   Gregory of Nyssa, *Against Eunomius*, I; PG, vol. 45, col. 369 D–372 A.

32   Gregory of Nyssa, *Against the Macedonians*, 22; PG, vol. 45, col. 1329 B.

33   Ibid.

34   Irenaeus of Lyons, *Five Books Against Heresies*, III 17.

35   Maximus the Confessor, *Comment on the Lord's Prayer*, S. *maximi Confessoris Operum*, vol. 1, Paris, 1675, p. 350.

36   Symeon the New Theologian, *Hymns on Divine Love* (*Divinorum Amorum*) 1; PG, vol. 120, col. 507–10.

24

Vladimir Lossky, "Redemption and Deification"

This text is classic because it says simply and straightforwardly what the Spirit adds – adds to the work of the Son. For that reason this article appears again and again on syllabuses. The Son redeems human nature in general; the Spirit, according to Lossky, *applies* that redemption to individuals. The Son saves; the Spirit picks out, molds, or individualizes. Or as Donald Winslow has put it, "What Christ has accomplished universally, the Spirit perfects particularly."[1] Lossky notes and repairs shortcomings characteristic of western theology, Catholic and Protestant, with the patristic pattern of "perfection."[2] Perfection, appropriated to the Spirit, Lossky takes as an individualizing, particularizing function. Christ saves the race; the Spirit makes Christians, and makes the particular, individual Christians they are. Son and Spirit, on this account, relate almost as nature and person.

Lossky might also serve as a stepping stone to Staniloae, who puts a similar insight in a more sophisticated way. Staniloae notices that you might read Lossky's formulation as functionalist: the Son provides, the Spirit applies. The Son works in general, for the human race; the Spirit particularly, for the human person. That interpretation makes Lossky's interpretation – however helpful – finally reductive. Staniloae seeks to de-functionalize and re-personalize Lossky's formulation, all the while using it to move forward. What Lossky puts in the language of appropriation, Staniloae puts in the language of indivisibility.

Vladimir Lossky, "Redemption and Deification," in *In the Image and Likeness of God*, ed. John H. Erickson and Thomas E. Bird (Crestwood, NY: St Vladimir's Seminary Press, 1974), pp. 97–110.

Redemption and Deification

Vladimir Lossky

"God made Himself man, that man might become God." These powerful words, which we find for the first time in St. Irenaeus,[3] are again found in the writings of St. Athanasius,[4] St. Gregory of Nazianzus,[5] and St. Gregory of Nyssa.[6] The Fathers and Orthodox theologians have repeated them in every century with the same emphasis, wishing to sum up in this striking sentence the very essence of Christianity: an ineffable descent of God to the ultimate limit of our fallen human condition, even unto death – a descent of God which opens to men a path of ascent, the unlimited vistas of the union of created beings with the Divinity.

The descent (*katabasis*) of the divine person of Christ makes human persons capable of an ascent (*anabasis*) in the Holy Spirit. It was necessary that the voluntary humiliation, the redemptive kenosis of the Son of God should take place, so that fallen men might accomplish their vocation of theosis, the deification of created beings by uncreated grace. Thus the redeeming work of Christ – or rather, more generally speaking, the Incarnation of the Word – is seen to be directly related to the ultimate goal of creatures: to know union with God. If this union has been accomplished in the divine person of the Son, who is God become man, it is necessary that each human person, in turn, should become god by grace, or "a partaker of the divine nature," according to St Peter's expression (2 Peter 1: 4).

Since, in the thought of the Fathers, the Incarnation of the Word is so closely linked to our ultimate deification, it could be asked whether the Incarnation would have taken place if Adam had not sinned. This question has often been raised, but it seems to us an unreal question. In fact, we have no knowledge of any condition of the human race except the condition resulting from original sin, in which our deification – the carrying out of the divine purpose for us – has become impossible without the Incarnation of the Son, a fact necessarily having the character of a redemption. The Son of God came down from heaven to accomplish the work of our salvation, to liberate us from the captivity of the devil, to destroy the dominion of sin in our nature, and to undo death, which is the wages of sin. The Passion, Death, and Resurrection of Christ, by which his redemptive work was accomplished, thus occupy a central place in the divine dispensation for the fallen world. From this point of view it is easy to understand why the doctrine of the redemption has such a great importance in the theological thought of the Church.

Nevertheless, when the dogma of the redemption is treated in isolation from the general body of Christian teaching, there is always a risk of limiting the tradition by interpreting it exclusively in terms of the work of the Redeemer. Then theological thought develops along three lines: original sin, its reparation on the cross, and the appropriation of the saving results of the work of Christ to Christians. In these constricting perspectives of a theology dominated by the idea of redemption, the patristic sentence, "God made Himself man that man might become God," seems to be strange and abnormal. The thought of union with God is forgotten because of our preoccupation solely with our own salvation; or, rather, union with God is seen only negatively, in contrast with our present wretchedness.

2

It was Anselm of Canterbury, with his treatise *Cur Deus Homo*, who undoubtedly made the first attempt to develop the dogma of redemption apart from the rest of Christian teaching. In his work Christian horizons are limited by the drama played between God, who is infinitely offended by sin, and man, who is unable to satisfy the impossible demands of vindictive justice. The drama finds its resolution in the death of Christ, the Son of God who has become man in order to substitute Himself for us and to pay our debt to divine justice. What becomes of the dispensation of the Holy Spirit here? His part is reduced to that of an auxiliary, an assistant in redemption, causing us to receive Christ's expiating merit. The final goal of our union with God is, if not excluded altogether, at least shut out from our sight by the stern vault of a theological conception built on the ideas of original guilt and its reparation. The price of our redemption having been paid in the death of Christ, the resurrection and the ascension are only a glorious happy end of His work, a kind of apotheosis without direct relationship to our human destiny. This redemptionist theology, placing all the emphasis on the passion, seems to take no interest in the triumph of Christ over death. The very work of the Christ-Redeemer, to which this theology is confined, seems to be truncated, impoverished, reduced to a change of the divine attitude toward fallen men, unrelated to the nature of humanity.

We find an entirely different conception of the redeeming work of Christ in the thought of St. Athanasius.[7] "Christ," he says, "having delivered the temple of His body to death, offered one sacrifice for all men to make them innocent and free from original guilt, and also to show Himself victorious over death and to create the first fruits of the General Resurrection with His own incorruptible body." Here the juridical image of the Redemption is completed by another image, the physical – or rather biological – image of the triumph of life over death, of incorruptibility triumphing in the nature which had been corrupted by sin.

In the Fathers generally, as well as in the Scriptures, we find many images expressing the mystery of our salvation accomplished by Christ. Thus, in the Gospel, the Good Shepherd is a "bucolic" image of the work of Christ.[8] The strong man, overcome by the "stronger than he, who taketh away his arms and destroys his power," is a "military" image,[9] which is often found again in the Fathers and in the Liturgy: Christ victorious over Satan, trampling upon the gates of hell, making the Cross his standard of triumph.[10] There is also a "medical" image, that of a sickly nature cured by salvation as the antidote to a poison.[11] There is an image which could be termed "diplomatic," the divine stratagem which deceives the devil in his cunning.[12] And so it goes. At last we come to the image used most often, taken by St. Paul from the Old Testament, where it was borrowed from the sphere of juridical relations.[13] Taken in this sense, redemption is a juridical image of the work of Christ, found side by side with many other images.[14] When we use the word "redemption," as we do nowadays, as a generic term designating the saving work of Christ in all its fullness, we should not forget that this juridical expression has the character of an image or simile: Christ is the Redeemer in the same sense that He is the Warrior victorious over death, the perfect Sacrificer, etc.

Anselm's mistake was not just that he developed a juridical view of the redemption, but rather that he wanted to see an adequate expression of the mystery of our redemption accomplished by Christ in the juridical relations implied by the word "redemption." Rejecting other expressions of this mystery as inadequate images, *quasi quaedam picturae*, he believed that he had found in the juridical image – that of the redemption – the very body of the truth, its "rational solidity," *veritatis rationabilis soliditas*, the reason why it was necessary for God to die for our salvation.[15]

The impossibility of proving rationally that the work of redemption was necessary, by making use of the juridical meaning of the term "redemption," was demonstrated by St. Gregory of Nazianzus in a magisterial *reductio ad absurdum*. He says: "We must now consider a problem and a doctrine often passed over silently, which, in my view, nevertheless needs deep study. The blood shed for us, the most precious and glorious blood of God, the blood of the Sacrificer and the Sacrifice – why was it shed and to whom was it offered? We were under the reign of the devil, sold to sin, after we had gained corruption on account of our sinful desire. If the price of our ransom is paid to him who has us in his power, I ask myself: Why is such a price to be paid? If it is given to the devil, it is outrageous! The brigand receives the price of redemption. Not only does he receive it from God, he receives God Himself. For his violence he demands such a disproportionate ransom that it would be more just for him to set us free without ransom. But if the price is paid to the Father, why should that be done? It is not the Father who has held us as His captives. Moreover, why should the blood of His only Son be acceptable to the Father, who did not wish to accept Isaac, when Abraham offered Him his son as a burnt-offering, but replaced the human sacrifice with the sacrifice of a ram? Is it not evident that the Father accepts the sacrifice not because He demanded it or had any need for it but by His dispensation? It was necessary that man should be sanctified by the humanity of God; it was necessary that He Himself should free us, triumphing over the tyrant by His own strength, and that He should recall us to Himself by His Son who is the Mediator, who does all for the honor of the Father, to whom He is obedient in all things. . . . Let the rest of the mystery be venerated silently."[16] What emerges from the passage we have just quoted is that, for St. Gregory of Nazianzus, the idea of redemption, far from implying the idea of a necessity imposed by vindictive justice, is rather an expression of the dispensation, whose mystery cannot be adequately clarified in a series of rational concepts. He says, in later passage, that "it was necessary for us that God should be incarnate and die that we might live again" (ch. 28). "Nothing can be compared with the miracle of my salvation: a few drops of blood re-make the whole universe" (ch. 29).

After the constricted horizons of an exclusively juridical theology, we find in the Fathers an extremely rich idea of redemption which includes victory over death, the first fruits of the general resurrection, the liberation of human nature from captivity under the devil, and not only the justification, but also the restoration of creation in Christ. Here the Passion cannot be separated from the Resurrection nor the glorious body of Christ, seated at the right hand of the Father, from the life of Christians here below. Even if redemption appears as the central aspect of the incarnation, i.e., of the dispensation of the Son toward the fallen world, it is but one aspect of the vaster dispensation of the Holy Trinity toward being created *ex nihilo* and called to reach deification freely – to reach union with God, so that "God may be all in all." The thought of the Fathers never shuts out this ultimate vision. Redemption has our salvation from sin as an immediate aim, but that salvation will be, in its ultimate realization in the age to come, our union with God, the deification of the created beings whom Christ ransomed. But this final realization involves the dispensation of another divine Person, sent into the world after the Son.

The work of the Holy Spirit is inseparable from that of the Son. To be able to say with the Fathers, "God became man that man might become God," it is not enough to supplement the insufficiencies of Anselm's theory by returning to the wider and richer idea of redemption found in the Fathers. We must, above all, recover the true place of the dispensation of the Holy Spirit, distinct but not separable from that of the Incarnate Word.[17] If the thought of Anselm could stop at the redeeming work of Christ, isolating it from the rest of Christian teaching, constricting the horizons of tradition, it was precisely because in his time the West had already lost the true idea of the Person of the Holy Spirit, relegating Him to a secondary position by making Him into a kind of lieutenant or deputy of the Son. We shall leave this question aside, for we have already attempted to analyze the dogma of the *processio ab utroque* and its consequences for all Western theology. We confine ourselves here to the positive task of showing why the idea of our ultimate deification cannot be expressed on a Christological basis alone, but demands a pneumatological development as well.

3

In the West, the theological thought of our day is making a great effort to return to the patristic sources of the first centuries – particularly to the Greek Fathers – in order to incorporate them into a catholic synthesis. Not only post-Tridentine theology, but also medieval scholasticism, with all its philosophical richness, nowadays appears theologically inadequate. A powerful effort is being made to put back into use the notion of the Church as the body of Christ, as a new creature recapitulated by Christ, a nature or a body having the Risen Christ as her Head.

Since the first Adam missed his vocation of free attainment of union with God, the Second Adam, the divine Word, accomplished this union of the two natures in His Person, when He was incarnate. Entering the actuality of the fallen world, He broke the power of sin in our nature, and by His death, which reveals the supreme degree of His entrance into our fallen state, He triumphed over death and corruption. In baptism we die with Christ, symbolically, to rise again, really, in Him, in the new life of His victorious body, to become members of this unique body, historically and concretely existing on earth, but with its Head in heaven, in eternity, in the mystery of the Holy Trinity. Christ, who is both the Sacrificer and the Sacrifice, offers on the heavenly altar the unique sacrifice which is done here below on numberless earthly altars in the eucharistic mystery. Thus there is no schism between the invisible and the visible, between heaven and earth, between the Head seated on the Father's right hand, and the Church, His body, in which flows unceasingly His most precious blood.

"That which was visible in our Redeemer now has passed into the sacraments."[18] This conception of the unity of the Christians who form the unique body of Christ is now being revived everywhere in the West. It is above all a liturgical and sacramental conception, which underscores the organic character of the Church, as our unity in the whole Christ.

It is unnecessary to emphasize the importance of this theology of the body of Christ, which recovers in a new way the riches of patristic tradition. What is important at present is to notice that this way of regarding the doctrine of redemption reopens the way to a wider Christology and a wider ecclesiology, in which the question of our deification, of our union with God, can again be raised. We can now say again what the Fathers said: "God became man, so that man might become God." But when one tries to interpret these words solely on a Christological and sacramental basis, in which the part of the Holy Spirit is that of a liaison between the heavenly Head of the Church and His earthly members, we get into grave difficulties and reach insoluble problems.[19]

In this conception of the Church as the body of the whole Christ, who contains in Himself the human beings who are members of the Church (a conception which we fully accept, in any case), there is a kind of Christian totalitarianism. Is it possible, one may ask, to safeguard the idea that all human persons are distinct from each other and, above all, from the unique Person of Christ, who here seems to be identified with the person of the Church? Is there not also a danger of losing the idea of personal liberty and of replacing the determinism of the sinful state from which we are saved by some sort of sacramental determinism, in which the organic process of salvation, accomplished in the collective totality of the Church, tends to suppress personal encounter with God? In what sense are we all one single body in Christ, and in what sense is it true that we are not and cannot be one without ceasing to exist as human persons or hypostases, each of whom is called to realize in his person union with God? For it would appear that there are as many unions with God as there are human persons, each person having an absolutely unique relation with the Divinity, and that as many possible sainthoods exist in heaven as there are personal destinies on earth.

4

When we wish to speak about human persons in relation to the body of Christ of which we are members, we should resolutely renounce the sense of the word "person" which belongs to sociology and to most philosophers. We should go to seek our norm or "canon" of thinking in a higher region, in the idea of person or hypostasis as it is found in trinitarian theology. The dogma of the Trinity, which places our spirit before the antinomy of absolute identity and of no less absolute diversity, is expressed in the distinction between nature and persons or hypostases. Here each person exists not by excluding others, not by opposition to the "Not-I," but by a refusal to possess the nature for himself (to use psychological language, which is very much out of place when we speak of the Trinity). Personal existence supposes a relation to the other; one person exists "to" or "towards" the other: *ho logos ēn pros ton theon*, as the preface to St. John's Gospel says. To put it briefly, let us say that a person can be fully personal only in so far as he has nothing that he seeks to possess for himself, to the exclusion of others, i.e., when he has a common nature with others. It is then alone that the distinction between persons and nature exists in all its purity; otherwise we are in the presence of individuals, dividing nature among themselves. There is no partition or division of nature among the three Persons of the Holy Trinity. The Hypostases are not three parts of a whole, of the one nature, but each includes in Himself the whole divine nature. Each is the whole, because He has nothing for Himself: even will is common to the Three.

If we now turn to human beings, created in the image of God, we can find, by taking the dogma of the Trinity as our starting-point, a common nature existing in many created hypostases. However, in the actuality of the fallen world, human beings tend to exist by excluding each other. Each affirms himself by contrasting himself with others, i.e., in dividing – in parceling out – the unity of nature, each owning a portion of human nature for himself, so that "my" will contrasts "myself" with all that is "not I." From this point of view, what we habitually call a human person is not truly a person but an individual, a part of the common nature, more or less like the other parts or human individuals of which humanity is composed. But in the measure in which he is a person in the true theological sense of the word, a human being is not limited by his individual nature. He is not only a part of the whole, but potentially includes the whole, having in himself the whole of the earthly cosmos, of which he is the hypostasis.[20] Thus each person is an absolutely original and unique aspect of the nature common to all. The mystery of a human person, which makes it absolutely unique and irreplaceable, cannot be grasped in a rational concept and defined in words. All our definitions inevitably have reference to an individual, more or less like other individuals; and the most perfect word for indicating personality in its absolute diversity will always be the wrong word. Persons, as such, are not parts of nature. Although linked with individual parts of the common nature in created actuality, they potentially contain in themselves, each in his fashion, the whole of nature. In our habitual experience we know neither true personal diversity nor true unity of nature. We see on the one hand human individuals, and on the other hand human collective totalities, in perpetual conflict.

We find in the Church the unity of our nature perpetually being realized, for the Church is more united than a collective totality: St. Paul calls it "the body." It is human nature, whose unity is no longer represented by the old Adam, the head of the human race in its extension into individuals. This human nature, ransomed and renewed, is reassembled and recapitulated in the Hypostasis or divine Person of the Son of God who has become man. If in this new reality our individualized natures are freed from their limitations (there is neither Greek nor Scythian, freeman nor slave), and if the individual, existing by opposition to his "Not-I," is called to disappear by becoming a member of a single body, this does not mean that human persons or hypostases are thereby suppressed. On the contrary. Only in the Church can they realize themselves in their true diversity. Not being parts of a common nature, as is the case with individuals, persons are not confused with each other on account of the unity of nature which is in the process of realization in the Church.[21] They do not become portions of the Person of Christ. They are not included in the Person of Christ as in a super-person. That would be contrary to the very idea of a person. We are *one* in Christ by virtue of our nature, in that He is the Head of our nature, forming in Himself one sole Body.

One conclusion must be drawn: if our individual natures are incorporated into the glorious humanity of Christ and enter the unity of His Body by baptism, conforming themselves to the death and resurrection of Christ, our persons need to be confirmed in their personal dignity by the Holy Spirit, so that each may freely realize his own union with the Divinity. Baptism – the sacrament of unity in Christ – needs to be completed by chrismation – the sacrament of diversity in the Holy Spirit.

5

The mystery of our redemption leads up to what the Fathers call the recapitulation of our nature by Christ and in Christ. This is the Christological foundation of the Church, which expresses itself above all in the sacramental life, with its quality of absolute objectivity. But if we wish to safeguard another aspect of the Church, which has a quality of subjectivity no less absolute, it must be based on the dispensation of another divine Person, independent, in His origin, of the Person of the Incarnate Son.[22] Without this, we risk depersonalizing the Church, by submitting the freedom of her human hypostases to a kind of sacramental determinism. On the other hand, if the subjective aspect alone is stressed, we will lose – along with the idea of the Body of Christ – the "logical," objective basis of the Truth and will fall into the vagaries of "individual" faith.

The point is that the Incarnation and the redeeming work of Christ, considered apart from the dispensation of the Holy Spirit, cannot justify the Church's personal multiplicity – something which is as necessary as her natural unity in Christ. The mystery of Pentecost is as important as the mystery of the Redemption. The redeeming work of Christ is an indispensable precondition of the deifying work of the Holy Spirit. The Lord Himself affirmed that when He said, "I came to cast fire on the earth, and would that it were already kindled!" (Luke 12: 49). But, on the other hand, one may say that the work of the Spirit serves that of the Son, for it is by receiving the Spirit that human persons can bear witness in full consciousness to the divinity of Christ. The Son has become like us by the incarnation; we become like Him by deification, by partaking of the divinity in the Holy Spirit, who communicates the divinity to *each* human person in a particular way. The redeeming work of the Son is related to our nature. The deifying work of the Holy Spirit concerns our persons. But the two are inseparable. One is unthinkable without the other, for each is the condition of the other, each is present in the other; and ultimately they are but one dispensation of the Holy Trinity, accomplished by two Divine Persons sent by the Father into the world. This double dispensation of the Word and of the Paraclete has as its goal the union of created beings with God.

Considered from the point of view of our fallen state, the aim of the divine dispensation can be termed salvation or redemption. This is the negative aspect of our ultimate goal, which is considered from the perspective of our sin. Considered from the point of view of the ultimate vocation of created beings, the aim of the divine dispensation can be termed deification. This is the positive definition of the same mystery, which must be accomplished in each human person in the Church and which will be fully revealed in the age to come, when, after having reunited all things in Christ, God will become all in all.

Notes

1　Donald F. Winslow, *The Dynamics of Salvation: A Study in Gregory of Nazianzus* (Cambridge, MA: Philadelphia Patristic Foundation, 1979), p. 129.

2　For an elegant and more charitable account that makes Anselm a deficient case of Athanasius's own logic, see David Bentley Hart, *The Beauty of the Infinite* (Grand Rapids, MI: Eerdmans, 2004), pp. 360–73.

3　*Adversus haereses* V, preface; PG [Patrologia Graeca] 7, col. 1120.

4　*De incarnatione verbi* 54; PG 25, col. 192 B.

5　*Poema dogmatica* 10, 5-9; PG 37, col. 465.

6　*Oratio catechetica magna* 25; PG 45, col. 65 D.

7　*De incarnatione verbi* 20; PG 25, col. 129 D–132 A. [David Hart's *Beauty of the Infinite* (pp. 360–73) corrects and supersedes Lossky. Editor.]

8　Matt. 18: 12–14; Luke 15: 4–7; John 10: 1–16.

9　Matt. 12: 29; Mark 3: 27; Luke 11: 21–2.

10　St. Athanasius, *De incarnatione verbi* 30; PG 25, col. 148.

11　St. John of Damascus, *De imaginibus* III, 9; PG 94, col. 1332 D. The image of Christ as the physician of human nature, wounded by sin, is often found in connection with the parable of the Good Samaritan, which was interpreted in this way for the first time by Origen, Homily 34 on St. Luke, PG 13, cols. 1886–8; *Commentary on St. John* 20, 28; PG 14, col. 656A.

12　St. Gregory of Nyssa, *Oratio catechetica magna* 22–4; PG 45, cols. 60–5.

13　Rom. 3: 24, 8: 23; 1 Cor. 1: 30; Eph. 1: 7, 14: 30; Col. 1: 14; Heb. 9: 15, 11: 35, with the sense of deliverance. 1 Tim. 2: 6; 1 Cor. 6: 20, 7: 22; Gal. 3: 13, with the sense of a ransom paid.

14　For St. Paul, the sacrificial or sacerdotal image of the work of Christ is basically identical to the juridical image – that of purchase or redemption properly so-called – but it also completes and deepens it. In effect, the idea of propitiation in blood (Rom. 3: 26) ties together the two images – the juridical and the sacrificial – in the notion of the expiatory death of the just man, a notion characteristic of the messianic prophecies (Isaiah 53).

15　*Cur Deus homo* I, 4; PL [Patrologia Latina]158, col. 365.

16   Oration 45, 22; PG 36, col. 653.
17   We find in St. Athanasius some hints of a pneumatological explication of the sentence: "God became man, that man might become god." This is above all manifest in the celebrated opposition of Christ, "God bearing flesh," and Christians, "men bearing the Spirit." The Word assumed flesh so that we might receive the Holy Spirit. *De incarnatione et contra Arianos* 8; PG 26, col. 996 C.
18   St. Leo the Great, Sermon 74, 2; PL 54, col. 398.
19   To have an idea of the difficulties in which Roman Catholic theology of our times flounders – hardly able to reconcile personal deification with the notion of the Church as the body of Christ – it is useful to consult Fr. L. Bouyer, *Mystère pascal* (Paris, 1945), pp. 180–94.
20   In speaking of the "earthly cosmos" – the nature of which man is the hypostasis (or the hypostases) – we are leaving aside the question of the "celestial cosmos," the angelic world. This is a completely different subject, not directly relating to the problem with which we are concerned here.
21   "In whatever way we are divided into well defined personalities, according to which someone is Peter or John, Thomas or Matthew, we are, as it were, established in one sole body in Christ, by being nourished by one sole flesh." St. Cyril of Alexandria, *Commentary on St. John* 11, 11; PG 74, col. 560.
22   "The Holy Spirit is found present in each of those who receive Him as though He had been communicated to him alone, and nevertheless He pours out complete grace on all." St. Basil, *De spiritu sancto* 9, 2; PG 32, cols. 108–9.

25

Dumitru Staniloae, *from* "Trinitarian Relations and the Life of the Church"

Vladimir Lossky described the work of Son and Spirit in a formulation that stresses their distinctiveness: the Son provides, the Spirit applies. The Son saves the race, the Spirit individualizes salvation. Staniloae prefers a formulation that stresses their interrelation: Son and Spirit together unite the particular and together diversify the general. Dmitru Staniloae makes Lossky's insight on Son and Spirit more sophisticated. He tries to save Lossky's insight without reducing it to a pair of principles or functions. In Staniloae, Son and Spirit do not reduce to functions. In Staniloae, they do what they do because of and out of their intra-trinitarian relationship. Union and diversity then come to human beings as they participate in the *relationship* of the Spirit and the Son. Unity and diversity emerge as Son and Spirit *interact*. The gifts of God do not arrive out of a mechanism: they emerge in a performance. That performance receives its particulars from the biblical narratives and language: the Spirit "rests" or "alights" on the Son. Union comes as the Spirit works union in human community *as the body of Christ*. Diversity comes as the Spirit distributes gifts *to the body of Christ*.

Staniloae allows several patterns to go without saying. First, he is working analogically. The resting of the Spirit on the Son does not name one thing, but identifies a pattern that repeats on multiple levels. The Spirit rests on the Son at the baptism of Jesus. The Spirit rests on the Son in the body of Christ that is the Church. The Spirit rest on the Son in the body of Christ that is the sacraments. And so on for many meanings of "the body of Christ." Second, Staniloae assumes a couple of root metaphors. One unstated comparison is that the Spirit relates to the Son as life to a body. Another is that unity and diversity relate as the gathering together and distribution of gifts that happens at the Eucharist. Neither

Dumitru Staniloae, "Trinitarian Relations and the Life of the Church," in *Theology and the Church* (Crestwood, NY: St Vladimir's Seminary Press, 1980), pp. 11–15, 20–9, 40, 43. Originally published in Romanian in *Ortodoxia* 19 (1967), pp. 503–25.

comparison is meant to work in a reductive way. So Staniloae would not say that the Son receives life from the Spirit because he lacked it on his own; rather he characteristically chooses to receive from another what he could have on his own. Or better, he choose to receive from another what he chooses not to have for himself alone. The life of the Son is not a transfer, it's a sharing and an opening. Similarly, the Eucharist too is not a transfer, but an inclusion within the trinitarian community of gift and gratitude. Those statements go rather farther than Staniloae, but (I think) in the same direction.

The accounts of Lossky and Staniloae, related but different, exemplify two strategies or practices for talking about the relations among the trinitarian persons: appropriation and indivisibility. Both attempt to carry forward biblical patterns. In the practice of appropriation, Christian thinkers note the Bible's tendency to *appropriate*, or assign, various works of the One God to particular Persons: the Father creates; the Son redeems; the Spirit sanctifies. In the practice of indivisibility, on the other hand, Christian thinkers note the Bible's tendency – constructed out of widely separated passages from different times and authors – to insist that the appropriation of a divine act to one Person must not exclude the others. So while creation tends to be appropriated to the Father, John 1 insists that without the Word "was not anything made that was made," and theologians sometimes read the Spirit hovering over the face of the waters in Genesis as a sign that it is biblical to talk also about creation by the Spirit. Similarly, the redemption appropriated to the Son includes the Father and the Spirit, while the sanctification appropriated to the Spirit includes the Father and the Son. The practice of indivisibility is summed up in the patristic maxim *Opera trinitatis ad extra indivisa sunt*, or "the works of the Trinity toward the outside are indivisible" (toward creatures or the world). Lossky does not violate that rule. He does *not* say that the Son redeems without the Spirit, or that Spirit applies without the Son. But Staniloae wants to complicate the matter, so that redemption and its participation arise from the relationships among the persons. He wants to set up a roadblock against thinking they acted alone or in series. He does not want to contrast Son and Spirit so that the Son (only?) generalized and the Spirit (only?) individualized, or that the Son unified and the Spirit diversified. "These are not two separate moments as Lossky thinks, but in virtue of the very fact that we are united to Christ through the Spirit, union with Christ also accentuates our growth as persons."

from **Trinitarian Relations and the Life of the Church**

Dumitru Staniloae

Ecclesiology is the central theme of the ecumenical movement. The Christian world's quest for unity is one with its quest for the Church; Christian unity means the Church, a Church in which all Christians wish to see themselves united. All who work for Christian unity must ask themselves therefore what kind of unity this is to be, or, in other words, what nature must the Church have so that she may correspond to God's plan for her and yet at the same time be the expression of the broadest and freest but also the closest fraternal union of all Christian men and women.

It is the Protestant world which is searching most assiduously for this unity which is the Church. But the unity and the Church which Catholicism offers do not attract the Protestant world because the unity and the Church which it is seeking cannot be marked by the hindering of personal freedom and diversity.

Protestants are looking for the signs of a Church which is fully satisfying, which transcends their own individualist form of Christianity. Catholics too will do the same when once they come to recognize certain deficiencies in their own ecclesiology.

Whether they are or are not acquainted in any detail with the Orthodox Church, we note with pleasant surprise that as often as some one or other group of these Christians sketches the image of the Church that it is seeking, the result, in principle, usually resembles Orthodox ecclesiology, and even at times the concrete form of the present-day Orthodox Church. Catholics aspire to the "sobornic" liberty of the Orthodox, and Protestants to their communitarian unity, while both groups consider that what they are seeking resembles most closely the form of ecclesial life which flourished in the earliest Church. It is obvious however that both groups also believe they can reach this true Church by penetrating more deeply into the very roots of their own form of Christianity. Nevertheless, as a concrete model to guide them in this search into the depths of their own Christian experience or as a confirmation of what they find there, they have before them the essential characteristics of Orthodox ecclesiology.

In order to encourage the use of Orthodox ecclesiology by the many Catholic and Protestant theologians who consider it to be the nearest approximation to the ecclesiology they are seeking, Orthodox strive to penetrate deeper themselves into the interpretation of their own ecclesiology, firstly, by indicating the presence of those dimensions for which the contemporary ecumenical perspective is searching, and secondly, by pointing out that these dimensions represent potentialities that could in fact be realized in a form adapted to the Church's contemporary mode of understanding, and thus become the expression of a united Christianity.

The present study attempts to make a partial contribution in this direction.

A unity such as the one we have sketched can exist only as a gift in Christ, and Christ is present only through the Spirit. Now it is a common observation of Western theologians that the life of Orthodox Christians bears the seal of a wholly remarkable feeling for the presence and the activity of the Holy Spirit. And it is this which gives to the Orthodox Church a note of unity in liberty that is unknown in either Catholic or Protestant ecclesiology. In a paper read at the World Conference of the Commission on Faith and Order of the World Council of Churches held in Montreal in July of 1963, Professor Roger Mehl said: "It seems to us that the refusal of the Orthodox Church [to recognize papal primacy] springs from an original conception of the relations between ecclesiology and pneumatology; that the exemplary seriousness with which Orthodoxy has always considered the doctrine of the Holy Spirit, the action of the Spirit in the Church, has preserved it from the pitfalls of an abstract legalism. In our encounters we must ask ourselves – after elucidating the relations between Christ and the Church – what is the place of the Holy Spirit in ecclesiology as a whole. The Churches of the Reformation must realize the fact that the theology of the 16th century did not devote sufficient consideration to the pneumatological problem. . . ."[1]

The lack of understanding of the pneumatological aspect of the Church in Catholicism has been illustrated recently by Pope Paul VI both in his opening address at the second session of the Second Vatican Council (29 September 1963) and in his encyclical *Ecclesiam Suam* of 6 August 1964. In both places it is only in function of Christ that the Pope describes the Church and calls for her renewal. We can see today in this predominant Christologism, which finds its natural expression in a "filioquism" subordinating the Holy Spirit to the Father and the Son, the root cause of the exaggeratedly institutional character of the Roman Catholic Church.[2]

The Orthodox theologian Nikos Nissiotis says: "The Roman neglect of the Holy Spirit is more evident than ever before; the schema *De Ecclesia*, though it begins with a trinitarian basis and by accepting the mystery of the Church, proceeds in its systematic exposition to overlook both things. The Holy Spirit, once mentioned, is entirely forgotten throughout the rest of the text. I do not mean by this remark that he is simply not mentioned, but the spirit that governs the schema and the Vatican Council as a whole shows a lack of consistent teaching about the Holy Spirit. In this way its right christological basis becomes in the end christomonism which is quite inflexible in the discussion of the particular controversial issues of ecclesiology. Thus the concepts of the hierarchy and the People of God, as well as the royal priesthood, are thought out on a sociological and juridical rather than a charismatic basis. The lines of succession Christ – Peter – Pope, and Christ – the Eleven – bishops become the inflexible *de jure divino* structure of a hierarchical institution which is obliged afterwards to set definite limits to the one Church, taking as criterion, not the wholeness of the sacramental charismatic life of the Church, but the discipline and order *sub Pontifice Romano*."[3]

To this institutionalism Protestants oppose an individualist and anarchical experience which some represent as the fruit of the Holy Spirit (though it surely cannot be this, for the Spirit is always the Spirit of the community: 1 Cor. 12), and others as an expression of an accentuated but isolated union with Christ which, inasmuch as it is incompatible with the restraints of institution or even of community, does away with all such restraints.

In the Orthodox Church preoccupation with Christ has not only been kept in balance by a similar preoccupation with the Holy Spirit, but it has always been the Orthodox judgement that union with Christ can be lived only in the Holy Spirit, and that the experience of being in the Holy Spirit is nothing other than union with Christ. The more vividly one knows Christ and the more one comes to live in him, the more one knows and lives in the Holy Spirit. The more spiritual a life one leads the more lovingly is one bound to Christ. By its own uninterrupted experience Orthodoxy confirms the words of St. Paul: "No one can say 'Jesus is Lord' except by the Holy Spirit." (1 Cor. 12: 3).

In this perspective we might say that from the Orthodox point of view the exclusive concentration on Christ in Western Christianity does not in fact suggest the presence of an ever more intimate union with him, for this union is not affirmed in the Holy Spirit. The proof is that Catholicism treats Christ as if he were removed from the Church – hence the need to have a vicar for him – while in Protestantism Christ is similarly thought to remain at a distance from the faithful – however movingly this is expressed – for he has no effect on the conduct of their lives or on their ecclesial union. In both traditions Christ is at a distance, because both have for all practical purposes forgotten the Holy Spirit through whom Christ is present. And the Church as the Body of Christ exists effectively where the Holy Spirit is present.

The indissoluble union between Christ and the Holy Spirit who truly constitutes the Church and sustains the life of the Christian within the Church has its profound roots in that indissoluble union which according to Orthodox teaching exists between them within the sphere of their inner trinitarian relations. We shall try to demonstrate this in what follows.

[The resting of the Spirit on the Son]

. . . Let us now however attempt another explanation of the "shining forth" of the Holy Spirit through the Son. It is our belief that such an explanation must begin with that "coming to rest of the Holy Spirit" upon the Incarnate Son which is spoken of both by the New Testament writings and by the Fathers of the Church. From this starting point we move to the conclusion that the same "resting" of the Spirit upon the eternal Son takes place before his incarnation. For when the Son becomes man, he receives as man what he has as God. "Rest" cannot be explained as the opposite of weariness – for the Spirit cannot grow weary – but as an "end to all further departing," as an "abiding" in the Son. This meaning is implied also by the word "procession" which does not mean a simple going forth of someone from another, as for example in the case of one being born; it means rather a setting forth from somewhere towards a definite goal, a departure from one person in order to reach another (*ekporeuomai* = I set out on the way in order to arrive somewhere). When the Spirit proceeds from the Father he sets out towards the Son; the Son is the goal at which he will stop. "Therefore we must ask ourselves," says St. Gregory Palamas, "when the Spirit goes forth from the Father in a movement we neither see nor understand: can we say that, according to the evidence of Scripture, he has someone in whom he can rest in a manner which befits God? If we search the Scriptures we discover that the Father of the Only Begotten God has seen fit to disclose this very thing to John the Precursor and Baptizer of the Lord who said: 'I myself did not know him; but he who sent me to baptize with water said to me, 'He on whom you see the Spirit descend and remain, this is He who baptizes with the Holy Spirit.' (John 1: 33). . . . And that no one may think that these things were spoken and accomplished by the Father with reference to the Incarnation of the Son . . . let us listen to the divine Damascene who writes in the eighth of the Dogmatic Chapters: 'We believe also in the Holy Spirit who proceeds from the Father and rests in the Son.' "[4]

This procession of the Spirit from the Father towards the Son in whom he "comes to rest," "abides," "remains," has a profound and double significance. Firstly, it means that the Spirit does not take his origin also from the Son, for this would mean that the Spirit goes forth from the Son instead of coming to rest in him. Were it true that the Spirit goes forth also from the Son, the Godhead would be capable of an infinite "unwinding," for just as the Son, though himself caused, would become a cause in his turn, so also there would be nothing to prevent that the Spirit, caused by the Son, would himself be able to become a cause and so on indefinitely. But in the Godhead only the uncaused Person – the Father – is cause; each of the other Persons who have come forth, comes forth immediately from the ultimate and absolute cause, having communion with that cause and partaking of it. Otherwise we would have a progressive watering-down of the divinity, an endless chain of Persons each further removed from the uncaused cause and hence participating in him to a correspondingly lesser degree.

In the second place, if the procession of the Spirit from the Father were not to have as its goal his "rest" in the Son, but instead a separate existence as Person alongside that of the Son, there would again be no compelling reason why still other Persons might not arise from the Father, having their existence alongside Son and Spirit and so on indefinitely. Is to be three in number a sufficient reason in itself why the divinity should not multiply continuously?

But because the Holy Spirit proceeds from the Father and comes to rest in the Son, and therefore is not begotten like the Son, an endless multiplication of the divinity is avoided, and a certain internal unity is achieved, for not only is the unity between Son and Spirit made manifest in this way, but that between the Father and the Son is also strengthened. The Spirit proceeding from the Father comes to rest in the Son who is begotten of the Father, and, like an arch, unites Father and Son in one embrace. Thus a unity among the three Persons is manifested which is distinct from their unity of essence. If there exists nothing between the two to unite them, the number two represents separation. The duality which appears at the begetting of the Son by the Father is reduced to a unity by the procession of the Spirit. St. Gregory Nazianzen says: "A complete trinity [is formed] from three perfect elements, for the monad is in motion because of its richness, but it transcends the dyad for it is beyond [the distinction of] matter and form from which bodies arise, and defines itself as trinity (for this is the first [stage] of synthesis beyond duality) in order that the divinity be neither too restricted nor overflow to infinity. For the first of these shows a lack of generosity and the latter a lack of order. The first is wholly Jewish, the second pagan and polytheist."[5] The third in the Trinity does not signify a further extension of the Godhead, but rather a bond between the two, and represents the perfection of the unity of the many. The Father causes the Spirit to proceed in order to unite himself with the Son and because he has begotten the Son. This would be a possible interpretation of the formula of St. John of Damascus: the Father causes the Spirit to proceed through the Son, that is, because of the fact of the existence of the Son.

We will not pursue all the consequences of the relation of Spirit and Son here, but only those which concern soteriology and ecclesiology in general.

The "rest" or "abiding" of the Spirit upon the Son or in the Son signifies not only the union of the one with the other in the order of eternity but also their union in the temporal order. The presence of Christ is always marked by the Spirit resting upon him, and the presence of the Spirit means the presence of Christ upon whom he rests. The Spirit is the one who shines forth, that is, the one who stands out over Christ like a light, and Christ is he who has led us into the light of the Spirit. If it was only at Pentecost that the Apostles fully recognized Christ as God, that was because it was only in the Ascension of Christ that the Spirit which rests upon him and shines forth from him as God was poured out upon him completely as man.

This is why Scripture never speaks of seeing the Spirit for his own sake, nor even of the vision of the Spirit in general – apart from the times when he showed himself symbolically as a dove, as tongues of fire, or as a cloud – but instead speaks only of seeing Christ "in the Spirit." Scripture speaks of "receiving" the Spirit, but not of seeing the Spirit. For the Spirit is only the spiritual light in which Christ is seen, as objects are seen in material light. And just as we cannot say that we see the material light, only other objects in it, in the same way we do not say that we "see" the Spirit, but Christ in or through the Spirit. The Spirit is the milieu in which Christ is "seen," the "means" by which we come to know him and to lay hold of and experience the presence of Christ. As such, the Spirit enters the system of our perceptual subjectivity. He is the power which imprints itself upon and elevates this subjectivity. In this sense the Spirit also "shines forth" through spiritual men, the saints.

Therefore, although there is no knowledge or experience of Christ as God apart from the Spirit, neither is there any experience of the Spirit by himself in isolation for he is only the means of supernatural perception.[6] If the Spirit is the means and the intensity of all knowledge of the transcendent Godhead, Christ as the Logos is the structured content of this knowledge.[7] Where this content is wanting the soul becomes lost in its own structures, in an inconsistent and disordered enthusiasm, and this has indeed happened with so many anarchical "experiences" and so many enthusiastic but destructive currents within Christianity which cannot be said ever to have possessed the Holy Spirit truly if it is true that the Spirit is not present apart from Christ. Moreover where the Spirit is absent as the means by which we come to the living knowledge of Christ, Christ becomes the object of a frigid theoretical science, of definitions put together from memorized citations and formulae.

The Holy Spirit is experienced as a kind of fluid spiritual atmosphere which rises within us and raises us up towards God in an ever greater understanding and love.[8] As such the Spirit can neither stand still nor can we take hold of him. He is like the air, like a fragrance which changes at every moment, like the soul itself for he is the supreme model of the soul. St. Cyril of Alexandria described the whole life of the saints as a perfume ascending to God. Such a life is steeped in the activity of the Holy Spirit. Just as in the Trinity the Spirit subsists in a continuous procession from the loving Father towards the beloved Son, and in a loving "irradiation" from the Son towards the Father, so within us the Spirit exists within a ceaseless flowing of the Son towards us and of ourselves towards the Son from whom we receive the Spirit. He is this flowing current of the love of the Son or, more exactly, of the Father, returning from us also as a current which is united with our loving affection for the Son or, more precisely, for the Father. He moves in us and from us in the way that light or perfume or the air moves, that is, without our being aware of him. "Let us not try to hinder the flight of the Dove towards the Lamb. It would be a temptation to interrupt this flight, to hold the Dove in our hands and feast our eyes as we please, to caress it, to study it carefully, to take our delight in contemplating it." The activity of the Spirit within us is such as to make us cry out: "O my dove, in the clefts of the rock, in the covert of the cliff, let me see your face, let me hear your voice, for your voice is sweet, and your face is comely" (Song 2: 14).[9]

The second consequence which follows upon this "resting" or "abiding" of the Spirit in the Son (apart from their indissoluble union with us) is that when the faithful receive the Spirit of Christ they do not receive him apart from Christ; they are not attached to him at a distance from Christ, but rather in Christ, because it is "in Christ" that they have been raised up. This would not be so if the Spirit were to proceed "and from the Son," or if, proceeding from the Father, he were not to rest in the Son. In that case the faithful might possess the Spirit without being in Christ, or they might possess Christ without being in the Spirit. We might better understand this by reference to a similar distinction: although we are "in Christ," nevertheless, because of the fact that the Son goes *forth* from the Father by generation, we are not also in the Father in exactly the same way that, once in the Spirit, we are consequently also in Christ. That is why the Western Christian world (Catholic and Protestant) sometimes affirms a presence which is said to be in the Spirit but not also in Christ, or speaks of one priesthood that is Christological-institutional and another that is pneumatological, an idea which can even be found in the works of some Russian theologians writing in the West (Lossky, Gillet).

According to Orthodox teaching the faithful can possess the Spirit only "in Christ" and vice-versa.[10] They are united with Christ through the Spirit who never leaves Christ, who "shines forth" from him but does not "come forth" from him. In this way the faithful participate with Christ in the "rest" of the Holy Spirit who comes upon him. Obviously, since the faithful, unlike Christ, are not divine hypostases they have only a partial share in the energy of the Spirit. Because the human hypostasis is not equal to the divine hypostasis, it cannot contain the fullness of the hypostasis of the Spirit, but inasmuch as it is united with Christ it is in a position to receive the abiding of the Spirit when he descends upon Christ, or better, inasmuch as it does receive the "rest" of the Spirit coming down upon it, it is therefore only that "rest," that "abiding" which has, in fact, come down upon Christ that the human hypostasis is able to receive. The Spirit never leaves this position of resting upon Christ, for his rest as an hypostasis is in Christ as the incarnate Son of God. But the Spirit can cease to rest upon man for there is no eternal hypostatic relation between men and the Spirit.

Inasmuch as through our union with Christ, with the incarnate hypostasis of the Son, we possess the Spirit, two things follow: on the one hand, we form, in a certain sense, one person with Christ; and on the other hand, because, unlike Christ, we do not possess the Spirit in his hypostatic fullness, but only as much as we can contain and as corresponds to the person of each of us, the Spirit simultaneously accentuates in us what is specific to us as persons. These are not two separate moments as Lossky thinks, but in virtue of the very fact that we are united to Christ through the Spirit, union with Christ also accentuates our growth as persons.

Everything that has been said here about the faithful must be understood to refer to them as members of the Mystical Body of Christ. The Spirit "comes to rest" (alights) upon the Church and in the Church because he comes to rest upon Christ, its head, and because the Church is united with Christ. Since even the term "irradiation" does not, as we have seen, mean that the one who shines forth also *comes* forth from the one in whom he radiates his light, it does show that when the Spirit communicates himself to us, he does not as a consequence come forth from or leave Christ, and therefore we do not possess him in isolation from Christ. Rather the Spirit unites us in Christ and gathers us together in him. But inasmuch as we are united with Christ, the Spirit who shines forth from Christ also shines forth from us, or from the Church. He does not however shine forth as a complete hypostasis in the manner in which he shines forth from Christ, and this for two reasons: firstly, because unlike Christ the faithful are not divine hypostases, and secondly, because the shining forth of the Spirit from the faithful is in proportion to their respective stages of growth in virtue, and this could scarcely be the case were the Spirit to shine forth from them in the fullness of his Person. In other words the human persons of the faithful are penetrated only by the activity of the Spirit who, as Person, is united with Christ the divine Head of the Body and Head of every believer who is a member of his Mystical Body. Hence as human beings the faithful cannot have that same integral personal relation with the divine Persons which these Persons have among themselves on the basis of their common essence: they can have only a relation "through grace," that is, through communion or through the activity, the energy of the Spirit.

For this reason Gregory of Cyprus avoids giving the name "irradiation" to the manifestation of the Spirit through the saints. Nevertheless the tradition of the Church strongly affirms this "irradiation" while obviously distinguishing it from the "shining forth" of the Spirit from Christ. The measure of this irradiation of the Spirit in the saints is proportionate to their growth in Christ and to the presence and effective activity of Christ within them.

St. Symeon the New Theologian, describing the fright which took hold of his soul at the sight of God's glory, and his own attempt to hide from it; continues in these words: "But you my God seized me all the more/ Ever more you enfolded me and embraced me/ Within the bosom of your Glory, my God,/ Within the folds of your garments,/ Gathering me in and covering me with your light."[11] And elsewhere he says: "For the mind is lost in your light/ And is filled with irradiation and becomes light/ Similar to your Glory."[12]

Where the experience of the Spirit in the Church and in the faithful grows weak, there appears a Church which is predominantly juridical and institutional, or a religious life characterized by an exaggerated individualism. It is not because the presence of Christ apart from the Spirit produces these phenomena – as some Western theologians and even some Orthodox authors hold – for Christ does not in fact abide in the Church and in the faithful apart from the Spirit. Rather it is because he is conceived either as a remote figure who has left behind a vicar to guide the Church according to his commands (Catholicism), or else as the one who allows each believer to guide himself according to the reasonings of his own conscience (Protestantism).

. . .

If the variety of gifts derives from the same Spirit who is at work in all and is revealed in the service of the common good, then we can conclude that the institution is not devoid of spirituality while spirituality on the other hand is not inevitably lacking in structure and institutional order. An institution with a weakened spiritual life would give proof of a weakening of the actual presence of Christ as well, while a disordered spirituality which does not maintain ecclesial unity would indicate in turn a weakening of the true presence of the Holy Spirit. The true Church is christological *and* pneumatological, institutional and spontaneous at the same time, or rather it is christological because it is pneumatological and vice-versa.

The institution cannot be compared merely to a vessel in which the spiritual life is stirred around; it is also the expression of the real and coordinated activity of the gifts (charisms and ministries) which come from the same Spirit, just as the variety of spiritual gifts and ministries is the means of the fullest possible expression of the spiritual wealth of the Church. The Spirit active in the Church through Christ not only imparts the variety of charisms but also creates unity among those who have been given these gifts in Christ. A so-called pneumatological individualism which does not possess Christ because it does not build up the faithful into the Body of Christ, does not possess the Spirit of Christ either. Nor does a non-pneumatological institutionalism from which the Spirit of Christ is absent possess Christ himself as an adequate effective presence.

. . . This teaching saves the creature both from being isolated from God and also from being confused with the Spirit.

. . . The life of the Church is full of transcendent divine transsubjectivity which has ultimately become her own by virtue of the fact that it is life in that Spirit who is consubstantial with and inseparable from the Son.

Notes

1   ["The Ecumenical Situation," *Ecumenical Review* 16 (1963–4), pp. 1–13; here, p. 9.]
2   N. Nissiotis in *Le Monde*, 6 October 1964, p. 10. [Discussion of Clement and Bouyer omitted.]
3   "Is the Vatican Council Really Ecumenical?" *Ecumenical Review* 16 (1964), p. 365.
4   See the reference in PG [Patrologia Graeca] 150, 833 to a work entitled *Two Apodictic Treatises Proving the Holy Spirit Does Not Proceed from the Son but Only from the Father*.
5   *Oratio* 23 (*De Pace* 3) 8, PG 35, 1160 C–D.
6   "Any attempt in this direction is doomed to fail should we try to draw near and capture the Dove as a reality independent from that of the Lamb. When the Spirit is examined apart from the Beloved Son, he flees and disappears; nothing as it were remains in our hands. We do not attain to the Dove except by uniting ourselves with his flight towards the Lamb and by accepting from the Dove the presence of the Lamb." "La Colombe et l'Agneau," *Contacts* 15 (1963), no. 41, p. 13.
7   "Le Colombe et l'Agneau," p. 12: "It might be said – without pressing these philosophical terms too hard – that because the Spirit identifies with us, though without any confusion of natures, he thereby makes himself the *subject* of our life as Christians, a subject filled with yearning and aspirations, while Jesus is the *object*, the model, the immediate goal of our striving; the Spirit is the consciousness of prayer while Christ is its content" (1 Cor. 14: 14–15).
8   Ibid., p. 14: "The Spirit is not the final goal of our prayer. He is 'what is between' us and the goal of our prayer. He is an *élan* which moves towards the Son. He is also an *élan* moving us towards the Father but towards the Father as found in the Son."
9   Ibid.
10   Acts 2: 33; 1 Cor. 12: 3.
11   *Hymns of the Divine Love*, 24, 261–5.
12   *Hymns of the Divine Love*, 39, 61–3.

VII
Mystical Resources

26

Symeon the New Theologian, from The Discourses

Symeon the New Theologian bears that title, "theologian," together with only two other Eastern Orthodox figures: John the Theologian, the Evangelist; and Gregory the Theologian, Gregory Nazianzen. A "theologian" in this restricted sense identifies God in a new way. John the Evangelist identifies Jesus as God in the prologue to his Gospel. Gregory Nazianzen identifies the Holy Spirit as God in various orations. Now, historically, the title is not bestowed by any particular body for any particular reason; there is no investigative body as for Catholic saints. All the more reason to ask how Symeon might identify God in a new way.

One candidate suggests itself from the way that Symeon defines "blasphemy against the Holy Spirit," that notorious but difficult-to-identify sin that two gospels (Luke 12: 10 and Matt. 12: 32) call unforgivable. In the heat of controversy against opponents suspicious of Symeon's claims to mystical experience, Symeon declares that "to deny that at this present time there are some who love God, and that they have been granted the Holy Spirit and to be baptized by Him as sons of God, that they have become gods by knowledge and experience and contemplation, that wholly subverts the Incarnation of our God and Savior Jesus Christ (Titus 2: 13)."[1] "By knowledge and experience and contemplation" means by grace, not by nature — distinguishing deified human beings from the Deity. Symeon, therefore, identifies God as continuing the incarnation in the Church by the Holy Spirit's presence in at least some living people.

This experience comes as illumination — sometimes a rapture of which Symeon cannot say whether it is in or out of the body — that the Holy Spirit bestows in prayer, described in the passages below. In what kind of prayer? Symeon dates his own illumination to a mental recitation of the prayer from Luke

Symeon the New Theologian, *The Discourses*, trans. C. J. deCatanzaro (Mahwah, NJ: Paulist Press, 1980), pp. 195–6, 198–203, 339–46.

18: 13, "God, have mercy on me, a sinner."[2] This practice prepares for the later use of the "Jesus Prayer" as a constant mental mantra in literal fulfillment of the commandment to "pray without ceasing" (1 Thess. 5: 17). The Jesus Prayer consists of the words "Jesus Christ, Son of God, have mercy on me, a sinner"; the practice of praying it "unceasingly" is called hesychasm.[3]

from The Discourses

Symeon the New Theologian

Chapter XV The Light of God

[§3. God as the Light of the Soul]

Let no one deceive you! God is light (1 John 1: 5), and to those who have entered into union with Him He imparts of His own brightness to the extent that they have been purified. When the lamp of the soul, that is, the mind, has been kindled, then it knows that a divine fire has taken hold of it and inflamed it. How great a marvel! Man is united to God spiritually and physically, since the soul is not separated from the mind, neither the body from the soul. By being united in essence man also has three hypostases by grace. He is a single god by adoption with body and soul and the divine Spirit, of whom he has become a partaker. Then is fulfilled what was spoken by the prophet David, "I have said, ye are gods, and ye are all the sons of the Most High" (Ps. 82: 6), that is, sons of the Most High according to the image of the Most High and according to His likeness (Gen. 1: 26). We become the divine offspring of the Divine Spirit (John 3: 8), to whom the Lord rightly said and continues to say, "Abide in Me, that you may bring forth much fruit" (John 15: 4, 8). He speaks of the multitudes that are being saved by them as "fruit." He adds, "Unless the branch abides in the vine it withers, and is cast into the fire" (John 15: 4, 6), therefore "abide in Me, and I in you" (John 15: 4). How He abides in us and how we in turn abide in Him, the Lord Himself taught us when He said, "Thou, Father, art in Me, and I in Thee (John 17: 21), and they are in Me, and I in them" (John 17: 23, 21). Desiring to confirm this He resumes his discourse and says, "That they may be in Me, and I in them, even as Thou, Father, art in Me, and I in Thee" (John 17: 21, 23). To assure His hearers He adds these words besides, "As Thou hast loved Me, so have I loved them" (John 17: 23), "and they have known that Thou hast sent Me" (John 17: 25). It is evident that just as the Father abides in His own Son (John 14: 10) and the Son in His Father's bosom (John 1: 18) by nature, so those who have been born anew through the divine Spirit (John 3: 3, 5) and by His gift have become the brothers of Christ our God and sons of God and gods by adoption, by grace abide in God and God in them (1 John 4: 12ff.).

Chapter XVI [Ecstasy in the Light]

[§1. The story of a novice – the pursuit of the light]
Brethren and fathers and children,

A young man has told me this story:[4]

"I was the apprentice of a venerable father, of one who was equal to the great and exalted saints. From him I often heard of divine illuminations sent from heaven to those engaged in the spiritual struggle, consisting in a flood of light, and conversations between God and man thereby, and I marveled. So great", said he, "was my desire and longing for such a blessing that as I thought thereof I forgot all things earthly and heavenly, to the extent even of eating and drinking and bodily relief.

"This man, however, was a great saint (he is now among the saints!), a man endowed with the gift of prophecy. When he saw me carrying out the things that he enjoined on me to the exclusion even of eating and drinking, wholly absorbed in myself and as though I was wasting away through some poison, out of endless compassion he gave me a strict command and so, unwillingly, I ate, for," as he said. "I was afraid of being charged with disobedience. The more I partook of food, the more the fire consumed me and I could not bear the constraint. I poured out tears like rivers and so I often left the table. In my senselessness I thought that he was setting obstacles in the way of my desire out of ignorance of the great pain that I suffered within. In this state, I, miserable wretch, did not know that he was aware even of the hidden thoughts of my heart, as will appear from what follows.

"It happened one day that we were going into the city[5] in which he had his dwelling, in order that we might visit his spiritual children. We spent the whole day among them, for there were many whom he helped even by his mere presence. At evening we came back to our cell, hungry and thirsty from much labor and the heat, for, however hot the day, he would never take the slightest nap, in spite of his age, though he was about sixty years old. When we sat down to partake of some bread I did not eat, for I was worn out by fatigue. I thought that if I were to take food and drink I should not at all be able to stand for prayer and seek what I desired. These," said he, "were my thoughts, as I was sitting, as though I were beside myself."

[§2. The counsels of Symeon the Pious]
"When the saint saw me and considered the labor that I had endured with him he realized why I had undergone these things, since, as I have mentioned, he was endowed with prophetic insight. Moved with great compassion he spoke to me and strictly commanded me, 'Eat, my child, and drink, and from henceforth be not sad. Had not God willed to have mercy upon you, it would not have pleased Him that you should come to us.' So we ate," said he, "and drank, and more than we needed, for he too ate to put himself on the level of my weakness. Then when the meal was finished he said to me, 'Know this, my boy, that it is neither fasting, nor vigil, nor bodily effort, nor any other laudable action that pleases God so that He appears to us, but only a soul and heart that is humble, simple, and good.' When I heard this I marveled at the words and the admonition of the holy man. More than ever

I was burning with ardor. With keenness of mind I called to mind in a single instant all my sins and was flooded with tears. I fell at his holy feet and laid hold of them and said, 'Pray for me, O saint of God, that I may find mercy through you, for none of the good things that you have mentioned belong to me, but only many sins, as you well know.' The holy man showed me even more compassion and shed tears. Then he bade me rise from the ground and said, 'I am confident that God, who has bestowed abundant grace on me, will bestow a double portion thereof on you simply because of the faith you show toward Him and toward my humble self.' So I received this word as though it came from God Himself and thought of that which Elijah did to Elisha (2 Kings 2: 9–10). I believed that however unworthy I was, yet God is gracious to men, and quick to fulfill the desire of those who fear Him (Ps. 145: 19). So again I made a bow of reverence and asked for his prayer and departed for my cell, having been told by him merely to recite the Trisagion[6] and go to sleep."

[§3. The light and the ecstasy]
"So I entered the place where I usually prayed and, mindful of the words of the holy man I began to say, 'Holy God.' At once I was so greatly moved to tears and loving desire for God that I would be unable to describe in words the joy and delight I then felt. I fell prostrate on the ground, and at once I saw, and behold, a great light was immaterially shining on me and seized hold of my whole mind and soul, so that I was struck with amazement at the unexpected marvel and I was, as it were, in ecstasy. Moreover 1 forgot the place where I stood, who I was, and where, and could only cry out, 'Lord, have mercy,' so that when I came to myself I discovered that I was reciting this. But Father," said he, "who it was that was speaking, and who moved my tongue, I do not know – only God knows. 'Whether I was in the body, or outside the body' (2 Cor. 12: 2, 3), I conversed with this Light. The Light itself knows it; it scattered whatever mist there was in my soul and cast out every earthly care. It expelled from me all material denseness and bodily heaviness that made my members to be sluggish and numb. What an awesome marvel! It so invigorated and strengthened my limbs and muscles, which had been faint through great weariness, that it seemed to me as though I was stripping myself of the garment of corruption. Besides, there was poured into my soul in unutterable fashion a great spiritual joy and perception and a sweetness surpassing every taste of visible objects, together with a freedom and forgetfulness of all thoughts pertaining to this life. In a marvelous way there was granted to me and revealed to me the manner of the departure from this present life. Thus all the perceptions of my mind and my soul were wholly concentrated on the ineffable joy of that Light."

[§4. The pain caused by the withdrawal of the light]
"But when that infinite Light which had appeared to me – for I can call it by no other fitting or appropriate name," so he continued, "in some way had gently and gradually faded and, as it were, had withdrawn itself, I regained possession of myself and realized what its power had suddenly done to me. I reflected on its departure and considered how it had left me again to be alone in this life. So severe was the

grief and pain that overcame me that I am at a loss properly to describe how great it was: A varied and most vehement pain was kindled like a fire in my heart. Imagine, father, if you can," said he, "the pain of being separated from it, the infinity of love, the greatness of my passion, the sublimity of this greatest of blessings! I on my part cannot express in words or comprehend with my mind the infinity of this vision."

[§5. The enjoyment of such a light]
"But tell me, most venerable father and brother," said I, "more clearly and exactly what were the effects of what you have seen." But that dear man, full of the divine Spirit, who had been found worthy of such contemplation, at once replied with a voice most gentle and flowing like honey, "Father, when it appears it fills one with joy, when it vanishes it wounds. It happens close to me and carries me up to heaven. It is a pearl [of great price] (Matt. 13: 46). The light envelops me and appears to me like a star, and is incomprehensible to all. It is radiant like the sun, and I perceive all creation encompassed by it. It shows me all that it contains, and enjoins me to respect my own limits. I am hemmed in by roof and walls, yet it opens the heavens to me. I lift up my eyes sensibly to contemplate the things that are on high, and I see all things as they were before. I marvel at what has happened, and I hear a voice speaking to me secretly from on high, 'These things are but symbols and preliminaries, for you will not see that which is perfect as long as you are clothed in flesh. But return to yourself and see that you do nothing that deprives you of the things that are above. Should you fall, however, it is to recall you to humility! Do not cease to cultivate penitence, for when it is united to My love for mankind it blots out past and present failures.' "

When I had heard these things from him, fathers and brethren, I was almost ecstatic and trembled all over. I noted at once the great height of contemplation and knowledge to which he had readily ascended, solely because he loved and trusted his spiritual father. From mere beginnings he had been granted to see and enjoy such great blessings, as if he had already cast human weakness aside and become an angel instead of a man.

[§6. The pursuit of purity of heart]
I therefore entreat you, brethren in Christ, let us cast far from us every attachment and every care of this present life. Let us hate the pleasures of the flesh, bodily comfort, slackness, and idleness, by which that which is worse prevails over that which is better. Come, let us arm ourselves with genuine faith (cf. Eph. 6: 16) toward God and toward our fathers and teachers who live according to God. Let us acquire a contrite heart, a soul humbled in mind, and a heart that by means of tears and repentance is pure from every stain and defilement of sin. So shall we too be found worthy in due time quickly to rise to such heights that even here and now we may see and enjoy the ineffable blessings of the divine light, if not perfectly, at least in part, and to the extent to which we are able. So shall we both unite ourselves to God and God will be united to us. To those who come near us we shall become "light" and "salt" (cf. Matt. 5: 13–14) to their great benefit in Christ Jesus our Lord, to whom be glory forever. Amen.

Chapter XXXIII On partaking of the Holy Spirit

[§1. The need for kindling the lamp of the soul]
Brethren and fathers,

God is fire (cf. Heb. 6: 4) and He is so called by all the inspired Scripture (cf. Heb. 12: 29). The soul of each of us is a lamp. Now a lamp is wholly in darkness, even though it be filled with oil or tow or other combustible matter, until it receives fire and is kindled. So too the soul, though it may seem to be adorned with all virtues, yet does not receive the fire – in other words, has not received the divine nature and light and is still unkindled and dark and its works are uncertain. All things must be tested and manifested by the light (cf. Eph. 5: 13). The man whose soul's lamp is still in darkness, that is, untouched by the divine fire, stands the more in need of a guide with a shining torch, who will discern his actions. As he has compassion for the faults he reveals in confession he will straightway straighten out whatever is crooked in his actions. Just as he who walks in the night cannot avoid stumbling, so he who has not yet seen the divine light cannot avoid falling into sin. As Christ says, "If anyone walks in the day, he does not stumble, because he sees this light. But if any one walks in the night, he stumbles, because he has not the light in him" (John 11: 9–10). When He said "in him," he meant the divine and immaterial light, for no one can possess the physical light in himself.

[§2. To the light of the Holy Spirit and of Christ]
Just as it is no use to him who walks in darkness to have many and very beautiful lamps all extinguished (cf: Matt. 25: 8), for they cannot help him to see either himself or any one else, so he who appears to have all virtues in him (even if it were possible) (cf. Luke 8: 18), but has not the light of the Holy Spirit in him, can neither see his own actions properly nor have sure knowledge whether they are pleasing to God. He is unable either to lead others or to teach them the will of God, nor is He fit to hear [in confession] the thoughts of others, even were He to become patriarch by man's appointment, until he has the light shining in him. For Christ says, "Walk while you have the light, lest the darkness overtake you; he who walks in the darkness does not know where he goes" (John 12: 35). If, then, he does not know where he goes, how will he show the way to others? What is the use if someone puts an extinguished lamp on another stand (cf. Matt. 5: 15; Luke 8: 16, 11: 33) when he lacks a burning and shining fire? This is not what he should do! "Then what should He do? That which God who is above all (Rom. 9: 5) has determined, for He says, "No one after lighting a lamp puts it in a cellar or under a bushel, but on a stand, that those who enter may see the light" (Luke 11: 33). When he says this He adds also the characteristics of the lamp, which both guides and possesses the light in itself, by saying, "The lamp of the body is the eye" (Luke 11: 34). What else does He mean by "the eye" than simply the mind, which will never become simple, unless it contemplates the simple light (cf. Luke 11: 34ff)? The simple light is Christ. So he who has His light shining in his mind is said to have the mind of Christ (1 Cor. 2: 16). When your light is thus simple, then the whole immaterial body of your soul will be full of light. But if the mind be evil, that is, darkened

and extinguished, then this body of yours will be full of darkness (cf. Luke 11: 34). " 'Therefore be careful lest the light in you be darkness" (Luke 11: 35). So He tells us, take heed lest you think that you have what you do not possess (cf. Luke 8: 18). See how the Master Himself addresses us in the same way as His own servants, when He tells us, "Take heed that you do not deceive yourself and think that you have light within you, when it is not light but darkness." See to it that we too utter the same words as the Master to our fellow-servants and do not say anything that is perverted or false.

So we say: See to it, brethren, that while we seem to be in God and think that we have communion with him (1 John 1: 6) we should not be found excluded and separated from Him, since we do not now see His light. If that light had kindled our lamps, that is, our souls, it would shine brightly in us, just as our God and Lord Jesus Christ said, "If your whole body is full of light, having no part dark, it will be wholly bright, as when a lamp with its rays gives you light" (Luke 11: 36). What other witness greater than this shall we adduce to make the matter clear to you? If you disbelieve the Master, how will you, tell me, believe your fellow-servant?

[§3. The key of knowledge]
But what shall I say to those who want to enjoy a reputation, and be made priests and prelates and abbots, who want to receive the confidence of others' thoughts, and who say that they are worthy of the task of binding and loosing? (Matt. 16: 19, 18: 18)? When I see that they know nothing of the necessary and divine things, nor teach these things to others nor lead them to the light of knowledge, what else is it but what Christ says to the Pharisees and lawyers: "Woe to you lawyers! For you have taken away the key of knowledge; you did not enter yourselves, and you hindered those who were entering" (Luke 11: 52). But what is the key of knowledge other than the grace of the Holy Spirit given through faith? In very truth it produces knowledge and understanding through illumination and opens our closed and veiled mind (cf. Luke 24: 45) through many parables and symbols, as I have told you, as well as by clear proofs.

[§4. The key, the door, and the house]
I will tell you yet again, the door is the Son, for, says He, "I am the door" (John 10: 7, 9). The key of the door is the Holy Spirit, for He says, "Receive the Holy Spirit. If you forgive the sins of any, they are forgiven; if you retain the sins of any, they are retained" (John 20: 22–3). The house is the Father, for "in My Father's house are many mansions" (John 14: 2). Pay careful attention, therefore, to the spiritual sense of the passage. Unless the key opens – as He says, "To him the porter opens" (John 10: 3) the door is not opened. But if the door is not opened, no one enters into the Father's house, for Christ says, "No one comes to the Father, but by Me" (John 14: 6).

[§5. The key – symbol of the Holy Spirit]
But that the Holy Spirit first opens our minds and teaches us the things concerning the Father and Son, He Himself again said, "When He, the Spirit of truth comes,

who proceeds from the Father, He will bear witness to Me (John 15: 25), and will guide you into all the truth" (John 16: 13). Do you see how through the Spirit, or, rather, in the Spirit, the Father and the Son are made known inseparably? Again He says, "If I do not go away, the Paraclete will not come to you (John 16: 7). But when He comes, He will bring all things to your remembrance," and again, "If you love Me, you will keep My commandments; and I will pray to the Father, and He will give you another Paraclete, to be with you forever, even the Spirit of truth" (John 14: 15ff.). A little later He says, "In that day" – that is, when the Holy Spirit comes to you – "you will know that I am in the Father, and you in Me, and I in you" (John 14: 20), and again, "John baptized with water, but you shall be baptized with the Holy Spirit" (Acts 1: 5). Rightly so, for unless one is baptized with the Holy Spirit, he does not become a son of God or a fellow-heir with Christ (cf. Rom. 8: 17). He also says to Peter, "I will give you the keys of the kingdom of heaven" (Matt. 16: 19), not keys of bronze or iron, but keys worthy of that house. What is the nature of that house? Listen to Paul as he speaks in the epistle to Timothy, "In the presence of God who gives life to all things, and of Christ Jesus" (1 Tim. 6: 13) I charge you," and a little later, "The blessed and only Sovereign, the King of kings and Lord of lords, who alone has immortality and dwells in unapproachable light" (1 Tim. 6: 15–16). For if, as He says, the house is unapproachable, it is clear that the door of the house is light and is itself unapproachable. But if you speak of one thing as being approachable and the other as unapproachable, that which is approachable will be consumed by that which is not, nor will the key ever be able to open it, unless it too is unapproachable and partakes of the same nature, but will be burned up by the door or door by the house, and so will become equally inaccessible to all. Or rather, it is our faith that will be destroyed, in that the Trinity is divided into that which is accessible and that which is not, into greater or less.

But beware as you hear these things, that you do not take the images of literal houses and doors and permit the physical pattern to be imprinted on your minds, so that your soul falls into doubt and blasphemy. You must reflect on all these images in a proper way, in a manner that befits God, if you are able, according to the rule and standard of the spiritual interpretation, and so you will find the right interpretation of them all. But if you are incapable of so understanding them in a manner that befits God, then receive them by mere faith and refuse all curious inquiry.

[§6. The dwelling of God]

The Holy Ghost is spoken of as a key because through Him and in Him we are first enlightened in mind. We are purified and illuminated with the light of knowledge; we are baptized from on high and born anew (cf. John 3: 3, 5) and made into children of God. As Paul says, "The Spirit Himself intercedes for us with sighs too deep for words" (Rom. 8. 26), and again, "God has given His Spirit in our hearts, crying, 'Abba!, Father!'" (Gal. 4: 6). This indicates to us that the door is light; the door shows us that He who dwells in the house is Himself unapproachable light (1 Tim. 6: 16). He who dwells therein is no other than God, His house is nothing else but light. Likewise the light of the Godhead and God are not two different things. He is one and the same, the house and He who dwells in it, just as the light and God are the same. In theological terms we use the term *house* of the Son, even as we use it of the Father, for He says, "Thou, O Father, art in Me, and I in them, and they in Me, and I, O Father, in Thee, that we may be One" (cf. John 17: 21, 23). Similarly, the Spirit says, "I will live in them and move among them" (2 Cor. 6: 16). "I and the Father will come and make our home with him" (John 14: 23). This He says through the Spirit, as Paul says, "Now the Lord is the Spirit" (2 Cor. 3: 17). If, then, the Lord is the Spirit, and the Father is in Him and He is in Him, and we likewise are in Him, then He is with God the Father and God is in Him.

[§7. The Persons in the Trinity]

If there is need to state anything more precisely, that which the One is, the other Two are as well. For the Three are in the same (cf. 1 John 5: 8) and are thought of as one Essence and Nature and Kingship. If a name is attributed to One, it is by nature applied to the others, with the exception of the terms *Father, Son,* and *Holy Ghost,* or the terms *beget, begotten,* and *proceeding,* for these alone indisputably apply to the Holy Trinity by nature and in distinctive fashion. As for an interchange of names, or their reversal, or their change, that we are forbidden to think or speak about. These terms characterize the three Persons, so that in this way we cannot place the Son before the Father nor the Holy Ghost before the Son. We must speak of them together as "Father, Son, and Holy Ghost," without the slightest difference of duration or time between them. The Son is begotten and the Spirit proceeds simultaneously with the Father's existence.

[§8. The unity of the divine nature]

In all other cases, the same name or comparison is attributed to each Person by Himself as well as to all Three together. So, if you speak of "light" (1 John 5: 8), then both each Person is light and the Three are one light; if you speak of "eternal life," so each of Them is likewise, the Son, the Spirit, and the Father, and the Three are one life. So God the Father is Spirit (cf. John 4: 24), and the Spirit is the Lord (2 Cor. 3: 17), and the Holy Spirit is God. Each Person is God by Himself and together the Three are one God. Each One is Lord and the Three are Lord. There is one God who is above all (Rom. 9: 5), Creator of all things; each One is that by Himself, and they are one God and Maker of all things. The Old Testament also says, "In the beginning God created heaven and earth. And God said, 'Let there be light,' and there was light" (Gen. 1: 1, 3). Thus the expression gives us to understand about the Father. When David says, "By the word of the Lord were the heavens made," we understand that this applies to the Son, "and all the host of them by the breath of His mouth" (Ps. 32: 6), we consider to be spoken of the Holy Ghost.

As for John, the "son of thunder" (Mark 3: 17), he says in the Gospels, "In the beginning was the Word, and the Word was with God" – that is the Father, "and the Word was God" – that is, the Son. "All things were made by Him, and without Him was nothing made that was made" (John 1: 1, 3).

[§9. Obtaining the true knowledge of God]

I beseech you therefore, you who bear the name of children of God (1 John 3: 1) and who think that you are Christians, learn these things! You priests and monks teach others with vain words and think that you are rulers – but falsely! Ask your elders and high priests, gather yourselves together in the love of God, and first seek to learn and experience these things in fact, and then have the will to see this and by experience become like God. Be anxious not merely to act a play and wear the garment thereof and so to approach apostolic dignities. Otherwise, as you in your imperfection rush to rule over others, before acquiring the knowledge of the mysteries of God, you will hear these words, "Woe to those who are wise in their own eyes, and shrewd in their own sight! Woe to those who put darkness for light and light for darkness!" (Isa. 5: 21, 20).

So I entreat you all, brethren in Christ, first to lay a good foundation (cf. Heb. 6: 1) of humility as you build up virtues. Then through training in godliness (1 Tim. 4: 7) raise the house (cf. Matt. 7: 24–5) of the knowledge of the mysteries of God (cf. Matt. 13: 11; Luke 8: 10) and so be enlightened by the divine light and see God with the purified eye of the heart (cf. Matt. 5: 8), as far as it is possible for us men. Then become initiated more perfectly into the mysteries of the kingdom of heaven (cf. Matt. 13: 11). Thus you will proceed from this knowledge, which is given from on high by the Father of lights (Jas. 1: 17), to the word of teaching (cf. Rom. 12: 7; 1 Tim. 4: 6) that you may instruct your neighbors "what is the will of God, what is good and acceptable and perfect" (Rom. 12: 2). Thus through our teaching we will bring "a people of His own" (Titus 2: 14) to God, who by His Holy Spirit has appointed us teachers of His Church, so that we will not be cast out from Christ's wedding feast as contemptuous and without a wedding garment (Matt. 20: 10ff.). Rather, as wise stewards (Luke 12: 42) who have duly dispensed the word of teaching among our fellow-servants, and above that duly ordered our own lives, may we enter in to Him without hindrance in the brightness of our lives and of heavenly knowledge. So may we be luminous and filled with the Holy Spirit and reign with Christ (2 Tim. 2: 12), as fellow-heirs with Him of that which belongs to the kingdom of God the Father in the Holy Ghost, the ever-living and immortal Fountain and Life. To him are due all glory, honor, and worship, now and ever, and to ages of ages. Amen.

Notes

1 *Discourses*, XXXII, p. 336.
2 *Discourses*, XXII, p. 245.
3 For nineteenth- and twentieth-century descriptions, see *The Way of a Pilgrim* (anonymous, in several editions) and Irénée Hausherr, *Hésychasme et Prière* (Rome: Orientalia Christiana Analecta, 1966).
4 Nicetas Stethatos, the biographer of Symeon, followed by other ancient editors, identified the "young man" in question with Symeon himself, and does not hesitate to incorporate the data in his life of Symeon. His spiritual father would thus be Symeon the Pious. There are some problems about the details. It would appear that the vision described in Catechesis

22 [§3] was experienced by Symeon while he was still a layman aged twenty, while this vision took place when Symeon had entered the monastery of Studion some eight years later, in 977. Stethatos's own explanation, . . . that these were two separate experiences, would seem to be most satisfactory, though it does not eliminate all difficulties.

5   i.e., toward the center of Constantinople, since the monastery of Studios was on its western outskirts.

6   The hymn "Holy God, Holy Mighty, Holy Immortal: have mercy upon us," one of the most frequently used forms of prayer in the Orthodox Church, occurring in the Divine Liturgy and the offices as well as in private devotion.

27

John Ruusbroec,
from The Spiritual Espousals

John Ruusbroec (1293–1381), a Dutch theologian and mystic, wrote treatises on the spiritual life developing trinitarian doctrines of deification, or how God joins the human being to the triune life. The content of the doctrines derives from Augustinian and Thomistic accounts, but Ruusbroec's versions differ in their remarkable vividness of tone. In particular, they use traditional designations of the Spirit as "love" and "fire" to extraordinary effect, and extend traditional exegesis of the Song of Songs as an allegory of the union of God and the soul. The pressure of Song exegesis, together with Jesus' parables comparing the king-dom of God to a wedding feast, have prompted many writers (including, in the present volume, John of the Cross, Matthias Scheeben, Hans von Balthasar, Adrienne von Speyr, Sarah Coakley, myself, and a host of others) to deploy metaphors of eros and marriage to explicate the Trinity, or its relation to the soul, or both. Others, on the other hand (Augustine and Richard of St Victor) warn *against* versions on the model of parent-parent-child, fearing that Christianity might turn into a fertility cult. In Ruusbroec, the Holy Spirit is in one place the priest, in another the dowry, and more often the fervor of the marriage.

"The nature of Love is to give and take," comments Rik van Nieuwenhove, in *Jan van Ruusbroec, Mystical Theologian of the Trinity*:

> and therefore we have to return to God in faith and works the love and grace we have received. [This return is the fruit of love, not the necessity of obligation.] Hereby a dynamic is generated of giving in order to enable the other to return the gift, and so forth, in a movement that is patterned according to the intra-trinitarian divine life in which the Spirit/Love is an active principle of love: the Spirit does not just "receive" the love of the Father and the Son but "returns" it and is thus the active principle of the divine *regiratio* whereby the divine Persons flow back into their shared unity . . . This is Ruusbroec's central intuition, which he elaborates in almost each area of his theology.[1]

John Ruusbroec, *The Spiritual Espousals and Other Works*, trans. and with an Introduction by James A. Wiseman (New York: Paulist Press, 1985), pp. 41–2, 75, 77, 78–81, 113–16.

from **The Spiritual Espousals**

John Ruusbroec

Prologue

"See, the bridegroom is coming. Go out to meet him" (Matt. 25: 6). These words, written for us by St. Matthew the Evangelist, were spoken by Christ to his disciples and to all persons in the parable of the virgins. The Bridegroom is Christ and human nature is the bride, whom God created according to his own image and likeness. In the beginning he placed his bride in the noblest place on earth, that is, Paradise. He subordinated all other creatures to her, adorned her with grace, and gave her a commandment so that through obedience to it she might deserve to be made firm and steadfast with her Bridegroom in eternal faithfulness and so never fall into any adversity or any sin. But then came an evildoer, the enemy from hell, who in his jealousy assumed the form of a cunning serpent and deceived the woman. They both then deceived the man, in whom human nature existed in its entirety. Thus did the enemy seduce human nature, God's bride, through deceitful counsel. Poor and wretched, she was banished to a strange land and was there captured and oppressed and beset by her enemies in such a way that it seemed she would never be able to return to her homeland or attain reconciliation.

But when it seemed to God that the right time had come and he took pity on his beloved in her suffering, he sent his only-begotten Son to earth into a magnificent palace and a glorious temple, that is, into the body of the glorious Virgin Mary. There the Son wedded this bride, our nature, and united her with his own person through the purest blood of the noble virgin. The priest who witnessed the bride's marriage was the Holy Spirit. . . .

Therefore Christ, the Master of truth, says, "See, the bridegroom is coming. Go out to meet him." Through these words Christ our Lover teaches us four things. First of all he gives a command, when he says, "See." Those who remain blind and ignore this command are all damned. Secondly, he reveals to us what we are to see, namely, the coming of the Bridegroom. Thirdly, he tells us what we are to do, when he says, "Go out." Fourthly, when he says "to meet him," he reveals to us the reward and end or our entire activity and our entire life, namely, a loving meeting with the Bridegroom.

"See"

. . .

Now the grace which flows forth from God is an interior impulse or urging of the Holy Spirit which drives our own spirit from within and urges it out toward all the virtues. This grace flows from within, not from without, for God is more interior to us than we are to ourselves,[2] and his interior urging and working within us, whether done naturally or supernaturally, is nearer and more intimate to us than are our own works. For this reason God works in us from within outward, whereas all creatures work from without inward. Grace and all God's gifts and inspirations thus come from within, in the unity of our spirit, and not from without, in the imagination by means of sensible images.

. . .

"The Bridegroom is coming."

. . .

The first coming of Christ in exercises full of desire is an interiorly felt impulse of the Holy Spirit which urges and impels us toward all the virtues. . . .

In his interior coming and through the power of his Spirit, Christ, the glorious sun and divine resplendence, enlightens, shines through, and enkindles the heart which is free, together with all the powers of the soul. This is the first effect of his interior coming in exercises full of desire. Just as the power and nature of fire enkindle material which is ready to be set aflame, so does Christ with the ardent heat of his interior coming enkindle the heart which is ready, free, and uplifted. At this coming he says, "Go out, through exercises which are in accord with this coming."

The effects of this coming and our response to it
This heat gives rise to unity in our heart, for we can attain true unity only if the Spirit of God enkindles his fire in our heart. This fire unifies all the things that it can master and transform, making them like itself. Unity means that a person feels interiorly gathered together with all his powers in the unity of his heart. Unity produces interior peace and restfulness of heart, and is a bond which draws together body and soul, heart and senses, and all the exterior and interior powers, enveloping them in the unity of love.

This unity produces interior fervor, for only a person who has been gathered together in unity can be interiorly fervent. Interior fervor means that a person is turned within to his own heart, so that he might understand and experience the interior working and inspirations of God. Interior fervor is a perceptible fire of love which God's Spirit has enkindled and fanned to a flame. Such fervor burns, drives, and urges a person from within in such a way that he does not know whence it comes or what is happening to him.

Interior fervor gives rise to a felt affection which penetrates a person's heart and the concupiscible power of the soul. Only a person who is interiorly fervent can have this affection, which is characterized by desire and by the perceptible savor which it produces in the heart. Felt affection and love consists in a desire, a taste, and a yearning which a person feels for God as an eternal good which includes all other goods. Felt affection lets go of all creatures as regards enjoying them, though not as regards making use of the them to the degree necessary. Fervent affection feels itself touched from within by an eternal love to which it must always be devoted. Fervent affection easily renounces and disdains all things so that it might obtain what it loves.

. . .

This fervent devotion gives rise to thanksgiving, for no one can thank and praise God so well as a person who is fervent and devout. It is right that we should thank and praise God, for he has created us as rational beings and has ordained that heaven and earth and the angels should serve us. Because of our sins he became a human being, teaching us, living for us, and showing us the way. He served us in a humble form, suffered an ignominious death for our sake, and promised us his eternal kingdom, where he himself will be our reward and our servant. He spared us in our sins and has fully forgiven us, even as he will forgive us in the future. He has poured his grace and his love into our souls and wishes to abide in us and with us for eternity. He has visited us with his noble sacraments in accordance with our needs and will continue to do so all the days of our lives. He has left us his body and blood to be our food and drink according to the hunger and desire of each of us. He has placed before us nature, Scripture, and all creatures to be a mirror and example in which we might observe and learn how to turn all our works into virtues. He has given us health, strength, and power, and has sometimes sent us sickness for our own good. He has provided for our exterior necessities and has laid within us the foundation of interior peace and tranquility. He has seen to it that we bear Christian names and that we have been born of Christian parents. For all these things we should thank God here on earth, so that we might eternally thank him in heaven.

. . .

Fervent thanksgiving and praise give rise to a twofold pain of heart and torment of desire. The first of these is that a person realizes that he is deficient in thanking, praising, honoring, and serving God, and the other is that he does not advance as much as he would like in charity, virtue, fidelity, and perfect behavior so as to be worthy of thanking, praising, and serving God as he deserves. This is the second pain. Together they are both the root and the fruit, the beginning of all interior virtues. The interior sorrow and pain which arise from our deficiencies in virtue and in praise of God constitute the highest activity in this first mode of interior exercise, and hereby this mode comes to its perfection.

. . . Consider now a comparison which will show what this exercise is like. When natural fire has, by means of its heat and its power, brought water or some other liquid to a boil, that is its highest activity. The water then reverses direction and falls back down to the bottom, where it is again raised up to the same boiling activity through the power of the fire, in such a way that the fire is constantly exerting its force and the water is constantly boiling. The interior fire of the Holy Spirit works in the same way. It drives, urges, and impels the heart and all the powers of the soul up to the boiling point, that is, up to the giving of thanks and praise to God in the way I have already described. Then a person falls back down to the same ground where the Spirit of God is aflame, so that the fire of love is constantly burning and a person's heart is constantly thanking and praising in word and deed and yet constantly remaining in humble lowliness, for such a person considers what he should do and would like to do to be something great and what he actually does to be something small.

. . .

The third coming, into the unity of the Spirit

The sublime, super-essential Unity of the divine nature, where the Father and the Son possess their nature in the unity of the Holy Spirit, lies in the bare, essential being of our spirit, beyond the comprehension and understanding of all our powers. In this sublime stillness God transcends every creature that is enlightened by a merely created light. This sublime Unity of the divine nature is both living and fruitful, for out of this same Unity the eternal Word is ceaselessly begotten of the Father. Through this birth the Father knows the Son and all things in the Son, and the Son knows the Father and all things in the Father, for they are one simple nature. From this mutual contemplation of the Father and the Son in eternal splendor there issues forth an eternal sense of well-being, a fathomless love, which is the Holy Spirit. By means of the Holy Spirit and of the eternal Wisdom, God inclines himself to every creature in distinct ways, bestowing gifts upon each one and enkindling each one in love according to his nobility and according to the state in which he has been placed and destined through his practice of virtue and through God's eternal providence. All good spirits in heaven and on earth are hereby moved to the practice of virtue and to righteousness.

. . .

. . . God's interior stirring and touch make us hunger and strive, for the Spirit of God is pursuing our spirit. The more there is of the touch, the more there is of the hunger and striving. This is a life of love at the highest level of its activity, above reason and understanding, for reason can here neither give love nor take it away, since our love has been touched by divine love. In my opinion, from this time on there can never again be any separation from God. God's touch within us, as far as we experience it, and our striving in love are both created and creaturely, and for this reason they can grow and increase as long as we live.

In this storm of love two spirits struggle – the Spirit of God and our spirit. God, by means of the Holy Spirit, inclines himself toward us, and we are thereby touched in love; our spirit, by means of God's activity and the amorous power, impels and inclines us toward God, and thereby God is touched. From these two movements there arises the struggle of love, for in this most profound meeting, in this most intimate and ardent encounter, each spirit is wounded by love. These two spirits, that is, our spirit and God's Spirit, cast a radiant light upon one another and each reveals to the other its countenance. This makes the two spirits incessantly strive after one another in love. Each demands of the other what it is, and each offers to the other and invites it to accept what it is. This makes these loving spirits lose themselves in one another. God's touch and his giving of himself, together with our striving in love and our giving of ourselves in return – this is what sets love on a firm foundation. This flux and reflux make the spring of love overflow, so that God's touch and our striving in love become a single love. Here a person becomes so possessed by love that he must forget both himself and God and know nothing but love. In this way the spirit is consumed in the fire of love and enters so deeply into God's touch that it is overcome in all its striving and comes to nought in all its works. It transcends its activity and itself becomes love above and beyond all exercises of devotion. It possesses the inmost part of its creatureliness above all virtue, there where all creaturely activity begins and ends. This is love in itself, the foundation and ground of all the virtues.

Now our spirit and this love are both living and fruitful in virtues, and for this reason the powers cannot simply remain in the unity of the spirit. God's incomprehensible resplendence and his fathomless love hover above the spirit and from there touch the amorous power, and at this the spirit falls back into its activity, this time in a more sublime and fervent striving than ever before. The more fervent and noble the spirit, the faster will it transcend its activity and come to nought in love; then it falls back into new works. This is a heavenly way of life. In its craving, the spirit constantly intends to consume and devour God, but in fact it remains itself swallowed up in God's touch, becomes unable to proceed in all its activity, and itself becomes love above all works. In the unity of the spirit there is a union of the higher powers, and here grace and love abide essentially, above works, for this is the source of charity and all the virtues. Here there is an eternal flowing out in charity and in virtues, and an eternal movement inward marked by an interior hunger for savoring God, and an eternal abiding in simple, undifferentiated love.

All this is in a creaturely manner and beneath God. This is the most interior exercise a person can practice when enlightened by created light, whether in heaven or on earth; above this is only the contemplative life, which is lived in the divine light and after God's own manner. In this exercise a person cannot go astray or be deceived. It begins here in grace and will last eternally in glory.

Notes

1 Rik van Nieuwenhove, *Jan van Ruusbroec* (Notre Dame, IN: Notre Dame University Press, 2003), p. 99.
2 The expression "more interior to us than we are to ourselves" is reminiscent of St Augustine's well-known phrase *interior intimo meo*: God is "deeper within me than my own inmost being" (*Confessions* 3.6).

28

St John of the Cross,
from "The Inhalation of the
Air," in The Spiritual Canticle

St John of the Cross (1542–91), Carmelite reformer and Spanish mystic, composed and commented in prose upon his own poetry, in which he paraphrased the Song of Songs. This selection comes from John's prose commentary on the phrase "the inhalation of the air" from his *Spiritual Canticle*. Like Song commentaries generally, John's poem is a love-dialogue between God and the Soul. In this passage, the Holy Spirit teaches the soul to breathe the divine atmosphere shared by the Father and the Son, which is itself the Holy Spirit. In a metaphor unavailable to John, it is almost as if the Holy Spirit breathes Himself into the soul in a mouth-to-mouth resuscitation. The soul's breathing of the Spirit by the Spirit transports the soul into the divine atmosphere, the divine milieu, the divine life, and becomes a figure for deification.

from The Inhalation of the Air, in *The Spiritual Canticle*

St John of the Cross

This breathing in of the air is a disposition, the soul is saying, that God will give her there in the partaking of the Holy Spirit. This Spirit, by breathing with her His divine breath all of a sudden catches up the soul and refashions and disposes her so that she should catch her breath in God with the same breathing of love that the Father breathes with the Son and the Son with the Father. That breathing is the Holy Spirit Himself, who is breathing for her in the Father and the Son to unite

I owe the suggestion of this passage from *The Spiritual Canticle* to Sarah Coakley. The translation is my own. In making it from John's original Spanish, I found the version in Hans Urs von Balthasar, *Theo-Drama V: The Last Act*, trans. Graham Harrison (San Francisco: Ignatius Press, 1998), p. 432, very suggestive – even though (or just because) that version had passed through German on the way from Spanish to English.

her to them by refashioning her. For this refashioning would hardly be genuine and complete were the soul not transformed tellingly and manifestly into the three Persons of the Most Holy Trinity. And this breathing of the Holy Spirit into the soul, with which God refashions her into Himself, is such a sudden, delicate, and profound delight to her, that there is no mortal tongue to tell it, nor any human understanding in position to reach anything of it. For even the temporal transformation that accompanies the soul's partaking cannot be spoken, since the soul, united with and refashioned into God, breathes in God to God the same divine breath that God – she becoming transformed into Him – breathes in Himself for her.

. . .

And it is not to be regarded as impossible that the soul can do something so sublime, by way of participation, as to breathe in God as God breathes into her. For, given that God has the kindness to unite her into the Most Holy Trinity, in which he makes the soul deiform and God by participation, is it any more incredible that she should also work her own work of understanding, knowledge, and love? or, better, that she should have it worked for her in the Trinity together with her, as that the Trinity Itself should do it? But God works it in the very soul as partaken and shared, because this is to become transformed into the three Persons in power and wisdom and love. In this the soul is likened to God, and so that this could come to pass, He created her to His image and likeness.

And how this could be, there is nothing more to know or able to be said, without telling how the Son of God raised us up to this exalted estate and merited for us this high position of being able to be sons of God; and so He asked it of the Father Himself, according to St John, saying, "Father, I want those you have given me to be where I am, and those to be with me and to see the glory you have given me" [John 17: 24], which is to say: that they do by participation in us the very same work that I do by nature, which is breathe the Holy Spirit. And he says further, "But I do not pray, Father, only for these present, but also for those who by their teaching come to believe in me, that all of them would be one in the way that you, Father, are in Me and I in You, so that they may be one, as We are one. I in them, and You in Me, in order that they may be perfected in one, so that the world should know that You sent Me and loved them as You loved Me" [John 17: 20–3]. Which is sharing with them the same love as with the Son, although not naturally as with the Son, but, as we have said, by the unity and refashioning of love. Nor is it to be understood that the Son asks the Father that the saints be one by essence or nature, as the Father and the Son are, but that they become one in the unity of love. Whence souls enjoy these goods by participation which he has by nature, for which reason truly they are gods by participation, likened to God, and His companions. Whence St Peter says, "Grace and peace be complete and perfect in you in knowing God and Jesus Christ our Lord, so that every divine capacity is given to us for life and in compassion, by the acquaintance with the One Who calls us with His proper glory and power, by which He gives us very great and precious promises, in order that by these things we may be made partakers of the divine nature" [2 Pet. 1: 2–4]. So far they are the words of St Peter, which clearly mean that the soul will participate in God Himself, that she will be working in Him companionably with Him the work of the Holy Trinity in the way we have said, on account of the substantial union between the soul and God. And although it will be perfectly completed in the next life, already in this one, when the soul arrives at the perfected state that we have been saying the soul does reach here, she is extended a great scent and savor of it in the way that we are saying, although, as we have said, it cannot be expressed.

Oh, souls created and called to such great things, what are you doing? What are you waiting for? Our pretensions are embarrassments and our possessions are miseries. O miserable blindness of the sons of Adam, blind for so great a light and deaf for such great voices, not seeing that the more you seek greatness and glory the more you remain miserable and small, made ignorant and unworthy of such great goods!

29

Matthias Scheeben,
[The Spirit as Bride] in
A Manual of Catholic
Theology

Matthias Scheeben (1835–88), a Catholic mystic and dogmatician who taught theology in an episcopal seminary at Cologne, presents here a remarkable piece of trinitarian speculation, combining the traditions of regarding the Spirit as feminine with those of the Father and the Son. German Romantics from Goethe and Schleiermacher on played with eternal masculines and feminines in a way that later readers have hardly known what to do with. Similar uses of an eternal feminine in theology passed from Schelling into Russian sophiology (Soloviev, Bulgakov), where too, for better and worse, a feminine principle in the Godhead provides a creative ground and becomes "incarnate" in Mary. The tone if not the content of this example may strike some contemporary readers as bizarre.

And yet, if the surrounding culture interpreted masculine and feminine as complementary essences, and theological traditions assign male characters to the "Father" and the "Son," while making a feminine Spirit available in Semitic languages, then the question becomes not "what was he thinking?" but why wasn't there more of this sort of thing?[1] What were the mostly unspoken controls that kept divine brides down? One control was undoubtedly the strictures against a trinitarian fertility cult, here explicitly avoided. Another control was undoubtedly a misogynist distaste for ascribing any feminine characteristics to God at all. A third control would have been the difference in gender rhetorics between the medieval West and the German and Russian Romantics: their medieval predecessors did not essentialize gender in God and assign it modally to different

Matthias Scheeben, *A Manual of Catholic Theology Based on Scheeben's "Dogmatik,"* 3rd, rev. edn., by Joseph Wilhelm and Thomas B. Scannell (London: Kegan Paul; New York: Benziger Brothers, 1906), pp. 333–6. The work of Wilhelm and Scannell was to translate, edit, abridge, and paraphrase rather than to compose anything new. I owe my attention to Scheeben to Lewis Ayres.

persons, but delighted to *bend* gender by assigning a womb to the Father or breast milk to Jesus.[2] Nineteenth-century Romantics innovated in segregating female characteristics in the Spirit. The problem, continued in first-wave twentieth-century feminisms, caused the Persons of God to embody rather than transcend a gender. The way the Romantics did it put the eternal feminine on such a pedestal as to give stylites a bad name.

[The Spirit as Bride] in *A Manual of Catholic Theology* based on Scheeben's *Dogmatik*

Matthias Scheeben

Although no human person furnishes an adequate analogue for the Third Person in the Blessed Trinity, still we can point to one who approaches as near as the diversity between Divine and human nature allows. This human person is none other than the bride, who, as spouse and mother, stands between father and son in the communication and representation of human nature, and is as essentially the third member of the human community, or the connecting link between father and son, as the Holy Ghost is the Third Person in the Divinity.

1.   The analogy is easily understood if the bride be considered in her ideal, ethical position in the human family, as wife and mother. Here she stands out as the representative of the union of father and son; as the focus in which the mutual love of father and son centres; as love personified and as the soul of the family. The differences arising from the diversity of Divine and human nature are: (a) In the Trinity the Personified Love is only a bond – not a mediator – between Father and Son, and consequently, is not the mother of the Son. (b) The Person of Love cannot be considered as the wife of the Father, because this Person is not a co-principle with Him, but only proceeds from Him. (c) The Person of Love stands in the same relation to the Son as to the Father; hence, as regards origin, the Son comes between the Father and the Substantial Love of Both. The intermediate position of the human mother between principle and product; her function of nourishing, fostering, cherishing, and quickening, and of being the centre where the love of father and child meet, find their analogue in the relations of the Holy Ghost to the external products of Father and Son, viz. to created natures.

2.   Considering the wide differences between the "Person of Love" in God and in mankind, human names cannot be unreservedly applied to the Holy Ghost. The names "mother" or "wife" must be excluded altogether; the name "bride" might be applied in the restricted sense that the Holy Ghost is the original and bridal partner of Father and Son. He is a bridal partner, because in virtue of their love He constitutes a substantial unity with them; He is a virginal partner, because He is with Father and Son, not as supplying a want of their nature, but as a Gift; He is the bridal partner of Both, because He bears the same relationship of origin to the Father and to the Son.

3.   The constituents of the analogy in question are sufficiently expressed by the name "Holy Ghost" (which in Hebrew is of the feminine gender, *ruach*, like *anima* in Latin), inasmuch as it designates the Third Person of the Trinity precisely as the focus of a mutual love that is purely spiritual, chaste, and virginal. We may further remark that the name *Holy* Ghost is derived from the name Ghost common to the other Two Persons, just as the name Eve, with respect to her relationship of origin, was derived from that of man (Gen. ii. 23). Moreover, the proper name which Adam gave to the wife taken from his side to signify her maternal character, is not only analogous in construction, but quite synonymous with the name Ghost; for Eve (*Chava*) signifies life, or, more properly, the outflowing life, the breath, i.e., that which, in analogy with breath, quickens and fosters by its warmth. And as herein is expressed the ideal essence of the universal mothership of the first woman ("And Adam called the name of his wife Eve, because she was the mother of all the living"), so also it expresses the characteristic of the Holy Ghost as principle of all the life of creation; wherefore also the Holy Ghost in this respect is called the "Fostering Spirit."

This analogy is completed by the origin of the first woman, an origin different from generation but similar to the origin of the Holy Ghost, and symbolizing the origin of the mystic bride of God. For the "taking" of Eve from the side of Adam, that is, from his heart, can only signify an origin by loving donation on the part of Adam, although this donation only gave the matter which, by the supernatural intervention of God, was endowed with life. Now, according to all the fathers, the origin of Eve was the type of the origin of the Church, the virginal bride of Christ, from the side of her Bridegroom, nay, from His very Heart, and by virtue of His own vital force through the effusion of His life's Blood. But, on the other hand, the effusion of the Blood of Christ being the vehicle and the symbol of the effusion of the Holy Ghost, being the bride of Christ, we have here an illustration of the character of the eternal procession of the Holy Ghost Himself, which bears the closest relation to the emission of the breath from the heart.

4.   In order to preserve all the force of this human analogy, and, at the same time, to do away with its inherent imperfections, and to point out the elements which do not appear in it, Revelation itself represents the Holy Ghost, with regard to this origin and position, under the symbol of an animal being, viz. the Dove. He appeared in the form of a dove on the Jordan (Matt. iii. 16), but already in the narrative of creation (Gen. i. 2) this form is hinted at. The dove, in general, is the symbol of love and fidelity, especially of chaste, meek, patient, and innocent love, and so it illustrates nearly all the attributes of the Spirit of Wisdom, described in Wisd. vii., that is, in one word, His Holiness. But the Divine Dove represents also the Holy Ghost as the Spirit of God – that is, as the Spirit proceeding from Father and Son and uniting Them. Like a dove, the Holy Ghost ascends from the heart of Father and Son, whilst in Him they breathe their Love and Life or Soul; and, like a dove, with outspread wings and quiescent motion, He hovers over them, crowning and completing their union, and manifesting by His sigh the infinite felicity and holiness of Their love. In short, this image shows the Holy Ghost as the hypostatic "Kiss," "Embrace," and "Sigh" of the Father and the Son, that is, in His character of Their virginal Bride.

The same image also represents the Holy Ghost in His relation of "Virginal Mother" to creatures. As a dove He descends from the heart of God upon the creature, bringing down with Him the Divine Love and its gifts, penetrating creatures with His warming, quickening, and refreshing fire, establishing the most intimate relations between God and them, and being Himself the pledge of the Love which sends Him and of the love which He inspires; and lastly, in the supernatural order, penetrating into the creature as into His temple to such a degree that the creature in its turn becomes the virginal bride of God and the virginal mother of life in others, and thus receives itself the name of dove – a name applied especially to the Blessed Virgin Mary, the Church, and the virgins of Christ, and generally to all pious souls (Canticles/Song of Songs ii. 10).

Notes

1 For commentary on something at least somewhat similar, see Alexander Golitzin, "Adam, Eve, and Seth: Pneumatological Reflections on an Unusual Image in Gregory of Nazianzus's 'Fifth Theological Oration,'" *Anglican Theological Review* 83 (2001), pp. 537–46.

2 The Womb of the Father derives from christological readings of Ps. 110: 2, "out of my womb I bore you" in the Vulgate, prominent in Augustine's *Enarrationes in Psalmos* 109.10 and canonized at the Council of Toledo in 675. For traditions of Jesus' breast milk, see Caroline Walker Bynum, "Jesus as Mother and Abbot as Mother: Some Themes in Twelfth-Century Cistercian Writing," in *Jesus as Mother: Studies in the Spirituality of the High Middle Ages* (Berkeley, CA: University of California Press, 1982), pp. 110–69. For a critique of nineteenth-century German essentializing of the feminine, see Marilyn Chapin Massey, *Feminine Soul: The Fate of an Ideal* (Boston: Beacon, 1985). For gender-bending in theological context, see Eugene F. Rogers, Jr., "Annunciation," in *After the Spirit: A Constructive Pneumatology from Resources outside the Modern West* (Grand Rapids, MI: Eerdmans, 2005; London: SCM Press, 2006), pp. 98–134.

30

Adrienne von Speyr,
from "Prayer in the Trinity"

Adrienne von Speyr was a twentieth-century mystic whose spiritual director was Hans Urs von Balthasar. One pattern of mystical experience shares the suffering of Christ on Good Friday. The "normal" thing for such a mystic is to go into a trance at noon and come out at three, the time when Jesus was hanging on the cross. But von Speyr didn't come out of the trance until Easter morning, which meant, in her case, that she experienced the descent into hell on Holy Saturday.

But this essay is not about that. Rather, it applies trinitarian principles to the passage in Romans 8 that keeps coming up among authors in this volume. According to some trinitarian logics – including hers – if the Persons of the Trinity do something in the world, that's because their activity in the world reflects their relations among themselves in the Trinity. So if the Holy Spirit prays for human beings, teaching them to take on the identity of the Son and call God "Father," then what does that mean about the Trinity's inner life? It means that the Persons of the Trinity pray to one another also among themselves.

This answers a conundrum about human prayer. How can human beings pray "hard enough" for their prayer to reach up to God? Why shouldn't human words simply hit the ceiling and bounce back down again? What if only God's own words are high enough or adequate enough for God? Von Speyr's account reveals such worries to be misplaced. Prayer is not fundamentally a human activity, but a *divine* activity – the speech and Word of God to God – in which God invites human beings to share. The prayer of the Trinity catches human beings up into what *God* is doing, so that the weakness and finitude of human activity becomes no barrier to prayer.

Adrienne von Speyr, "Prayer in the Trinity," in *The World of Prayer* (San Francisco: Ignatius, 1985), pp. 28–37, 40–2, 57–67, 69–72.

from **Prayer in the Trinity**

Adrienne von Speyr

Expectation and fulfillment

Prayer has no beginning because Father, Son and Spirit have been in conversation from all eternity, united in an eternal expectation and an eternal decision. The Father possesses one Word – the Son. The Son is his Word, and the Father is continually bringing forth this one Word, who is always being fulfilled in him and in the Spirit. All that the Father intends, thinks and utters is always expressed in the Son as Word, intelligible and understood. And the Word of the Father is prayer, since he is simultaneously a conversation with the Father and the Spirit. The uttered, emitted Word of the Father replies in his own words, his own speech, always in accord with the expectation that lies in the Father's will. It is no meaningless conversation, no superfluous disclosure of what is already fixed and settled. In this dialogue, plans are continually being proposed and carried out. Every word spoken is both adoration and commitment: It is adoration of the God who is addressed, but it is a fulfilled adoration, for the word lays a divine commitment on the speaker. A commitment of this kind can be seen in the decision to proceed with the Incarnation, for the Son is committed to the Father's will, the Father to the path the Son has set before him, and the Spirit to both. What has been promised will be performed: Every guarantee has been furnished.

From all eternity the Father has needed to love perfectly. And since, in God, need and fulfillment are one, this need caused him from all eternity to beget the Son. The first thing they do together is to send forth the Spirit from them both, thus extending this love of theirs which has achieved a divine objectivity. And as it was the Father's nature so to love that he must beget the Son, so too this extension is so much part of the Father's nature that both Spirit and Son possess that nature. They are not afterthoughts or adopted strangers: Their origin is directly from the Father, and they share his nature. And the first thing the Son and Spirit do is to thank the Father. They thank him for having begotten them and breathed them forth, for having allowed them to be of the same nature as himself and for endowing them, in the act of bringing them forth, with a divinity that develops freely in his love. They thank him that they are eternally bound to him through sharing the one nature but also that they may eternally meet him in contrast and confrontation, so that reciprocal exchange is possible. And the Father accepts these thanks because he is perfect love, of his nature bestowing love, and thus cannot seek to avoid their thanks. But he does not accept their gratitude in order to hide it within himself; instead, he passes it on to them again, grateful that they have undertaken to share his nature with him. Eternally brought forth, eternally becoming, they correspond to his will, expectation and love.

Thanks is the first declaration of this love which has come to be. The Father wishes to beget the Son and expects him to be as he wants him to be. And in coming forth, the Son perfectly fulfills the Father's expectation from the outset, so that the Father feels bound to him in gratitude from that first moment. The Father's perfection begets the Son's perfection, and yet at that moment when he is before the Father it is as though the Son has exceeded the Father's boldest expectations. For he is not a life-less replica but a living Thou with the infinite fullness of divinity. In the result of the begetting of the Son we see for the first time the excess, the "greater-than," of the divine being. The Son is the overfulfillment of the Father's expectation. But there is no time when the Father is alone in God, still planning the Son – no time prior to the begetting. So the expectation does not precede the overfulfillment but is one with it. Similarly, there is no time in God when the Son was still becoming and not yet really fully in being (as a human child develops after conception and only later wakens into consciousness): Rather, right at his origin in the Father's begetting of him, the Son participates in his own begetting. Thus fulfillment is never separated from expectation but rather is one with it; and at the same time there is room within this unity for the infinite "greater-than" of the fulfillment. A person in love who is waiting for the beloved knows who is coming, and yet the actual arrival of the beloved brings a fulfillment greater than the expectation. Instead of a correspondence between them, there is a relation of superabundance. Even when love knows what it may expect, namely, "more," the "more" of fulfillment is not simply a replica of the expected "more." The Son is the Father's first expectation and his first fulfillment, and for eternity he remains what he was and is: expecta-tion and fulfillment, expectation which, though unsurpassable, is surpassed by the fulfillment. The Son is for the Father the perpetual proof that in God there are no limits, no disappointments. Far from a minimal fulfillment that is just enough to vindicate the expectation, here we have a prodigality outstripping the most daring hopes. This superabundance occurs again in the procession of the Holy Spirit, when Father and Son see their mutual love surpassed as it issues forth from them as a third Person, standing bodily before them and expressing their innermost being.

In this "more" of God's nature lies prayer's ultimate root: in the fruitfulness of the divine nature, containing the threeness of Persons in the oneness of nature. In the divine love which unites them they adore each other with the entire spirit of God. God stands in the presence of God. God the Father stands before God the Son and God the Spirit, perceiving God in each of them. But what the Father adores in them is not the nature which is his but that which is distinctively theirs. And the Son and Spirit adore the Father in the same way. Though they share in a divine nature, they are distinct; each sees in the other what is uniquely his. All three are one in their origin from the Father but distinct through their different relation to the origin. They are related as Persons fundamentally united by the divine love, yet who carry on a conversation among themselves from the primal beginning and for all ages, a conversation whose nature is prayer. Nothing they expect of, perform for or com-municate to one another is outside of divine love and thus outside of prayer.

The Father's expectation lay in his infinite intention to create an object for his perfect, divine love. Since he was Almighty God, divinely perfect in himself, his will knew no greater yearning than to give his love an object like himself. And since the Father knows and sees everything from eternity, he knows eternally that, beside the Son, he will create creatures who are to love him but who, because they are creatures and not of one nature with God but different from him, will disappoint him. But since he begets the eternal Son prior to all creation, he sees that he will never be disappointed by his love and that neither of them will be so disappointed in the creation that their love will grow cold, for this love has been cultivated from all eternity. From the Son, who never disappoints, the Father draws strength, as it were, to bear all the coming disappointments from creatures. And in the conversation which they carry on from eternity, which is prayer, they lay the foundation for all coming conversations between God and creatures and for all the prayers which are to arise from the world to God.

The eternal dialogue is prayer first and foremost because it is divine vision: vision as the core of contemplation, as a silent listening, a reciprocal beholding, being led, adjusting to the other and getting to know him more, a reciprocal expectation and response. This abundant life streams from one Person to another, since each one always stands in view of the others. There is no self-concealment or reserve between them, only a constant acceptance and surrender, self-opening and self-disclosure, showing and loving.

As soon as Father and Son are together, they cause the Spirit to proceed as the witness to their living bond, to the life which consists of their being in unity. And at once, at the very origin of his procession, the Spirit takes on this role of witness to their life. From the very beginning the dialogue between Father and Son sees the signs of fruitfulness in the Spirit, and from the beginning the Spirit, bearing witness, receives a share in their fruitfulness. To the Father he bears witness to the Son's equality of nature; to the Son he testifies to the Father's equality. And the Spirit so fulfills and overfills the expectations of Father and Son that they see more in him than they looked for: In him they experience a totally unsuspected proof of their love. So they are bound to him in gratitude, just as he to them. Immediately and without any rehearsal he is in the midst of their prayer and dialogue, sharing in their knowledge, discernment, speech, obedience and silence, ensuring that this prayer is a constant adoration and fulfillment. It is adoration because God is in the presence of God; it is fulfillment because God may expect everything from God.

So great is their joy in the reciprocity of their going forth and being that, in a certain respect, the Father cannot cease begetting the Son, and Father and Son cannot cease from causing the Spirit to proceed; and in a more passive manner the Son and Spirit cannot but place themselves at the disposal of their generation in a process of becoming which always exhibits all the qualities of being. And this eternal, amazing relationship of joy lays the foundation for the world and mankind to be taken up one day into the divine joy, just as the communion of true lovers is always a preparation for the adoption into the relationship of others who do not yet love.

[Faith in the Trinity]

God the Father stands eternally vis-à-vis the Son and the Spirit. Their features have always been known to him. Yet in his fellowship with them it is as though he is always positing a new beginning, a beginning rooted in himself and partaking of that primal foundation in him which, beyond time, gives rise to faith, hope and

love. Faith, because God the Father knows and expects himself and in this knowledge and expectation continually discovers afresh God the Son and God the Spirit;
faith, since he continually finds his expectation fulfilled in the others; faith which
is never disappointed in God the Son and God the Spirit because his expectation
corresponds exactly with the result, since their superabundant response is perfect.
This fulfilled knowledge and expectation contain in themselves the origin of faith,
for the relationship of trust is always totally new, and the response to it comes
fresh each time. The Father's prior knowledge is never an obstacle to his love
relationship with the Son and Spirit, causing the Father to find in himself the fulfillment which the Son and Spirit offer him. Rather, he finds this fulfillment in them
as their continual gift to him. His infinite knowledge does not impede him if he
wishes to be in a state of perpetual expectation. The moment he wishes to put his
knowledge at love's service – and he does this from eternity, since he eternally
begets the Son and sends forth the Spirit – knowledge, faith and trust become one
in him. This faith is anchored in divine love, which guarantees that there can be
no disappointment because divine love is always perfect and, in its perfection,
participates in God's perfect nature. What in God and in the Father can be called
faith and trust is there only to provide love with every opportunity for development,
to give it the room which it would lack if everything were stale foreknowledge
– room which it needs, for it cannot exist without self-surrender, movement and
flight. Love always has this element of trust, this kind of yearning, this reverent
waiting upon the other's freedom, waiting for his spontaneous disclosure, his
incalculable gift. To try to remove this element is to kill love. This reverent, divine
waiting contains the source, the first cell of hope, that hope which the Father puts
in the Son and the Spirit. He gives them such a full participation in his nature that
they are equal in nature to him. Thus the Father's hope, love and faith are found
the same and undiminished in the Son and Spirit, so that even though the Father
remains Father eternally, just as the Son and Spirit remain themselves forever,
they encounter each other in an equal power and intensity of divine experience,
expectation and fulfillment. The participation of each in what the other has is
undiminished; in every relationship and surpassing response there is an equal strength,
equally transmitted.

Among men, where two equally gifted people love each other, one partner will
still be stronger and one weaker at different times in the exchange of love; a negative
element will meet a positive one. And the exchange of love will grow and improve
to the extent that these supportive movements occur. Not so in God: In God the
tension arises not only through the heterogeny but also through the homogeny, where
the one discovers and fulfills himself in his equal. No tedium arises because the
tension does not slacken; it always springs fresh from its source bearing all the
characteristics of the divine: perfect, self-surpassing correspondence. In God, therefore, one can no more speak of a faith prior to sight than of an expectation prior
to fulfillment. In God, faith is always fulfilled in sight; yet, since it is based on love,
it continually renews itself from contemplation.

Certainly there is something unsatisfactory and misleading in speaking of an
element, in God, of faith. And yet the concept is indispensable, particularly when

we speak of prayer in God. If we were to give up the concept of faith in order to clarify our idea of the divine life, then that life would no longer be at all access-ible to us. In initiating us into his inner-divine world of love, showing us ways to his trinitarian nature and guiding us into the "greater-than" of his being, God lets us keep our human concept with all its inadequacy because it can be transformed through grace. And precisely those highest gifts of God which come directly from his inner-divine life, faith, love and hope, are far better adapted to reveal his nature than any powers of our creaturely nature as such. We must use what experience we as Christians have of God as access to his nature, as a means of interpreting his being. To renounce this would be to shut ourselves in our earthly world and reject the most precious gifts which give access to God. It would be to hold the strange opinion that God had given us something perfectly good which, on enter-ing heaven, we found to be earthly, temporal, ephemeral and useless. Of course our faith will be transformed when we enter heaven. God will fulfill it beyond our boldest expectations, for God, when he reveals himself, will be the One who is always greater. And the direct vision he then will give us will be a much more concrete, proven and evident form of faith. But far from destroying faith, this vision will fulfill it. Faith will be the root from which vision arises. Now faith is revealed and sight is concealed; then sight will be revealed and faith will be its hidden precondition.

A kind of transitional state, connecting on earth both links of the chain, is mystical contemplation.[1] Mysticism is always an expression of faith; it can only take place within faith. Faith loses its abstract, speculative character in order to take into itself an element of experience of divine reality. But one cannot use vision in order to take a rest from faith. Moreover, the faith which does not see cannot be defined as a state of loss of vision. Faith after a vision is not very different from faith before it; perhaps it is not even different from faith during the vision. And it is certainly not the case that the more a mystic sees, the less he has to believe. The truth is that in mysticism faith and sight form a unity in tension which is emphasized in the one or other direction at different times, according to how God fashions the given situation.

Something of the simultaneity of faith and sight in earthly mysticism is taken up into the beatific vision in heaven, just as something of our earthly life of faith, of the most personal aspect of our Christian existence – this absolutely special gift of God's grace – will enter into our eternal vision. The little child wants to delight his father by bringing him the little things he finds; his love means it very seriously. Later, when the child is grown up, he can give "valuable" gifts; but this does not mean that the love and devotion have also grown. The father accepts both with equal love. Thus God will not despise the fruits of our faith and accept only the fruits of our vision. And the fruits are not separable from the act. When the Lord was a child on earth he possessed vision (as *comprehensor*) and faith (as *viator*). If he had only seen and known and not *also* believed, he would not have been the first Christian and everything would have gone much too easily. He possessed a boundless, childlike trust in the Father's guidance. He had the will to accept everything the Father offered him without examining whether it was hard or easy, intelligible or unintelligible. He did not want to play the grown-up, judging every-thing himself, but to accept everything from the Father, sight unseen. And he kept this attitude all his life. So too for the mystic, much more perfectly for the Son on earth, and ultimately for the blessed in heaven, there can be a simultaneity of seeing and believing. (Just as on earth true love knows a simultaneity of penitence and joy, of being caressed and being humbled. We human beings arc accustomed to experience in succession things which in reality can exist entwined in a unity, in love, in the Christian life, in mysticism, in Christ, in heaven.) This simultaneity proves that there is something eternal in faith and that, by analogy, one can speak of a faith in the midst of the vision of the trinitarian God.

[Vision in the Trinity]

. . .

In eternal vision and love, consequently, two things are united which in the earthly vision and love are separate, namely, *act and state*. In sexual love, for instance, the encounter of man and woman is a process in which elements of state and act alternate; state is emphasized more in the case of the woman, act more in the man's case. In God both are present in principle: The Father begets and loves the Son without interruption, and yet this love and begetting is event at every point; at every point he brings forth the Spirit together with the Son. One can say that God's state is that of an eternal, personal love which acquires a certain actuality in the acts of begetting, breathing and beholding; or, equally, that his state is his eternal begetting and beholding, and within this state the reciprocal love of the Persons is what has the character of act.

Love between man and woman can be inspired and shaped from two sides: by prior experiences that brought fulfillment and by present needs and expectations, not by each partner making his or her own plans, but in mutual accommodation. In this way a rich texture arises through the interplay of fulfillment and expectation, what is present and what is yet to be discovered, state and act – an interplay that creates love's vitality and inexhaustibility. True love can never be boring; it is self-renewing. But this continual motion of human love is only a reflection of the infinite movement of divine love. For instance, a man may plan for himself, but in the center of his planning his expectation of the woman's response plays a role. The Father also plans, as it were, with regard to what he expects from his Son, but he leaves room for the Son's response. And the Son's response will always be totally divine and therefore totally personal. In the scope between the divine and the personal, divine love shows itself in its fruitfulness and wealth of creativity. The woman responds both as a lover and as a woman to the man's expectation, which is both loving and masculine. Again, if he is not only a man but also a lover, the man's masculine expectation is quite different from the same expectation in the absence of love. In one way it is more sensitive, nuanced, discerning and appropriate, and in another way more differentiated and more characteristically masculine: as if only love's unity could bring out the true differences of sexes and persons.

Finally, sexual love provides us with another analogy in the fact that the lovers know exactly what they are doing and at the same time do not know at all. The man already knows the nature of their union, but he does not know how the woman will receive him on this occasion; he can only hope that it will happen in love, awakening in her an even greater love for him. The point of departure is a solitary planning; the fulfillment of these plans becomes more and more a mutual affair and at the same time robs the two individuals of absolute power and control. The man does retain a certain primacy, yet in such a way that he only takes the lead by surrendering and losing himself. In an analogous way, all processes in God are based on an initial vision: the Father's plan, ordering all things. The act of begetting the Son is as if included in this primal vision, as is the Son's act of co-operation in his begetting and the Spirit's procession, like an action within an all-embracing contemplation. In the same way, Mary's assent to the angel is an act within an all-embracing assent of contemplation. The difference is that in God there can be no moment which is only planning and vision, without action and begetting: The Father's vision is the begetting of the Son, and the vision of Father and Son is the spiration of the Spirit. It is as if this vision is so overpowering that it constitutes, in itself, the bringing forth of what it envisages, and thus the overwhelming and inundation of the observer by the reality of the beloved and the mutuality of love.

Action springs from vision, but vision immediately acquires new substance through action and its result. Thus God is infinite to himself: Every infinity of his being opens new doors to the infinity of his understanding, which in turn is the creative source of new infinity of his being. It is one of the laws of love that the lover cannot completely fathom the essence of the beloved. No human being can calculate or possess another's reactions in advance, or count on them as if they were not the expression of a free personal nature. If anyone could do this, the other person would instantly cease to be a spiritual being. Love is built up essentially on the incalculability of the beloved. He must always disclose and surrender himself afresh, continually surprising and overwhelming the lover. If ever this movement were to stop, to be replaced by a conclusive knowledge of each other, love would come to an end. What seemed to be complete knowledge would be the sign of a real finitude. But in God nothing is finite.

. . .

It is as if the Spirit is witness that the distance between them can never be separation because he constantly bridges the permanent, perpetual distance with the love of him who proceeds. Thus in triune being, distance and union are motive forces which can only increase and which are rooted so deeply in the life of God that they keep it forever new and fruitful.

One can get some notion of the infinite multiplicity of relations in God by contemplating the world: If the world's variety is so colorful, fascinating, exciting and inexhaustible, how rich must the source of this variety be! And if God delights in man whom he has caused to live in his grace, never tiring of taking pleasure in man's joys, man's love, and the millions of possibilities open to him of relationships with

God and his fellows, how much greater must be his delight in the infinity of his own omnipotence and the inventive love of his eternal intercourse! The Father sees all that the incarnate Son undertakes together with his brothers; the Son sees the plans the Father has for mankind and how he is carrying them out; and both observe how the Spirit carries out the most surprising initiatives and miracles in the world. It is all such a spectacle that even a God cannot see enough of it. And yet all that God undertakes in the world is a drop in the ocean of the divine tensions, distances and unions within the one divine love.

. . .

Petition

. . . And now, as the Three face each other, their will seems to have acquired a new color. What up to now was bound in the nature of God is now, through the process of generation and spiration, in a certain sense free: It receives a form which is no longer bound to any necessity of essence. Each one sees this divine will in the other. But whereas, in the context of the necessity of the processions, the will was of necessity bound as it passed from Father to Son and from both to the Spirit, in a sequence determined as of nature, the will demonstrates, in its freedom and unity, a hierarchy established by the processions. Freedom in God knows about the priority of the necessary processions, and they determine a hierarchical priority within freedom.

This is freedom's primal shape. In order for a will to be free, it must be part of a hierarchy. Even the freest freedom must manifest something of the precedence of the Father over the Son and of the Father and Son over the Spirit; man must remember that the preeminent will resides in the Father. Thus Christian obedience is an act of a free will. The Son and Spirit must recognize the Father's precedence, and the Father must be aware of them. Only in this way can he permit the Son to say: "Not my will but thine be done."

The Father's first, primal purpose is not free. Or rather, in its absolute sovereignty it is beyond necessity and freedom. Once the Son is begotten, however, he adopts the Father's will by freely desiring to be what the Father's purpose has determined. And now, from the vantage point of this free will, it is as if even the Father's begetting and the Son's being begotten acquire characteristics of freedom, as if in their freedom Father and Son recapitulate their natural relationship, in order freely to be what they are of necessity. In fact, this is the opposite of what takes place in the human relationship, where the man freely decides on the act of generation which, however, once begun, takes a necessary and natural course. But in God necessity is not a blind necessity of nature, preliminary to his qualities of mind and personhood. It is a divine necessity which expresses his spiritual nature. It has no parallel among us creatures; we can only describe it as lying beyond all creaturely freedom and necessity.

Each of the three divine Persons is free. But the Father's will takes precedence over the Son's, and the Father's and Son's over the Spirit's: The Son can send forth the Spirit. But one cannot say that, because the Spirit is dependent on two Persons, he is more bound than the Son. . . .

So the Spirit proceeds, seeming on the one hand to be the most bound of the Persons, and on the other to possess free will in a perfect measure. Will is his essential character: He blows where he will. He is bound to the necessary will of the Father and to that of the Son, and also to the Son's free will. And as he sees how the Son restrains his free will in favor of the Father and is obedient to him, the Spirit wishes to exercise the same obedience toward both Father and Son. Now it is as though Father and Son observe this restraint, this reserve, this kind of self-abnegation on the part of the Spirit, and immediately cry "No!", definitively bestowing on him complete divine freedom. The Spirit is no late arrival in God, the last of a series originating in the Father, in which the Son imitates the Father and the Spirit imitates the Son. Rather, his relationship to Father and Son is totally new and original, determined by his twofold bond; yet it immediately bursts this bond with the demand that he be *will*. It demands that he manifest something of the Father's paramount will and something of the Son's subordinate will in an original and unified way, in which the relationship of superordination and subordination is no longer completely visible; instead something arises that is most intimately connected with the way he was brought forth, revealing him vis-à-vis the Father and Son as the possessor of a complete freedom. He exercises this freedom but always between Father and Son; it always fulfills the purposes of Father and Son, yet does so in a free manner. Hence it belongs to him particularly to choose. Freedom of choice is not only a precondition for his operations; it is an inner quality of them. It is visible in God's "election of grace" in the world, his favoring of this person rather than that one, the fact that, out of all the apparently identical seeds, he causes this one to sprout rather than that one. The Spirit manifests himself in this elective quality in his continual blowing between Father and Son. And one can no more ask why there is a Holy Spirit than why he chooses this person and not that one, irrespective of any response or merit on man's part. This freedom of the Spirit is rooted in his position between Father and Son; it is something internal to God, not dependent on creation.

The Spirit is like someone who may do whatever he will. But he can only do what is between Father and Son, from whom he proceeds. In his freedom he is always being adopted into the divine conformity between Father and Son, although everything is given to him, everything is permitted. So too the Christian is bound precisely because he is free in the deepest sense; he believes freely, yet he is held firm by the law of his free faith. For him, every step outside the freedom of his faith would be a falling into slavery; therefore he will only operate within the conformity of his faith. The Spirit is free in his divinity (he cannot be other than he is) and hence free in his standing and his moving between Father and Son, in the eternal worship and contemplation of Father and Son, in their purposes and the implementing of them in the Spirit. The Christian puts his will into his faith, summons his will to realize itself within his faith and sets faith before his will as its law. The law for the Spirit's will is his relationship to Father and Son. But in this he need not imitate the Son. He must be himself, the free Spirit of Father and Son. That is why he can be a "Rule" for the incarnate Son, for he is free and yet sums up in himself the essence of the intentions of Father and Son. They are not imposed on him, but out of love he gives them whatever corresponds with the love of the Father and of the Son and will help realize them. The distance between the Persons becomes important again here: The Spirit is not stifled between Father and Son but has more and more room for his freedom. He can freely do whatever he can devise to promote the love of Father and Son.

Having said all this, we have exposed the roots of petitionary prayer in God. When the Father sees the Son before him and sees how spontaneously love answers him in the Son, how the Son both worships him and accepts his worship, contemplates him and accepts his contemplation, the Father introduces petition. He asks the Son to help promote the fatherly purposes he has revealed in contemplation. Everything which has the nature of purpose in him he hands over to the Son, showing him possibilities of action which are not already contained in his fatherly nature. The Father's intentions, now committed to the Son, are like preludes, beginnings taken up by the Son to be realized. Here we have a parallel to the Son's words, "Into your hands, Father, I commend my spirit." For here the Father gives his spirit (his purposes, his work, his creation) into the Son's hands. . . . But one cannot say that the Father delights in granting his own request; rather, he delights in the Son. The joy of granting the request is at most an anticipatory joy, inseparable from its fulfillment in the Son, just as all expectations are already fulfilled in God from all time. The Father eternally looks forward to the Son; but the Son who eternally stands before him is infinitely more than what the almighty and all-knowing Father expects, and his delight is infinitely more than his anticipatory joy. His begetting has resulted in more splendid fruit. And so he knows that his granting of the Son's request will also contain a divine "more-than"; that this heightening, this surprise, this superabundance is a divine aspect reappearing everywhere, so that God's joy can never be exhausted. This is the experience he wishes to give the Son immediately: Even before the Son asks him, the Father wants to make his request, as if to give the Son precedence in the delight of granting. Ultimately it is only on the basis of the divine joy in granting requests that the Spirit can be understood as having perfect freedom. Father and Son together create a mode of granting requests which lies behind the Spirit's freedom. They ask the Spirit, as it were, to dispose freely over their plans.

Thus the begetting itself seems to contain a kind of petition, but one which is already granted: Even as the Father begets, the Son has always been. As the Father is about to give the kiss of love, the Son has already offered his cheek. So the Son takes from the Father the intention which is just developing and carries it out – as the Father's deed and plan – by making himself ready for it. In God everything is full of these loving details which contribute essentially to understanding the Trinity, full of these prior ententes built into and fulfilled in reality. . . .

Leaving the other free is something which goes back to the distance which is established in the begetting. The Father does not beget within himself but out of himself. In true love the lovers do not cling to each other: They have the distance which is essential if they are to see and encounter each other completely. In God the gift is always just what he wanted, yet a certain "time" and opportunity is left to desire it and a certain "time" for the gift to be got ready. The Son gives the

Father the opportunity of making his will known so that he can accept it. Similarly, in marriage, the husband must let his wife have time to be a woman, and vice versa. And perhaps there are certain wishes of the Father which the Son does not carry out, so that the Spirit may do so. . . . In God, of course, the Third Person is never excluded, but he is able to be present and to make his contribution in different ways, perhaps simply by making room for the others to act. Definite forms are exhibited by the will, by love, by wishes. Results do not flow automatically from a characterless amalgam. The same result can be achieved by the most diverse constellations of causes. One cannot deduce from equal total sums that their component numbers are the same.

. . .

[How Mary embodies trinitarian prayer]

At the point where the triune God decides upon the creation of the world, where there is no talk yet of future sin, where the Son affirms the Father's plan in everything, at that point he puts himself at the disposal of creation, to take up his dwelling there. It is like an intimation of the Eucharist, not yet in sacramental form and with no reference to suffering or even to a body. Rather, the Son sees initially the great similarity between his eternal begetting and the procession from God of a creation imbued with grace; he imagines all the Father's joy at encountering his Son in the world. To delight the Father he wants this encounter to take place in every human being. And as if to clothe the Son's wish with a concrete form, to create a central point from which the Son's Eucharist can flow and spread forth; Father, Son and Spirit together choose one human being for the Son to dwell in: a woman. This one woman will receive the Son and be his mother. In this sense, Eve is already a woman in God's foreknowledge before Adam becomes a man. For, mysteriously, Christ and Mary are the first couple but are held as it were in reserve like a hidden basis. The ultimate, normative distance from God is determined by Christ and Mary, and not by Adam and Eve, who are drawn from the first separation from God in which they existed into the final distance determined by Christ and Mary. The Son's plan of glorification, prior to and more final than that of redemption, has always continually involved Mary and, through her, all creatures who join in the Father's praise. Just as the Father has his plan in creation which is particular to his fatherly point of view, so the Son has his according to his filial point of view; and the Spirit has his plan as well, since he carries out the plan of Father and Son in the freest possible manner. He brings about the Immaculate Conception; he overshadows the Mother; he works the miracle of the Virgin Birth. Thus all three Persons are involved in the origin of this first couple, who embody the epitome of creation. But the functions exercised by each Person in the work of creation are ultimately determined in the context of the divine petitionary prayer, not only in the contemplation from which action issues as its fruit. Certainly these functions are outlined here, but they only become concrete when Son and Spirit offer themselves for the sake of the Father's work, when they ask to be allowed to cooperate in it and when the Father asks for their collaboration. They want to explore and experience in eternity what mankind will do and experience later in petitionary prayer. The Lord's word, "All that you ask the Father in my name will be done for you," is to have its basis in God himself. And just as all three Persons petition each other together, they also grant fulfillment to one another. The whole work of creation lies in this divine granting. Each one gladly does the will of the other because in love he wants to delight him, because it is something which corresponds to his own will, and finally because his own will is completely shaped by the will and the judgment of the other. But this loving game of asking and granting in creation is seen most clearly at its highest point, in God's primal creation: Mary.

[The Eucharist in the Trinity]

... Divine prayer has the character of decision, a character that expresses a trait of the divine nature: In God nothing is undecided. It is the nature of God that he is differentiated as Father, Son and Spirit, and that in this threefold being he is perpetually deciding. He decides both to give and to receive. ...

An analogy for this is the Son's Eucharist, in which he is always sharing himself out; yet the more he is shared out, the more he strives to recapture unity. The Son's integrity is heightened by every Communion. In a similar way there is a communion in God, an exchange of the divine nature in which differentiation and unification are one. And this exchange in God is something quite concrete. ... The Lord on earth ... is not a memory but a living, real presence, the concrete offering of himself; the triune life is the basis for this. Whoever rejects the Lord's real eucharistic Presence, therefore, is without access to the trinitarian fellowship. People very often speak of "mere symbols" when they can go no further, when they can no longer rise to the significance of what, for God, is a pure reality. With its realism, the Eucharist is a bridge to heaven for believers. It shows that in heaven there are decisions and concretizations, decisions which are as concrete in God as the Lord is for the believer when he has the Host on his tongue.

Note

1   To be joined in this way, the links must first be open. Thus even in God there is an opening which is the precondition for the eternal closing. Father and Son are not parallel, and they do not merely touch like two rings; they are in one another, penetrating and encompassing one another. To do this, however, they must have an open place. The Father's opening is in begetting and conceiving the Son, and the Son's opening is in his cooperation in being begotten and in his return to the Father. Something analogous can be said of faith and vision.

VIII
Late Twentieth-Century Applications

31

Stephen E. Fowl, *from* "How the Spirit Reads and How to Read the Spirit"

Twentieth-century American Protestantism has debated over and over again the idea that the Holy Spirit inspires the words of the biblical text. That idea differs considerably from traditional versions of the inspiration of the Holy Spirit, both at and before the Reformation. The traditional view saw the Holy Spirit working in the heart of the *reader*. In this essay, Stephen Fowl attempts to recover for contemporary Christians the idea that the Spirit affects and effects the interpretation of Scripture by working in communities of readers. He argues from the way the Spirit inculcates a new interpretation of Scripture among the communities of Acts.

New Testament authors did not have the New Testament to go by: Scripture for them was the Greek version of the Hebrew Bible, the Septuagint, which Christians would later come to call the "Old Testament." But as the New Testament was being written, the Septuagint wasn't "old," it was the only Bible they had. The Book of Acts records a massive change in the interpre-tation of the Hebrew Bible and the debates about it. Both the change and the debates appealed to the Holy Spirit. Both the change and the debates treated an issue of great import-ance: who belongs in the community.

First-century Jewish ideas about the end of the world, or eschatology, foresaw one of two possible outcomes. Either the Messiah would come and all human beings, Jews and Gentiles, would acknowledge the God of Israel as the one true God, by observing Torah, including circumcision and keeping kosher. In short, Gentiles would acknowledge the God of Israel by becoming observant Jews. *Or* the Messiah would come and all human beings, Jews and Gentiles, would acknow-ledge the God of Israel as the one true God, but Gentiles would *not* be circumcised or observe kosher laws. In that case, Gentiles would acknowledge

Stephen E. Fowl, "Reading the Spirit and How the Spirit Reads," in *Engaging Scripture* (Oxford: Blackwell, 1998), pp. 97–9, 113–27.

the God of Israel without taking on all marks of Israel. Paul thought he had *empirical* evidence that the end was arriving, the Messiah had come, the Gentiles were coming to acknowledge the God of Israel as the one, true God – and that God was following Plan B. Gentiles were acknowledging the God of Israel without circumcision and keeping kosher, and God was pouring out the Holy Spirit on them anyway. That meant that, empirically speaking – Paul could see it – both identifiable Jews and identifiable Gentiles could receive the Spirit of the Messiah – that "in Christ there is no Jew or Gentile," even if in Torah-observance there still was.

Well, Plan B was a big surprise. It was one of the possible eschatologies, but it involved a lot more change, even a reversal. Plan A would have been more modest. Plan A would have shown a clearer continuity with God's history with Israel. But in Plan B, apparently under way, God seemed to be pouring out the Holy Spirit not only on Israel but also on Gentiles *who retained distinguishing Gentile characteristics*. Paul's Letter to the Romans shows that he is shocked. God seemed to be acting excessively, beyond nature, like a bigamous husband or a crazy farmer (Rom. 11). Acts reports that Peter is indignant. It takes a dream and a confrontation to bring him around. The coming in of Gentiles without circumcision represents the biggest change that the messianic community ever underwent. Indeed, that marked the beginning of Gentiles taking it over.

In this chapter, Steven Fowl surveys and improves attempts to use the great eschatological change of the coming in of the Gentiles to evaluate other proposed changes in what is now Christianity. The coming in of the Gentiles overturned expectations, including moral expectations; it caused extensive, prolonged reinterpretation of scripture; and it provoked community-dividing disagreements about what scripture meant. The coming in of the Gentiles, especially as depicted in Acts, came to serve as a model – much appealed to, and much disputed – for how the Spirit changes the community, or how the community discerns the Spirit. Here, Fowl evaluates and suggests ways of using the coming in of the Gentiles in Acts as a model for negotiating current disputes about rule-keeping and Spirit-discernment in the contemporary Church on a more recent issue that most divides it in the early twenty-first century: homosexuality.

from How the Spirit Reads and How to Read the Spirit

Stephen E. Fowl

Introduction

In the previous chapter [of *Engaging Scripture*] I addressed the objection that my account of underdetermined interpretation left Christians with no resources for resisting their tendency to read scripture in ways that supported their own sinful beliefs and practices. I argued that the resources for resisting this tendency lie not in theories of textual meaning, but in Christians' abilities to exercise a particular

sort of vigilance and to engage in practices of forgiveness, repentance, and reconciliation which will themselves lead Christians to grow in virtue. It is important to
remember, however, that, in and of themselves, these resources will not work to
eliminate interpretive disputes among Christians. Indeed, this side of the kingdom
an absence of interpretive dispute is not necessarily a desirable result. Rather, because
no particular scriptural passage is self-interpreting, Christians will always need to
debate with each other over how to interpret and embody scripture in the various
contexts in which they find themselves. In this situation of ongoing debate, argument, and struggle, the resources [for vigilance, forgiveness, repentance, and rec-
onciliation] displayed in the previous chapter will do more to direct these debates,
arguments, and struggles towards generating faithful living and worshipping than
theories of textual meaning.

This, however, is but one of the ways in which Christians' convictions and practices need work to determine their interpretation of scripture. Clearly, there is a
vast array of convictions and practices which should shape and be shaped by Christian
interpretation of scripture. Further, these convictions and practices should not be
taken to operate in isolation from each other. Rather, they should work together
in ways that enhance and illuminate each other. . . . I am simply pointing out some,
but by no means all, of the important convictions and practices which should play
a role in Christian interpretation of scripture. In part, the selection of issues in this
book reflects my views that these topics are particularly in need of attention. In
this light, the current chapter will turn to explore how Christian convictions about
the Holy Spirit bear on issues of interpretation.

I will begin by looking at John's gospel to make some general comments about
the role of the Spirit in scriptural interpretation [omitted here]. These comments will
indicate that the Spirit's intervention and interpretive work is crucial if the followers
of Jesus are faithfully to carry on the mission Jesus gives them. This is because the
Spirit enables believers to understand the words of Jesus in the light of his death
and resurrection. Further, because the Spirit speaks in unison with the Father and
Son, all Spirit-directed actions will also conform to God's will. These considerations
will provide a _rinitarian grounding to my discussion about the role of the Spirit
in interpretation. The aim of this is to keep the Spirit from seeming to be a free-
floating entity operating in distinction from the other persons of the Trinity.[1]

I will then move to a closer examination of Acts 10–15 [abridged here] and the
issues surrounding the inclusion of Gentiles in the church. Here the Spirit plays
a decisive role in a particular set of disputes involving scriptural interpretation. What
is striking about this passage is that the characters demonstrate a remarkable
facility for recognizing, interpreting, and acting upon the work of the Spirit. I argue
that this facility is underwritten by two interconnected elements. The first is the
ability to bear witness to the work of the Spirit in the lives of others. The second
is the way that this ability is sustained by the particular friendships that these Christians
are able to form.

I then conclude by looking at two arguments for reading the contemporary
disputes over the role of homosexuals in the church as an analogous extension of
the disputes over the inclusion of Gentiles in the church in Acts 10–15. To even

be in a position to debate, and perhaps enact, this type of analogical extension, Christians will need to begin by opening themselves to the sorts of friendships with homosexuals that would enable them to testify about the work of the Spirit in the lives of their friends. Without this step, Christians will neither be able to read the Spirit nor read with the Spirit. . . .

. . .

Reading the Spirit as essential for reading with the Spirit

Thus far I have relied on John's gospel to provide a trinitarian grounding for the importance of the role of the Spirit in interpreting and embodying scripture. My discussion of Acts 10–15 has presented a specific narrative example of the Spirit's role in a dispute among the earliest followers of Jesus. This dispute involved questions both about how to interpret scripture and about how to interpret the work of the Spirit in displaying the will of God. At this point I will try to state what the narrative only implies about how to recognize, interpret, and act upon the work of the Spirit.

As Luke Johnson has repeatedly stressed in regard to James' judgment, the interpretation of scripture is guided by the testimony about the Spirit's work, rather than the other way around.

> What is remarkable, however, is that the text is confirmed by the narrative, not the narrative by the Scripture. As Peter had come to a new understanding of Jesus' words because of the gift of the Spirit, so here the Old Testament is illuminated and interpreted by the narrative of God's activity in the present.[2]

As we will also later see with Paul, experience of the Spirit's work provides the lenses through which scripture is read rather than vice versa. This is perhaps the most significant point the New Testament has to make about the hermeneutical significance of the Spirit; this point runs against the grain of modern interpretive presumptions. Nevertheless, we should not treat the pattern of the priority of Spirit experience to scriptural interpretation as an abstract hermeneutical rule. On the one hand, Johnson's observations – along with Richard Hays's parallel ones . . . – are a useful corrective to the presumption that in the New Testament exegesis according to abstract principles shapes the way the work of the Spirit is understood. On the other hand, seeking to demonstrate the priority of either Spirit experience or exegesis is to bind oneself to false alternatives. The pattern of reading scripture found in Acts and elsewhere in the New Testament cannot be easily or profitably separated from the very specific types of ecclesial contexts in which that reading takes place. As my overview of Acts 10–15 has indicated, the Spirit's activity is no more self-interpreting than a passage of scripture is. Understanding and interpreting the Spirit's movement is a matter of communal debate and discernment over time. This debate and discernment is itself often shaped both by prior interpretations of scripture and by traditions of practice and belief. This means that in practice it is probably difficult, if not impossible, to separate and determine clearly whether a community's scriptural interpretation is prior to or dependent upon a community's experience of the Spirit. Experience of the Spirit shapes the reading of scripture, but scripture most often provides the lenses through which the Spirit's work is perceived and acted upon. Even here the notion of an "experience of the Spirit" should not be taken as a reference to an internal mental transaction, immediately perceived and understood by isolated individuals. . . .

The difficulty, if not impossibility, of clearly separating moments of scriptural interpretation from moments of interpretation of the Spirit's activity is not a reason simply to dissolve or subsume reflection and debate about the Spirit into reflection and debate over scripture. Such a reduction will leave us merely paying lip-service to the hermeneutical significance of the Spirit. Instead, if Christians are to follow the examples found in Acts 10–15 and read scripture with the Spirit, that is, as the Spirit reads, then it will be essential to learn to read the Spirit, to discern what the Spirit is doing. In this section I would like to point out several practices, habits, and structures related to the specific contexts of Acts 10–15 which appear to be crucial for the characters' abilities to discern what the Spirit is doing and to act upon this discernment.

It is clear that in both Acts 11 and 15 Peter's testimony (among others') that Gentiles had received the Spirit upon hearing the Gospel is the primary component persuading those in favor of Gentile circumcision that this was not necessary.[3] It is perhaps not surprising to claim that both the practice of testifying or bearing witness and the practice of listening wisely to such testimony are essential to a community's ability to "read the Spirit."[4]

From law courts to shows such as Donohue and Oprah, we can find numerous types of utterances which might count as testimony. In fact, it may well be that our society and our churches are overrun with "testimony" of one sort or another. There are, however, several distinguishing features about the practice of testifying in Acts 10–15 that separate this type of speaking from both the adversarial nature of a law court and the self-promotional context of a television talk-show.

First, it is testimony about the Spirit by those who are already recognized as people of the Spirit. Peter stresses that God has poured out the same Spirit on the Gentiles as he and his fellow Jews had received. It is the Gentiles' reception of this same gift, apart from circumcision, that is ultimately decisive here. The basis for Peter's claim is his, and his fellow Jews', prior reception of the same Spirit. . . . For now, it is sufficient to note that Peter's status as one who already knows the Spirit lends weight to his testimony about the Spirit's work in the lives of others. It may well be the case, then, that giving testimony about the Spirit is not something that normally can be done well by just anybody. Testimony about the Spirit's work in others tends to be done best by those who have experienced the Spirit's work themselves.

While noting that those who are recognized as people of the Spirit are likely to be the best ones to testify about the Spirit's work, it is also crucial to note that Peter's testimony is in two crucial respects not *his* testimony. That is, there are two respects in which Peter is not the subject of his testimony. First, Peter's testimony is not so much about what he has done as what he has seen God doing. In the various accounts he offers, Peter makes it plain that the inclusion of the Gentiles is not his pet project; rather it is the work of God. This is made most clear in 15: 8 when he claims that God has testified (*emartyrsen*) to the "cleansed hearts" of the Gentiles by "giving them the Holy Spirit." Here God not only becomes the subject of Peter's testimony, but the primary witness to it as well.[5]

The second respect in which Peter's testimony is not strictly his testimony concerns the fact that his account is not so much about what God has done to him (although that figures in passages such as 10: 34) as about what God had done to others. Peter's testimony is not about himself and his experience of the Spirit. Rather the subject of Peter's testimony is the work of the Spirit in the lives of others. Moreover, in the case of the visit to Cornelius, Peter's testimony is attested to by "those of the circumcision" who went with him from Joppa to Caesarea.

To be able to read the Spirit well, Christians must not only become and learn from people of the Spirit, we must also become practiced at testifying about what the Spirit is doing in the lives of others. In our present age, which favors self-authentication above all else, we may find it hard to recognize this as a crucial element in testimony about the Spirit's work. One example of this might be found in the emphasis in so much work in contemporary pastoral care and group process on getting people to make "I statements." Presumably the intentions here are to keep people focused on what they know and, thus, to shield their comments from certain sorts of criticisms. Nevertheless, this emphasis seems to contribute to moving us further and further away from a situation in which we might be expected to render an account of what the Spirit is doing in the lives of others – let alone articulate the type of judgment James does, which then becomes the basis for communal consensus.

Both ecclesially and socially we can become so isolated from others that when we must make judgments about scripture, about our common life, or about others, we have little recourse but to rely on the self-authenticating testimony of virtual strangers or merely to repeat the practices, demands, and strictures we have used before. This is not to say that we should always innovate, ignoring or actively transgressing past convictions and commitments. At the Jerusalem Council past commitments and convictions are articulated and applied in what seems to be an obvious way – Gentiles joining this Jewish body must be circumcised and obey Torah. The burden of proof seems to lie with those who would innovate. In response, Peter (along with Paul and Barnabas) testifies to the work of the Spirit in the lives of Gentile converts, interpreting this work in such a way that indicates that God does not demand circumcision. James articulates a judgment that both accounts for the Spirit's creative movement and, by means of both his scriptural citation and reliance on the Torah-based practical "burdens" to be placed on the Gentiles, aims to retain both long-range continuity with God's work among the people of Israel and practical continuity exhibited in a unified table fellowship.

Of course, such continuities are always contestable matters of interpretation. There are no guarantees that our attempts to follow the Spirit will always result in belief, practice, and worship that faithfully continue the life of the people of God.

Christians can hope in God's providential care. This, however, cannot be an excuse for inaction. Moreover, as I have already noted, simply repeating what has been done before will not insure fidelity. Changing historical circumstances will change the significance, meaning, and effects of traditional words and practices whether we like it or not. Christians have no choice but to struggle, argue, and debate with one another over how best to extend our faith, worship, and practice in the present and into the future while remaining true to our past. In this struggle, testimony about the Spirit's work in the lives of others must become as central to contemporary Christians as it was to the characters in Acts.

The only way to counter the privatizing tendencies of contemporary church life, which make it unlikely or impossible that Christians would be in a position to testify about the work of the Spirit in the lives of their sisters and brothers, is to enter into friendships with them. There are at least two respects in which the practice of testifying depends upon Christians' abilities both to overcome their tendencies towards isolation and to nurture and sustain certain types of friendships. First, no matter how acute our spiritual insight, we will not be able to detect the Spirit's work in the lives of others unless we know them in more than superficial ways. While the narrative of Acts 10–15 is quite compressed, we still get a hint of the importance of forming particular sorts of friendships through the brief but significant announcements of hospitality and welcome being extended. When they finally meet, Cornelius is not exactly a stranger to Peter. Those sent to Joppa to find Peter informed him (testified?) about Cornelius. They stayed with Peter and traveled from Joppa to Caesarea together. Cornelius, too, extends hospitality to Peter. Initially, we must assume that Peter would have called Cornelius "unclean." In the course of directly encountering him and speaking the good news to Cornelius in his home, Peter is able to recognize the Spirit being poured out on Cornelius and his household and to come to see the practical significance of this in regard to all Gentile converts. We do not know if Peter would have called Cornelius a friend. We do know that Peter did not consider him some alien element who can only be labeled "unclean." Further, when Paul, Barnabas, and the others from Antioch arrive in Jerusalem they are welcomed and experience the hospitality of Christians there (15: 4). Moreover, the "burdens" placed on the Gentiles seem primarily directed towards allowing Jewish and Gentile followers of Jesus to sit at table together. Throughout this narrative the offering and receiving of hospitality always seems to be in the background supporting and enabling the sorts of friendships that allow Christians with differing convictions to listen together to the voice of the Spirit.

Secondly, the formation of friendships is crucial to Christians' abilities to be wise hearers of testimony. I will say more about this in the next chapter [of *Engaging Scripture*] regarding Paul and the churches in Galatia. In the case of Acts, it seems likely that Peter's relationships with the various parties whom he confronts in Jerusalem affect the ways in which his testimony is received. We are more likely to respond wisely to the testimony of someone we know. Unlike the adversarial nature of a law court, where we look for jurors who do not have connections to either the defendant or witnesses, wise listening in the church is usually founded on friendships between witnesses and listeners.

Even within the context of specific friendships, which can sustain and act upon testimony about the Spirit's work, discerning the work of the Spirit takes time.[6] It is only on the third time of reflecting on the events surrounding his visit to Cornelius that Peter comes to the conclusion that the upshot of God pouring out the Spirit on Gentiles apart from their circumcision indicates that the church should not require that Gentile converts become Jews as well. Even for the most insightful testifiers, and for the wisest listeners, interpreting the Spirit so that one can interpret with the Spirit demands patience, or what Luke Johnson calls "the asceticism of attentiveness."[7] More basically, simply forming the friendships needed to be able to detect, much less interpret, the Spirit's work in the life of another is time consuming. Rushing into judgments risks lapsing into the patterns of discrimination characterized in Acts by the use of *diakrino* as opposed to the *krino* offered by James which "seems good to the Holy Spirit and to us." It is only within communities that both sustain and nurture certain types of friendship and exhibit patience in discernment that we will find the sort of consensus emerging that is narrated in Acts. I am not claiming that such consensus is always necessary. In fact, without the communal friendships and patience needed to testify to the work of the Spirit, Christians should not really expect such consensus to emerge. In such cases, however, the remedy is not further reflection on the processes needed to achieve consensus, but more fundamental revisions to a common life that is not yet adequate to consensus-forming. As an illustration of this I want to turn to a set of issues that currently occupy many American churches.

Thus far, I have argued that close study of Acts 10–15 provides crucial insights into the hermeneutical significance of the Spirit. This narrative (among other passages) indicates that if Christians are to interpret with the Spirit, they will also need to learn how to interpret the Spirit. Further, our prospects for interpreting the Spirit are closely linked to our proficiency at testifying to the Spirit's work, particularly the Spirit's work in the lives of others. Such testimony depends on the forming and sustaining of friendships in which our lives are opened to others in ways that display the Spirit's working. Welcoming strangers and the extension of hospitality become building blocks for such friendships. Finally, building such friendships, becoming people of the Spirit, and recognizing and interpreting the work of the Spirit all take time and demand patience from us. I would now like to turn to two recent attempts to read a contemporary ecclesial interpretive dispute – the role and status of homosexual Christians – through Acts 10–15. While these proposals open up promising options, they also point out how difficult it is to attempt to read with the Spirit in the absence of the ecclesial practices that enable us to read the Spirit.

Homosexual Christians and Gentile inclusion

Over the past fifteen years or so, all of the mainline churches have engaged in discussion and debate over the role and status of homosexual persons in the church.[8] Despite the differences in these debates there are at least two elements that always seem to be evident. First, aside from the subject-matter, the public discussion and debate closely resembles the most bitter partisan political debates one might hear on the floor of Congress, though members of Congress tend to be a bit more charitable to their opponents. The debates are adversarial, divisive, and acrimonious; there is an absence of interpretive charity; posturing prevails over persuasion, lending credence to Alasdair MacIntyre's claim that politics in liberal democracies (such as most churches aim to be) is civil war carried out by other means.[9]

Secondly, there are always appeals to and/or discussions about scripture. This, of course, is as it should be. The focus of these discussions is almost always of the sort "What (if anything) does the Bible say about homosexuality?" Typically, texts such as Gen. 1–2, 19 (Sodom and Gomorrah); Lev. 18: 22, 20: 13; Rom. 1: 26–7; 1 Cor. 6: 9, and 1 Tim. 1: 10 become the focus for debate. As those who have studied this issue will attest, there is an abundance of scholarly and popular literature on these passages and how they should be read. While there are several exegetical questions surrounding these passages, the real issues seem to focus on which, if any, of these texts are most apposite to our present situation.

Recently, two New Testament scholars have proposed that the most apposite text for discussing the role and status of homosexuals within the church is Acts 10–15. In what follows, I would like to examine this move further. My discussion here about the possible analogical extension of Acts 10–15 to address contemporary debates about homosexuality within the church should not be taken as a full-fledged argument about the subject. Even if one is persuaded about the relevance of Acts 10–15 to this issue, there are still a number of outstanding issues that would need to be addressed. For my purposes, I will focus on those who have recently argued that Acts 10–15 is particularly important for this debate.

In a brief article which first appeared in *Commonweal*, Luke Johnson has raised the possibility that just as experience of the Spirit in Acts convinced someone like Peter to argue for Gentile inclusion without circumcision, so recognition of the Spirit's work in the lives of homosexual Christians might lead the church to re-consider the moral status of homosexuality.[10] In regard to Acts, Johnson notes,

> On the basis of this experience of God's work, the church made bold to reinterpret Torah, finding there unexpected legitimation for its fidelity to God in surprising ways (Acts 15: 15–18). How was that work of God made known to the church? Through the narratives of faith related by Paul and Barnabas and Peter, their personal testimony of how "signs and wonders" had been worked among the Gentiles. (Acts 15: 4, 6–11, 12–13)[11]

Johnson concludes his essay by asking whether there are narratives of homosexual holiness, analogous to the narratives of Gentile holiness related by Peter, Paul, and Barnabas, to which the church ought to begin listening. Such testimonies might lead the church to raise the question, "Is homosexual covenantal love according to the 'mind of Christ', an authentic realization of that Christian identity authored by the Holy Spirit, and therefore 'authored' as well by the Scripture despite the 'authorities' speaking against it?"[12]

Johnson rightly emphasizes the role of testimony in the church's decision-making in Acts. Further, I agree that any analogous application of Acts 10–15 to issues of homosexual inclusion will need to be grounded in testimonies of "homosexual holiness." Johnson's comments, however, indicate that the burden of providing such testimony is on homosexual Christians. This is a departure from the testifying practices of Acts. It is crucial that Peter, Paul, and Barnabas were all circumcised Jews testifying about the work of the Spirit in the lives of uncircumcised Gentile believers. It is not the responsibility of the Gentiles to provide testimony to their own reception of the Spirit. It should not, then, be the responsibility of homosexual Christians to provide "narratives of homosexual holiness." Instead, the onus is on other Christians who may enter (or have already entered) into friendships with homosexual Christians out of which they might offer testimony of their friends' holiness. Alternatively, it may be the case that such friendships generate calls to repentance from one friend to another.[13] Several things need to be said in this regard. First, the point of such friendships is not simply to be able to make inquiries and judgments about the sexual practices of another person. Friendships are not to be a form of fieldwork from which one can then make judgments about others. That is, like all friendships between Christians, these friendships are to be marked by the habits, practices, and dispositions that enable friends to deepen their communion with each other and with God. Through prayer, conversation, argument, tears, and laughter, these friendships are to be part of the transformations that God seeks to work in both friends' lives, conforming them ever more nearly into the image of Christ. Christian friends both assist in each others' struggles to live faithfully before God and exemplify for each other the shape of faithful living in particular contexts.[14] Of course, and perhaps most importantly, this cannot happen in the absence of habits of hospitality. That is, Christians have no reason to think they understand how the Holy Spirit weighs in on the issue of homosexuality until they welcome homosexuals into their homes and sit down to eat with them.

Jeffrey Siker, a New Testament scholar and Presbyterian minister, offers this sort of testimony in a recent essay.[15] Having surveyed various analogies used to situate homosexual Christians within the church, Siker argues, "I believe a more appropriate constructive analogy . . . is to view homosexual Christians today in the same way the earliest (that is, Jewish) Christians approached the issue of including Gentile Christians within the community."[16]

As Siker rightly notes, Acts initially indicates that for the earliest Jewish Christians (and all other Jews), Gentiles *qua* Gentiles could not be members of the people of Israel, even the eschatologically reconstituted Israel represented by the followers of Jesus. Gentiles were, by definition, unclean, as attested by Peter in Acts 10.[17] "And yet the experiences of Peter and Paul led them, and eventually many others, to the realization that even as a Gentile one could come to know God, worship God, and to receive and show the Spirit of God."[18] Siker recognizes that for the earliest Christians, the decisive argument for including the Gentiles as Gentiles is the recognition (through the testimony of Peter in particular) that God's Spirit had been poured out on the Gentiles. In this light, Siker goes on to "confess:"

> Before I came to know various Christians who are also homosexual in their sexual orientation, I was like the hard-nosed doctrinaire circumcised Jewish Christians who denied that Gentiles could receive the Spirit of Christ as Gentiles. But just as Peter's experience of Cornelius in Acts 10 led him to realize that even Gentiles were receiving God's Spirit, so my experience of various gay and lesbian Christians has led me to realize that these Christians have received God's Spirit as gays and lesbians, and the reception of the Spirit has nothing to do with sexual orientation.[19]

In a footnote to this quote, Siker relates that it was a particular friendship with a gay Christian which brought this home to him. In the light of my earlier comments on Acts 10–15, it strikes me that this note should have played a more central role in Siker's argument. It is the one point where he gives specific testimony to the presence of the Spirit in the life of a particular homosexual Christian.

There is much in Siker's argument I have not addressed here. Further, I am not sure the conclusions that follow from seeing issues surrounding homosexual Christians as analogous to issues surrounding Gentile inclusion in Acts are as clear and straightforward as Siker thinks. For example, there is a built-in ambiguity in the notion of including Gentiles as Gentiles that would need to be clarified in any attempt to draw analogies between Acts 10–15 and the present. On the one hand, being a Gentile simply designates a non-Jew. In this sense, by accepting Gentiles as Gentiles, the first followers of Jesus did not require these non-Jews to become Jews. On the other hand, the designation "Gentile" could also implicate one in a host of unacceptable practices such as idolatry which needed to be abandoned upon entering the church (cf. Eph. 2). These practices seem to be in view in the "burdens" placed on Gentiles in Acts 15: 19–21. In this respect, Gentiles were not straightforwardly accepted as Gentiles.[20] Leaving these issues aside for the moment, I do have to say that Siker has opened up a new avenue in this debate, drawing some promising analogies that might allow us beyond our present sterile, if not acrimonious debates.

The obvious question one must ask is how does one know that God's Spirit has been poured out on homosexual believers?[21] It is at this point that Siker's argument begins to wind down. Rather than focus on his own testimony of witnessing the work of the Spirit in the life of a homosexual friend, Siker begins to tackle this question by drawing an analogy to the way Paul in Gal. 3 addresses this same issue of whether Gentile believers need to be circumcised and obey Torah:

> Paul calls upon them, and us, to pay attention to their experience of the Spirit. Did they recognize the Spirit through a doctrinal orthodoxy and orthopraxy now being called for by troublemakers who insisted that the only good Gentile was a "Jewish Gentile"? Or did they recognize the Spirit through their faith? And so today we are called to ask an analogous question: Despite our experience, do we insist that homosexual Christians can only have the Spirit of God if they are "heterosexual homosexual" Christians? Or with Peter and Paul are we up to the challenge of recognizing, perhaps with surprise and with humility, that even gay and lesbian Christians, as gays and lesbians and not as sinners, have received the Spirit in faith?[22]

I will address the specifics of Galatians 3: 1–5 in the next chapter [of *Engaging Scripture*]. For now, I want to note that Siker's conclusion here is underdeveloped.

Spirit experience, in both the New Testament and the present, is not self-interpreting. It is often quite difficult to read the Spirit.[23] As I have already indicated, as related in Acts, the very manner in which the Gentiles were included as full members of the people of God presupposes a whole set of ecclesiological practices which are largely absent from Christianity in the US. Most churches do not train and nurture people in forming the sorts of friendships out of which testimony about the Spirit's work might arise. Moreover, Christians are generally suspicious about claims concerning the Spirit; we are not generally a people who either testify well or listen wisely to the testimony of others. We largely favor self-authentication and despise common patterns of discernment. We abhor the notion that our lives ought to be disciplined by a concern for one another. In short, most Christian communities lack the skills and resources to debate what a life marked by the Spirit might look like in the present. In the absence of these ecclesial practices and structures one cannot be hopeful that most Christian churches will be able to follow Siker's proposal here without replicating the same sorts of indecisive, divisive, and acrimonious debates that have already marked discussion of this issue. In short, Siker's essay nicely illustrates that reading with the Spirit cannot be done apart from reading the Spirit's work. Further, it provides a sort of testimony to the work of God in the lives of homosexual Christians. What it falls short of recognizing, however, is that Christians cannot aspire to either of these apart from forming and nurturing certain types of common life.

It should be clear that my reservations about Siker's argument are different from those raised by Christopher Seitz in his attack on Siker's position. The most important claim Seitz makes is that one cannot invoke the Spirit to override the "plain sense" of Old Testament texts without taking a supersessionist view of the Old Testament. Although he does not give a comprehensive list, on Seitz's view the texts whose "plain sense" is threatened by Siker's approach would be those texts forbidding sex outside of marriage and those prohibiting same-sex sexual contact. Seitz seems to miss the point of Acts 10–15. It seems quite clear that the initial presumptions of the characters in Acts are that the "plain sense" of texts such as Gen. 17: 9–14 demands that Gentiles joining themselves to the people of Israel must be circumcised. It is recognition of the Spirit's work through the testimony of Peter, Paul, and Barnabas that leads James to invoke Amos 9: 9–12 as part of a decision to include Gentiles without forcing them to be circumcised.[24] I will address more fully the question of whether or not this counts as a supersessionist approach to the Old Testament in the next chapter [of *Engaging Scripture*]. For now let me simply say that I do not think it is supersessionist in any sense of that term that might lead Christians to opt for something like Marcion's approach to this issue. It does, however, raise again the sharp issue about how compatible a static notion of the "plain sense" of scripture, a plain sense located in the text rather than the believing community, is with Christian theological approaches to the Old Testament.[25]

Conclusion

Thus far, I have argued that Christians have every reason to expect the Spirit to play a role in scriptural interpretation. From a reading of John's comments on the

Spirit it is clear that the role that the Spirit plays and the interpretation the Spirit enables will faithfully display the will of the triune God. Even in a case like John 12: 16, it is evident that Spirit-inspired interpretation is going to involve innovative re-readings of scriptural texts in the light of the life, death, and resurrection of Jesus. The issue of the inclusion of the Gentiles in Acts 10–15 gives a more detailed account of Spirit-directed interpretation. This narrative makes it clear that if Christians are to read with the Spirit (as they agree they must) then they must also become adept at reading the Spirit's activity in their midst. The good working of this process depends on Christians' abilities both to testify to the work of the Spirit in the lives of others and to listen wisely to such testimony. These abilities are directly related to the forming and maintaining (through acts of hospitality) of certain types of friendships.

I then examined some attempts to bring the patterns of reasoning related in Acts 10–15 to bear on the contemporary issue of how and under what circumstances homosexuals are to be recognized and included in the church. These attempts will fail as long as the ecclesial practices of forming friendships through acts of hospitality which then enable Christians to testify about the work of the Spirit are in disrepair.

At this point there are still several questions about how Spirit experience and Spirit-inspired interpretation might be connected to each other. In this chapter I have focused on how reading the Spirit and reading with the Spirit are connected to specific structures in the common life of Christian communities. In addition to these, it is also clear that both reading the Spirit and reading with the Spirit involve individuals in acts of interpretive power. In the next chapter [of *Engaging Scripture*] I want to explore the nature of this interpretive power and its close connection to the character of the interpreter.

Notes

1   I do not say a great deal about scripture and the Trinity here. I presume the persuasiveness of David Yeago's account which shows the connection between scripture and the trinitarian doctrines of Nicea. See his "The New Testament and Nicene Dogma," in *The Theological Interpretation of Scripture: Classic and Contemporary Readings*, ed. S. E. Fowl (Oxford: Blackwell, 1997), "the Nicene *homoousion* is neither imposed *on* the New Testament texts, nor distinctly deduced *from* the texts, but, rather, describes a pattern of judgments present in the texts, in the texture of scriptural discourse concerning Jesus and the God of Israel" (p. 87).

2   L. T. Johnson, *Scripture and Discernment* (Nashville, TN: Abingdon Press, 1996), p. 105.

3   As will become clear in the next chapter's discussion [in *Engaging Scripture*] of Galatians, Peter seems to change his mind. My points about Peter in Acts are separable from Galatians and discussions about the historical Peter.

4   Robert C. Tannehill's comment (*The Narrative Unity of Luke–Acts*, 2 vols. (Philadelphia and Minneapolis: Fortress Press, 1986–90), vol. 2, p. 130), regarding 10: 1–11: 18 is applicable to the entirety of this section, "Study of the composition of the narrative also reveals another important factor in discernment of the will of God: the sharing of divine promptings with other persons."

5   See also Peter's claim in 5: 32, "And we are witnesses of these things, and so is the Holy Spirit whom God has given to those who obey him."

6   L. Gregory Jones has provided an important homiletical meditation on this point in "Taking Time for the Spirit," *The Christian Century* (April 29, 1992), p. 451.

7   See "Debate and Discernment, Scripture and the Spirit," *Commonweal* (January 28, 1994), pp. 11–13. This is now part of Johnson, *Scripture and Discernment*, p. 144.

8   In general I am not persuaded that there is a single issue called "homosexuality" about which Christians must have a position. (On this point see Stanley Hauerwas, "Gay Friendship: a Thought Experiment in Catholic Moral Theology," *Irish Theological Quarterly* 58/2 (1992), pp. 141–53; repr. in Eugene F. Rogers, Jr., ed., *Theology and Sexuality* [Oxford: Blackwell, 2002], pp. 289–305.) My purposes here are primarily concerned with these issues as they involve scriptural interpretation.

9   See *After Virtue*, 2nd edn. (Notre Dame, IN: University of Notre Dame Press, 1984), p. 253. I think, however, that Jeffrey Stout is right to note that civil war carried out by other means is still preferable to real civil war.

10   Johnson, *Scripture and Discernment*, p. 145.

11   Johnson, *Scripture and Discernment*, p. 147.

12   Johnson, *Scripture and Discernment*, p. 148.

13   I gather this might be the force of the story Richard Hays tells in his essay, "Awaiting the Redemption of Our Bodies," *Sojourners* 20 (July 1991), pp. 17–21.

14   "By spending time together with people who are good, by sharing and delighting with them in our mutual love for the good we are more fully impressed with the good ourselves. Friendship is not just a relationship; it is a moral enterprise. People spend their lives together doing good because that is what they see their lives to be." Paul Wadell, CP, *Friendship and the Moral Life* (Notre Dame, IN: University of Notre Dame Press, 1989), p. 62. See also Hauerwas, "Gay Friendship," for a further account of the moral significance of friendship.

15   Jeffrey Siker, "Homosexuals, the Bible and Gentile Inclusion," *Theology Today* 51 (July 1994), pp. 219–34.

16   Siker, "Homosexuals, the Bible," p. 229. Christopher Seitz in a long footnote attacks Siker's article on several fronts. See "Human Sexuality Viewed from the Bible's Understanding of the Human Condition," *Theology Today* 52 (July 1995), p. 240 n.3. One of Seitz's points is that attempts to justify homosexual practice as simply a natural inclination that must be allowed in the loving community of Jesus' followers despite explicit prohibitions against it, both run counter to Jesus' own practice and leave one in the position of adopting a supersessionist approach to the Old Testament. Siker's position, however, need not entail the claim that Christians should always be free to follow their natural inclinations.

17   Here it is important to note that although Siker's wording is ambiguous, a charitable account of his position would take his claims about the "earliest Christians'" views about Gentiles to be fairly straightforward inferences and deductions based on what Seitz would have to call a "plain sense" reading of Acts 1–11. Seitz, alternatively, reads Siker's claims about the "earliest Christians" to be an attempt to set up an original moment as a sort of straw figure which is then easily undermined from a modern perspective. As Seitz notes, this would be a mistake. This is not the only way to read Siker's claims, however.

18   Siker, "Homosexuals, the Bible," p. 230.

19   Siker, "Homosexuals, the Bible," p. 230. The final clause of the quote, "the reception of the Spirit has nothing to do with sexual orientation," deserves some comment. If all

Siker means by this is that the reception of the Spirit is not dependent upon one's sexual orientation, then his point is clear and follows well from his previous argument. If he means reception of the Spirit has no bearing on one's sexual orientation and practice, then one would have to say that this is not a claim justified by the evidence he cites.

20   In his recent book, *The Moral Vision of the New Testament* (San Francisco: Harper San Francisco, 1996) Richard Hays briefly addresses Johnson's and Siker's arguments, calling them "richly suggestive" (p. 396), but ultimately rejecting them until such time as those advocating this view can (as Paul does with the issue of Gentile inclusion) offer readings of scripture to show that "this development can be understood as a fulfill-ment of God's design for human sexuality as previously revealed in Scripture" (p. 399). Hays is skeptical that such a reading can be offered. It may well be the case, however, that there is more scope here than Hays thinks. First, as Hays himself knows, Paul's readings of scripture were quite audacious and ran against what most would consider to be the preponderance of scriptural testimony. Secondly, Hays may have artificially prejudiced the matter by requiring that such readings fit into God's design for human sexuality. Christians need to remember that "human sexuality" is a modern notion that may include a variety of assumptions and presuppositions that fit badly with Christian convictions about God's design for humans and creation. If this is the case, then there may be ways of reading scripture that fit certain types of relationships and practices which we now cover under the term "homosexuality" within an account of God's economy in ways that do not fit under the description "human sexuality."

21   Towards the end of the essay Siker raises these very questions very briefly. Unfortunately, he does not really tie these issues together with his own testimony about the role of the Spirit in his friend's life. Nor does he explore ways in which these questions are addressed in the narrative of Acts 10–15.

22   Siker, "Homosexuals, the Bible," p. 234.

23   In response to comments I made to Siker on this essay, he added some comments recognizing the difficulties in recognizing Spirit reception both in Acts and in the pre-sent when the essay was reprinted in *Homosexuality in the Church: Both Sides of the Debate,* ed. J. Siker (Louisville, KY: Westminster/John Knox Press, 1994), pp. 178–94. These additional comments did not change the substance of his argument.

24   Seitz's claim that in Acts 13: 47 Paul uses Isa. 49: 6 to justify going to the Gentiles *qua* Gentiles is simply inaccurate. Paul uses Isa. 49: 6 to justify going to the Gentiles in the light of rejection by the Jews in Psidian Antioch. This passage is completely silent about whether these Gentiles should become Jews upon hearing the gospel. It is only the Spirit's work that resolves this question later.

25   This is what I take to be the difference between Frei's and Tanner's notion of the "plain sense" (discussed in chapter 1 [of *Engaging Scripture*]) and the view Seitz lays out by implication. I think the fact that Seitz is a professional Old Testament scholar and the fact that Frei was and Tanner is a theologian accounts for much of this difference. This raises the further question of the extent to which one can simultaneously function as a professional scholar of the Old Testament and as a Christian theologian. See fur-ther Jon Levenson's *The Hebrew Bible, the Old Testament and Historical Criticism* (Louisville, KY: Westminster/John Knox Press, 1993).

32

Bruce D. Marshall, *from* "The Epistemic Role of the Spirit"

What's marvelous about this selection is Marshall's concept of the Spirit providing "habitability." What he means is that the Spirit makes living within the moral
and intellectual demands of Christianity attractive and plausible: the Christian world
becomes *habitable*. But the word packs in more than it says. The world that the
Spirit makes habitable recalls the Spirit's hovering over creation, to make it
friendly to human beings. The world that the Spirit makes habitable recalls the
Spirit's gathering a community in the church, to make a habitat for the faithful.
The world that Spirit makes habitable recalls the Spirit's habituating believers
with faith, hope, and charity, the qualities that make the Christian life plausible
and possible. Marshall has chosen a word that ramifies through many features
of God's action in the world traditionally appropriated to the Spirit: In making
Christianity habitable, the Spirit brings life, gathers community, initiates identity,
inspires virtue, sustains sacraments, inculcates holiness. All of those things make
Christianity habitable as an extension of God's triune life.

Marshall's larger project proposes a distinctively trinitarian theory of truth in an
analytic philosophical register. Thus his discussion of habitability forms a section
of a chapter, "The Spirit's Epistemic Role" – in conforming the mind to the
truth. The Trinity brings it about that true beliefs are true, say that "Jesus is risen."
The acts of the three Persons of the Trinity, Father, Son, and Holy Spirit, remain
indivisible but appropriate to each. So the Father raises Jesus; the Son shows
himself raised; the Spirit prepares the mind to believe it, in part by establishing
a habitable community. In the resurrection, the Father generates the truth; the
Son bears the truth; the Spirit leads into truth. Or the Father makes true beliefs
true; the Son proves them true; and by the Spirit human beings come to hold

Bruce D. Marshall, "The Epistemic Role of the Spirit," in *Trinity and Truth* (Cambridge: Cambridge
University Press, 2000), pp. 180–2, 204–7, 211–12.

them true. The Father conforms reality to the truth; the Son conforms the appearances; and the Spirit conforms minds and communities. In this activity, however, the Trinity is bringing it about not so much that beliefs as that human beings become true: they "will bear the image of the man of heaven."

from The Epistemic Role of the Spirit

Bruce D. Marshall

We recognize the ultimate epistemic right which belongs to Jesus Christ by organizing our total system of belief around the narratives which identify him, crucified and risen. If we ascribe this epistemic significance to Jesus, we shall be unwilling to hold true any belief which we recognize to be inconsistent with these narratives, and, conversely, unwilling to regard these narratives as false for the sake of holding true any other belief, should that belief conflict with them. Whence, though, comes this willingness to hold the narratives true in the face of whatever epistemic opposition the believer may encounter? How – without recourse to foundations or epistemic dependence – do we succeed in recognizing the epistemic ultimacy of Jesus the Son?

To this question the tradition has tended to respond by appealing to a distinctive epistemic role of the Holy Spirit: "No one can say 'Jesus is Lord,' except by the Holy Spirit" (1 Cor. 12: 3). If the Gospel of John identifies "the truth" with Jesus Christ, the Word incarnate (14: 6; cf. 1: 14, 17), 1 John identifies "the truth" with the Holy Spirit, precisely in virtue of the Spirit's faithful witness to Jesus Christ: "the Spirit is the truth" (1 John 5: 6).[1] The Spirit's role as witness comes through with equal clarity in the Gospel's farewell discourses (cf. John 15: 26: "he will testify on my behalf," also 14: 26; 16: 13–14). In virtue of the Spirit's own unique location within the triune life of God, these passages suggest, he must be the one who empowers us to recognize the epistemic ultimacy of Jesus Christ – who teaches us how to order all of our beliefs around the narratives which identify the Father's crucified and risen Son. As Thomas Aquinas puts the point, "To make the truth manifest belongs uniquely to the Holy Spirit (*convenit proprietati Spiritus sancti*). For it belongs to love to disclose hidden things," and in God the love which opens up that which is hidden is the Holy Spirit himself: "the Holy Spirit is nothing other than love."[2]

The Son's distinctive epistemic role is therefore inseparable not only from that of the Father . . . but also from that of the Spirit. That both the faith which assents to the church's central beliefs and the wisdom which judges all other beliefs accordingly depend on the continuing action of the Holy Spirit already indicates, as Christian theologians have long maintained, that there is no hope of generating what William James calls "coercive arguments" for the church's chief convictions (though the Christian community expects that it will be able, at least in the long run, to meet almost any argument which is brought against these beliefs, by showing that objections to them are not rationally coercive, either). The Spirit's epistemic work is thus to teach us how to believe – and to judge all things in accordance with – claims whose denial will always, at least in this life, be rationally plausible.

How does the Spirit do this? Acquiring a Christian view of the world calls for a persistent willingness to overturn the epistemic priorities (though not the totality of belief) we would otherwise be inclined to have. In at least this sense, ordering one's beliefs such that Jesus Christ has unrestricted epistemic primacy requires a change of heart and not simply a change of mind. The gospel of Jesus Christ, it seems, proclaims a truth which cannot be known unless it is also loved (see 2 Thess. 2: 10). More than that: grasping the truth of the church's beliefs apparently requires a life which enacts a wide range of dispositions rooted in a Spirit-wrought love for God and neighbor. "Whoever says, 'I have come to know him,' but does not obey his commandments, is a liar, and in such a person the truth does not exist" (1 John 2: 4). The Spirit's induction of human beings into the Christian community's way of belief thus seems bound up with the creation of that purity of heart or holiness without which, as the New Testament has it, "no one will see the Lord" (Heb. 12: 14; cf. Matt. 5: 8).

Stirred by texts like these, Christian theologians have long sought to forge strong links between grasping the truth of the church's central beliefs and following from the heart a way of life these beliefs commend. "Anyone who does not love the truth," Gregory the Great observes in comment on 1 John 2: 4, "has not yet known it (*adhuc minime cognovit*) . . . I tell you that it is not by faith that you will come to know the light of truth [= Christ], but by love; not by mere conviction, but by action."[3]

. . .

How, though, does the Spirit create a willingness to judge all beliefs by their coherence with the church's central convictions? We get needed purchase on the epistemic role of the Spirit by tracking the links between practice and meaning. But this leaves unsettled the question of how we become persuaded to believe that the church's central beliefs are true, with the unrestricted epistemic primacy which the church attributes to them. It is of course quite possible for someone to mean by central Christian sentences just what the Christian community means by them, and to hold them false. We need, therefore, not simply an account of how the Spirit's action fixes the contents of central Christian beliefs, but an account of how the Spirit persuades people to hold these beliefs true.

As the problems faced by the pragmatic thesis show, a successful account of the Spirit's persuasion will have to avoid treating (descriptions of) the practices the Spirit creates as some form of evidence for the truth of Christian belief. There is no evidence for beliefs beyond the totality of belief to which any contested claims also belong, and the epistemic role of the Son already accounts for the distinctively Christian way of structuring this total field of belief. In the nature of the case the Spirit will not persuade by adding something to the totality of belief, by giving us reasons or evidence we do not already have, but by eliciting our assent to a way of structuring the whole.[4]

To fix the contents of the church's beliefs is to know what the world would be like if these beliefs were true. Willingness to hold these beliefs depends, presumably, on the attractiveness and the habitability of the world they describe – the world there must be if the beliefs are true. The community's beliefs will be attractive to hold if what they are about attracts: if, roughly put, the triune God who in love creates, redeems, and perfects all things is a being whom it would be desirable to be created, redeemed, and perfected in love by. But attractiveness alone is not enough for willingness; one might find a description of the world both plausible and attractive, but nonetheless regard it as imaginary. Willingness to believe thus seems to require an incentive beyond the attractiveness of what the beliefs are about.

The life of the Christian community constitutes the needed incentive, by displaying the habitability of the world which Christian beliefs describe. Communal success at holding these beliefs and living accordingly – the encounter with actual public willingness to suppose that the world described by these beliefs is not simply desirable but real – encourages and prompts its like.

This can happen in many ways. For example, people sometimes become especially attracted – or remain attracted, having been drawn from earliest memory – to the unmerited forgiveness which, so the church proclaims, the triune God bestows upon the undeserving in Jesus Christ. People may find themselves attracted, that is, to the triune God's will, which nothing can vanquish, to make right humanly irreparable wrongs. God's will to forgive, so the church supposes, reaches us in the most elemental way in public communal practices which are the Spirit's work – in baptism, confession and absolution, the preaching of the gospel, and the eucharist. One cannot coherently be attracted to this particular sort of forgiveness without also desiring to belong to this community and to believe its central claims (though of course a person might not realize this right away).

There are, of course, shades of desire or attraction here, and with that shades of belief. One might simply wish there were an omnipotently forgiving God, as one might wistfully desire to relive one's vanished youth. Such attraction does not require that one believe the truth of the church's central claims to be a serious possibility, any more than one believes time travel to be a serious possibility. One might positively desire the divine forgiveness of which the church speaks, but without actually partaking of the communal rites by which it is received. This does require taking the truth of the beliefs which identify the triune God, and specify the grounds for supposing that this God is unquenchably forgiving, as a serious possibility. It seems impossible genuinely to desire (and not just idly wish for) a good which one is committed to believing cannot be obtained.

One might, however, actively seek to receive the forgiveness which the triune God gives by accepting a share in the Christian community's life, and participating in those communal actions by which the triune God accomplishes his own forgiveness of sinners. This would seem to require not simply being open to the truth of the church's central claims, but actually believing them, since it seems impossible to seek forgiveness from a God whom one does not believe to be (that is, identifying descriptions of whom one does not hold true), or whom one does not believe acts forgivingly. One might, though, seek forgiveness without fully believing that the church's claims about this God are true, retaining some insecurity as to whether the forgiveness one is looking for has actually been received. One might, finally, trust in God's free and undeserved mercy in Christ, confident in the triune God's forgiveness in spite of one's sinful failings, and this would seem to require being fully convinced that the beliefs which identify and describe the forgiving God are true.

The Christian community's life displays the habitability as well as the attractiveness of a world in which God freely forgives sinners. In this community, people not only desire and seek forgiveness, but have utter confidence of receiving it, in spite of the wrongs which they themselves cannot make right. Members of this community display their trust in God's forgiveness not only by announcing their belief in it, but by forgiving those who have wronged them, even when this brings humiliation and suffering (not all do this, but some do it). As such they show that a world where the triune God freely forgives and commands us to do likewise is not only attractive, but viable. People actually succeed in living in this world; the sort of utter trust in God's forgiveness which enables people freely to forgive even those who hate them is, to be more precise, not simply possible but actual.

If, though, I want the forgiveness of this God to reach me such that I can know it and rely upon it, I have to hold true the church's central beliefs. At this point the manifest habitability, and not simply the attractiveness or desirability, of a world in which God freely forgives sinners plays a crucial role in eliciting belief that God forgives – belief that this is the way the world is.

It seems unlikely, though perhaps not impossible, that my desire alone, or even my active quest for forgiveness, could induce me to hold the beliefs without which I cannot trust or be confident in God's forgiveness. Since these beliefs cannot be regarded, epistemically, as either unavoidable or inadmissible, holding them requires a measure of willingness. But doing so simply because I desire what they promise perhaps demands too much of the will. That I want a good is surely an incentive to believe that it can be received, but seems by itself inadequate to sustain this belief, still less the belief that it actually has been received. When, however, I behold a community of people presently enjoying the good which I desire – confidence in God's free mercy – the burden on the will is reduced. The good already enjoyed by this community greatly increases the incentive to find my desire fulfilled by sharing in its life, and with that to hold the beliefs I must hold in order to enjoy the good which I seek.

The Spirit of course invites participation in the church's life in many other ways, and so has many other ways of eliciting assent to the beliefs which are necessary to enjoy the goods particular to that way of life. Perhaps more than anything else, so Christians hope and believe, the publicly visible love of this community's members for one another and for the world will invite all of humanity to share in that love, and so in the communal life constituted by it. Especially as it reaches to enemies and persecutors, this love displays itself as the Spirit's gift in its tendency to outrun the strength of those who, nonetheless, most dearly enjoy and enact it. But the features of Christian communal life which might elicit willing assent to the church's belief system are probably too numerous and diverse to systematize. Some basic patterns of attraction will no doubt be easy to observe, but the Spirit who lives in the church will endlessly fashion novel ways of inviting the world to share in its life.

. . .

Thus the Spirit's persuasion makes the church habitable for us. The Spirit draws us into that community structured by practices and beliefs which together give us a share in the forgiving and demanding love which is the life of the triune God. Seeing the Spirit's epistemic role in terms of his donation of a share in God's community-forming love may help us understand those scriptural texts which forge strong links between holding Christian beliefs and engaging in specific practices, and thus may seem to support the pragmatic thesis. "Whoever does not love" – which is to say, more specifically, "whoever does not obey his commandments" – "does not know God, for God is love" (1 John 4: 8; cf. 2: 4). This need not be taken to suggest that the sinful failure of those who profess Christian beliefs is by itself incompatible with actually holding those beliefs. There is no one-to-one correlation of action with belief, and so no way to read off from any one act, either in our own case or that of others, an absence of Spirit-wrought love or desire for God, and with that of Christian belief. But the willingness actually to hold these sentences true has to come from the Spirit's donation of a share in the love which God is. And this donation cannot be without love toward companions who share it, and toward enemies who refuse it – cannot, in other words, be without obedience to the commandments of the God who is love. In just this sense, though not as pragmatic evidence for the truth of Christian beliefs, "anyone who resolves to do the will of God will know whether the teaching [of Christ] is from God" (John 7: 17).

Notes

1 Ignace de la Potterie makes much of this last passage, together with 1 John 4: 6, in *La Vérité dans Saint Jean*, 2 vols. (Rome: Biblical Institute Press, 1977); see especially pp. 286–328, and the summary, pp. 1012–14.

2 *In Ioannem* 14, 4 (no. 1916). The last thought is, of course, characteristically Augustinian.

3 *Homilia in Evangelia* 14, 3–4 (PL [Patrologia Latina] 76, 1129A–B).

4 Bonaventure suggests the notion of "persuasion" to characterize this aspect of the Spirit's epistemic role: "In faith, even though the intellect of the believer does not have a reason on account of which he ought to assent to the truth, it has the authority of the highest truth, who persuades his heart" (*In* III *Sent.* [Aquinas's Commentary on the *Sentences* of Peter Lombard, Book III], 23, 1, 1, ad 3; *Opera Selecta* III, p. 463a).

Further Reading

Especially useful readings are marked with one or two asterisks (*).

Ambrose of Milan. *The Holy Spirit*. In *Theological and Dogmatic Works*. Trans. Roy J. Deferrari. Fathers of the Church, vol. 44. Washington, DC: Catholic University of America Press, 1963.

*Athanasius of Alexandria, Saint. *The Letters of Saint Athanasius Concerning the Holy Spirit*. Translated with Introduction and Notes by C. R. B. Shapland. New York: Philosophical Library, 1951.

Augustine. *De Trinitate*. Trans. Stephen McKenna. Fathers of the Church, vol. 45. Washington, DC: Catholic University of America Press, 1963.

Balthasar, Hans Urs von. *Creator Spirit: Explorations in Theology*, vol. 3. Trans. Brian McNeil, CRV. San Francisco: Ignatius Press, 1993.

Balthasar, Hans Urs von. *Prayer*. Trans. Graham Harrison. San Francisco: Ignatius Press, 1986.

Bar Hebraeus. *Bar Hebraeus's Book of the Dove*. Trans. A. J. Wensinck. Leyden: E. J. Brill, 1919.

Barth, Karl. *Church Dogmatics*, 4 vols. in 13. Trans. G. W. Bromiley et al. Edinburgh: T. & T. Clark, 1936–75, esp. sections 6, 12, 16, 62, 63, 67, 68, 72, 73.

Brock, Sebastian P. "Baptismal Themes in the Writings of Joseph of Serugh." In *Symposium Syriacum 1976*, ed. Arthur Vööbus. Rome: Pontificium Institutum Orientalium Studiorum, 1978.

Brock, Sebastian P. *Spirituality in the Syriac Tradition*. Moran Etho Series, no. 2. Kerala, India: St Ephrem Ecumenical Research Institute, 1989.

Brock, Sebastian P. *Studies in Syriac Spirituality*. Syrian Churches Series, vol. 13. Poona, India: Anita Printers, 1988.

Brock, Sebastian P. "Studies in the Early History of the Syrian Orthodox Baptismal Liturgy." *Journal of Theological Studies* n.s. 23 (1972): 16–64.

Brock, Sebastian P. "The Holy Spirit as Feminine in Early Syriac Literature." In *After Eve*, ed. Janet Martin Soskice. London: Marshall-Pickering, 1990.

**Brock, Sebastian P. *The Holy Spirit in the Syrian Baptismal Tradition*, 2nd rev. and enlarged edn. Poona, India: Anita Printers, 1998. Reprinted: Piscataway, NJ: Gorgias Press, 2008.

Brock, Sebastian P. "The Mysteries in the Side of Christ." *Sobornost* 7 (1978): 462–72.

Brock, Sebastian P., ed. and trans. *The Syriac Fathers on Prayer and the Spiritual Life*. Cistercian Studies Series, no. 101. Kalamazoo, MI: Cistercian Publications, 1987.

*Bulgakov, Sergius. *The Comforter*. Trans. Boris Jakim. Grand Rapids, MI: Eerdmans, 2004. Esp. ch. 4.

Burgess, Stanley M. *The Holy Spirit: Ancient Christian Traditions*. Peabody, MA: Hendrickson Publishers, 1984.

Burgess, Stanley M. *The Holy Spirit: Eastern Christian Traditions*. Peabody, MA: Hendrickson Publishers, 1989.

Burns, J. Patout and Gerald M. Fagin, eds. *The Holy Spirit*. Message of the Fathers of the Church, no. 3. Wilmington, DE: Michael Glazier, 1984.

Cantalamessa, Raniero. *Come, Creator Spirit: Meditations on the* Veni Creator. Trans. Denis Barrett and Marlene Barrett. Collegeville, MN: Liturgical Press, 2003.

Cantalamessa, Raniero. *The Holy Spirit in the Life of Jesus: The Mystery of Christ's Baptism*. Collegeville, MN: Liturgical Press, 1994.

Coakley, Sarah. *On Desiring God*, vol. I: *God, Sexuality and the Self: An Essay "On the Trinity."* Cambridge: Cambridge University Press, forthcoming.

Coakley, Sarah. "Traditions of Spiritual Guidance." In *Powers and Submissions: Spirituality, Philosophy and Gender*. Oxford: Blackwell, 2002.

*Coakley, Sarah. "Why Three? Some Further Reflections on the Origins of the Doctrine of the Trinity." In *The Making and Remaking of Christian Doctrine: Essays in Honour of Maurice Wiles*, ed. Sarah Coakley and David A. Pailin. Oxford: Oxford University Press, 1993.

*"La Colombe et l'Agneau: méditation sur le Christ et l'Esprit." Par un moine de l'Église d'Orient. *Contacts* (Paris) 15 (1963): 5–33.

Congar, Yves. *I Believe in the Holy Spirit*. Trans. David Smith. New York: Crossroad, 1997.

Dabney, D. Lyle. *Die Kenosis des Geistes: Kontinuität zwischen Schöpfung und Erlösung im Werk des Heiligen Geistes*. Neukirchner Beiträge zur Systematischen Theologie, Bd. 18. Neukirchen-Vluyn: Neukirchener Verlag, 1997.

D'Costa, Gavin. *Sexing the Trinity: Gender, Culture and the Divine*. London: SCM Press, 2000.

*Evdokimov, Paul. *L'Esprit Saint dans la tradition orthodoxe*. Paris: Éditions du Cerf, 1969.

**Florensky, Pavel. *The Pillar and Ground of the Truth*. Trans. Boris Jakim. Princeton, NJ: Princeton University Press, 1997.

Graves, Charles. *The Holy Spirit in the Theology of Sergius Bulgakov*. Geneva: World Council of Churches, 1972.

*Gregory of Nazianzus. *Theological Orations. Oration V: On the Holy Spirit*. In *Faith Gives Fullness to Reasoning: The Five Theological Orations of Gregory of Nazianzus*. Trans. and ed. Lionel Wickham and Frederick Williams, with Introduction and Commentary by Frederick W. Norris. Leiden and New York: E. J. Brill, 1991.

Gregory of Nyssa. *On the Holy Spirit*. In Nicene and Post-Nicene Fathers, 2nd series, vol. 5.

*Gregory of Nyssa. *To Abblabius: On Not Three Gods*. In *Christology of the Later Fathers*, ed. Edward R. Hardy. Library of Christian Classics, vol. 3. Philadelphia: Westminster Press, 1954.

Gross, Jules. *The Divinization of the Christian According to the Greek Fathers*. Trans. Paul Onica. Anaheim, CA: A. & C. Press, 2003.

Guerric d'Igny. Second Sermon for Annunciation. In *Liturgical Sermons*, vol. 1. Kalamazoo, MI: Cistercian Publications, 1971.

Harvey, Susan Ashbrook. "Feminine Imagery for the Divine: The Holy Spirit, the Odes of Solomon, and Early Syriac Tradition." *St Vladimir's Seminary Quarterly* 37 (1993): 111–39.

Hilary of Poitiers. *De Trinitate*. In Nicene and Post-Nicene Fathers, 2nd series, vol. 9.

Isaac of Nineveh. *Mystical Treatises*. Trans. A. J. Wensinck. Amsterdam: Koninklijke Akademie van Wetenschappen, 1923.

Jensen, David, ed. *Lord and Giver of Life*. Philadelphia: Westminster John Knox, 2008.

Jenson, Robert W. *Systematic Theology*. New York: Oxford University Press, 1997–9.

*Jenson, Robert W. "The Holy Spirit." In *Christian Dogmatics*, 2 vols., ed. Robert W. Jenson and Carl E. Braaten. Philadelphia: Fortress Press, 1984.

*Jenson, Robert W. *The Triune Identity*. Philadelphia: Fortress Press, 1982.

Jenson, Robert W. *Unbaptized God: The Basic Flaw in Ecumenical Theology*. Minneapolis: Fortress Press, 1992.

John of Damascus. *The Orthodox Faith*. Trans. Frederic Chase. New York: Fathers of the Church, 1958.

Kilby, Karen E. "Perichoresis and Projection: Problems with the Social Doctrines of the Trinity." *New Blackfriars* 81 (2000): 432–45.

Laminski, Adolf. *Der Heilige Geist als Geist Christi und der Gläubigen: Der Beitrag des Athanasios von Alexandrien zur Formulierung des trinitarischen Dogmas im vierten Jahrhundert*. Leipzig: St Benno-Verlag, 1969.

Lampe, G. W. H. *God as Spirit*. The Bampton Lectures, 1976. Oxford: Clarendon Press, 1977.

**Lampe, G. W. H. *The Seal of the Spirit: A Study in the Doctrine of Baptism and Confirmation in the New Testament and the Fathers*, 2nd edn. London: SPCK, 1967.

Loughlin, Gerard. "Sexing the Trinity." *New Blackfriars* 79 (1998): 18–25.

Metéos, J[uan]. "L'action du Saint-Esprit dans la liturgie dite de s. Jean Chrysostome." *Proche-Orient Chrétien: Revue d'études et d'informations* 9 (1959): 193–208.

Milbank, John. "Can a Gift be Given? Prolegomenon to a Future Trinitarian Metaphysic." *Modern Theology* 11 (1995): 119–41.

Moltmann, Jürgen. *The Source of Life: The Holy Spirit and the Theology of Life*. Philadelphia: Augsburg Fortress Press, 1997.

Monloubou, Louis. *La Prière selon saint Luc: Recherche d'une structure*. Paris: Éditions du Cerf, 1976.

Philoxenus of Mabbug. *On the Indwelling of the Holy Spirit*. In *The Syriac Fathers on Prayer and the Spiritual Life*, ed. and trans. Sebastian P. Brock. Cistercian Studies Series, no. 101. Kalamazoo, MI: Cistercian Publications, 1987.

Photios, Saint. *The Mystagogy of the Holy Spirit*. Translated by the Holy Transfiguration Monastery. No place of publication. Studion Publishers, 1983.

*Prestige, G. L. *God in Patristic Thought*. London: SPCK, 1952.

Radner, Ephrem. *The End of the Church: A Pneumatology of Christian Division in the West*. Grand Rapids, MI: Eerdmans, 1998.

Rogers, Eugene F., Jr. *After the Spirit: A Constructive Pneumatology from Resources Outside the Modern West*. Grand Rapids, MI: Eerdmans, 2005.

Rogers, Eugene F., Jr. "Supplementing Barth on Jews and Gender: Identifying God by Anagogy and the Spirit." *Modern Theology* 14 (1998): 43–81.

**Schmemann, Alexander. *For the Life of the World*, 2nd edn. Crestwood, NY: St Vladimir's Seminary Press, 1998.

Schmeeman, Alexander. *Of Water and the Spirit: A Liturgical Study of Baptism*. Crestwood, NY: St Vladimir's Seminary Press, 1974.

Siman, Emmanuel-Pataq. *L'Expérience de l'Esprit par l'Église d'après la tradition syrienne d'Antioche*. Théologie historique 15. Paris: Beauchesne, 1971.

Soskice, Janet Martin. "Trinity and Feminism." In *The Cambridge Companion to Feminist Theology*, ed. Susan Franks Parsons. Cambridge: Cambridge University Press, 2002.

Soulen, R. Kendall. "YHWH the Triune God." *Modern Theology* 15 (1999): 25–54.

*Staniloae, Dumitru. "The Holy Spirit and the Sobornicity of the Church." In *Theology and the Church*. Crestwood, NY: St Vladimir's Seminary Press, 1980. (1st edn. 1974).

*Staniloae, Dumitru. "The procession of the Holy Spirit from the Father and his Relation to the Son, as the Basis of our Deification and Adoption." In *Spirit of God, Spirit of Christ: Ecumenical Reflections on the Filioque Controversy*, ed. Lukas Vischer. Faith and Order Paper no. 103. London: SPCK; Geneva: World Council of Churches, 1981.

*Swete, Henry Barclay. *The Holy Spirit in the Ancient Church: A Study of Christian Teachings in the Age of the Fathers*. London: Macmillan; reprint, Grand Rapids, MI: Baker Book House, 1966.

Swete, Henry Barclay. *The Holy Spirit in the New Testament*. Eugene, OR: Wipf and Stock, 1998.

Vischer, Lukas, ed. *Spirit of God, Spirit of Christ: Ecumenical Reflections on the Filioque Controversy*. Faith and Order Paper no. 103. London: SPCK, 1981.

Volf, Miroslav and Maurice Lee. "The Spirit and the Church." In *Advents of the Spirit: An Introduction to the Current Study of Pneumatology*, ed. Bradford E. Hinze and D. Lyle Dabney. Milwaukee, WI: Marquette University Press, 2001.

Wacker, Grant. *Heaven Below: Early Pentecostals and American Culture*. Cambridge, MA: Harvard University Press, 2001.

**Weinandy, Thomas G. *The Father's Spirit of Sonship: Reconceiving the Trinity*. Edinburgh: T. & T. Clark, 1995.

Welker, Michael. *God the Spirit*. Trans. John F. Hoffmeyer. Minneapolis, MN: Fortress Press, 1994.

*Winkler, Gabriele. "Eine bemerkenswerte Stelle im armenischen Glaubenserkenntnis: Credimus et in Sanctum Spiritum qui descendit in Jordanem proclamavit missum." *Oriens Christianus* 63 (1973): 130–62.

*Winslow, Donald F. *The Dynamics of Salvation: A Study in Gregory of Nazianzus*. Cambridge, MA: Philadelphia Patristic Foundation, 1979.

Yeago, David. *The Faith of the Christian Church*. Columbia, SC: Lutheran Southern Theological Seminary, n.d.

Zizioulas, John D. *Being as Communion: Studies in Personhood and the Church*. Crestwood, NY: St Vladimir's Seminary Press, 1997.

Scripture Index

Scriptural references appear in roman type, page numbers in *italic*.

Genesis, 1:1, *178*; 1–2, *25*; 1:2, *115, 117, 178, 147 n. 21, 160 n. 4*; 2:24, *96*; 3:8, *28, 42 n. 9*; *18, plate 1*; 18:11, *49*; 41:38, *118*

Exodus, 3:2, *160 n. 15*; 12:13, *126 n. 15*; 13:21, *160 n. 16*; 28:3, *117*; 31:3, *117, 147 n. 44*; 33:20, *42 n. 27*; 34:30, *160 n. 14*; 35:31, *117*

Leviticus, 18:22, *309*; 22:13, *309*

Numbers, 27:18, *114*

Deuteronomy, 4:24, *161 n. 53*; 32:11, *115*

Judges, 6:34, *117*; 11:29, *117*

1 Samuel, 16:14, *140 n. 7*; 16:23, *162 n. 61*; 19, *173 n. 17*; 19:20, 23, *117*

2 Samuel, 23:1–3, *196*

1 Kings, 18:12, *117*

2 Kings, 2:9–10, *264*; 2:11, *160 n. 17*; 2:15, *117*; 2:16, *117*; 19:34, *118*

1 Chronicles, 12:19, *117*; 17:10–14, *196*

2 Chronicles, 7:1, *120*; 24:20, *117*

Ezra, 3:12; *117*; 7:122, *118*; 8:3, *117*; 11:1, 24, *117*

Job, 1:10, *118*; 3:23, *118*; 33:4, *147 n. 43, 162 n. 57*; 38:4, *161 n. 51*

Psalms, 2:7, *203*; 5:10, *161 n. 51*; 7:17, *184 n. 8*; 8:3, *183 n. 6*; 10:7, *161 n. 30*; 21:17, *184 n. 40*; 23:5–6, *218*; 26:5, *184 n. 34*; 26:12, *183 n. 7*; 32:6, *269*; 33:6, *147 nn. 9, 45, 162 n. 56, 197*; 34:8, *161 n. 36*; 36, *161 n. 51*; 36:9, *147 n. 28*; 41:1, *173 n. 28*; 41:5, *184 n. 33*; 45:7, *23*; 51:8, *161 n. 28*; 51:11, *117*; 51:12, *114*; 52:2, *161 n. 29*; 56:2, *184 n. 45*; 57:4, *161 n. 29*; 60:4, *184 n. 36*; 60:10, *147 n. 35*; 60:12, *147 n. 40*; 70, *147 n. 40*; 77:20, *147 n. 54*; 78:53, *148 n. 56*; 80:1, *148 n. 55*; 82:6, *41 n. 15, 262*; 85:8, *160 n. 26*; 88:16, *184 n. 15*; 92:15, *147 n. 36*; 103:18, *184 n. 35*; 104:3, *123, 161 n. 54*; 104:30, *31, 117, 162 n. 58*; 108:2, *184 n. 9*; 110:2, *284 n. 2*; 111:5, *184 n. 21*; 112:1, *183 n. 4*; 117:15, *183 n. 3*; 117:26, *183 n. 5*; 119:103, *161 n. 37*; 119:105, *160 n. 13*; 120:6, *184 n. 38*; 125:2, *184 n. 14*; 138:8, *118*; 139:7–15, *161 n. 51*; 140:30, *147 n. 48*; 142, *161 n. 51*; 143:8, *160 n. 27*; 143:10, *117, 147 n. 34*; 145:19, *264*; 148:4, *161 n. 55*; 148:5, *184 n. 12*

Proverbs, 4:25, *160 n. 24*; 5:16, *173 n. 16*; 6:23, *160 n. 12*; 8:22, *26; 15, 135 n. 4*; 19:17, *184 n. 22*; 23:4, *140 n. 3*; 24:7, *140 n. 8*

Song of Songs, 2:14, *180, 184 nn. 32, 47*; 6:8, *123, 126 n. 36*; 8:5, *184 n. 46*

Isaiah, 1:4, *184 n. 18*; 2:10, *184 nn. 39, 41*; 3:34, *161 n. 33*; 4:6, *184 n. 37*; 6, *120*; 7:14, *23*; 8:14, *161 n. 46*; 11:1–3, *161 n. 51*; 11:2, *117, 147 n. 42*; 11:4, *184 n. 42*; 19:14, *126 n. 17*; 27:11, *117*; 31:5, *118*; 34:4, *31*; 40:9–11, *5 n. 2*; 42:1, *117*; 42:11, *184 n. 29*; 44:3, *117*; 48:16, *117, 146, 148 n. 52, 161 n. 51*; 53, *245 n. 14*; 60:19–20, *197*; 61:1, *23, 125*; 63:9, *117*; 63:10–11, *114*; 63:14, *117, 148 n. 53*; 64:4, *172 n. 2*

Jeremiah, 1:5, *98*; 13:14, *117*; 15:10, *184 n. 19*; 39:5, *147 n. 32*

Lamentations, 4:20, *147 n. 32*

Ezekiel, 11:19, *117*; 28:2, *140 n. 3*; 36:20, *173 n. 19*

Daniel, 6:22, *162 n. 64*; 7:9, *123*; 9:10, *94*

Joel, 2:28, *117, 213*

Amos, 7:14, *162 n. 62*; 9:9–12, *312*

Zecharia, 9:9, *184 n. 13*; 12:10, *117*

Malachi, 3:6, *161 n. 51*

Matthew, 1:20, *178*; 1:23, *23*; 2:9, *160 n. 19*; 3:11, *146 n. 2*; 3:16, *118, 173 n. 31, 283*; 3:17, *147 n. 16*; 4:1, *147 n. 18*; 5:8, *270, 318*; 5:13–14, *265*; 5:15, *266*; 6:7, *74*; 6:10, *231*; 6:12, *172 n. 4*; 6:14–15, *172 n. 8*; 6:26, *226*; 6:27, *226*; 6:28, *226*; 7:2, *160 n. 25*; 7:7, *71*; 7:22, *147 n. 19*; 7:24–5, *270*; 8, *173 n. 27*; 9:15, *219*; 11:20, *147 n. 19*; 11:27, *135 n. 10, 147 n. 25*; 12:28, *88, 147 n. 20*; 12:29, *245 n. 9*; 12:32, *135 n. 2, 261*; 12:40, *140 n. 2*; 13:11, *270*; 13:43, *160 n. 22*; 13:46, *265*; 16:19, *267, 268*; 16:37, *119*; 17:5, *118*; 18:3, *74*; 18:12–14, *245 n. 8*; 18:18, *267*; 20:10, *270*; 21:9, *183 n. 2, 184 n. 31*; 25:6, *273*; 25:8, *266*; 25:14, *184 n. 20*; 27:46, *210*; 27:51, *184 n. 27*; 28:19, *41 n. 13, 135 n. 3, 212*

Mark, 1:10, *118*; 1:11, *87*; 1:12, *76, 88*; 3:17, *269*; 3:27, *245 n. 9*; 4:1, *118*; 4:32, *119*; 6:14, *147 n. 19*; 9:7, *87, 118*; 14:36, *60*; 15:34, *210*

Luke, 1:28, *208 n. 7*; 1:31, *208 n. 7*; 1:35, *88, 116, 117, 118, 199, 208 n. 7*; 2:9, *160 n. 18*; 2:14, *147 n. 12*; 2:25, *118*; 3:8, *184 n. 28*; 3:21–2, *88*; 3:22, *118, 184 n. 10, 199, 201*; 4:1, *88, 118*; 4:12, *262*; 4:14, *88*; 4:18, *125, 236 n. 29*; 8:8, *173 n. 29*; 8:10, *270*; 8:16, *266*; 8:18, *266–7*; 9:32–4, *160 n. 20*; 9:34, *118*; 9:35, *184 n. 10*; 10:13, *147 n. 19*; 10:21, *88*; 10:35, *184 n. 24*; 11:9–10, *266*; 11:12, *231*; 11:13, *118*; 11:21–2, *245 n. 9*; 11:33, *266*; 11:34, *266–7*; 11:35, *267*; 11:36, *267*; 11:52, *267*; 12:10, *261*; 12:12, *118, 219*; 12:25, *226*; 12:35, *266*; 12:42, *270*; 12:49, *244*; 14:16, *161 n. 39*; 15:4–7, *245 n. 8*; 17:21, *231*; 18:13, *261*; 19:38, *184 n. 49*; 19:40, *184 n. 25*; 20:13, *87*; 23:34, *172*; 23:46, *88*; 24:45, *267*; 24:49, *206, 207*

John, 1:1, *147 n. 10*; 1:1–5, *226, 269*; 1:3, *26, 31, 178, 196*; 1:5, *161*; 1:9, *147 n. 29, 160 n. 10*; 1:14, *118, 161 n. 51, 234 n. 5*; 1:18, *26, 29, 262*; 1:32, *83, 118*; 1:33, *88, 147, 173 n. 32, 252*; 3:3, *162 n. 59, 213, 262, 268*; 3:5, *24, 207, 213, 262, 268*; 3:8, *118, 161 n. 44, 207, 262*; 3:24, *161 n. 51*; 3:34, *207*; 4:14, *135 n. 5*; 4:24, *147 nn. 27, 31, 269*; 7:17, *321*; 7:38–9, *135 n. 6*; 7:39, *60, 188*; 10:1–16, *245 n. 8*; 10:3, *267*; 10:7, *9, 267*; 10:30, *204*; 11:9–10, *266*; 12:3–5, *124*; 12:13, *184 n. 16*; 12:16, *313*; 12:28, *184*; 12:35, *266*; 14:2, *267*; 14:6, *267*; 14:10, *262*; 14:15, *268*; 14–16, *59*; 14:16, *147 n. 39*; 14:9–10, *204*; 14:17, *147 n. 37, 191*; 14:20, *268*; 14:23, *269*; 14:26, *118*; 15:4, *262*; 15:6, *262*; 15:8, *262*; 15:13, *172 n. 6, 173 n. 21*; 15:25, *268*; 15:26, *83, 86, 89, 147 n. 41, 161 n. 51, 212, 317*; 16:7, *206, 268*; 16:7–15, *60*; 16:8–11, *78*; 16:13, *118, 147 n. 37, 148 n. 57, 219*; 16:13, *268*; 16:13–14, *135 n. 11*; 16:14, *88 n. 5*; 16:14–15, *161 n. 51*; 16:15, *89 n. 5, 89 n. 7*; 17:3, *201, 203*;

John (*cont'd*)
   17:20–3, 279; 17:21–3, 262, 269;
   17:24, 279; 17:25, 262; 19:30, 206;
   20:22, 118; 20:22–3, 147 *n.* 22, 267;
   20:28, 161 *n.* 35; 20:31, 189
Acts, 1:2, 88; 1:4, 206; 1:5, 268; 1:7,
   228–9; 1:8, 117; 2:3, 153, 161 *n.* 32;
   2:16, 213; 2:17–18, 118; 2:22, 144,
   147 *n.* 19, 208; 2:23, 24, 206–7; 2:26,
   118; 2:33, 257 *n.* 10; 2:38, 24; 4:8,
   208 *n.* 6; 4:31, 208 *n.* 6; 5:9, 4, 143,
   147 *n.* 6; 5:15, 118; 5:41, 208 *n.* 6;
   8:39, 118; 9:3, 152, 160 *n.* 21; 9:31,
   118; 10–15, 301–2, 304, 307–13, 315
   n. 23; 10:20, 146, 148 *n.* 50; 10:38,
   125, 144, 147 *n.* 17, 231; 10:44, 118;
   11:15, 118; 13:2, 146, 148 *n.* 51, 158,
   161 *n.* 51; 13:47, 315 *n.* 24; 15:4–13,
   309; 15:15–18, 309; 17:28, 37; 19:11,
   144, 147 *n.* 19; 19:16, 117; 20:23,
   118
Romans, 1:1–5, 98; 1:4, 207; 2:7, 153,
   161 *n.* 31; 2:10, 118; 4, 100, 158,
   161 *n.* 51; 6:3–4, 24; 8, 44–8, 50,
   61, 68, plates 2 and 3; 8:3–4, 44–50,
   68, 285; 8:9, 72, 80 *n.* 2; 8:11, 137,
   206–7; 8:14–17, 46, 59; 8:14–27, 71;
   8:16, 99; 8:26, 5 *n.* 4, 11, 45, 49, 75;
   8:26–7, 46; 8:27, 71; 8:29, 160 *n.* 5;
   8:35, 140 *n.* 6; 9, 98; 9:7–8, 98;
   15:29, 146 *n.* 1
1 Corinthians, 1:30, 245 *n.* 13; 2:9, 166,
   172 *n.* 3; 2:11–15, 99; 2:16, 266;
   3:13, 142, 146 *n.* 3; 6:9, 309; 6:11,
   41 *n.* 13, 146, 147 *n.* 46; 6:12–20, 95,
   213; 6:14, 211; 6:20, 245 *n.* 13; 7:22,
   245 *n.* 13; 7:28, 144, 147 *n.* 23; 8:6,
   26, 31; 11, 49; 11:29, 169, 173 *n.* 18;
   12, 213, 250; 12:1, 4, 132; 12:3, 33,
   59, 144, 147 *n.* 13, 26, 251, 257
   n. 10, 317; 12:7, 188; 12:7–11, 134,
   135 *n.* 9; 12:11, 133, 135 *n.* 8,
   143–4, 147 *n.* 8, 24; 12:12–13, 24;
   12:28–30, 59; 13:4–6, 143, 147 *n.* 7;
   13:8, 88; 14, 74; 14:14–5, 257 *n.* 7;
   14:15, 80 *n.* 2; 14:19, 75; 14:24–5,
   143, 147 *n.* 5; 15, 94; 15:28, 214;
   15:44–5, 207, 211

2 Corinthians, 1:21, 40 *n.* 13; 3:3, 192;
   3:6, 118, 191; 3:8–9, 145, 147 *n.* 38;
   3:17–18, 59, 207, 211, 269; 4:13,
   211; 6, 61; 4:14, 206; 6:16, 269; 12,
   48; 12:2–3, 264; 12:9, 118; 13:13, 87;
   17, 146, 147 *n.* 49
Galatians, 1:1, 206; 2:19–20, 93, 100;
   2:20, 170, 173 *n.* 23, 210; 3, 100;
   3:1–5, 311; 3:5, 144, 147 *n.* 19;
   3:7–9, 96; 3:8, 98, 104 *n.* 26; 3:13,
   245 *n.* 13; 3:14, 96; 3:26–9, 98;
   3:27–8, 24; 3:28, 97; 4:4, 88; 4:6,
   24, 60, 83, 88, 118, 146, 147 *n.* 47,
   206, 229, 268; 4:6–7, 59; 5:16–24,
   97, 207; 5:22–3, 59
Ephesians, 1:6, 87; 1:7, 239, 245 *n.* 13;
   1:20, 206; 2, 311; 3:13, 161 *n.* 42;
   4:6, 31; 4:13, 137, 140 *n.* 1; 4:30,
   118; 5:13, 140 *n.* 1, 266; 6:16, 265;
   6:18, 80 *n.* 2
Philippians, 2:7, 201; 4:7, 147 *n.* 30
Colossians, 1:14, 87, 245 *n.* 13; 1:15–16,
   31; 1:18, 160 *n.* 6; 2:9, 200; 2:12,
   206; 3:3, 184 *n.* 48
1 Thessalonians, 5:17, 71, 262; 5:19, 118
2 Thessalonians, 2:10, 318
1 Timothy, 1:10, 309; 2, 49; 2:6, 245
   n. 13; 3:16, 207, 211; 4:6–7, 270;
   6:13, 268; 6:15–16, 268; 6:16, 160
   n. 9, 268
2 Timothy, 1:12, 184 *n.* 23; 1:14, 118;
   2:5, 161 *n.* 48; 2:12, 270
Titus, 2:13, 144, 147 *n.* 14, 261; 2:14,
   270; 3:5, 118
Hebrews, 1:9, 231; 2:10, 172, 173 *n.* 33;
   5:9, 191; 6:1, 270; 6:4, 266; 7, 96,
   98; 7:20, 161 *n.* 52; 8:8–10, 190;
   9:8, 118; 9:14, 88, 158, 161 *n.* 51,
   207; 9:15, 245 *n.* 3; 10:15, 118;
   10:28–9, 191; 11:13–14, 229;
   11:33–40, 229; 11:35, 245 *n.* 3;
   12, 156, 161 *n.* 45; 12:14, 318;
   12:20, 159, 161 *n.* 52; 12:29, 266
1 Peter, 1:1, 41 *n.* 13; 1:12, 203; 2:8, 156,
   161 *n.* 46; 3:18, 206–7, 211; 3:19, 88;
   3:21, 160 *n.* 7; 4:14, 117
2 Peter, 1:2–4, 280; 1:4, 238; 1:17,
   199

1 John, 1:5, *160 n. 8, 262;* 1:6, 267; 1:20,
   147 n. 33; 2:4, *318, 321;* 3:1, *270;*
   3:2, *227;* 4:2, *59;* 4:4, *172 n. 5;*
   4:4–12, *166;* 4:5, *172 n. 7;* 4:6, *172*
   n. 10, 321 n. 1; 4:7, *172 n. 11–12;*
   4:7–8, *172 n. 13;* 4:8, *87, 321;* 4:9,
   173 n. 20; 4:9–10, *173 n. 24;* 4:11,
   173 n. 25; 4:12, *173 n. 26, 262;* 4:13,
   140 n. 4; 4:15, *140 n. 5;* 4:16, *87;*
   5:6, *147 n. 375, 207, 317;* 5:6–9, *59;*
   5:7, *59;* 5:8, *269*

Revelation, 10:5–7, *220*

General Index

Aaron, 121
Abba, 24, 32, 46, 60–1, 64, 88, 99, 146, 228–9, 268
Abel, 120
Abraham, 95–8, 100, 121, 159, 182, 240, *plate 1*
Adam, 31, 36, 94–6, 98, 238, 241, 243, 280, 283, 296
adoption, 46, 58–61, 69, 91, 98–9, 142, 158, 228, 262, 288
Aëtius of Antioch, 27
Albertoni, Ludovica, *plate 3*
Ambrose of Milan, 49, 89 nn. 5, 6, 322
Amos, 159
Andrew, 159
angel(s), 95, 111, 120–1, 149, 152, 156, 181, 202, 220, 265, 275, 292
Anglican(s), 54, 69–70, 73–6, 78
Annunciation, 2, 116, 118, 180
Anointed (one), 20, 23, 109, 124–5, 145, 149, 152, 231
Anselm of Canterbury, 218, 239–41
Aphrahat, 114, 120
Apostles, 88, 132–4, 143–4, 157, 167, 169–70, 181, 187–8, 190–1, 196, 253
Aquinas, Thomas, xi, xv, 5 n. 3, 35–6, 42 n. 45, 43 n. 49, 67 n. 53, 88 n. 4, 89 nn. 6, 8, 90 nn. 13, 14, 185–6, 317
Arius, 26–7, 198
  Arians, 125, 138–9
  Neo-Arianism, 27–8

Ascension, 3, 156, 158, 206–7, 239, 253
Athanasius of Alexandria, xi, xiv, 4, 26, 39, 43 nn. 52–4, 48, 85, 89 n. 7, 136–7, 198, 234 n. 8, 238–9, 245 n. 10, 246 n. 17, 322
Augustine of Hippo, xi, xiv, 13, 42 n. 46, 50, 72, 75, 83, 87, 89 nn. 5–6, 90 n. 14, 165, 173 n. 14, 187–92, 198, 202–3, 204 n. 1, 3, 277 n. 2, 284 n. 2, 322
Awad, Najeeb G., 161 n. 40

Bagger, Matthew, 103 n. 20
Balai, 120
baptism, 3, 23–5, 31, 57, 63, 69, 80, 98, 115, 119, 131, 141–2, 146, 153, 268
  as gift, 149–51, 156, 169, 172, 177–9, 201, 212, 241, 244, 319
  with oil, 109–10, 120–1, 123–5, 132–4
Barnabus, 146, 309–10, 312
Barth, Karl, 4, 9–17, 17 n. 4, 22–5, 54, 58–60, 65 n. 12, 66 n. 33, 217, 322
  Kirchliche Dogmatik, 11–13, 16, 22, 57, 65 n. 4, 66 n. 23, 38
  prophetism, 12–13
Bartholomew I, 82
Basil of Caesarea, xi, xiv, 4, 20, 23, 27, 29, 33, 38, 40 n. 8, 41 n. 17, 42 n. 44, 66 n. 45, 84, 105 n. 43, 110 n. 1, 141–2, 222–3, 234 n. 8
Bedjan, Paul, 125 n. 9, 126 nn. 28, 36

Bernard of Clairvaux, 72, 78–9, 184 n. 32
Bernini, Gian Lorenzo, *plate 3*
binitarianism/binity, 11–12, 16, 54, 56, 221
bird(s), 94, 119, 123, 177, 179, 226
blood, 63, 97, 120, 122, 142, 160, 169, 183, 207, 220, 240, 242, 275, 283
body, 3, 95, 120, 122, 137, 149–50, 155, 169, 214, 220, 242, 262, 275, 296
Boethius, 37
Bolotov, B., 88 n. 1
Bonaventure, 200, 321 n. 4
Book of Common Prayer, 20, 40 nn. 1–2, 4–5
Bowker, J., 65 n. 13
bread, 3, 111, 119–22, 149, *plate 4*
breath, 23, 30, 36, 47, 50, 94, 109, 111, 143, 159, 183, 197–8, 233, 278, 283
Brock, Sebastian, xi, xiv, 5 n. 2, 113, 322
Brunner, Peter, 13
Bulgakov, Sergei, 4, 217, 323
Bultmann, Rudolph, 93, 102 nn. 10, 12, 103 n. 15
Burgess, Stanley, 323
Burns, J. Patout, 323
Bynum, Caroline Walker, 284 n. 2

Caiaphas, 61
Cain, 120
Cantalamessa, Raniero, 323
Cappadocians, 19, 21, 25–8, 30, 32–3, 36, 38–9, 42 n. 46, 79, 83, 85, 91
Cassian, John, 76
Chabot, J. B., 137 n. 38
charismata, 59–60, 62, 211, 213
charismatic(s), 54, 57, 64, 68–70, 72–5, 78–80
charity, 138, 166–72, 183, 188, 275, 277, 309
Charlemagne, 85
Chenu, Marie-Dominique, 217
Christ, 5, 9–10, 12–18, 21–2, 26–9, 32, 46, 53, 57, 59–60, 62–3, 68, 78, 88, 95–101, 109–11, 118, 132, 134, 138–9, 144, 146, 151, 156–60, 167, 169, 172, 177–81, 190–1, 195, 200, 203–4, 206–9, 213, 222–3, 226–7, 229, 231, 237–42, 245, 261–2, 270,

274, 279, 291, 296, 303–4, 309–11, 318–20, *plates 2 and 3*
as anointed one, 109, 124–5
ascension of, 3, 156, 158, 206–7, 239, 253
baptism of, 19–20, 23–5, 31, 36, 88, 120, 122–3, 142, 178, 195, 199, 243, 247, 252
body of, 3, 20, 93–5, 120, 149–50, 155, 220, 241–2, 244, 247, 251, 255–6,
as Bridegroom, 153–4, 183, 273, 283
death of, 54, 58, 61, 77–8, 92, 100, 124, 182–3, 211, 238–40, 242, 313
as door, 267
images of, 2–3, 98
life of, 205
narratives of, 2–3, 317
the Pearl, 122
poverty of, 62
relationship to believers, 92
role in creed, 82
role in prayer, 71
role in Trinity, 1–2, 4, 23, 50, 56, 136, 249, 251, 255
Christianity, 1, 3, 11, 24, 54, 68, 70, 73, 100–1, 113–14, 120, 131, 149–50, 219, 238, 249, 251, 302, 316
Christians, 1, 3, 19–20, 22, 24, 37, 68–70, 75, 77, 81, 83, 93, 101, 131, 134, 167, 169, 196, 200, 220–1, 229–30, 238, 270, 302–4, 306–13
Christmas, 205
Christology, 55, 58, 62, 80, 241–2, 244, 250, 254, 256
Chrysostom, John, 79, 161 n. 49
Church, 3, 9–10, 12, 16, 38, 47, 55, 59–60, 63, 69, 78, 80, 82–4, 87–8, 124–5, 144, 172, 180, 207–8, 210, 220–2, 225–7, 230–1, 238–9, 241–5, 251, 256, 270, 283, 309–11, 317, 319–21
as Christian unity, 249, 255, 316
relationship to Spirit, 250
Church of England Doctrine Commission, xiii, 68
Climacus, John, 225
Coakley, Sarah, xi, xiii, 4, 19, 44, 51 n. 1, 53, 68, 91, 272, 323

Commentary on St John X, 83, 184 n. 4, 245 n. 11, 246 n. 21

Communion, *see* Eucharist

community, 3–4, 12, 15–16, 63, 114, 150, 210, 224, 301–2, 312–13, 316–20
  through prayer, 44, 137, 208
  of Trinity, 2, 15, 248, 250

Congar, Yves, 323

Coptic Gospel of Philip, 116

Cornelius, 179, 231, 306–8, 311

Council of Nicaea, 26–7, 32

creation, 1–3, 10, 24–5, 27–8, 30–1, 34–5, 38, 43 n. 56, 48, 56, 92, 111, 120, 143, 145–6, 159, 177, 179, 181, 196–8, 201, 203, 212–14, 219–20, 225–26, 228, 230, 241, 283, 288, 294, 296, 316

Creator, 25, 27–9, 36–7, 41 n. 22, 150–1, 198–200, 202–4, 213, 225
  as Spirit, 174

creatures, *see* humanity

cross, 53, 58, 61, 64–5, 88, 168, 183, 206–7, 210–11, 238–9

crucifixion, 53, 65, 100, 133, 182, 205, 211, *plate 2*

Cunningham, David, 135 n. 1

Cyril of Alexandria, 39, 83, 85–6, 89 n. 7, 90 n. 11, 214 n. 2, 254

Cyril of Jerusalem, xi, xiv, 131, 135 n. 12, 203, 209, 246 n. 21

Dabney, D. Lyle, 214 n. 3, 323

Dahl, Nils, 97, 104 n. 29

Daniel, 159

Daniel of Tella, 127 n. 38

David, 159, 169, 180, 195–6, 202, 262, 269

D'Costa, Gavin, 323

de Halleux, André, 125 n. 6, 126 n. 29

Deity, 22, 25–30, 33–5, 37, 153, 157
  deification, 155, 158, 218, 227, 238, 241–2, 245, 272, 278–9

de Lubac, Henri, 217

depression, 68, 76–7

Descartes, René, 93, 100

Desert Fathers, 75

devils, 134, 144, 181

Diadochus of Photice, 77, 79

Didymus the Blind, 89 n. 7

DiNoia, J. A., 19

Dionysius, 50, 235 n. 11

distance-crossing, 1–3, 53

divinization, 62, 69, 141, 245

dogma, 21–2, 86, 145, 192, 221–3, 238–9, 241, 243
  dogmatics, 57, 64, 221, 224, 252

dove, 2, 20, 23, 36, 78, 119, 121–4, 172, 180, 182–3, 199–202, 229, 253–4, 283–4, *plate 4*

Dryden, John, xiv, 174

Easter, 63, 205–6, 211, 228

ecclesiology, 16, 63, 242, 249–50, 253

Ecclestone, Alan, 66 n. 44

Edsman, C. M., 126 n. 21, 24

Ehrman, Bart, 101 n. 2

ekporeusis, 82–7, 223, 251

ekstasis, 45, 50

election, 10, 15, 174

Elias, 152

Elijah, 264

Eliot, T. S., 78

Elisha, 264

energeia, 33–4, 42 n. 44, 88

Enlightenment, 22, 151, 160 n. 2, 217

Ephraim, 75

Ephrem the Syrian, xi, xiv, 105 n. 44, 109–10, 113–14, 119, 122–4, 126 n. 34, 127 n. 37, 225

Epictetus, 97, 104 n. 31

Epiphanius of Salamis, 89 n. 7

Erickson, John H., xv n. 24, 237

Ern, V. F., 235 n. 16

Esau, 98

Eucharist, 3, 19–20, 63, 82–3, 111, 120, 122, 131, 149, 248, 296–7, 319, *plates 1 and 4*
  eucharistic prayer, 21

Eunomius, 27

Evdokimov, Paul, 67 n. 49, 214 n. 6, 217, 323

Eve, 96, 283, 296

Fagin, Gerald M., 323

faith, 16, 21–2, 25, 30, 36, 48, 63–4, 71, 83–7, 92, 96, 98, 100–1, 119–20,

133–4, 142, 181, 187, 190–2, 198, 200, 203, 207–8, 213, 221, 224, 226, 229, 231, 244, 264–5, 268, 272, 288–91, 294, 307, 309, 311

Farrer, Austin, 65 n. 3

Father, 19, 21–2, 24–7, 30, 32, 59, 62–4, 69, 87–8, 99, 122, 133, 137, 154, 157–8, 160, 167, 169–70, 174–5, 177–8, 180–2, 196, 200–1, 203–7, 209–10, 212–13, 218, 221–3, 225, 228–9, 234, 240, 246, 248, 248, 279–80, 291–7
  as Anointer, 109, 231–2
  in *filioque* controversy, 81–2
  as God, 57, 115, 132, 138–9, 198, 202
  as *hypostasis*, 34, 37–8
  language, 52 n. 2
  relationship to prayer, 285–6
  relationship to Son, 10, 14–16, 20, 23, 31, 33, 38–9, 44, 47, 60–1, 79, 83, 86–7, 91, 134, 138, 199, 211, 252–4, 262, 268, 276, 282, 287–9, 316
  relationship to Spirit, 38–40, 43 n. 52, 46–8, 58, 68, 72, 83, 85–7, 91, 134, 143–5, 155, 185, 199, 211, 250, 252–4, 268, 276, 282, 288–9, 316
  role in Trinity, 23, 56, 84, 136, 139, 141–2, 152, 165, 269, 285, 303
  source, 131
  as sun, 119–20

Fellowship community, 70, 73–6

filioque, 13, 66 n. 30, 68, 81, 84–7, 88 n. 1, 89 n. 5, 224, 250

fire, 3–4, 51, 78, 113, 119–22, 131, 142, 152, 158–9, 174–5, 229, 253, 262–3, 265–6, 272, 274–7, 284

Florensky, Pavel, xii, xv, 217–18, 323

forgiveness, 59, 132, 303, 319–20

Fowl, Stephen E., xii, xvi, 301–2

freedom, 58–9, 61, 64, 80, 100, 186, 209, 223, 227, 230, 244, 249, 264, 289, 293–5

Freud, Sigmund, 50, 61

Frothingham, A. L., 126 n. 20

Gabriel, 116, 199

gender, 24, 45–6, 48, 51, 101, 116, 177–8, 217, 281–2

Genesis, 96, 98, 148, 248
  creation story, 25
  Homilies on Genesis 2.5, 40 n. 12, 197

Gentiles, 61, 96–8, 100–1, 179, 189, 228, 301–13

Gero, S., 126 n. 32

Gethsemane, 61, 77, 210

gift(s), 31, 33, 44, 58–9, 62, 64, 68, 70, 74–5, 87–8, 97, 100, 125, 137, 139, 142–5, 158–9, 169, 175, 187–8, 191, 213, 227, 247–8, 262, 272, 274, 276, 289–90, 295, *plate 4*
  of Christ, 249
  of the Spirit, 24, 40, 59, 132, 134, 146, 149–51, 153, 203, 256

gnosis/Gnostics, 3, 25, 27, 41 n. 22

God, 1–3, 10–11, 16–17, 19–20, 22–4, 53–5, 57, 59, 62–4, 69, 71, 74, 77–9, 84, 91, 94–101, 111, 118, 120, 122, 133–4, 140, 146, 149–50, 153, 157–60, 165, 167–71, 179, 181–3, 186–92, 196–200, 203–4, 206, 208, 210, 214, 218–20, 222, 225, 229, 232–3, 238–42, 245, 254, 256, 261–6, 269–70, 272–8, 281, 284, 291–7, 303–6, 308, 310, *plates 2 and 3*
  absence of, 61, 64
  desire for, 45–6, 49–51, 71–2, 76
  as Father, 57, 115, 132, 138–9, 142–5, 195, 199–200, 202, 285, 287–9
  as fire, 159, 266
  image, 31–2, 243, 279
  of Israel, 301–2
  as light, 152, 197, 267
  likeness of, 32
  as love, 166, 169
  nature of, 25–40, 41 n. 22, 42 n. 48
  relationship to mediator, 2, 26, 56
  relationship to Word, 58, 226–7
  as Son, 200, 253, 289
  as Spirit, 71, 79, 155–6, 169, 289
  triunity, 12–15, 21, 34, 46–7, 195, 201, 290–1, 313, 316–17, 319–21
  will, 31, 61, 88

Goethe, J. W. von, 281

Golitzin, Alexander, 284 n. 1

Good Friday, 63, 205, 285

gospel, 12, 16, 96, 160, 167, 171, 178, 189–192, 239, 305, 317–19
grace, 3, 24, 47–8, 57, 59, 63, 69, 79, 132–4, 139, 142, 144–5, 149, 151, 153, 175–6, 178–9, 182, 185–92, 195, 219, 224–5, 230, 238, 255, 262, 264, 267, 272–5, 277, 290, 292, 294, 296
Graves, Charles, 323
Greer, Rowan A., 52 n. 5
Gregory of Cyprus, 255
Gregory of Nazianzus, xi, xiv, 27–8, 33, 40, n. 8, 41 n. 26, 42 n. 40, 43, 83, 90 n. 10, 149–50, 230, 235 n. 10, 238, 240, 252, 261, 323
Gregory of Nyssa, 27–8, 33, 38, 40 n. 8, 41 n. 24, 42 n. 32, 42, 46–7, 43 n. 53, 90 n. 11, 126 n. 36, 224, 231, 235 nn. 10, 12, 236 nn. 25, 26, 30–2, 238, 245 n. 12, 323
Gregory, S., 161 n. 41
Gross, Jules, 323
Guerric of Igny, xi, xv, 180, 184 n. 44, 323
Gunton, Colin, 41 n. 18

Haenchen, E., 66 n. 37
Hahm, David, 103, n. 21
Hannah, 49
Hanson, R. P. C., 57, 62
Hart, David Bentley, 245 n. 2
Harvey, Susan Ashbrook, 5 n. 2, 324
Hauerwas, Stanley, 314 nn. 8, 14
Hausherr, Irénée, 270 n. 3
Hays, Richard, 93–4, 101 n. 2, 102 nn. 11, 13, 103 nn. 14, 15, 18, 23, 304, 314 n. 13, 315 n. 20
heaven, 1–2, 30–1, 56, 111, 120, 122, 133, 142, 150, 152–3, 156, 158, 172, 175–6, 178, 197–8, 200–1, 205, 210, 212, 214, 219–20, 222, 238, 242, 263, 265, 268, 270, 273, 275–7, 290–1, 297, 317
Hebrew, 96, 98, 113, 117–18
Hector, Kevin, 161 n. 40
Hegel, G. W. F., 209, 217
hell, 54, 205, 223, 273
Hengel, M., 65 n. 13

Henneke, E., 125 n. 4
Hermas, 28, 42 n. 28, 56–7, 66 nn. 16, 18, 221
Hilary of Poitiers, 89 n. 5, 324, 203
Hippolytus, 48, 51 n. 4, 60
Hodge, Caroline Johnson, 97, 104 nn. 25–8, 32, 34, 97, 105 nn. 35, 38
Holy Ghost, *see* Spirit
Holy Spirit, *see* Spirit
homosexuals, 303–4, 308–13
Hooker, Richard, 21
Huetter, Reinhard, 17 n. 1
humanity/human beings, 2–3, 9–10, 12, 14, 19–20, 22–32, 34–7, 40, 41 n. 22, 53–4, 57, 60, 63–4, 92, 94, 97, 99, 101, 150–2, 165–6, 174, 178, 187–90, 198–203, 213, 220, 237, 243, 246, 248, 274–7, 284, 287–8, 293, 296–7, 316, 318, *plate 1*
as bride, 282
relations/ships, 91, 96–8, 101
suffering of, 30, 59, 63, 76–7, 99, 209, 219
union with Christ, 255–6
union with God, 44, 136–7, 159, 185, 239, 247
hypostasis(es), 30, 32–5, 37–9, 47, 56–7, 116, 145, 218–19, 222–6, 232, 242–4, 254–5, 262

idolatry, 29
Ignace de la Potterie, 321 n. 1
Illumination, 56, 63, 145, 149, 151–3, 220, 222, 227, 230, 261, 263, 267–8
incarnation, 122, 136–7, 149–51, 238, 241, 244–5, 251–52, 261
interpretation, 1–2, 21–2, 56, 58, 60, 74, 80, 94, 97, 101, 115, 134, 138, 201–2, 206, 237, 249, 253, 268, 301–6, 312–13
Irenaeus of Lyon, 19–28, 30–3, 36, 38–9, 40 n. 9, 42 n. 33, 48, 51 n. 3, 105 n. 43, 110 n. 1, 232, 236 n. 34, 238
Irigaray, Lucy, 50, 52 n. 8
Isaac, 96, 98
Isaac of Nineveh, xi, xiv, 111, 113, 324
Isaac the Syrian, 225

Isaiah, 121, 197
Ishmael, 98

Jacob, 116, 120, 196
Jacob of Serugh, 116, 120, 122–3, 126
    n. 34
James, 118, 304–8, 312
James, William, 317
Jenkins, David, 67 n. 54
Jenson, David, 324
Jenson, Robert W., xi, xiii, 4, 9–10, 17
    n. 1, 18 n. 14, 19, 44, 166, 172 n. 1,
    217, 324
Jerome, 114, 179
Jesse, 196
Jesus, *see* Christ
Jews, 92, 100–1, 179, 196, 199, 301–2,
    305, 308, 310
Joel, 207
John, 23, 32, 59, 60, 77, 111, 125, 138–9,
    142, 172, 206–7, 220, 223, 226, 243,
    246 n. 21, 248, 269, 312
   the Gospel of, 86, 115, 195–6, 303, 317
   Homily on the First Epistle of, xiv n. 15,
    165
John Damascene, 84, 87, 90 n. 12, 90
    n. 13
John of Damascus, 39, 234, 245 n. 11,
    253, 324
John of the Cross, xii, xvi, 47, 63, 67
    n. 51, 76–7, 272, 278
John the Baptist, 23, 115, 252, 268
John the Evangelist, 178, 261
Johnson, Luke, 304, 308–10, 313 n. 2, 314
    nn. 10–12, 315 n. 20
Johnston, Timothy, xiii
Jonah, 15, 58–60, 138–9
Jones, L. Gregory, 314 n. 6
Joseph, 146
Joshua, 114
Judaism, 55, 59, 92–3, 120
Judas, 169–70
Jüngel, Eberhard, 54

Kant, Immanuel, 217
Kelly, J. N. D., 66 n. 14
Kilby, Karen E., 214 n. 1, 324
King, Gundaphor, 115

King Robert II, 174
Koyré, Alexandre, 103 n. 16
Krueger, Derek, xiii
Küng, H., 54

Laminski, Adolf, 324
Lampe, G. W. H., 57, 65 n. 12, 66 n. 15,
    324
Lamy, T. J., 126 n. 35
Langton, Stephen, 174
Larentin, R., 208 n. 7
Last Supper, *plate 1*
Lazarus, 159
Lee, Maurice, 325
Leo the Great, 246 n. 18
Levenson, John, 315 n. 25
Levi, 96
light, 109, 119, 133–4, 142, 145, 150–2,
    156, 158–9, 171, 174–6, 196–7, 222,
    233, 253, 255–6, 262–70, 276
Logos, *see* Word
Lohse, F., 208 n. 2
Lombard, Peter, 166, 321 n. 4
Long, A. A., 105 n. 40
Lord, *see* God
Lossky, Vladimir, xii, xv, 4, 64, 65 n. 11,
    66 n. 47, 217, 237, 247–8, 255
Loughlin, Gerard, 324
love, 14, 16, 19, 26, 28, 35, 40, 47, 50–1,
    53, 79, 87–8, 111–12, 144, 157, 166,
    168–72, 174, 181, 185, 187, 205,
    211, 213, 220, 228, 231–2, 254, 265,
    272, 274–9, 282–3, 286–93, 295–7,
    317–21
Loyola, Ignatius, 71
Luke, 37, 59, 60, 62, 64, 80, 199, 207–8,
    231, 245 n. 11
Luther, Martin, xi, xv, 10, 60–1, 63–4,
    71, 195

Macarius the Great, 225
Macdonald, Paul, 102, n. 12
Macedonius, 84
MacIntyre, Alasdair, 309
mankind, *see* humanity
Marcion, 312
Mark of Ephesus, 223
   Unpublished Works of, 235 n. 9

Marshall, Bruce D., xii, xvi, 316
Martin, Dale B., 103, nn. 17, 22
Marx, Karl, 217
Mary, 3, 88, 116, 122–4, 180, 197, 199,
    202, 273, 280, 292, 296–7
Massey, Marilyn Chapin, 284 n. 2
Matthew, 159, 232, 246 n. 21, 273
Maximus the Confessor, 84–6, 90 n. 11,
    232–3, 236 n. 35
McVey, Kathleen, 105 n. 44, 109
Meade, G. H., 42 n. 49, 110 n. 2
mediator, 2, 26, 56, 59–60, 62, 64
Medieval Cistercian, 180
Mehl, Roger, 250
Melchizedek, 96
Metéos, Juan, 324
Michelangelo, *plate 3*
Milbank, John, 324
Mill, John Stuart, 235 n. 17
Mingana, A., 126 n. 23
miracles, 134, 144, 146, 187–9, 201–2,
    224, 240
Moltmann, Jürgen, xii, xv, 54, 61, 209,
    324
monarchy, 56, 83–4, 86, 145
Monloubou, Louis, 324
Moses, 118, 121, 152, 159, 197
Moshe bar Kepha, 115, 127 n. 40
mother, 97, 101, 114–15, 177, 179,
    282–4, 296
Moule, C. F. D., 65 nn. 2, 3
Mühlen, H., 65 n. 1, 214 n. 4
Murray, Robert, 105 n. 43, 110 n. 1, 125
    n. 5, 137 n. 39
mystics, 4, 117, 123, 217, 223, 272, 278,
    281, 290–1

Narsai, 121
Nathan, 196
Neale, John Mason, 175
New Testament, 2, 4, 14, 21, 25, 59–60,
    77, 80, 91–3, 95, 101, 116–19, 132,
    178, 190–2, 195, 207, 212–13, 251,
    301, 304, 312
Nichols, Aidan, 205
Nissiotis, Nikos, 18 n. 15, 250
Noah, 124
Norris, Richard, xi, xiii, 4, 19–20, 44

O'Connor, E. D., 65 n. 1
oil, 109–10, 113, 119–20, 124–5, 131,
    150, 153, 231
Old Testament, 49, 114, 116–18, 120,
    132–3, 178, 188–90, 225, 229, 269,
    301, 304, 312
O'Neill, J. C., 65 n. 13
Origen, 40 n. 12, 44–5, 48–9, 51, 51 n. 3,
    52 n. 6, 114, 221–2
ousia, 25, 27, 32–3, 38, 42 n. 39
Overbeck, J. J., 126 nn. 22, 36

Palamas, Gregory, 4, 73, 251
Pannenberg, W., 13
Paraclete, 59–60, 69, 89 n. 5, 139, 145,
    174–5, 206, 245, 268
paradise, *see* heaven
participation, 92–3, 95–96, 98–101, 150,
    186, 279
passion, *see* Christ, death of
Paul, 5 n. 4, 23–4, 31–2, 40 n. 14, 45–8,
    50, 57–61, 64, 71, 78–9, 80 n. 2,
    91–101, 143, 146, 152, 159, 169,
    207, 213, 230–1, 239, 243, 245 n. 14,
    268, 302, 304, 306–7, 309–12
Peirce, Charles, 217–18
Pentecost, 3, 10, 12, 16, 47, 79, 133, 155,
    174, 189, 200, 206, 208, 222, 244,
    253
    pentecostalism, 54
perichoresis, 39, 43 n. 55
Peter, 32, 143, 159, 170, 179, 250, 268,
    302, 304–12, 313 n. 3, 314 n. 5
Philip, 204
Philo, 42 n. 29, 99
Philoxenus of Mabbug, 116, 122, 324
Photios, 324
pneuma, 57, 84, 94–9, 101, 206–7
pneumatology, 54–5, 57–60, 62, 65, 65
    n. 4, 180, 223, 241, 250, 254, 256
*Pontifical Council for Promoting Christian
    Unity*, xiv, 81–2
Pope John Paul II, 90 n. 15
Pope Leo III, 85
Pope Paul VI, 250
prayer, 1, 4, 44, 51, 63, 69, 72, 75, 80, 80
    n. 2, 120, 122, 137, 167, 174, 208,
    222–3, 228, 290, 295–7, 310

relationship to sexuality, 48–9
relationship to Spirit, 45, 69–71, 73, 76,
    78–9
relationship to trinitarianism, 45–7,
    285–7
Prestige, G. L., 42 n. 41, 324

Rabanus, 187
Radner, Ephrem, 324
Rahner, Karl, 35, 42 n. 41, 54
Ramsey, A. M., 65 n. 2
Ratzinger, Joseph Cardinal, 16, 18 nn. 17,
    18
redemption, 10, 30, 33–4, 175, 181,
    237–45, 296
Régamey, P., 66 n. 43
Reitzenstein, Richard, 102 n. 8
Resch, A., 208 n. 7
resurrection, 3, 12, 24, 58, 67 n. 54, 92,
    95, 98–100, 111, 146, 149, 151, 156,
    158–9, 206–7, 210–12, 220, 227, 229,
    233, 238–41, 313, 316, *plate 3*
revelation, 2, 10, 22, 24–5, 33, 36, 55, 58,
    88, 201, 225, 233
Ricoeur, Paul, 66 n. 42
Rogers, Eugene F., Jr., 4, 5 n. 1, 4, 19,
    44, 160 n. 1, 272, 284 n. 2, 314 n. 8,
    324
Rousseau, A., 42 n. 35
Rupert of Deutz, xi, xiv, 177
Ruusbroec, John, xii, xv, 272

Sabellius, 199
sacrifice, 120, 122, 170, 211, 223, 233,
    240, 242
Sahdona, 122
salvation, 10, 12, 14, 62, 88, 100, 134,
    142, 150, 153, 155, 170, 176, 181,
    191, 205, 218–19, 222, 229, 239–41,
    245, 247
Sambursky, Samuel, 105 n. 37
2 Samuel, 195
Sanders, Ed, 92–4, 100, 101 n. 2, 102
    n. 10
Sands, Kathleen M., 52 n. 9
Sapphira, 143
Sarah, 49
Saul, 139, 146, 159, 169

Savior, *see* Christ
Scheeben, Matthias, xii, xvi, 272, 281
Schelling, F. W. J. von, 217
Schillebeeckx, 54, 67 n. 48
Schleiermacher, Friedrich, 10, 22, 280
Schlier, H., 208 n. 1
Schmeeman, Alexander, 324
Schneemelcher, W. 125 n. 4
Schniewind, J., 206
Schweitzer, Albert, 92–4, 100, 102 nn. 7,
    8, 103 n. 14
Seidensticker, P., 208
Seitz, Christopher, 312, 315 n. 24
Seraphim of Sarov, 226
Severus, 116, 122, 125, 125 nn. 8, 11
sexuality, 44–7, 55–1, 95–6, 302,
    309
    relationship to prayer, 48–9
Siker, Jeffrey, 310–12, 314 nn. 15–19,
    315 nn. 21–3
Siman, Emmanuel-Pataq, 325
sin, 24, 49, 58–60, 77, 79, 96, 98, 100,
    112, 121–3, 133, 138–9, 143, 146,
    150–1, 158–9, 167–8, 174, 178, 182,
    190–2, 230, 238–41, 264–7, 273,
    275, 296
Sölle, Dorothy, 61
Solomon, 120
Son, 19, 21–2, 24–7, 58–60, 62, 64, 69,
    100, 132–3, 137, 157–9, 167, 170,
    175, 177–8, 180–2, 187–9, 196,
    200–3, 205–7, 209–10, 212–13, 218,
    221–3, 228, 234, 238, 240–1, 244,
    278–81, 291–7
    as Anointed, 109, 124–5, 231–2
    divinity of, 141–2
    as dove, 123
    in *filioque* controversy, 81
    as God/Creator, 198, 225
    as *hypostasis*, 34, 36–8, 224
    as light, 119–20
    as love, 166
    relationship to Father, 10, 14–16, 20,
        23, 33, 38–9, 43 n. 52, 44, 47, 60–1,
        79, 82, 86–7, 91, 134, 138, 199, 211,
        252–4, 262, 268, 276, 282, 287–9,
        316
    relationship to prayer, 285–6

Son (*cont'd*)
  relationship to Spirit, 39, 43 n. 52, 47–8,
    56, 58, 72, 80, 83–6, 91, 134, 143–5,
    155, 185, 199, 211, 237, 247–8,
    250–4, 268, 276, 282, 288–9, 316
  role in Trinity, 23, 56, 136, 139, 152,
    165, 169, 255, 269, 285, 303
  sonship, 19, 47, 59–63, 72, 82–3, 91
  wellspring, 131
  as Wisdom and Word of God, 29–32,
    35, 42 n. 33
Son, Aaron, 201 nn. 2, 4
Song of Songs, 49, 51, 151, 184 n. 32,
    151, 272, 278, 284
  Commentary On, 52 n. 6
  Targum, 126 n. 30
Soskice, Janet Martin, 324
soul, 47, 63, 72, 78, 121–2, 132–4, 146,
    151–4, 159–60, 175, 182, 188–90,
    212, 219–20, 223, 226–7, 231, 233,
    253–4, 256, 262–8, 272, 274–5,
    278–80, 283–4
Soulen, R. Kendall, 183 n. 1, 324
source, 11, 16, 25–6, 32–3, 46–7, 50, 57,
    63, 79, 82–90, 119, 125–7, 129, 145,
    158, 174, 178, 222, 227, 233, 277,
    289, 292
Spirit, 1, 4–5, 9, 11, 16–17, 19, 21–2,
    24–5, 48, 53–4, 59–64, 73, 77–8, 80,
    88, 110–11, 118, 132–4, 137, 139,
    146, 150–1, 158–60, 175, 178–81,
    186–91, 195–7, 200, 203–10, 212–14,
    217–34, 238–9, 241, 243, 256, 261,
    265–7, 270, 273–5, 278–84, 287,
    291–7, 301–2, 304–13, 316–21,
    plates 2 and 3
  baptism in, 71
  bodily experience of, 68, 71
  as Creator, 174, 198, 202, 248
  doctrine of, 10, 57, 221
  as dove, 122–4, 172, 199
  as fire, 119–22
  as gift, 149–50, 153
  as God, 141, 155–6, 169
  as *hypostasis*, 33–4, 37–8, 222, 224
  images of, 2–3, 20, 36, 109, 119–23,
    131, 177
  as key, 268
  as Kingdom of God, 231
  as mediator, 56, 60, 62, 64
  as mother, 115–16
  narratives of, 2–3, 12–14
  as oil, 109, 124–5
  origin of, 87
  Paul's account of, 91
  Pentecostal coming of, 12
  relationship to Church, 250
  relationship to Father, 38–40, 43 n. 52,
    46–8, 58, 72, 83, 85–7, 91, 134,
    141–5, 185, 199, 211, 250, 252–4,
    268, 276, 282, 288–9, 316
  relationship to prayer, 45, 48–50, 69–71,
    73–6, 78–9, 285–6
  relationship to Son, 39, 42 n. 33, 43
    n. 52, 47–8, 56, 58, 72, 80, 83–6, 91,
    93, 134, 143–5, 185, 199, 211, 237,
    247–8, 250–4, 268, 276, 282, 288–9,
    316
  role in prayer, 45
  role in Trinity, 1–2, 4–5, 14–15, 23, 44,
    85, 136, 139, 152, 165, 249, 251,
    255, 269, 285, 303
  in Syriac, 113–19
  as water, 131, 133
  as Word, 27, 30–2, 39, 58
Spirit-talk, 9, 150
spirituality, 53, 57, 61, 63–4, 156, 220,
    230
Staniloae, Dumitru, xii, xv, 4, 217, 237,
    247, 324
Steffen, B., 214 n. 5
Stendahl, Krister, 100
Stout, Jeffrey, 314 n. 9
Stowers, Stanley, xiv, 91
Styers, Randall, 102 n. 10
substance(s), 89, 94–5, 100, 134, 145,
    150, 158–9
Swete, Henry Barclay, 324
Symeon the New Theologian, xii, xv, 4,
    69, 72, 226, 233, 236 n. 36, 256, 261
Syriac Christianity, 113–14
Syriac texts, 114–19, 122–5

Tannehill, Robert C., 313 n. 4
Tarasius, 84
Targum, 114, 120

Tatiana, 49
Tavard, George, 81, 88 n. 2
Taylor, J. V., 65 n. 2
Temple, William, 78
temptation, 13, 60, 156, 166, 254
Teresa, 75
Tertullian, 37, 41 n. 14, 88 n. 5, 89 n. 6,
    105 n. 39, 221, 234 n. 5
Theodore of Mopsuestia, 116
Theodosius, 120
theologian(s)/theology, 5, 9, 11, 21, 35–6,
    70, 73, 77, 91, 111, 149, 205, 224,
    238, 261, 272, 281, *plate 2*
  apophatic, 26, 29–30, 36–7, 42 n. 30
  Christian, 17, 56–7, 62, 94, 248–50,
    256, 317–18
  of the creed, 81
  of deification, 150
  Eastern Orthodox tradition, 55
  feminist, 51 n. 2
  of God's identity, 28–30
  of the Holy Spirit, 10, 53–5, 62–5, 68,
    79, 141
  of human sexuality, 46
  Protestant, 10, 249
  Russian, 217, 254
  Syriac, 113, 115
  of the Trinity, 2–4, 55–6, 72, 80, 88
    n. 5, 99, 243
  western, 12–14, 237, 241, 249
Thomas, 153
Thomas, Judas, 115
Timothy, 120
Tolstoy, Leo, 228
tongues, 73–6, 134, 143–4, 153, 158–9,
    175, 179, 200, 202–3
Tracy, D., 65 n. 10
Transfiguration, 3, 118, 206, 213–14, 219
trinitarianism, 3, 10–15, 25–6, 32, 34,
    36–7, 39, 48, 50–1, 58, 78–80, 83–4,
    87–8, 109, 136, 150, 165, 195–6,
    205, 211–12, 214, 218, 243, 251,
    280, 303–4, 316
  community, 15, 248, 250
  intratrinitarian, 82, 247
  relationship to prayer, 45–7, 49, 72
Trinity, 4–5, 16, 25–6, 28–9, 31–2, 34–5,
    37, 40 n. 3, 43 n. 52, 48, 50–1, 60,

84, 88, 133, 178, 185, 195, 198–9,
    202–3, 208–9, 211–12, 214, 218–19,
    223, 225, 232, 234, 242, 245, 252–4,
    269, 279–82, 295, 317, *plates 1 and 2*
  Christian worship in, 19–20
  Christ's role in, 1–2
  as community, 44, 137
  as Creator, 200
  doctrine of, 1, 11–13, 20–3, 25, 30,
    38–40, 45, 72, 157
  dogma of, 20, 22, 243
  example of sun, 119
  Holy Spirit's role in, 1–3, 23, 47, 83, 87
  linear model of, 53
  nature of, 157, 248
  as prayer, 137, 285
  psychological analogy of, 165
  theology of, 2–4, 55–6
triunity, 12–15, 34, 227
Trocmé, E., 66 n. 36
truth, 16, 24–5, 30, 45, 57–60, 63, 85,
    132, 134, 143–5, 156, 158, 167–8,
    175, 218–19, 240, 244, 268, 290,
    316–21
Tugwell, S., 65 n. 1, 67 n. 50

unction, 3, 20, 144, 149, 151, 174

van Nieuwenhove, Rik, 272, 277 n. 1
Veni Spiritus, xiv, 174
Vischer, Lukas, 324
Volf, Miroslav, 324
von Balthasar, Hans Urs, xi, xv, 4, 53–4,
    77, 205, 272, 285, 322
von Speyr, Adrienne, xii, xvi, 4, 19, 91,
    272, 285

Wacker, Grant, 325
Wadell, Paul, 314 n. 14
water, 3, 23–4, 40, 109, 113, 115,
    119–24, 131, 133, 142, 150–1, 159,
    177–9, 207, 248, 275
Watson, David, 69
Weber, O., 214 n. 7
Weinandy, Thomas, 4, 19, 214 n. 2, 325
Welker, Michael, 325
Whiteley, Denys, 105 n. 41
Wickens, U., 208 n. 3

Williams, Rowan, xi, xiii, 19, 44, 53
wind, 94, 109, 114, 123, 131
wine, 3–4, 112, 119–20, 149
Winkler, Gabriele, 5 n. 2, 105 n. 43, 110
    n. 1, 325
Winslow, Donald F., 237, 245 n. 1, 325
Word, 22–6, 36, 38, 41 n. 23, 47, 49,
    55–7, 59–60, 62–4, 84, 87, 136,
    138–9, 143–4, 151, 153, 156, 158–9,
    197–8, 201, 221, 223, 226–7, 229,
    241, 245, 248, 269, 276, 317
  as feminine, 115
  as human, 137
  nature of, 137
  as Power, 116
  as prayer, 286

  as Son, 29–32, 35, 132, 149, 195–6,
    286
  as Spirit, 27, 30–2, 39–40, 58
world, 2–3, 12, 19–20, 26–9, 34–5, 37,
    55–64, 72, 78, 92–5, 99, 101, 111,
    119, 132–4, 138, 142, 145, 152, 159,
    166–70, 174, 179, 181–2, 190–1, 204,
    206–7, 209–14, 226, 241, 243, 245,
    296, 316, 319–20
Wrede, William, 100
Wright, M. R., 103 n. 16
Wright, William, 126 n. 19

Yeago, David, 19, 44, 313 n. 1, 325

Zizioulas, John D., 325